Rome
and Latium

Further titles available
in the
Phaidon Cultural Guides
series:

Athens and Attica
Austria
Florence and Tuscany
France
Germany
Great Britain and Ireland
Greece
Holland
Italy
Jerusalem and the Holy Land
The Loire Valley
Paris and the Ile de France
Provence and the Côte d'Azur
Spain
Switzerland

Rome and Latium

A Phaidon Cultural Guide

with over 300 colour illustrations
and 8 pages of maps

Phaidon

Contributors: Dr Marianne Albrecht-Gott, Gernot Kachel, Martin Locher, Dr Marianne Mehling, Dr Elisabeth Nowak, Maria Pauker M.A., Dr Helmut Scharf

Photographs: Fratelli Fabbri Editori S.p.A., Milan, Ernst Höhne, Franz N. Mehling, SCALA Istituto Fotographica Editoriale, Florence

Maps: Herbert Winkler, Munich

Ground-plans and town-plans: Karl Schneider, Solms; Hans-Jürgen Schäfer, Mücke

Phaidon Press Limited, Littlegate House, St Ebbe's Street, Oxford OX1 1SQ

First published in English 1987
Originally published as *Knaurs Kulturführer in Farbe: Rom und Latium*
© Droemersche Verlagsanstalt Th. Knaur Nachf. Munich 1985
Translation © Phaidon Press Limited 1987

British Library Cataloguing in Publication Data

Rome and Latium.—(A Phaidon cultural
  guide)
  1. Rome (Italy)—Description—1975-
  —Guide-books 2. Lazio (Italy)—
  Description and travel—Guide-books
  I. Albrecht-Gott, Marianne II. Knaurs
  Kulturführer in Farbe, Rom und Latium.
  English
  914.5'63204928   DG804

  ISBN 0-7148-2393-7

Translated and edited by Babel Translations, London
Typeset by Hourds Typographica, Stafford
Printed in West Germany by Druckerei Appl, Wemding

Cover illustration: Rome, Colosseum (photo: © Tony Stone Associates Ltd.)

Preface

No traveller can fail to be overwhelmed by the grandeur that is Rome. The city's origins are shrouded in legend. Built on its Seven Hills, it was first ruled by Etruscan kings and later guided by elected magistrates, the Consuls taking the vow of office in the Temple of Jupiter crowning the original Capitol. By the time Julius Caesar was murdered in 44 BC the Roman Republic had made herself mistress of the Mediterranean. Augustus and the emperors succeeding him consolidated and extended the colonial territory until Latin became the language of law and administration from the Atlantic to the Black Sea. There its daughter languages are still spoken today, while Latin is also a vital strand in some other languages, English among them. Christianity had flourished at Rome, mostly underground, since the martyrdom of the Apostles Peter and Paul until it was established by the Emperor Constantine in 325. During the next hundred years the Empire was assailed by barbarian hordes and finally collapsed. Henceforth Rome was ruled by the Popes – many of them discerning patrons of arts and letters – until it became the capital of a united Italy in 1871.

The present guide will introduce the visitor by word and picture to the sights of a city that is heir to an incomparable artistic legacy. Ancient buildings and monuments still abound, medieval churches with glorious mosaics a thousand years old stand within a few minutes' walk of St. Peter's Basilica and other majestic architectural masterpieces of the Renaissance and the Baroque. Michelangelo and Raphael were employed by the Popes to decorate rooms in the Vatican Palace, and some of Bernini's greatest sculptures are to be found in St. Peter's, in front of which he also designed the breathtaking colonnade. Palaces, fountains and equestrian statues bear eloquent witness to the city's age-old artistic tradition. Churches and museums house many of the finest paintings and sculptures to be found in Europe, and many an English-speaking visitor still makes, as thousands have done before him, the pilgrimage to the tombs of Keats and Shelley and to the two poets' memorial house at the foot of the famous Spanish Steps.

The sights of the Eternal City, 100 of which are illustrated in colour, are the subject of the first part of this guide. The second is devoted to Latium, which extends in a semicircle of about 100 km. around Rome. Before the rise of Rome this region was settled by the Latins and other peoples, and some of its cities by the Etruscans, whose elaborate tombs and other remains – many touched by strong Greek influences – are perhaps the most fascinating sights for the traveller. But there are also many unspoilt towns and villages in this antique land, with Roman remains, fine old churches and civic buildings, and medieval monasteries of historic importance.

The Latium section starts on page 129. As with other guides in the series the text in this section is arranged in alphabetical order of place name for easy reference. The link between places which are geographically close but separated in the text because of the alphabetical arrangement is provided by the maps on pages 320–3. They show all the principal towns described in the text and also, in the same colour, those subsidiary places mentioned in the environs section at the end of each entry.

The heading to each entry gives the post-code and name of the town and, below, its geographical region and a reference to the map section, giving page number and grid reference. Within each entry the main sights are printed in bold type: less significant objects of interest appear under the heading **Also worth seeing** and places in the vicinity under **Environs.** At the end of the book is an index listing the principal sights in Rome and an index of places mentioned in the text.

Rome

Organization of the Rome article:

---

00 100 Roma/Rome

p.322□D4

O Roma felix, quae duorum Principum
Es consecrata glorioso sanguine
Horum cruore purpurata ceteras
Excellis orbis una pulchritudines.

Thus 'happy' Rome is celebrated in a medieval hymn. The Emperor Hadrian called the city 'Roma Aeterna', eternal Rome. And the adjectives 'happy' and 'eternal' still fit this city of three million people, despite excess population, apparently insoluble traffic problems, and the often impoverished population living in the ghetto-like outer suburbs. Rich and distinguished noble families, like the Colonnas and the Orsinis, still exist almost as they did six hundred years ago. Just as in ancient times, beggars and the rich, almost surfeiting on la dolce vita, live side by side.
The most attractive feature of Rome

View of St.Peter's and St.Peter's Square

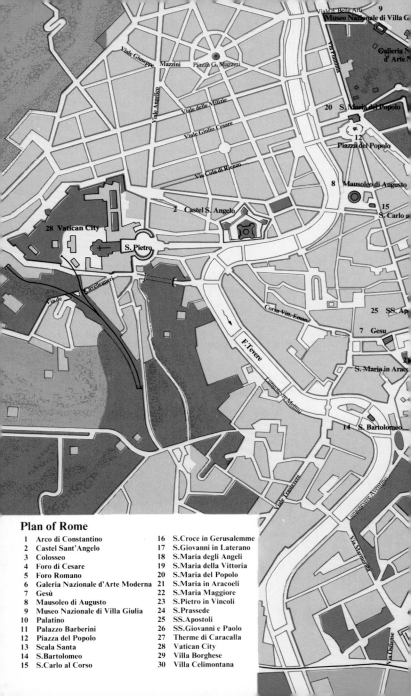

Plan of Rome

is the ancient city, rediscovered by the world of art in the 15C and the academic world in the 18C. Here we find Marcus Aurelius in person—when repairs are finally completed and he is replaced—on the Capitoline, the hill upon which stood the first castle of all. The still older Capitoline Wolf is also there, a relic left over from the ancient Etruscan past—a copy in the square and the original in the nearby museum. Here the Pantheon can be admired, the first building in which the Romans were able to show the Greeks something new, and the Colosseum. A walk through the Forum Romanum is accompanied by history and legend from the earliest times.

But it is not just antiquity which draws us to Rome. Rome is also Roma Sacra, the city of Peter and of Paul, the city of the catacombs, of the persecution of the Christians and worldwide conversion to Christianity. Rome is the city of the Pope.

The eternal splendour of Rome was dimmed for only a short time, in the late Middle Ages, when ancient times were forgotten and the seat of the pontifex maximus of the Roman Catholic church moved to Avignon. At that time the population of Rome, in ancient times almost one and a half million, declined to 20,000. Grass grew among the ruins. Sheep grazed on the Forum Romanum. But soon the Pope returned, and in the 15C the importance of ancient history and culture were recognised, and the city rose to another commanding peak, for art the highest peak of all: the Renaissance, and after it the baroque, created a new Rome. The early Christian churches were extended and built higher, as in the cases of S.Giovanni in Laterano, S.Maria Maggiore and St.Peter's. New cathedrals and palaces were built, new streets, new houses, new fountains and new gardens. The city has a bloody history, but much beauty in its culture.

Rome is the city of Michelangelo, the city of Raphael. Rome is a city of wonderful museums, of universities and opera houses, a city so richly endowed with treasures that it is almost idle to expect to taste them to the full. It would take a lifetime. In

Vanvitelli: View of the Castel Sant'Angelo and St.Peter's, National Gallery

the 18C, archaeologists' trowels dug deep into the town. The 19C, which idolized history and the importance of classical antiquity, chose the most important of all the cities of antiquity as capital of a united Italy in 1871, the city whose ancient empire stetched from Spain to England, through the whole of Europe to Asia and North Africa. Care was taken to enhance the splendour of the town with magnificent buildings, as is shown by the Ara Patriae, the monumental memorial for Vittorio Emanuele, smooth and gleaming white on the slope of the Capitoline.

Ancient Rome was built on seven hills, the Capitoline, the Palatine with the forums of the emperors, the Aventine, the Caelian with the Lateran in the E., the Esquiline with Nero's Golden Palace and the Baths of Trajan, the Viminal and the Quirinal. Today the city sprawls for miles, and has assimilated surrounding towns and villages like a gigantic Moloch. For the traveller and the wealthy Roman living in an exclusive villa on the Aventine, the Parioli or the Via Appia, ancient Rome with its three thousand years of history has survived, almost entirely spared by the Second World War: Roma Aeterna with all her culture, her own and the treasures she has assembled from all over the world in her museums. For hippies and clerics, proletariat and capitalists, beggars and the better-heeled, Japanese, Indians and Americans—Rome is the meeting-place of the world.

Chronology

11–10C BC: The first Italian migration of the peoples between the 12&11C BC, during which Latins and Faliscans settled in the valley of the Tiber, was followed from the 11C by the migration of the Italicae, various primitive tribes, who did not settle until the 10C, when they practised agriculture and cattle breeding.

10–9C BC: First proven settlement on the Palatine by Italacae of a Latin tribe, presumably shepherds, who lived in huts made of straw and clay.

8C BC: Proven settlements by the Sabine tribe on the Esquiline and Quirinal.

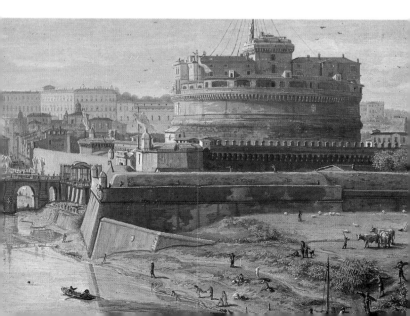

753 BC: The ancient historian Varro (116–127) wrote that Rome was founded on 21 April 753 BC. Presumably it was approximately then that the various hill settlers united as a small village community which can be seen as the beginnings of the later city of Rome, above all from the point when the plains between the three hills were settled as well.

616 BC: The legendary kings Romulus, Numa Pompilius, Tullus Hostilius and Ancus Marcius were followed in 616 BC by the first historically documented king, Tarquinius Priscus, an Etruscan conqueror. He built important features such as a drainage channel for the forum, a temple of Jupiter on the Capitoline; and the first town boundary wall.

579–509 BC: More Etruscan kings ruled in Rome, Servius Tullius and, from 534 BC, Tarquinius Superbus. It is assumed that the first town fortifications were built under Servius Tullius, and these were strengthened in 396 BC. Remains of this so-called 'Servian Wall' can still be seen by the Termini Station.

509 BC: The last Etruscan king of Rome, Tarquinius Superbus, was deposed c. 509. Two consuls became the heads of state. The Republic began with the introduction of the Senate and the people's assembly. The plebians were granted their own assemblies, and were represented by two tribunes of the people.

450 BC: The Decemvirate (rule of the ten) was introduced, and also the Law of the Twelve Tablets, the oldest Roman laws, which were published to the people on twelve bronze or wooden tablets.

387 BC: In the 4C BC republican Rome was attacked by her Latin and Etrurian neighbours but defended herself successfully. In 387 BC the Gauls penetrated as far as Rome and set the city on fire. The 'Servian city wall' was constructed when the city was rebuilt.

380 BC: Foundation of the harbour town of Ostia.

338 BC: Rome becomes supreme overlord of Latium.

343–290 BC: Samnite Wars for supremacy over Campania.

280–146 BC: War against Tarentum.

264–146 BC: During the three Punic

Capitoline Wolf suckling the twins Romulus and Remus

Wars against the Carthaginians the Romans gradually conquered Sicily, Sardinia, Corsica, and also parts of Spain and North Africa. Hannibal, a young Carthaginian general, marched to Italy over the Alps from Spain with 36 elephants. He was not able to conquer Rome, however. In 146 BC the Romans finally destroyed Carthage.

102 BC: Rome's victory over the Cimbri and Teutons under Consul Gaius Marius. Civil war broke out as a result of disputes between the supporters of Marius and those of Sulla.

73–41 BC: Slaves' revolt led by Spartacus. In 62 BC, Rome was ruled by the Triumvirate of Pompey, Caesar and Crassus; Caesar was so successful abroad (in particular in conquering Gaul) and at home that he was elected dictator for life.

44 BC: The Republicans felt so threatened by the tyranny of Caesar that they decided to kill him. He was murdered by the conspirators on 15 March.

30 BC: Before he died, Caesar had named his successor, his great-nephew Octavius. In 30 BC he became dictator, and was later given the title Augustus by the Senate. He became the first Emperor of Rome.

27 BC–AD 14: Reign of Augustus, the 'Golden Age'. He was followed by: **14–37:** Tiberius, **37–41:** Caligula, **41–54:** Claudius, **54–68:** Nero.

61: St.Paul the Apostle in Rome. Christianity spread as a counter-movement to the opulent lifestyle of the Romans. The persecution of the Christians started shortly afterwards (AD).

64: Nero set Rome on fire.

69: After a short period of anarchy the Flavian emperors came to power: Vespasian, Titus, Domitian, Nerva, and finally Trajan.

94: Beginning of one of the worst Christian persecutions.

98–117: Reign of the emperor Trajan. In the meantime the Romans had conquered half the world. The Roman Empire now stretched from Spain to Armenia, from Egypt to Britain. Rome had a million inhabitants and fine internal organisation. Under Trajan attempts were made to secure justice for every citizen, and also to support the poor.

117–193: From 117 Hadrian ruled as

Tomb relief of a Roman married couple, 1C BC

The Emperors

Octavianus Augustus	27 BC–AD 14	Gallienus	260–268
Tiberius	14–37	Claudius Gothicus	268–270
Caligula	37–41	Aurelianus	270–275
Claudius	41–54	Tacitus	275–276
Nero	54–68	Florianus	276
Galba	68–69	Probus	276–282
Otho	69	Carus	282–283
Vitellius	69	Carinus	283–285
Vespasian	69–79	Numerianus	283–284
Titus	79–81	Diocletian	284–305
Domitian	81–96	Maximian	285–305
Nerva	96–98	Constantius I Chlorus	305–306
Trajan	98–117	Galerius	306–311
Hadrian	117–138	Licinius	311–324
Antoninus Pius	138–161	Constantine (I) the Great	312–337
Marcus Aurelius	161–180	Constantine II	337–340
Lucius Verus (Co-Regent)	161–169	Constans I (West Rome)	337–350
Commodus	180–192	Constantius II (East Rome)	337–361
Pertinax	193	Julian the Apostate	361–363
Didius Julianus	193	Jovian	363–364
Septimius Severus	193–211	Valentinian I (West Rome)	375–392
Caracalla	211–217	Valens (East Rome)	364–378
Geta (Co-Regent)	211–213	Gratian (West Rome)	375–383
Macrinus	217–218	Valentinian II (West Rome)	375–392
Elagabalus	218–222	Theodosius I	379–395
Alexander Severus	222–235	Maximus (West Rome)	383–388
Maximinus the Thracian	235–238	Eugenius (West Rome)	392–394
Gordianus I	238	Honorius	395–423
Gordianus II	238	Valentinian III	425–455
Pupienus	238	Petronius Maximus	455
Balbinus	238	Avitus	455–456
Gordianus III	238–244	Majorianus	457–461
Philippus the Arab	244–299	Livius Severus	461–465
Decius	249–251	Anthemius	467–472
Trebonianus Gallus	251–252	Romulus Augustulus	475–476
Aemilianus	253		
Valerianus	253–260	End of the imperial line in West Rome	

Prima Porta Augustus, 1C AD

Vespasian's arrival in Rome, 1C AD

Departure of Emperor Domitian, 1C AD

Apotheosis of Antoninus Pius, relief on base of Antoninus Pius column, AD 161

the first Antonine emperor, followed by Marcus Aurelius from 161–180 and finally Commodus until 195. Rome was considered to be the centre of the world.

193: The Severine emperors ruled from 193, including Caracalla from 211–16.

235–284: Period dominated by military anarchy.

253: Roman Empire under Emperor Valerianus Galerius divided into an eastern and a western empire for the first time.

270–275: Reign of Emperor Aurelianus, who built the 'Aurelian Wall' after the Germani attacked Italy.

293: Diocletian founded the Tetrarchy, or rule of four emperors (two Augusti and two Caesars), with Maximinian as his Augustus, or co-regent. Galerius and Constantius Chlorus were the Caesars. Their residences were in Nicomedia, Milan, Sirmium and Trier or York.

303–311: Persecution of the Christians.

306: From 306 the 'Second Flavians' ruled, after Maxentius, the son of Maximinian, had seized power in Rome. Rome once more became the capital of the Roman Empire.

311: Constantine I, the Great, put a stop to the persecution of the Christians.

330: Constantine I transferred his residence to Byzantium, which was consecrated as his capital and thereafter known as Constantinople.

395: After the death of Theodosius the empire was divided into Eastern Rome and Western Rome. Arcadius ruled in Constantinople; Honorius in Milan, then later in Ravenna. Rome was never again the capital of the whole empire, yet never really lost her significance.

408: Ravenna became capital of the western empire.

410: Rome conquered by Alaric the Visigoth.

455: Rome conquered by Vandals under Geiserich.

476: End of the Western Roman Empire. Emperor Romulus Augustulus dethroned by the German Odoacer. The Eastern Roman Empire survived until 1453, when the Turks seized Constantinople.

535–553: Rome under Byzantine rule.

540: Theoderich the Ostrogoth became ruler in Ravenna.

546: Totila the Ostrogoth conquered Rome; the population had shrunk to 30,000, but in the meantime the power of the Popes had increased, and with it the significance of the city.

590: Consecration of Pope Gregory the Great. The Langobards, who had already overrun North and Central Italy, were at the gates of Rome.

754: Pope Stephen II had sought assistance from Pepin III (the Short) against the Langobards. Pepin defeated the Langobards and made over territory in Ravenna and Rome to the church.

800: At Christmas Pope Leo III crowned Charlemagne emperor in St.Peter's in Rome; he had defeated the Langobard King Desiderius. This was seen as a renewal of the Roman imperial concept, and from this point onwards Rome was the capital of the Western world. The concept of the Holy Roman Empire of German Nations was born.

846: The Saracens attacked Rome.

916: Destruction of the Saracens.

962: Otto I crowned emperor in Rome.

1000: Emperor Otto III in residence on the Aventine. Rome had become the centre of the Christian world. Beginning of the struggles between Pope and Emperor began.

1054: Schism between the churches of Rome and Byzantium.

1078: Normans sack Rome under Robert Guiscard. Internal intrigues among the nobles (Frangipani, Pierleoni, Colonna and Orsini) and power struggles between the Pope and the nobility led to blood feuds.

Bust of Caesar in the National Museum in Naples ▷

1143: Roman commune set up to counter the aristocracy and the Pope.

1155: Execution of Arnold de Brescia, who had opposed the Pope's political power.

1220: Imperial coronation of Frederick II in Rome. Internal political feuds became civil wars.

1300: Annus mirabilis under Boniface VIII.

1309: Pope Clemens V moved the papal residence to Avignon, which considerably reduced the importance of Rome; the population was reduced to 17,000. The buildings of antiquity fell into ruin and were forgotten.

1347: Cola di Rienzo wanted to return to the splendour of ancient Rome, which had become idealized in the popular mind, and so proclaimed the Roman Republic from the Capitol. The nobility rose against him. Cola di Rienzo murdered in 1354.

1348–9: Outbreak of plague; town rocked by earthquakes.

1377: Pope Gregory XI returned from Avignon to Rome; the papal residence was moved from the Lateran to the Vatican.

1378–1418: Schism in the Western church.

1408: Rome conquered by King Ladislaus of Anjou.

1420: Pope Martin V in Rome. Ideas of humanism and Renaissance emanating from Rome also influenced politics, but led above all to the astonishing upsurge of a new Roman culture, which affected the rest of the world for centuries.

1495: Charles VIII in Rome.

1506: Renewal of the church state under Pope Julius II.

1527: Sacco di Roma: Charles V's soldiery, under the influence of the Reformation, laid waste the city.

1540: The Jesuit Order founded as a result of the Counter-Reformation by Ignatius Loyola, who came from Spain. The baroque age also had its origin in Rome.

1626: Pope Urban VIII consecrated the new St.Peter's; building had begun in 1452.

1708: Rome besieged by Emperor Joseph I.

1721: City plundered by Imperial, Neapolitan and Spanish troops.

Bust of Brutus, Musei Capitolini

Terracotta head, 1C BC, Museo Etrusco

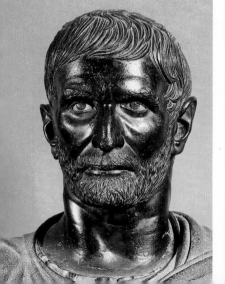

1798: Rome occupied by General Berthier in the course of the French Revolution; he declared the Roman Republic and stripped the Pope of his office.

1801: Concordat between Napoleon I and Pius VII.

1809: The church state fell to France on the exile of Napoleon.

1815: Church state returned to the Pope by the Congress of Vienna.

1848: National consciousness aroused in Italy. In 1848 Pius IX did not wish to become involved in Italy's war against Austria. He was forced to flee and was unable to return until 1850, with the help of the French army. Garibaldi fought for the unification of Italy.

1869–70: First Vatican Council.

1870: French troops withdrawn from Rome during the Franco-Prussian War. The Italian army of General Cadorna defeated papal troops in Rome, marking the end of the Pope's temporal power.

1871: Rome became capital of Italy united under King Victor Emanuel II. The population began to rise (1870: 200,000, 1900: 400,000, now almost 3 million). The city began to expand.

1922: March on Rome. Rise of Italian fascism under Benito Mussolini.

1929: Vatican declared an independent city state under the church by the Lateran Treaty between the church and the Italian state.

1944: Rome fell to the Allies without resistance.

1946: Italy became a republic. Rome remained capital.

1948: New republican constitution effective from 1 January.

1957: The heads of government of six of the Montan Union states signed the treaty founding the European Economic Community, the 'Treaty of Rome'.

1960: XVII Summer Olympics in Rome.

1962–5: Second Vatican Council.

Cultural Chronology

1300–1200 BC: An early settlement is assumed to have existed near the Tiber S. of the Capitoline (Bronze Age vessels excavated).

1000–900 BC: Early Iron Age

Leo the Great meets Attila, Raphael's Stanze

cremation sites (Forum Romanum) point to an early Latin settlement.

800 BC: The nucleus of the later city came into being with the amalgamation of the settlements which had developed on the Palatine, Esquilan and Quirinal.

750 BC: Necropolis on the later Forum Romanum.

700–600 BC: Introduction of Greek ceramics, the Etruscan Heroon, said to be the grave of Romulus, on the Forum Romanum. First bridge over the Tiber built towards the end of the 7C BC.

600–500 BC: Building of a sewerage system, the so-called cloaca maxima, with a threefold layer of wedge-shaped stones. Bucchero vessels with Etruscan inscriptions found on the Capitoline, Palatine and Aventine, and a stone with an Etruscan inscription on the Forum Romanum. The first Circus Maximus also dates from this period.

509 BC: Dedication of the Temple of Jupiter on the Capitoline.

498 BC: Consecration of the Temple of Saturn in the Forum Romanum.

493 BC: Consecration of the Temple of Ceres, Liber and Libera on the Forum Boarium.

484 BC: Consecration of the Temple of Castor in the Forum Romanum. The original bronze statue of the Roman Wolf dates from this period. Fine sculptures influenced partly by the Etruscans and partly by the Greeks were made, for example the marble Dioscuri with horses from the Lacus Juturnae.

431 BC: Consecration of the Temple of Apollo on the Campus Martius.

378 BC: Building of the Servian Wall in Cappellaccio tufa.

344 BC: Consecration of the Temple of Juno Moneta on the Capitol.

312 BC: Opening of the Via Appia, which led from Rome to Capua.

293 BC: Consecration of the Temple of Quirinus on the Quirinal.

◁ *Emperor Lucius Verus (2C),*
Museo Civico, Bologna

c. 280 BC: Esquiline fresco fragment.

c. 270 BC: Scipio tombs on the Appian Way.

221 BC: Building of the Circus Flaminius on the Campus Martius.

Into the 3C BC peasant feasts and religious rites, accompanied by music on the lyre and the tibia (a kind of clarinet), were held. After this the influence of Greece began to show. All sorts of works of art were brought to Rome as a result of state plunder and private purchase in Greece. Copies of Greek masterpieces became the fashion. Early Roman literature was based entirely on Greek models. Livius Andronicus (*c.* 284–203), Naevius, Ennius and Cato the Elder (234–149) translated and adapted original Greek texts. Cato became the father of Latin prose. Plautus (250–184) and Terence (185–159, originally a Carthaginian slave) created Roman comedy, which was successful for hundreds of years, on the Greek pattern.

200 BC: Hellenisitic sculptors and architects, painters, philosophers and poets came to Rome from Asia Minor and influenced every aspect of cultural development, as Attic artists had done 20 years before. Musical instruments now included the flute, the Pan pipe and trumpet, tuba, lyre, cymbal and tambourine.

181 BC: Temple of Venus Erucina on the Quirinal.

179 BC: Pons Aemilius.

170 BC: Basilica Sempronia on the Forum Romanum.

116 BC: Birth of the Roman scholar and historian Varro (116–27).

106 BC: Birth of the philosopher and rhetorician Cicero (106–43).

100 BC: Temple of Fortuna in Praeneste and circular temple in the Forum Boarium.

99 BC: Birth of the philosopher Lucretius, who taught an expanded version of Epicurean philosophy in Rome, and committed suicide on 10.10.55 BC. Scholars place his date of birth between 99 and 94 BC.

90–10 BC: Architectural and representational painting have survived to some extent. Sculpture was dominated by realistic portraits.

86 BC: Birth of the historian Sallust (d. 35).

86–78 BC: Tabularium on the Capitol.

84 BC: Birth of the poet Catullus (d. 54).

70 BC: Birth of the poet Virgil (d. 19).

65 BC: Birth of the poet Horace (d. 8).

62 BC: Building of the Pons Fabricius to the Tiber island.

60–50 BC: Building of the Casa Republicana with frescoed walls on the Palatine.

59 BC: Birth of the historian Livius Titus (Livy) (d. AD 17).

55 BC: Building of the Theatre of Pompey on the Campus Martius.

51–46 BC: Building of the Forum of Caesar.

43 BC: Birth of the poet Ovid (d. AD 17 or 18).

c. 40 BC: Gardens of Sallust on the Quirinal, tomb of Caecilia Metella.

40–30 BC: House of Augustus on the Palatine.

33 BC: Vitruvius wrote a manual of architecture and technology dedicated to Augustus in 25 BC. The age of Augustus was known as the 'Golden Age of Poetry', in which Maecenas among others placed his fortune at the disposal of poets.

30 BC: House of Livia on the Palatine.

28 BC: Consecration of the Temple of Apollo on the Palatine and Mausoleum of Augustus on the Campus Martius.

13 BC: Building of the Balbus Theatre on the Campus Martius.

c. 12 BC: Pyramid of Cestius and Theatre of Marcellus.

9 BC: Consecration of the Ara Pacis on the Campus Martius.

4 BC: Birth of the Roman philosopher Seneca, in Córdoba. He became famous in Rome as Nero's tutor and as a politician, tragic playwright and Stoic. He was condemned to commit suicide in AD 65.

2 BC: Consecration of the Forum of Augustus.

AD 35–100: Period of trompe l'oeil painting.

43: Temple of Isis and Serapis on the Campus Martius.

c. 63: Baths of Nero.

66: Death of the writer Petronius.

Coronation of Charlemagne, detail, Raphael's Stanze

80: Consecration of the Flavian Amphitheatre (Colosseum); Baths of Titus.
81: Arch of Titus.
91: Equestrian statue of Domitian.
94: The Greek philosopher Epictetus taught the Stoa in Rome until this date.
112: Forum of Trajan.
120–125: Birth of the writer and lawyer Apuleius (d. 180).
126–134: Villa Adriana.
130–200: Necropolis under St.Peter's.
134: Pons Aelius.
139: Consecration of the Mausoleum of Hadrian.
c.161: Equestrian staue of Marcus Aurelius on the Capitol.
c. 180: First Christian painting in the catacombs.
193: Marcus Aurelius column on the Campus Martius.
203: Arch of Septimus Severus. Early Christian writers, later known as the Fathers of the Church, wrote from the 3C to disseminate their views on faith and doctrine.
216: Baths of Caracalla; the site of the Mithras cult now under S.Clemente dates from roughly the same period.

From 270: Aurelian Wall: statue of the Good Shepherd.
304: Fabius Pictor is said to have been the first painter of towns. In the 4C remarkable stucco and mosaic work thrived alongside the painting of late antiquity.
305: Baths of Diocletian.
306: Basilica of Maxentius in the Forum Romanum.
313: Arch of Constantine.
315: Lateran basilica. The Christian church building developed from the ancient basilica, originally the hall of the king, and then a public building for cult worship and trade; the Pope bestowed the name basilica in special cases.
330: Building of St.Peter's.
334: Equestrian statue of Constantine in the Forum Romanum.
339: Birth of Ambrosius, one of the four great Church Fathers of the West (d. 397).
354: Birth of Augustine, the greatest of the Western Church Fathers and philosophers (d. 430); he lived in Rome until 384.
From 336: Memorial tablets to the martyrs placed in the catacombs.

Apollo Belvedere, 4C BC, Vatican

Hera Barberini, Vatican

386: The Basilica of St.Paul (S.Paolo fuori le mura) was rebuilt, and mosaics added in S.Pudenziana.

403: Reinforcement of the Aurelian Wall.

432: S.Maria Maggiore.

c. 460: S.Stefano Rotondo.

480: Birth of the statesman and philosopher Boethius, executed in 524.

500: Christian hymns introduced in churches alongside folk music.

c. 530: Apse mosaic in SS.Cosma e Damiano and frescos in the crypt of S.Clemente.

c. 590: Mosaics in the triumphal arch of S.Clemente.

600: Pope Gregory I introduced Gregorian chant, which developed in subsequent centuries in Italy, and also particularly in Belgium and Burgundy. This music reached its height in the works of Giovanni Pierluigi Palestrina (1526–94).

c. 650: More churches with mosaics and frescos built. Sacred art displaced secular art in Rome.

c. 720: Building of S.Maria in Cosmedin.

From 730: The Byzantine painting dispute overflowed to Rome.

c. 830: Building of the Zenon chapel in S.Prassede.

c. 850: Vatican Wall built by Leo VI.

c. 920: Building of S.Bartolomeo on the Tiber island.

c. 1000: The philosophy of scholasticism began to spread in Italy, and gained more and more ground in the 11&12C (Petrus Lombardus, 1100–64). From the 12–14C mysticism flourished (Bonaventura 1221–74).

c. 1120: Mosaic in S.Maria in Trastevere.

c. 1150: The Cosmati began to be predominant in Rome; they were families of artists in which the name Cosmas occurred frequently, and who provided Rome and the surrounding area with outstanding mosaics until well into the 14C.

1220: Building of cloisters in the Lateran and S.Paolo fuori le mura.

1225: Birth of the great theologian and philosopher Thomas Aquinas, who taught in Rome among other places and died in 1274.

1230: Birth of the poet Jacopo da Todi (d. 1306) who, in the dialogue of his Laudes, wrote precursors of the medieval mystery plays, which

Laocoön group (2C BC), Vatican

Bust of Antinous, after 130, Vatican

reached their peak in the 14C. In the 13C the music of courtly love developed in Sicily, and later in Tuscany. Florence and other Italian cities began to rival Rome as centres of culture, and indeed eclipsed it in the 14&15C.

1240: Birth of the sculptor and architect Arnolfo di Cambio (d. 1302) who created the tabernacle in S.Paolo fuori muri. In the late 13C he led the team of builders of Florence cathedral. He was one of the first great artistic personalities of the proto-Renaissance in Italy and a pupil of Nicolo Pisano.

1280: Building of S.Maria sopra Minerva.

1295: Mosaics in S.Maria Maggiore.

1300: Annus mirabilis, presided over by Pope Boniface VIII. Giotto (1266–1337), the greatest painter of his time, and father of Italian art, worked in Rome. He was responsible for the frescos in the Lateran Palace, now lost.

1321: Death of Dante (b. 1265), who wrote his 'Divina Commedia' in Tuscan. In the 13C the Italian vernacular had developed from Latin in various regional forms which later came closer to each other. Until the late Middle Ages, and then again in the Renaissance, poets wrote alternately in Latin and Italian. The discovery of the vernacular is also essentially due to the Humanists. In Umbria St.Francis of Assisi wrote his 'Song of the Sun'; the Dominican Jacobus a Voragine (c. 1229–98) published a collection of legends of the saints, the 'Legenda aurea'. In the 14C secular poetry began to hold its own with religious works.

1341: Franceso Petrarca (1304–74) was crowned poet on the Capitoline in Rome. He was a friend of Boccaccio (1317–75), who wrote his 'Decamerone', which was to be influential for centuries, in Florence. Even at this time interest in antiquity was beginning to revive.

1401: Birth of the painter Masaccio (d. 1428), who worked with Masolino in S.Clemente. He was also responsible for important work in Florence and Pisa, and is considered to be one of the most important early figures of the Italian Renaissance.

1415: Birth of Johannes Argyropulos (d. 1487), who taught Greek in Rome.

Odysseus in the Country of the Laestrygones (50 BC), Vatican Museums

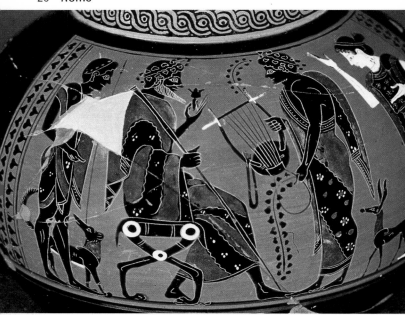

Detail of an Attic jug, Museo Gregoriano Etrusco

He translated Aristotle. The neo-Platonists were teaching in Florence, and in the latter part of the century the Renaissance began to make its mark in Italy.

1427: The painter Masolino (1383–1440) worked from 1427 in the Cappella di S.Caterina in S.Clemente.

1428: Birth of Pomponio Leto (d. 1497), who founded the first academy for research into antiquity in Rome. The study of antiquity soon became a school subject.

1447–49: Fra Angelico (1400–55) painted the Nicholas V chapel in the Vatican.

1452: Rebuilding of St.Peter's begins. Birth of the universal genius Leonardo da Vinci (d. 1519), who lived in Florence, then Milan from 1481.

1470: Melozzo da Forlì lived in Rome from 1470. His work can be seen in the pinacoteca of the Vatican Museum.

1480–4: Painters Pinturicchio (1454–1513) and Perugino (1450–1523) at work in the Sistine Chapel.

1488–93: Filippino Lippi (1457–1504), son of the painter Filippo Lippi, created the frescos of the Caraffa Chapel in S.Maria sopra Minerva.

1499: Michelangelo's Pietà. Michelangelo Buonarotti (1475–1564), sculptor, painter, architect and poet, was the most imposing and perfect sculptor of all time after the Greeks. He took the Roman and Florentine Renaissance to heights which were never reached again.

1502: Bramante (1444–1514), whose work as an architect made a major contribution to the development (lucidity, harmony and beauty of form) and pefection of the Renaissance, created the Tempietto di S.Pietro in Montorio. The monastery courtyard of S.Maria della Pace was

Achilles and Ajax throwing dice, black-figured amphora, Vatican

started by him in 1504; he was in charge of the rebuilding of St.Peter's from 1506.

From 1508: Raphael's 'Stanzi' in the Vatican. The painter and architect was famous in his lifetime. In 1515, after the death of Bramante, he was put in charge of building work in St.Peter's. As a painter he was a powerful influence on subsequent centuries up to the time of the Pre-Raphaelites (19C).

1508–1511: Building of the Villa Farnesina under the direction of Baldassare Peruzzi (1481–1536), who took over the building of St.Peter's after the death of Raphael.

From 1513: Michelangelo created the figure of Moses on the tomb of Julius II (now in S.Pietro in Vincoli); the statue of Christ in S.Maria sopra Minerva dates from 1519–21.

1513: The universal genius Leonardo da Vinci came to Rome. Paintings by him are on show in the pinacoteca of the Vatican Museum.

1514: Building of the Palazzo Farnese.

1517: The poet Pietro Aretino (1492–1556) spent time in Rome. At the same time Niccoló Machiavelli was working in Florence.

1525: Birth of Pierluigi Palestrina (d. 1594) in Rome. He was organist and choirmaster at St.Peter's, then at the Lateran Basilica, at S.Maria Maggiore, at the Collegium Romanum and finally at S.Peter's again. His style of composition was generally acknowledged as a model for church music.

In the 16C Commedia dell'arte developed in Italy; it has survived until today in various versions.

1536: Michelangelo's plans for the Piazza di Campidoglio (Capitol Square), and his enormous Last Judgement in the Sistine Chapel.

1544: Birth of the poet Torquato

Tasso, who lived in Rome and died in 1595, when he was crowned 'poetus laureatus'. In the 16C Rome had also become a centre of poetry. In ancient times Rome to a large extent imitated Greek culture; in the Renaissance she reached unsurpassed heights in her own right.

1545: Birth of G.B.Nanino, the founder of the so-called Roman School of music.

1568–75: Church of 'Il Gesù' built under the direction of G.B.Vignola. It is considered the first baroque building, and was a seminal influence on the European architecture of subsequent centuries.

1591–1606: Michelangelo Caravaggio (d. 1610) worked in Rome. His paintings created a new style (dramatic forms and stark realism, with marked chiaroscuro); he influenced Frans Hals, Rubens, and above all Rembrandt.

1595: The Carracci brothers started work on the fresco cycle of the Palazzo Farnese in Rome.

1599: Death of Luca Marenzio, who felt an obligation to the Roman school of music.

1600: Immediately after the peformance of 'Euridice' by Peri (libretto by Rinuccini) in Florence, the first opera to reach the stage, Cavalieri's 'Rappresentazzione di anima e di corpo' had its first performance in Rome. Opera as a new art form was consolidated by Monteverdi from Mantua from 1607. In 1600 the philosopher Giordano Bruno (1548–1600) was burned as a heretic in Rome, after seven years under arrest.

1603: Carlo Maderna (1556–1629), a pupil of Domenico Fontana, (1543–1607), created the façade of S.Susanna. He was put in charge of the building of St.Peter's, and was responsible for the façade, among other features. He was the most important Roman architect of the early 17C, and was already building in the baroque style, which like that of the Renaissance, was to spread all over Europe from Rome.

1605: Gian Lorenzo Bernini (1598–1680) came to Rome from Naples, where he became one of the most outstanding baroque sculptors and architects. He worked in the service of the Popes until his death.

1608: Birth of G.A.Borelli (d. 1679), who fled to Rome from Messina for political reasons in 1674. He was the principal 17C exponent of iatrophysics.

1612: Death of G.B.Guarini (b. 1538), who created pastoral theatre.

1620: The architect Francesco Borromini (1599–1667) worked in Rome, under Carlo Maderna, on St.Peter's and the Palazzo Barberini, until 1629.

1629: End of the stay of Tommaso Campanella (1568–1639), the Italian philosopher and utopian, in Rome; in 1591 he was accused of heresy and thrown into prison.

1630: Galileo Galilei in Rome to acquire permission to publish his astronomical writings. He faced the Inquisition in 1632, and recanted in 1633, against his better judgement.

1635–50: Pietro da Cortona (1596–1669) created the frescos in the Palazzo Barberini and thus revealed himself as one of the first important baroque painters. He lived in Rome from 1613, and also designed baroque façades like that of S.Maria della Pace from 1656-7.

1637–50: Francesco Borromini worked on the Convent and Oratory of S.Filippo Neri.

1638–41: Borromini in charge of the building of the church of S.Carlo alle Quattro Fontane. He did not add the façade until 1665-8. The church shows his mastery of late baroque.

1642–50: S.Ivo alla Sapienza built under the direction of Borromini.

1644–55: Piazza Navona built.

1653: Birth of Arcangelo Corelli, who lived as a composer in Rome and was later recognised as the creator of modern violin technique.

1656–67: Bernini designed St.Peter's

Self-portrait of Raphael (left) from the 'Stanze' ▷

square; the colonnades date from 1663.

From 1658: Bernini directed the building of S.Andrea al Quirinale.

1681: The writer and law scholar Andrea Pozzo (1642–1709) came to Rome and was a co-founder of the Accademia dell'Arcadia and in 1711 the Accademia dei Querini.

1698: Birth of the opera librettist and oratorio writer Pietro Metastasio (d. 1782).

1721–5: Building of the Spanish Steps.

From 1728: Pompeo Batoni, a popular painter of the time, worked in Rome.

1735: Ferdinando Fuga (1699–1781) built the neoclassical Palazzo della Consultà.

1736: Death of the architect Alessandro Galilei (in Rome from 1691) shortly after he had completed the Corsini funerary chapel in the Lateran and above all the façade of S.Giovanni in Latero.

From 1740: The engraver and architect Giovanni Battista Piranesi (1720–78) came to Rome for the first time. He became famous for his pictures of ancient buildings.

1741: A.R.Mengs (1782–79), the German painter and art scholar, stayed in Rome, where he drew a great deal in the style of Raphael. In 1746 he became court painter in Dresden, but often returned to Rome.

1743: Fernando Fuga built the façade of S.Maria Maggiore. The same year saw the death of the composer Luigi Boccherini.

1749: Birth of Vittorio Alfieri (d. 1803), who lived in Rome among other places, and wrote tragedies in the classical style. At the same time Carlo Goldoni (1707–93), who perfected commedia dell'arte, and Carlo Gozzi (1720–1806), who wrote fairy-tale dramas, were writing in Venice.

1760–1: Mengs painted his famous 'Parnassus' ceiling fresco in the Villa Albani in Rome.

1762: Building of the Fontana di Trevi and birth of Giuseppe Valadier (d. 1839), who worked in Rome as a town planner, neoclassical architect and archaeologist (restoration of the Arch of Titus).

Bust of a woman (100–110), Vatican Museums

Sarcophagus with harbour scene (3C AD), Vatican

1778: The writer Vicenzo Monti (1754–1828) came to Rome. Among other things he translated the Iliad in 1806&7, and became a member of the Accademia dell'Arcadia. Ugo Foscolo was born in the same year; his poetry contains the first hints of Romanticism. Alessandro Manzoni was born in 1785.

1779: The neoclassical sculptor Antonio Canova (1757–1822) moved to Rome. He created statues and tombs. The marble sculpture of Paolina Borghese (Venus) became especially famous.

1791: Birth of Giuseppe Gioacchino Belli (d. 1863), who wrote in Roman dialect.

1792: Birth of Gioacchino Rossini; Gaetano Donizetti was born in 1797 and Vincenzo Bellini in 1801. Italian opera began to achieve world fame. The Palazzo Braschi was built in neoclassical style by Cosimo Morelli.

1810: The 'Nazarenes' (League of Luke) came to Rome: they were a group of German Romantic painters (J.F.Overbeck, F.Pforr etc, then later P. von Cornelius, W.Schadow and J.Schnorr von Carolsfeld). They lived in the deserted monastery of Sant'Isodoro. They hoped to achieve an ethical and religious basis for painting, and the renewal of old German and old Italian painting.

1813–20: Giuseppe Valadier redesigned the Piazza del Popolo and the adjacent Pincio building.

1813: Birth of Giuseppe Verdi. Ruggiero Leoncavallo was born in 1858, and Pietro Mascagni in 1863; the latter became director of the Scuola di Musica in Rome and died there in 1945. Famous operatic performances in the Teatro Argentino.

1822: The lyric poet Giacomo Leopardi (1798–1837) spent time in Rome.

1826: Giuseppe Valadier designed the façade of S.Andrea delle Fratte.

1849: The politician and philosopher Giuseppe Mazzini (1805–72) directed the defence of the Roman Republic against French troops, along with Giuseppe Garibaldi.

1858: Birth of Giacomo Puccini (d. 1924), and also of the dialect poet Cesare Pascarella (d. 1940).

1866: Birth of the Hegelian philosopher Benedetto Croce (d. 1952).

1867: Birth of Luigi Pirandello, who studied at the university of Rome among other places, worked there as a journalist, and taught the history of Italian literature at the university from 1897. His plays were influential throughout the world.

From 1870: Large-scale rebuilding of the city: the Corso Vittorio Emanuele II was built, and old buildings pulled down to create new suburbs.

1876: Death of the historical philosopher G.Ferrari (b. 1811).

1879: Birth of the composer Ottorino Respighi (d. 1936); he became teacher of composition at the Conservatorio di Santa Cecilia in 1913, and director of that institution from 1932–5. He was the leading exponent of Italian instrumental music in the early 20C.

1885: Birth in Rome of the symbolist poet Arturo Onofri (d. 1928).

1888: Birth in Greece of Giorgio de Chirico, the painter who was to become the leading exponent of Italian Surrealism.

1889–1900: Building of the Palazzo della Giustizia, one of the principal works of 19C Italian architecture.

1890: World premiere of Pietro Mascagni's 'Cavalleria Rusticana' in the Teatro Costanzi in Rome.

1895: Building of the Garibaldi monument (equestrian statue of the national hero) on the Gianicolo.

1895–1911: National memorial for Vittorio Emanule II built by G.Sacconi in the Piazza Venezia.

1900: Birth of the Italian author Ignatio Silone, later secretary of the Socialist Youth in Rome. He was the editor of the Roman weekly paper, and a founder member of the Italian Communist Party in 1921. He was exiled in Switzerland for a time, but returned to Italy in 1945.

1900: Premiere of Giacomo Puccini's 'Tosca' in the Teatro Costanzi in Rome.

1904: Birth of one of the leading contemporary composers, Luigi Dallapiccola; Luigi Nono was born in Venice in 1924.

1906: F.Marinetti (1876–1944) published his first futurist manifesto.

1907: Birth of the author Alberto Moravia in Rome.

1908: Birth in Bergamo of the graphic artist and sculptor G.Manzù, who

Miniature from the Vatican Vergil (5C), Vatican Museums

designed the bronze doors for St.Peter's in Rome.

1912: Birth of Renato Guttuso, one of the principal exponents of modern Italian painting. In Rome he also worked as a stage designer at the Opera (Carmen).

1913/14: Designs for a Città Nuova by A.Sant'Elia. First reinforced concrete buildings in Milan.

1915: The composer, conductor and music critic Alfredo Casella (1883–1947) taught at the Liceo Musicale di S.Cecilia in Rome, and from 1933 also at the Accademia di S.Cecilia. He composed 30 operas, and other works.

From 1917: The philosopher and politician G.Gentile (1875–1944) was professor in Rome.

1919–23: Publication of the Roman magazine 'La Ronda'.

1920: Surrealism established itself as a dominant force in painting.

1928: Building of the Foro Italico, the sports centre in the N. of the town. The olympic stadium is next to it.

1938: Building of the main station in Rome begins. The Stazione Termini were completed in 1950 by the archi-tectural team of L.Calini, E.Montuori and A.Vittelozzi.

After the Second World War Rome became a centre of cross-fertilization for international cultural trends.

1938: Adalberto Libera built the Palazzo dei Congressi (EUR).

1942: The satellite town to the S. of Rome with the Palace of Heroes was further extended after the Second World War (skyscrapers). Giuseppe Ungaretti became professor of modern Italian literature in Rome.

1950: Death of the Roman poet Tri-lussa (b. 1875).

1953: Death of the important Italian dramatist Ugo Betti (b. 1892) in Rome.

1957: Completion of Diego Fabbri's (b. 1911) 'Trial of Christ'. Fabbri was for a time director of the Vatican Film Office in Rome. His effective plays were influenced by Pirandello and Betti. The novelist Giuseppe Tomasi di Lampedusa died in Rome (b.1896).

1960: Stadio Flaminio on the Viale Tiziano in the N. of the city, an all-purpose stadium for the Olympic Games, designed by Nervi.

St.Laurence before the Emperor Decius (detail), fresco in the Nicholas V chapel in the Vatican

1964–71: Pier Luigi Nervi built the audience hall behind the colonnade of St.Peter's Square.

1966: Death of the painter and art historian Carlo Carrà (b.1881).

1973: Death of the author Carlo Emilio Gadda (b. 1893).

1975: Murder of the Roman poet and film director Pier Paolo Pasolini (b. 1922) in Ostia.

I. Ancient and Early Christian Monuments from A-Z

The early Christian catacombs had attracted the attention of pilgrims and scholarly humanists in the 15C, but it was the discovery of the *Laocoon Group* (1506) which stimulated Renaissance interest in antiquity. Raphael was commissioned by Pope Leo X (1513–21) to devise the first overall plan for the restoration of ancient Rome, but it was centuries before archaeologists were able to put it into practice. In the Renaissance little was done to maintain ancient buildings, and when ancient art began to be a matter of interest again at the turn of the 17&18C it was principally pictorial works which attracted attention. At this time there were several private collections of antiquities in Rome, including that of Cardinal Albani, which was first catalogued on historical principles by Johann Joachim Winckelmann (1717–68). The Vatican Museum of Antiquity came into being in 1770 under Winckelmann's successor as Commissioner of Antiquities, Giovanni Battista Visconti. In the early 19C the first excavations began; previously, ancient buildings had simply been restored or made safe; excavation in accordance with scientific principles became more and more precise in the early 20C. Recently archaeologists have come into conflict with town planners: the hoped-for excavation of the Forum of Vespasian is going ahead on a very modest scale for the time being.

Ara Pacis Augustae/Altar of the Augustan Peace (Piazza Augusto Imperatore): Augustus' peace altar, started in 13 BC and consecrated in 9 BC, first stood in the Campus Martius and was reconstructed near the Mausoleum of Augustus after the final sections had been excavated in 1937. The altar is entirely in marble, and consists of an almost square enclosure (38 ft. by 35 ft.) with two entrances, one opposite the other, and the actual altar, which is set a little higher, and forms three sides of square open to the front. The outer sides of the enclosing wall have pilasters at the corners and a plain entabulature and are divided into two by a double meander frieze. The lower section is decorated with an acanthus motif, the upper section has two self-contained reliefs on the entrance sides, and on the S. and N. sides is the famous *frieze of figures* representing the dedicatory procession consisting of Augustus and his family, the most distinguished citizens of the empire and members of senatorial families. At the head of the procession in the SW corner are 4 lictors with fasces; they are facing Augustus, who is wearing a wreath and about to perform the sacrifice. Then come the consuls, priests and members of the imperial family. The other side is of lower artistic calibre, and shows the procession of senators and high officials, with the massed ranks of spectators in the background. The single relief on the N. side shows *Tellus*, the Roman goddess of the earth, surrounded by personifications and symbols of the elements responsible for the fertility of the earth. Very little remains of the *relief of Roma* on the opposite side: only part of a pile of weapons, evidence of her victories which have helped to bring about peace. On the right near the S. entrance is a representation of the sacrifice made by *Aeneas* to the Penates on landing in Latium. What little

Dante, detail from Raphael's Stanze ▷

remains of the relief on the left suggests that it showed the shepherds finding *Romulus and Remus*. The interior of the surrounding wall, which is about 20 ft. high, is of similar design to the exterior. The lower slabs are decorated with plain strips, the upper ones have garlands of fruit and bucranes (bulls' skulls). The 3 walls of the altar itself were decorated inside and out with pictorial friezes showing the sacrifice on the altar of peace; only about a third of the frieze has survived.

Arco degli Argentarii/Arch of the Moneychangers (Piazza della Bocca della Verità): This single arch, now partially incorporated into the church of S.Giorgio in Velabro, was built in AD 204 by the moneychangers and merchants of the Forum Boarium; the reliefs show the Emperor Septimus Severus and his wife Julia Domna making a sacrifice; on the other side is their son Caracalla; the relief of his wife Plautilla was removed after her murder in 211.

Arco di Costantino/Arch of Constantine (Via di S.Gregorio): This tripartite arch was built by the Senate for Constantine and his Augustus of the West Licinius after the victory over Maxentius in AD 312. The arch is 69 ft. high, 84 ft. wide and 24 ft. deep, was completed in 315 and is the best-preserved ancient monument in Rome. The *N. side* of the arch is lavishly decorated and faces the Colosseum; above the central opening is a large inscription recording the Senate's decision to build; the tablets over the two side openings congratulate Constantine on the tenth anniversary of the beginning of his reign and offer good wishes for the next decade. In the spandrels of the principal opening are victories with trophies, winter and spring; the spandrels of the side openings depict river gods. The circular reliefs on the side openings, set above friezes with figures, show Constantine hunting lions and boars and Licinius sacrificing to Hercules and Apollo. The vertical rectangular reliefs on the attica are of an earlier date, showing incidents from the life of the Emperor Marcus Aurelius in AD 174 and 176. In front of the

Arch of Constantine

attica pilasters are statues of captured Dacians, on the bases of the columns victories with Roman legionaries and captured Germani. The *S. side* and the *narrow sides* of the arch follow the same pattern. The sections built especially for the arch are in white marble, the yellow marble columns are from an earlier building; the Dacian figures and reliefs from a building of the time of Trajan are in Phrygian marble. The reliefs taken from buildings of the period of Trajan and Marcus Aurelius and from a hunting memorial to Hadrian were adapted to suit the scale of their new site, and the features of the older emperors were also changed to those of Constantine. The friezes showing the deeds of Constantine and the reliefs on the column bases were created especially for this building, which despite its disparate elements forms a harmonious whole. It was influential in the design of Renaissance and baroque façades and fountains.

Basilica di Porta Maggiore/Basilica Sotteranea (Piazza di Porta Maggiore): This building, 46 ft. under the ground, was discovered in 1917, though its function was not clear. The basilica dates from the 1C AD and consists of a narthex, a central space 40 by 30 ft., divided by massive piers into three tunnel-vaulted aisles of equal height, and a semicircular apse. The floor is covered with white mosaic with geometrical patterns; the vaults are decorated with excellent stucco of Greek mythology. Plan and decoration anticipate basic patterns of later Christian church architecture.

Castel S.Angelo/ (Mausoleo di Adriano/Mausoleum of the Emperor Hadrian) (Lungotevere di Castello): The building was started by the Emperor Hadrian (AD117–138) in 135 as a mausoleum for himself and his successors and completed by Antonius Pius in 139. Septimus Severus was the last Emperor to be buried here in 211. After the building of the Aurelian Wall in 271 the building became a bastion in the fortifications, and was strongly fortified under the Emperor Honorius (395–423), and christened Castel S.Angelo by

Colosseum

Pope Gregory the Great in 590 (after seeing a vision of the Archangel Michael here). Pope Nicholas III joined the Castel S.Angelo to the Vatican Palace with a crenellated wall in 1277; Alexander VI built 4 corner towers, depots and living quarters; Sixtus V made the Castel S.Angelo into a treasury in the late 16C. The building was still used as a prison and barracks in the 19C, and became a museum in 1933&4. Access to the mausoleum was by the *Pons Aelius* across the Tiber; its three central arches were incorporated into the present Ponte S.Angelo, with 10 angel statues created by Lorenzo Bernini and his colleagues in 1660–7. The massive central walls of the rotunda, almost 66 ft. high, and a grave chamber reached by an approach slope have survived, though without the original interior and exterior decoration. A castellated wall with 4 round bastions shows the line of the square podium of the old mausoleum. Since 1447 the *papal buildings* have stood on the base of the old rotunda; in the *Cortile dell'Angelo* is a marble angel dating from 1577, which topped

the basilica until 1752, when it was replaced by a bronze angel. The finest of the papal rooms are the *Apollo chamber* with its splendid 16C frescos, the wonderful Sala del Consiglio or *Sala Paolina*, the *Perseus Room*, the *Stanza dell'Adriano* with an important Madonna painted by Luca Signorelli (*c.* 1450–1523) and the *Saletta dei Festoni*.

Catacombe di S.Callisto/Calixtus catacomb (110 Via Appia Antica): The corridors of this extensive underground burial place have been extended ever since the late 2C AD, and are about 6 miles long; it is estimated that there are about 170,000 graves, with the oldest nearest the surface and the most recent further underground. In the 6 *Cubicila*, the sacramental chapels, are late 2C and early 3C frescos of baptism, confession and the Last Supper. Pope Sixtus II was buried in 258 in the *Cappella dei Papi*, the burial place of numerous 3C Roman bishops. Next to this is the *burial chamber of S.Cecilia*, with 7&8C wall frescos and a copy of a marble statue of Stefano

Pantheon

Maderna, dating from 1599&1600, from the church of S.Cecilia in Trastevere, to which Pope Paschal I (817–824) had the relics of the Saint taken.

Catacombe di Domitilla/Domitilla catacomb (282 Via delle Sette Chiese): This is probably the largest catacomb in Rome and grew up around the burial place of Christian members of the Flavian imperial house, which included Domitilla, the grand-daughter of the Emperor Domitian. The *Basilica di SS.Nereo e Achilleo* at the entrance to the catacomb was built 390–395 and rediscovered in 1874. To the right of it is a *cubiculum* with fresco of S.Petronilla, and to the left the *Flavian funeral precinct* with 1C AD walls, and some wall paintings of the same period. Just beyond this is a grave chamber with 2C wall paintings. Other parts of the catacombs with lavish fresco decoration date from the 3&4C. This catacomb is practically a museum of the development of early Christian painting.

Catacombe di SS.Marcellino e

Inside the Pantheon

Pietro (Via Casilina): A particularly fine 3&4C Christian painting has survived in this catacomb (the name probably comes from a particular burial place in the Via Appia Antica known as 'ad catacumbas' meaning 'in the hollow', which was then applied to all cemeteries). The central panel shows Christ as teacher and 4 Apostles, above this the Annunciation, and below it the Three Wise Men from the East. On the left are two Wise Men with the Madonna, and on the right is the Baptism of Christ.

Catacombe di Priscilla (Via Solaria): Very old Roman burial places (the first date from 191 BC), connected to a large catacomb in the 4C AD. The lavish early-Christian painting includes an Annunciation, Noah with the Dove, Abraham's Sacrifice and the Resurrection of Lazarus, as well as a unique picture of the Eucharist, the so-called Panis Fractio.

Colombario di Pomponio Hylas/Columbarium of Pomponius Hylas (between Via Appia Antica and Via Latina): Columbarium is the

Basilica of Constantine

name used for a grave chamber with wall niches for urns. The grave of the freedman Pomponius Hylas was built under Tiberius (AD 14–37) and was used until AD 150. The walls are articulated with pilasters, half columns, cornice and pediment and also have paintings on them.

Colosseo / Colosseum / Flavian Amphitheatre (Via dei Fori Imperiali): The first three tiers of this massive building were begun by the Emperor Vespasian in AD 72; Titus added the fourth tier and had the amphitheatre dedicated in the year 80 with a festival which lasted for 100 days. It was christened Colosseum in the Middle Ages, after the colossal statue of Nero which used to stand beside it. The building was neglected in the Christian period and the section on the Caelian side was destroyed in the earthquake of 1348. The Colos-

seum was built for gladiatorial games, animal fights, athletic contests and also dramatic performances; it accommodated about 50,000 spectators, mainly seated. The oval design of the amphitheatre developed from the stadium and the Greek theatre; it reached supreme heights in the Colosseum, which was designed by an unknown architect. It is 465 ft. long, 386 ft. wide and 118 ft. high. The *façade* is made up of three tiers of vaulted galleries in grey Travertine marble; the protruding half-columns are Doric in the first tier, Ionic in the second and Corinthian in the third. The closed wall of the uppermost tier is built in yellowish Travertine marble; there used to be bronze shields between the small square windows. The interior decoration and equipment are lost; the arena once had a planking floor with space for stage machinery, animals and

Forum Romanum, Temple of Castor and Pollux

contestants underneath it, but all that remains is the exposed substructure, although it is still clear how brilliantly the three *tiers for spectators* and the access to them were designed.

Domus Aurea di Nerone/Nero's Golden Palace (Via Labicana): After his Domus Transitoria on the Palatine was destroyed by the disastrous fire of the year AD 64, Nero began to build a new palace with extensive gardens. These gardens were wrecked by his successors and a fire in the year 104, and later the site was built on; the Colosseum occupies the site of the artificial lake. Substructure and ground-floor rooms were revealed in the Renaissance; rediscovered works of art included the Laocoon group (now in the Vatican Museum). Parts of the imperial residence, once magnificently decorated with gold, jewels and ivory and out-

standing examples of painting and sculpture, have been excavated: a long *cryptoportico* (vaulted corridor on the lower floor of a columned hall) with ceiling paintings, *rooms* with paintings in the fourth Pompeian style, the so-called *Hall of the decorated ceiling* with paintings by Fabullus, the *Sala quadrata* and the octagonal *domed room* among others.

Fori Imperiali/Imperial forums (Via dei Fori Imperiali): The Forum Romanum was extended by taking over a residential area to the N. of it, started by Julius Caesar in 54 BC, and continued by Augustus, Vespasian, Nerva and Trajan.

Foro di Augusto/Forum of Augustus: Octavius Augustus dedicated the Temple of Mars Ultor in 2 BC and surrounded it with a colonnaded square. Later Emperors restored and extended the buildings, which were used by Basilian monks in the 9C and later by the Order of St.John. Only the central part of the podium, column stumps and 3 reconstructed columns with pediment have survived of the *Temple of Mars Ultor*, a peripteral temple with 8 tall Corinthian columns on either side. The *Hall of Kolosses*, on the left by the temple, dates from the late imperial period, and its surrounding wall is still standing, along with a circular wall from the N. exedra which forms the lower part of the *Priory of the Knights of Malta*. The *Antiquario del Foro di Augusto* (Via Tor de'Conti) houses finds from the Forum of Augustus.

Foro di Cesare/Forum of Caesar: The centre of the new colonnaded square was the *Temple of Venus Genetrix*, consecrated by Julius Caesar in 46 BC and rebuilt by Domitian and consecrated by Trajan in AD 113. The three reconstructed columns and section of the entablature are evidence of the artistic quality of the building. Two storeys of some of the *shops* on the S. side of the square have survived, and there are also substantial remains of the *Basilica Argentaria*, which used to house the moneychangers and the stock exchange. Two rows of columns from an *ancient hall* have been reconstructed near the temple.

Foro di Nerva/Forum of Nerva: Domitian started to develop this area, which is also known as the *Forum Transitorium*, between the Forum of Augustus and the Forum of Vespasian (Templum Pacis), which has not yet been excavated. It was once dominated by the *Temple of Minerva*, later pulled down by Pope Paul V. Two stunted columns, fragments of the frieze and sections of the entablature have survived from the *colonnade* on the right.

Foro Romano/Forum Romanum

(Via dei Fori Imperiali): This low-lying site was drained *c.* 510 BC, and much built on in the 5C: the temples of Saturn and Castor, the Regia and the Temple of Vesta. Later additions were the Comitium precinct, where the citizens assembled, judges sat and parliament met; it also housed the Curia of the Senate, the Rostra (speakers' platform) and the Graecostis (stand for ambassadors from other countries), and a market. Julius Caesar began to rebuild the Forum, and work was completed by Augustus. Later Emperors also built in the Forum Romanum, which meant that it was very crowded by the end of the imperial period.

Starting to walk round from the E., the first feature to be reached is the **Arch of Titus** on the Velia, the saddle between the Palatine and the Esquiline, built in AD 81 by Domitian, after the death of Titus. It is the oldest surviving triumphal arch in Rome, and consists of a plain base with plain and fluted Corinthian columns with composite capitals at the corners beside the round arch. Above the jutting cornice is a plain attica. The triumphant quadriga has not survived, but the artistically perfect reliefs on the side walls showing Titus' procession of triumph over the Jews are still there.

To the right of the Arch of Titus is the **Temple of Venus and Roma**, designed by the Emperor Hadrian and consecrated in AD 136. This double temple is a Corinthian peripteral temple with 10 granite columns on the short sides and 44 on the long sides; the E. section was dedicated to Venus (the mother of the line of Roman Emperors) and the W. section to Roma. A row of reconstructed columns, part of the substructure and the two apses which housed the images of the gods have survived.

Statue of Marcus Aurelius on the Capitol ▷

Somewhat further forward and on the right are the massive ruins of the **Basilica of Constantine or Maxentius**, begun in AD 306–310 by Maxentius and completed by Constantine in 330. Like the basilicas of Julia and Aemilia it was used for legal and trading purposes, but was far more ambitiously conceived and built than these. Constantine moved the entrance of the huge basilica (the nave was 262 ft. long, 82 ft. wide and 115 ft. high) with nave and two aisles to the S., and built a second large apse on the N. wall. Its decline began under Pope Honorius I (625–638), who used the bronze tiles for the old St.Peter's. The nave and S. aisle collapsed, probably as a result of the earthquake of 847; only the monumental brick core of the N. aisle survived.

W. of this is the **Temple of Romulus**, a circular brick building built by Emperor Maxentius in AD 307 for his son Romulus, who died young. The two bronze doors from the columned portal survived; even without the pictorial decoration on the panels they were important as models for medieval cathedral doors. The *library* of the Forum of Vespasian behind the Temple of Romulus is now the church of *SS.Cosma e Damiano*.

S. of the Via Sacra is the House of the Vestal Virgins, the **Atrium Vestae**, opposite the Temple of Romulus. The building was rebuilt for the last time under Septimus Severus (AD 193–211), but all that has survived is the substructure, numerous bases for statues of the Vestals, and individual statues; the aedicule has been reconstructed. PNW by the Atrium Vestae is the reconstructed **Circular**

Forum Romanum 1 Arch of Titus **2** Temple of Venus and Roma **3** Basilica of Constantine or Maxentius **4** Temple of Romulus **5** Atrium Vestae **6** Temple of Vesta **7** Temple of Antoninus Pius and Faustina **8** Regia **9** Temple of Caesar **10** Temple of Castor and Pollux **11** Juturna spring **12** Temple of Augustus **13** S.Maria Antiqua **14** Julia Basilica **15** Temple of Saturn **16** Arch of Tiberius **17** Miliarium Aureum **18** Rostra **19** Lacus Curtius **20** Equestrian statue of Domitian **21** Equestrian statue of Constantine **22** Lapis Niger **23** Diocletian base **24** Comitium **25** Curia Julia **26** Basilica Aemilia **27** Temple of Concordia **28** Temple of Vespasian **29** Hall of the Dei Consentes **30** Arch of Septimus Severus

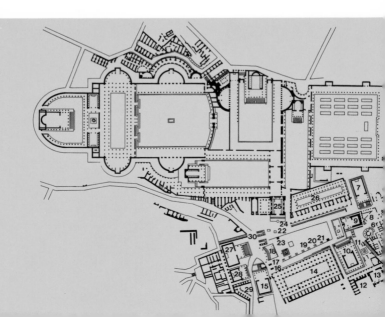

Temple of Vesta, in which the Vestal Virgins watched over the eternal flame. Rebuilt for the last time by Septimus Severus; sacrificial vessels and symbols of Roman priests can be seen on the entablature frieze.

Opposite and to the N. is the **Temple of Antonius Pius and Faustina**, built by the Emperor Antonius Pius in AD 141 in honour of his wife Anna Galeria Faustina the Elder, and also dedicated to him after his death in 161. In the Middle Ages the temple became the church of *S.Lorenzo in Miranda* (first mentioned in 1150); six columns from the temple façade and 2 columns from the long side have survived in front of the baroque church façade of 1602. On the left behind the church is a *prehistoric cemetery*; in front of the temple are remains of the Regia, the official residence of the pontifex maximus. W. of the Regia are the foundations of the *Temple of Caesar*, consecrated in 29 BC. Between the Temple of Caesar and the Temple of Castor and Pollux was the triumphal arch of Augustus dating from 20 BC.

Fragments of the podium of the **Temple of Castor and Pollux**, rebuilt in 117 BC, have survived; the first temple was consecrated in 484 BC; there are three 40 ft. high Corinthian columns with rich entablature from Tiberius' building of AD 6. E. of the temple was the *Well of Juturna*; legend has it that this is where Castor and Pollux watered their horses after announcing in the Forum the victory over the Tarquinians in 499 BC.

S. of this, at the end of the Vicus Tuscus, are ruins of the so-called **Temple of Augustus**; probably this rectangular brick building was part of the residence built by Domitian on the Palatine. In the imperial buildings next to it the church of **S.Maria Antiqua** was built in the 6C, adjacent to a Greek monastery. Pope Leo IV (847–855) transferred the monastery to the Temple of Venus and Roma. The church was restored in the 13C after a period of neglect, and rebuilt in 1617 at a higher level as S.Maria Liberatrice. With the exception of the ancient walls, on which fragments of outstanding 6–8C Romano-Byzantine

Arch of Titus with S.Maria Nuova

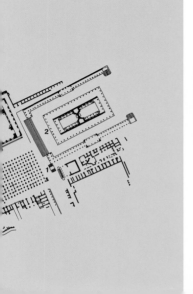

frescos have survived, it was pulled down in 1901&2. On the other side of the Vicus Tuscus opposite the Temple of Castor and Pollux are the foundations of the **Basilica Julia**, started *c*. 54 BC for Julius Caesar and consecrated by him in 46, but only finally completed by Augustus, who rebuilt it after a fire.

Only 8 Ionic columns have survived of the new **Temple of Saturn** built in the 4C. E. of this are foundations of the *Arch of Tiberius* and the square of the former *Miliarum Aureum*, the bronze-clad marble column of Augustus dating from 29 BC. Next to it, in front of the foundation walls of the *rostra* is a 2C 45 ft. high column, rebuilt in 608 as *Phocas' Column of Honour*. To the E. are then the *Lacus Curtius*, the foundations of a large *equestrian statue of Domitian* and a masonry *base*, presumably for an equestrian statue of Constantine the Great.

The triumphal arch of **Septimius Severus** was built in AD 205 for the tenth anniversary of his reign; the reliefs show events from the Emperor's campaigns. E. of the arch is the *Lapis Niger*, a black marble square said to mark the grave of Romulus. The surviving pedestal of the so-called *Diocletian monument* (built in AD 303 to celebrate the twentieth anniversary of Diocletian's reign) shows various sections of a sacrificial procession on its four sides.

The last feature of the NE area of the **Comitium** is the **Curia Julia**, the meeting-place of the Senate. After the first building rebuilt in 52 BC was destroyed, a new building was completed by Augustus in 29 BC. This was destroyed by fire in the 3C, and another new building was erected in 303 under Diocletian, and this was restored after 410. In the interior of the hall, 88 ft. by 59 ft., fragments of the coloured marble floor have survived; here too are the so-called *Trajan*

anaglyphs, marble barriers decorated with excellent reliefs, probably dating from the reign of Hadrian (117–138).

The **Basilica Aemilia** was founded in 179 BC by the censor Marcus Aemilius Lepidus, enlarged in 78 BC by Marcus Aemilius Paulus, rebuilt in the reign of Augustus after a fire, and restored in the 3C AD.

At the W. end of the Forum Romanum are the ruins of the **Temple of Concordia** at the foot of the Capitol, with remains of the building rebuilt by Tiberius in 10–7 BC; the temple was founded in 367 BC. Next to thisK are the remains of the *Temple of Vespasian* dating from 79 BC. 3 fine Corinthian columns from the six-columned narthex have survived. Some columns with entabulature of the adjacent *Hall of the Dei Consentes* have been reconstructed; the hall dates from the 2 or 3C BC, was rebuilt in the Flavian period and restored in AD 367.

Foro Traiano/Forum of Trajan/ Mercati Traianei/Market place of

Forum Romanum

Trajan: This is the largest and best-preserved imperial forum, built by the architect Apollodorus of Damascus in AD 107–112; a memorial temple to Trajan was added in the reign of Hadrian (117–138). The focal point was the bronze equestrian statue of the Emperor Trajan; the long sides of the square were taken up with colonnades, access was via the triumphal arch built in 116. At the end of the square was the *Basilica Ulpia*, a hall 427 ft. by 410 ft. still marked by a row of broken-off porphyry columns. Behind this was another square with the Column of Trajan of 113, library buildings and the pseudo-peripteros built by Hadrian at the W. end. The most important surviving feature of this splendid set of buildings is the 125 ft. high *Triumphal Column of Trajan*; the ashes of the Emperor were buried in a golden urn at its base. Most famous of all is the sculptural frieze which spirals from the base to the balcony and represents the Dacian wars of 101&2 and 105&6. The *Market place of Trajan* was excavated in 1908; the impressive remains of the great hall on the Via IV Novembre give a good impression of how a Roman shop used to look.

Janus Quadrifons/Arch of Janus (Piazza della Bocca della Verità): This marble building dating from the 4C AD covered up a junction which had been used as a meeting-place by the merchants of the Forum Boarium. There are large round-arched vaulted gates on the four sides, each with a picture of a god on the keystone. The outer walls consist of base and two storeys with shell niches and Corinthian columns.

Mausoleo di Augusto/Mausoleum of the Emperor Augustus (Piazza Augusto Imperatore): The Emperor Augustus built this burial place for himself and his family *c*. 28 BC; it is in the form of an earth mound surmounted by a stone circle. The marble-clad cylinder was 285 ft. in diameter and 144 ft. high. In the Middle Ages the building was used as the citadel of Colonna, destroyed in 1241, rebuilt as a villa in the 16C and used as a concert hall until 1936. After that all later accretions were removed,

Forum Romanum

Façade of the Capitol with Marcus Aurelius

with a result that today all that can be seen are three tiers of bare round walls, with cypresses growing on the lowest tier.

Palatino/Palatine: On the Palatine, one of the seven hills of Rome, was the oldest Roman settlement, documented from the 8C BC. Under the Republic it was a residential area (Cicero lived here), and in the imperial period it was covered with temples and other buildings. It declined in the Middle Ages but flourished again in the Renaissance; vineyards, gardens and pleasances were built. At the same time interest in the buildings of antiquity was aroused, but despite meticulous exploration right up to the present day only a fraction of the important monuments documented in written sources has been discovered.

The greater part of the *Domus Tiber-* *iana*, the palace of Tiberius, is under the **Farnese Gardens**, designed in the mid 16C for Cardinal Alessandro Farnese and completed in the early 17C by Girolamo Rainaldi. Parts of the podium of the *Temple of the Magna Mater*, completed in 191 BC have survived among remains of older houses. The outlines and holes scratched in the rock are evidence of *prehistoric huts.*

There are important Roman wall paintings in the so-called second Pompeian style in the surviving sections of the *House of Livia*, the consort of the Emperor Augustus. The rooms have no windows, and are decorated with illusionistic architectural painting, enchanting landscapes, and figures.

The *cryptoporticus*, a semi-underground corridor with tunnel vault over 400 ft. long, linked the individual sets of rooms in the imperial palace.

Forum Romanum with Temple of Saturn, Triumphal Arch of Septimus Severus and Basilica Ulpia

The **Flavian Palace** was built under Domitian (AD 81–96); the foundations of the peristyle, the triclinium and the imperial hall have survived. This consisted of the smaller Hall of the Lares (household gods), the central Aula Regia and a room called a basilica, probably used for court sessions.

The two-storey 2C BC **Gryphon House** is the oldest surviving private house from the Republican period, and was rebuilt in the middle of the first century BC. It is named after the two painted gryphons in one of the rooms.

The **Baths of Tiberius or Livia** were probably part of the Domus Transitoria or Nero's Domus Aurea; they have side rooms with floors in various kinds of marble and painted vaults.

There are surviving sections of the living rooms grouped around two spacious courtyards of the **Domus Augustana**, the imperial palace. The so-called *Stadium of Domitian*, over 450 ft. long, was presumably a garden laid out like a stadium. The earliest section which could have been used for sporting purposes was the small 6C elliptical area in the S.

The surviving substructure of the *Baths of Septimius Severus* (193–211) is one of the most splendid ruins on the Palatine.

The *Paedagogium* (the name is scribbled on the wall in various places) dates from AD 1 or 2 and was probably the living quarters of the imperial staff.

Pantheon/S.Maria della Rotonda (Piazza della Rotonda): The temple known as the Pantheon was consecrated in the Baths of Marcus Agrippa in 27 BC; it burned down in AD 110 and was replaced by the Emperor Hadrian in 120–5 with the present building, the most impressive circular building in the history of world architecture, and the ancient Roman building which has survived in the best condition. Pope Boniface IV (608–615) made the temple into the church of *S.Maria ad Martyres* and had the bones of many martyrs interred here. The exact purpose of the building has never been established, and the name of the architect is also not known. A wall 20 ft. thick forms a circle 142 ft. in diameter at its base; this supports a dome on stepped coffers which taper as they rise, leaving a circular opening 29 ft. in diameter. The interior is 142 ft. high, and could therefore contain a complete sphere. The walls are articulated with two-dimensional niches, columns and pilasters; the coloured marble cladding of the lower storey is ancient, the stucco on the upper section dates from 1747 (the original articulation has been exposed at one point). The temple-like façade outside the rotunda has eight columns, and a massive bronze door with two leaves leads from the portico into the interior. The interior is decorated with altars and tombs in rounded niches.

Piramide di Gaio Cestio/Pyramid of Cestius (Porta S.Paolo): In 11 BC C.Cestius, Praetor and tribune of the people, commissioned a pyramid in the cemetery on the road to Ostia; it was to be his tomb. There are still remains of frescos in the grave chamber, 13 ft. by 20 ft. The pyramid was rebuilt under Honorius (395–423) and is now 13 ft. underground.

Ponte Fabricio (Isola Tiberina): Built in 62 BC as Pons Fabricius, the bridge is the oldest in Rome; its two arches each has a span of 80 ft. The balustrade was added in 1679.

Ponte Mollo/Ponte Milvio/Mil-

Forum of Augustus, excavations in the Piazza Venezia

Excavations in the Area Sacra del Largo Argentina, Republican Temple, near Piazza di Calcori

vian Bridge: The 4 central arches of
the bridge were part of the new structure built in 109 BC by the Censor
Marcus Aemilius Scaurus. In 1805
Pope Pius VII commissioned Giuseppe Valadier to turn the bridge
tower, added in the 15C, into a triumphal arch. The baroque statues
represent St.John Nepomuk, John the
Baptist, the Baptism of Christ and the
Immaculata.

Porta Appia/Porta S.Sebastiano:
This city gate flanked by massive
square towers was rebuilt under
Emperor Honorius (395–423) and
restored again *c.* 530; above the
recessed round-arched door are two
rows of windows. Inside in front of
the Porta Appia is the so-called *Arch
of Drusus,* an arch from the Aqua
Marcia, probably built *c.* AD 200 and
incorporated in the Porta Appia by
Honorius.

Porta Maggiore: This city gate was
originally a way underneath the Aqua
Claudia and Anio Novus aqueduct,
built AD 38–53. It was incorporated in
the Aurelian city wall to form a small
fortified yard, lost in the 19C. As well
as the walls of the gate the late-
Republican *tomb of a Roman couple*
and the *tomb of M.Virgilius Eurysaces,*
once enclosed by a round tower, and
built by the baker and redemptor for
himself and his wife Atistia in the
second quarter of the 1C BC.

Porta Tiburtina: This arch was
built by Augustus in 5 BC for the
Aqua Marcia, Tepula and Julia, and
rebuilt by Titus in AD 79 and Caracalla in 212/3; a gateway with two
massive square flanking towers was
built in front of the arch under
Honorius (395–423).

**Portico d'Ottavia/Portico of
Octavia** (Via del Progresso): This
hall with two rows of columns was
built by Quintus Caecilius Metellus
Macedonicus in 148–146 BC and contained the Temple of Jupiter Stator

S.Maria in Cosmedin

and Juno Regina. Augustus rebuilt it
in 27 BC and dedicated it to his sister
Octavia; Septimus Severus and Caracalla rebuilt it after the fire of 205.
The columns and fragments of entabulature are now part of the porch of
the church of *S.Angelo in Pescheria.*

**Sepulcro degli Scipione/Tomb of
the Scipios** (Via di Porta S.Sebas-
tiano): The tomb of the famous
Roman Scipio family was hewn into
the rock, extended and provided with
gate and columned portico, parts of
which have survived. From the early
3C to the late 2C BC the Scipios were
buried in sarcophaguses here.

City wall: The so-called *Servian
Wall* was not built under King Servius Tullius (*c.* 550 BC), but at the
time of the Gallic invasion of 398 BC.
The most substantial remains are by
the Capitol and in front of the Sta-

Triumphal Arch of Septimus Severus

zione Termini. Once the people of the North began to invade Italy, the Emperor Aurelianus started c. AD 270 to build a wall to enclose the parts of the town which had grown up outside the Servian Wall. The enormously long *Aurelian Wall* was completed by the Emperor Probus (276–282); it was almost 12 miles long and had 380 towers 97 ft. apart (100 Roman ft.). The walls and gates were raised and partially rebuilt in AD 402 by Stilichio, Honorius' general. The Aurelian Wall was maintained and extended until the 19C, when individual sections were pulled down because of traffic problems.

Teatro di Marcello/Theatre of Marcellus (Via del Teatro di Marcello): This theatre in the N. of the Forum Holitorium (vegetable market) was built by Augustus in 17–13 BC in memory of his nephew Marcellus,

who died young. In the Middle Ages it was used as a fortress and residence; the accretions were removed in 1926, with the result that the exterior of the two magnificent tiers of arches gives a striking impression of how the original building must have been.

Tempio Circolare di Vesta/ Temple of Vesta (Piazza della Bocca della Verità): This circular temple in the Forum Boarium was never dedicated to Vesta, but to Portunus or the sun; it consists of a tufa base, a round cella and 20 slender fluted columns with (reconstructed) Corinthian capitals. The white marble building is presumed to date from the Augustan period, and was later used as a church, known in the late 17C as S.Maria del Sole.

Tempio di Adriano/Temple of the Emperor Hadrian (Piazza di Pie-

Via Appia Antica

Pantheon 1 Annunciation fresco ascribed to Melozzo da Forli **2** Tomb of Victor Emmanuel II (d.1878) **3** Tomb of Cardinal and Secretary of State Consalvi by Bertel Thorvaldsen, 1824 **4** Tomb of Raphael (1481–1520), on the altar is the statue of the Madonna del Sasso by Raffaello da Montelupo after a model by Raphael, on the left, bust of Raphael **5** Tomb of King Umberto I (d.1900), under it, tomb of Queen Margherita (d.1926) **6** Tomb of the painter and architect Baldassare Peruzzi (1481–1536) **7** Tombs of Taddeo Zuccaro, Pierin del Vaga and Flaminio Vacca

tra): Antonius Pius built this temple in AD 145 for his adoptive father, the deified Emperor Hadrian. Remains of the cella wall and 11 marble columns with Corinthian capitals have survived; they are now part of the wall of the Rome Stock Exchange.

Tempio della Fortuna Virile/ Temple of Fortuna Virilis (Piazza della Bocca della Verità): The so-called Temple of Fortuna Virilis dates from *c.* 100 BC and was probably dedi-

cated to Portunus, the god of harbours and gates, and thanks to the fact that it became the church of S.Maria Egiziaca in the 9C, it is the one temple to have survived almost complete from the Republican period. An open staircase leads to the 4 Ionic columns of the vestibule, and over their plain entablature is a pediment. In the interior outstanding 9C Carolingian wall paintings have survived; they show Peter and John at the empty tomb and Joachim with his shepherds.

Tempio di Minerva Medica/ Temple of Minerva Medica (Via Giovanni Giolitti): This building once stood in the Licinian Garden of the Emperor Gallienus (259–268); from the 17C, when a statue of Minerva with the snake was found here, the symbol of medicine, it was called the Temple of Minerva

Via Appia Antica

Medica. It may have been a lavishly decorated nymphs' shrine dating from the time of Constantine, and formerly had a dome (collapsed in 828) used as a model by Renaissance and baroque architects.

Templi repubblicani/Republican Temples (Largo di Torre Argentina): When a whole row of houses was being demolished in 1926–30, 4 temples from the Republican period were excavated here; it was impossible to establish with any certainty to which gods they were dedicated, and so they are identified with letters. 15 columns have survived from the 3C BC *Temple A*, and also a crypt and two apses with remains of frescos from the medieval church. *Temple B* was circular and dates from the 2C BC; *Temple C* is presumably 3 or 4C BC, but fragments of terracotta decoration suggest rebuilding in the imperial period.

Temple D is only half excavated and is the most recent of the four buildings.

Terme di Caracalla/Baths of Caracalla (Via Guido Baccelli): The baths were started under Septimius Severus in 206 BC and opened under Caracalla in AD 216; they are a masterpiece of Roman architecture, and the most magnificent municipal baths in Rome. They were restored under Aurelius (270–5), and did not start to fall into disrepair until the Goths cut off the water supply in 537, by damaging the Aqua Marcia. The vaults collapsed in the earthquake of 847. Large baths in the imperial period were used principally for bathing, but also for gymnastics, recreation, socializing and popular education. You undressed in the apodyterium, could than take a warm bath (in the caldarium), a lukewarm bath (in the tepidarium) or a cold one (in the frigidarium), have a steam bath, or sunbathe on the terraces, have a swim in the open-air pool (natatio) or play sport in the palaestrae. There were restaurants, club rooms, libraries, lecture rooms and shops, and also extensive gardens. The complex is strictly symmetrical and essentially square, with sides just over 1,000 ft. long. A wall with colonnades to the left and right of the entrance enclosed the gardens and sports areas, the shallow apses to the E. and W. contained lecture halls and rooms for gymnastics. Between them was the massive bath house with its multitude of differently-shaped rooms with domes, half domes, tunnel, half-tunnel or groin vaults and walls of an equal variety of design. The surviving ruins still give an excellent idea of composition and scale, but not of the magnificent decoration and furnishing.

Terme di Diocleziano/Baths of Diocletian (Piazza della Repubblica): These were the largest baths in Rome; they cover an area of 1,168 ft. by 1,037 ft., and were started by the Emperor Diocletian in AD 298 and completed in 305. They have survived surprisingly well, principally because they were placed at the disposal of the Carthusians, who built cloisters and monastery buildings here from 1561, including Michelangelo's church of S.Maria degli Angeli. The baths museum has been housed here since the late 19C.

Terme di Traiano/Baths of Trajan (Via delle Terme di Traiano): Only fragments have survived of these baths built over Nero's golden palace after AD 104; the architect was Apollodorus of Damascus.

Tomba dei Valerii (Via Latina): This two-storey tomb, built in AD 159, contains splendid stucco reliefs with rosettes and individual figures in squares as well as dancing couples and nereids in circles. In the central panel a winged gryphon is leading a shrouded dead man to the gods.

Tomba di Cecilia Metella/Tomb of Cecelia Metella (Via Appia Antica): The mausoleum of Cecilia

Teatro di Marcello (Theatre of Marcellus)

Metella is an impressive rotunda 66 ft. in diameter and decorated with a relief frieze with garlands and bucranes. The battlements were added in 1299 when it became the castle of the Caetani.

Tomba di Pancrazi (Via Latina): One of the underground grave chambers is decorated with outstanding coloured stucco reliefs dating from the first half of the 2C AD. The walls are lavishly decorated with trompe l'oeil gods, centaurs and animals and the shallow tunnel vault has 4 mythological scenes on the model of Greek painting. The centrepiece shows Jupiter being carried into the sky by an eagle.

Via Appia Antica: This 'Queen of Streets' was built by the Censor Appius Claudius Caecus in 312 BC, at the same time as the first water system, the Aqua Appia; the Appian Way led from Rome to Capua, 200 km. away. It was later continued via Benevento and Tarento to Brindisi. As burial within the city was forbidden, graves were sited on the great roads which led out of it. The first tombs are immediately beyond the Porta Appia; the most important in this group is the tomb of the Scipios. The Via della Caffarelli branches off beyond the little church of 'Domine, quo vadis?' and on it is the so-called *Tempio del Dio Redicolo*, the lavishly decorated mausoleum of Annia Regilla, the wife of Herodes Atticus, dating from the 2C AD. The *Tomb of Romulus*, the son of the Emperor Maxentius, who died in AD 307, is just past the Calixtus catacomb and the church of S.Sebastiano. Beyond this are the ruins of the *Circus of Maxentius*, built in 309; the chariot racing track was over 500 yards long and 86 ft. wide. After the tomb of Caecilia Metella comes a stretch of the Via Appia Antica about 4 km. long; the ancient paving stones only show through in a few places, but there are many graves: the grave of Servilius, the tomb of the sons of Sextus Pompeius, the so-called grave of St.Uranus, the monument to Hilarius Fuscus, the grave of the Secundini, the tomb of the Rabieri. After this are some stones with inscriptions and the

Via Appia Antica

site if the *Villa of the Quintilines*, the so-called *Graves of the Horatii* and *Casal Rotondo*, a cylindrical tomb. A little further on is the the *Torre Selce* on a high grave pyramid, a 12C tower. After the *Torre Rossa*, a half-ruined 12&13C Saracen tower, and the 'Pillars of Hercules' the Via Appia Antica peters out into a country lane. Shortly after this, just outside the city, it joins the busy Via Appia Nuova.

II. The Churches of Rome

The basilicas, the first large Christian buildings, are the most influential contribution to the development of western ecclesiastical architecture. The largest are the 5 patriarchal basilicas (Basilicae maiores) S.Giovanni in Laterano, S.Pietro in Vaticano (Old St.Peter's), S.Paolo fuori le

Baths of Caracalla 1 Main entrance 2 Ancient entrances 3 Modern entrances 4 Adopteria 5 Natatio 6 Frigidarium 7 Tepidarium 8 Caldarium 9–12 Steam and massage rooms 13 Palaestrae 14 Instruction rooms 15 Exedrae 16 Sports area with spectator's stand, water container underneath 17 Libraries 18 Palaestrae 19 Conference and lecture rooms 20 Aqueduct

mura, S.Maria Maggiore and S.Lorenzo fuori le mura. With the exception of memorial and funerary buildings the rotunda was only integrated into Christian liturgy in the form of the baptistery (e.g. S.Giovanni in Fonte), although S.Stefano Rotondo is the exception which proves the rule. In the Middle Ages, because of papal problems, Rome was not the centre of church architecture. The only Gothic church of any size in Rome is S.Maria sopra Minerva. It was not until the papacy was strengthened and above all after the Council of Trent (1547) that church building began to increase again, with the lead coming from Rome. Bramante's Tempietto near S.Pietro in Montorio is an example of an almost revolutionary humanism, Michelangelo's version of New St.Peter's is the apotheosis of the monumental, Vignola's domed Il Gesù paved the way for the baroque. This new style, which could be said to have been born in Rome, was profoundly interlinked with the Jesuits and the Counter-Reformation: individual architectural elements can no longer be considered in isolation, architecture and decor-

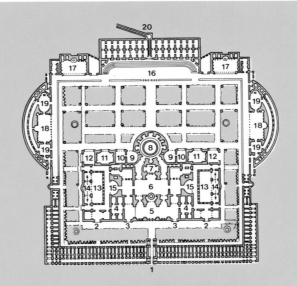

ation become a co-ordinated whole. The control of light becomes an essential element in composition, and the breadth of the space is the most striking feature of the church interior. The outstanding architects of the period are F.Borromini (S.Carlo alle Quattro Fontane, S.Ivo alla Sapienza, S.Agnese in Agone), G.L.Bernini (S.Andrea al Quirinale), G.della Porta (S.Andrea della Valle), C.Maderna (S.Susanna), P. da Cortona (SS Luca e Martina, S.Maria della Pace), C.Rainaldi (S.Maria in Campitelli) and D.Fontana (work on S.Giovanni in Laterano and S.Maria Maggiore).

Abbazia alle Tre Fontane (Via delle Tre Fontane): At the place where the Apostle Paul was executed, and where three springs burst forth when his severed head struck the ground three times, there are now three churches. An arch survives of the monastery founded in 625 and occupied by Cistercians from 1140. *Monastery church of SS.Vencenzo e Anastasio*: this brick basilica with a nave and two aisles was built in the austere style of Cistercian Romanesque and has a transept and straight choir. The point at which the intended tunnel vaulting was to spring can still be seen in the stark interior with its open beams. The window glass is 13C and there are 16C frescos. *S.Paolo alle Tre Fontane*: Centrally planned building built by Giacomo della Porta in 1599 on the site of an earlier 5C church; the interior contains three monumental symbolic fountains and remains of a late Roman mosaic floor. *S.Maria Scala Coeli*: Octagonal church built in 1583 by Giacomo della Porta; its crypt is held to have been St.Paul's prison.

S.Agata dei Goti (Via Mazzarino): This church of the Aryan Goths dating from the second half of the 5C became a Catholic churtch in 592, was rebuilt in the 16&17C and F.Ferrari added the narrow façade in 1729. In the interior the basic features of the early Christian basilica with a nave and two aisles can still be discerned, despite baroque decoration; the broad nave is divided from the aisles by ancient columns. The four-columned ciborium and the partially preserved floor were the work of 12 or 13C Cosmati artists; the flat ceiling dates from 1633; the frescos with the legend of St.Agatha on the upper walls of the nave date from the 17C.

S.Agnese in Agone (Piazza Navona): At the place where St.Agnes was to have been led naked before the crowd before her execution, an intention which was thwarted by the miraculous growth of her hair, there used to stand the stadium built by the Emperor Domitian in AD 86, the outline of which can still be made out in the present Piazza Navona. Pope Innocent X had a church built on the W. side of the square in memory of the martyr—together with the Palazzo Pamphili—and this was begun in 1652 by Girolamo Rainaldi and completed by Carlo Rainaldi in 1657–72. The broad, concave façade with two towers is dominated by the towering drum dome, and has a very fine monumental portal decorated with pilasters and pediments; it was a strong influence on the later baroque architecture of Central Europe. The tendency to centrality of the cruciform plan is emphasised by the dome, painted by C.Ferri, S.Corbellini and Gaulli (work completed in 1689). Interior: 3 17C altars with sculptural reliefs, tomb of Innocent X (1730, by G.B.Maini), underground remains of Domitian's arena containing an altar picture 'Miracle of St.Agnes' Hair' (*c*.1653, by A.Algardi).

S.Agnese fuori le mura (Via Nomentana): The original Basilica of St.Agnes was endowed in the 4C by Constantia, the daughter of Constantine. The present church was built under Pope Honorius I (625–638) and is on another site, reached through the columned courtyard of the Lateran

Canons. An early 16C Renaissance portal and a long marble staircase dating from 1590 lead into the vestibule into which the three portals of the plain façade open. In 1603 so much soil was removed from the area surrounding the church that it was possible to build free-standing side chapels. In the interior of the basilica with nave and two aisles, surrounded by galleries on the end and the long sides, the arches are supported by 16 columns; the columns are repeated at the level of the galleries. The high nave has a lavish wooden roof dating from 1600, and round-arched windows. The lower wall of the apse is clad with grey marble and porphyry; the apse mosaic with St.Agnes between Popes Honorius and Symmachus dates from the 7C, as does the stone bishop's throne. The baroque altar baldacchino dates from 1614, and the decoration on the triumphal arch from 1855.

S.Agostino (Piazza S.Agostino): This church, one of the most important of the Roman Early Renaissance, was endowed by Cardinal Guillaume d'Estrouville. It was built in 1479–83 as an Augustinian hermitage church by G.da Pietrasanta and S.Fiorentino, and altered in the mid 18C. The Travertine marble Renaissance façade is articulated with pilasters and has a higher pedimented central section with side scrolls; it is based on S.Maria del Popolo. The rather more conventional interior is dominated by the crossing dome; the circular design is an architectural innovation. The basilica with nave and two aisles has metric-system vaulting, side chapel and transept, and leads to a choir with a semicircular apse, and side choirs with straight apses. Furnishings: high altar (1627) with Byzantine Madonna (transferred from Hagia Sophia in 1453) and Bernini angels, 'Madonna del Parto', the revered miraculous image of the pregnant Mary (1518–21, by J.Sansovino). Other important works of art by Raphael, Caravaggio, Sansovino and Guernico.

S.Anastasia (Via di S.Teodoro): This titular church certainly existed in the second half of the 4C (derived from titulus, which means house inscription; the post-Constantine churches were built on house plots) and was originally a very short single-aisled building with a transept and apse; it was extended as a basilica with nave and two aisles, presumably by Leo III (795–816), and often altered later. The present façade was built between 1636 and 1644 by L.Arrigucci, a pupil of Bernini; the lively interior decoration dates from the most recent alteration in 1721&2. The figure of St.Anastasia under the high altar was the work of F.Aprile and E.-Ferrata, under the influence of Bernini. The little picture of Jerome in the choir at the end of the l. aisle is attributed to Domenichino. Substantial remains of a portico and a street with 2&3C houses have been revealed under the church.

S.Andrea al Quirinale (Via del Quirinale): Prince Camillo Pamphili commissioned a new building on the site of an earlier Jesuit church in 1658. His brilliant architect Gian Lorenzo Bernini built this major work of Roman baroque architecture on a small oval plan surrounded by 8 chapels and a larger altar niche. The pilastered façade has a triangular pediment and is almost entirely taken up by the portal, which is placed in context by the half oval of the approach staircase and the rounded temple portico. The interior is defined by the shallow dome with lantern and the alternating chapels. The altar niche opposite the entrance concludes in a massive aedicula with double columns. It contains the sculpture of the 'Martyrdom of St.Andrew', accentuated by the play of the light, and the altar picture of

S.Clemente, Annunciation, detail ▷

S.Clemente, bust of Apollo

smaller rectangular windows. The light dome soars over the crossing; the ground plan is cruciform, with side chapels. Dome frescos: 'Glory of Paradise' (1621–5, by G.Lanfranco) and Evangelists (1624–8, by Domenichino). Apse frescos: scenes from the life of the patron saint by Domenichino (*c.*1625) and Mattia Preti (1650–1). Piccolomini papal graves (*c.*1500). Cappella Lancellotti (1670, by Carlo Fontana).

S.Andrea delle Fratte (Via di S.Andrea): The nave of this imposing brick building, first mentioned in the 12C was rebuilt *c.*1600 in the style of Il Gesù and altered by Borromini (transept, dome and campanile) in 1653–6. The façade (1826) is by Valadier. The parts of the building designed by Borromini are the most remarkable features, above all the elegant bell tower with its bizarrely shaped top. Furnishings: 2 expressive Bernini angels by the high altar (created in 1667–70 for the Ponte S.Angelo), 19C artists' tombs (Angelika Kauffmann, R.Schadow).

SS.Apostoli (Piazza dei SS.Apostoli): This church, founded in the 6C, later became the private chapel of the nearby Palazzo Colonna and was rebuilt in 1702–8 by F. and C.Fontana. Façade by G.Valadier. It is the last of the great Roman basilicas, and has a wide, palace-like portico (begun *c.*1500 by B.Pontelli) with nine arches on the ground floor and a baroque upper storey pierced by windows. There are baroque sculptures of Christ and the Apostles (1681) on the columned balustrade at the top. The portico contains items of Roman and medieval art. The massive scale and high triumphal arch give nave, aisles and choir the appearance of a single, unified space. The central feature of the ceiling frescos is a depiction of the triumph of the Franciscan Order (1707, by Baciccia). In the Confessio are the bones of the Holy Apostles Philip and James. Splendid tomb of

the 'Crucifixion of St.Andrew' (1688, by Borgnone), supported by stucco angels. In the convent is the tomb of St.Stanislaus Kostka (*c.*1700, by P.Legros).

S.Andrea della Valle (Corso Vittorio Emanuele II): This church of the Theatine Order has one of the most impressive baroque façades in Rome; it was started in 1591 by Giacomo della Porta and completed in 1665 by Carlo Rainaldi. The incidental involvement of Carlo Maderna shows in the magnificent dome (1622–5), which is the largest in Rome after St.Peter's. The façade rises through two storeys, and is articulated with powerful double columns and topped with a massive pediment. The central section is slightly protruding, and has a portal at the bottom and a loggia at the top, while the side sections are decorated with niches with figures or

Pope Clement XIV (1787, by Antonio Canova) in a transitional style from baroque to neoclassicism. 15C cardinals' graves.

S.Balbina (Via di S.Balbina): This church consists of a rectangular room, with side walls opening into 6 alternately square and semicircular niches, and a semicircular apse to the E. The ancient building was restored in 1930; important remains of 9–14C wall paintings have survived. The tomb of Cardinal Surdi to the right of the entrance was created by G.di Cosma in 1303. The Crucifixion relief in one of the chapels is the work of Mino da Fiesole or G.Dalmata.

S.Bartolomeo all'Isola (Isola Tiberina): Only the brick tower remains of the memorial church founded c.1000 by Emperor Otto III for St.Adalbert of Prague. After destruction by floods in 1557 the church was rebuilt in 1624 by Orazio Torriani and dedicated to St.Bartholomew. The columned basilica with nave and two aisles has a nave with a flat ceiling, groin-vaulted aisles, narrow transept and main and side choirs. Relics of the patron saint under the high altar. Remarkable marble well (c.1000) above the spring of an old Aesculapian shrine with arch figures: St.Adalbert, Christ, the Apostle Bartholomew and Emperor Otto III.

S.Bibiana (Via Giovanni Giolitti): The original 4&5C church was restored in 1220 and formed the basis for radical rebuilding by Bernini under Pope Urban VIII. The basilica with nave and two aisles lies beyond a portico, and contains 8 ancient columns. There are relics of S.Bibiana under the high altar with a powerful sculpture of the martyr (1626, by Bernini). Wall frescos of the life of the saint by Pietro da Cortona and A.Ciampelli.

S.Clemente, Mary beneath the Cross ▷

S.Carlo ai Catinari (Piazza Benedetto Cairoli): This church was built in 1612–50 to designs by Rosato Rosati in the Catinari (basinmakers) quarter and dedicated to St.Carlo Borromeo. The sculpturally modelled pilastered façade with protruding central section is the work of G.B.Soria (1635). The crossing dome is supported by 4 piers and is the central point of the cruciform building. Dome frescos: 4 cardinal virtues (1630, by Domenichino). Apse frescos; 'Ascension of St.Charles' (1647, by G.Lanfranco).

S.Carlo al Corso (Via del Corso): The church was begun in 1612 by Onorio Lunghi and completed in 1672. G.B.Menicucci created the colossal columned façade in 1684. The dome (1668, by Pietro da Cortona) and ambulatory are the architectural highlights of the cruciform building. Furnishings: frescos (1623–91, by G.Brandi), high altar (*c.*1660, by Carlo Fontana) with painting (1685-90 by C.Maratta).

S.Carlo alle Quattro Fontane (Via delle Quattro Fontane): This is Borromini's first Roman church, built in 1638–41 and named after the four fountains (dedicated to the Tiber, the Aniene, Faith and Bravery) at the junction. It is one of his major works, and one of the treasures of baroque architecture. The rhythm of the curved columned façade, topped with cornice, balustrade and medallion, is concave-convex-concave on the lower storey and concave-concave-concave in the upper one. In the middle of the lower section is a portal topped with sculpture, and above it a curved balcony with a little oval temple, flanked by windows and sculpture niches. There is a turret above the fountain, which is an integral part of the façade. In the interior only the cornice follows the ground plan of the building: a rhombus with circular or elliptical corners. The rhombus is charmingly blurred by the organisation and resolution of the walls, and the entire interior is a continual source of optical surprises.

S.Caterina dei Funari (Via dei Funari): This church was built by

S.Clemente, temple and altar of Mithras, 2C BC

G.Guidetti on the site of an earlier 12C building; it has a decorative pilastered façade, bell tower with crown-shaped tip, vaulted nave, side chapels and tunnel-vaulted rectangular choir. High altar paintings 'Martyrdom of St.Catherine' and 'Annunciation' (by L.Agresti). On the side walls life of the patron saint (1571, by F.Zuccaro). Further paintings by Annibale, Muziano and Pulzone.

S.Cecilia in Trastevere (Via di S.Cecilia): According to legend this is the site of the house of St.Valerian, the husband of St.Cecilia, who was martyred under Marcus Aurelius (161–180). The first church was built in the 5C, rebuilt under Pope Paschal I (817–824) and altered later, particularly in the 19C. The fine façade with 12C and baroque elements is reached through a baroque portal which leads into the large courtyard. The five-storey brick bell tower with its massive cornices dates from the first half of the 12C. In the interior, a low basilica without transept, are the tomb of Cardinal Forteguerri (d.1473) by

Mino da Fiesole, the excellent tomb of Cardinal Herford, (d.1398) and the altar ciborium of A.di Cambio of 1293 and S.Maderna's masterly marble statue of St.Cecilia created in 1599&1600. The mosaic in the hemisphere of the apse showing Christ on the heavenly cloud dates from the 9C. The most important work of art in the church is P.Cavallini's Last Judgement of 1293, on the inner entrance wall of the church. This wonderful wall picture shows Christ in the mandorla as judge of the world, surrounded by angels, with the Madonna, John the Baptist and Apostles, including angels with trumpets. A vaulted passage with gargoyles by Paul Brill leads from the right aisle to the ancient calidarium, where the altar picture of the school of G.Romano and frescos narrate the legend of St.Cecilia and St.Valerian. There are remains of a floor mosaic in the ruins of a Roman house.

S.Clemente (Via S.Giovanni in Laterano): Pope Siricius (384–99) built a basilica over a shrine of Mithras, probably established in an older

S.S.Cosma e Damiano, courtyard and fountain

S.Clemente, St.Catherine and the Philosophers, detail

SS.Cosma e Damiano, angel in the apse mosaic

Roman building in the 3C; the basilica was destroyed in the 11C. Pope Paschal II (1099–1118) then built a new, smaller basilica on the base, raised by the dumping of rubble. *Mithraic temple*: some rooms of this large Roman building are accessible; the Temple of Mithras is a long tunnel-vaulted room with stone benches at the sides, and an altar with a relief of Mithras. *Lower church*: This columned basilica with nave and two aisles was not discovered and excavated until the 19C; it contains outstanding 8–12C Romanesque wall paintings, with 5–8C frescos in the aisles. *Upper church*: The courtyard outside the church is surrounded on three sides by a portico with columns taken over from ancient buildings, and on the fourth side is the façade rebuilt by C.S.Fontana in 1715. The basilica has a nave and two aisles with

arches supported by alternate fluted and smooth columns, and a fine marble floor, also a remarkable choir for which the 6C slabs from the lower church were used. The apse dome and the triumphal arch are decorated with early 13C mosaics. The splendid early Renaissance paintings in the Cappella di S.Caterina were endowed by Cardinal Castiglione and probably painted in 1425 by Masolino.

SS.Cosma e Damiano (Via dei Fori Imperiali): A building from Vespasian's Forum Pacis was transformed by Pope Felix IV (526–530) into the church of the oriental martyr-doctors Cosmas and Damian; baroque interior 1632. The excellent mosaics on the triumphal arch (in bad condition) and the apse hemisphere date from 526–30.

S.Constanza (Via Nomentana): The

daughter of the Emperor Constantine, Constantia (d.354), had her mausoleum built near the original basilica of St.Agnes. This brightly-lit annular building has arches supported by 12 double columns, and is surrounded by a dark, tunnel-vaulted ambulatory. In the surrounding wall there are small, alternately concave and convex niches, and a larger, taller one opposite the entrance containing the splendid marble sarcophagus copy; original in the Vatican Museum). The 4C dome mosiacs of Biblical scenes were lost; in the vaulting of the ambulatory are mosaics of vine tendrils with birds and putti, and scenes of the grape harvest as a symbol of changing nature and resurrection. Christian subjects are illustrated in two niches: Christ hands over the keys of heaven to St.Peter and the law to the Apostles.

S.Crisogno in Trastevere (Viale di Trastevere): The present basilica was built in 1123 over an 8C building which replaced the titular church of St.Crisogno, which occupied the site from the 5C. It was redesigned in the baroque style in 1618–26 and given a new façade. In the *lower church*, excavated *c*.1924 fragments of 8–11C wall paintings have survived. The *upper church* has 22 ancient granite columns with a remarkable mosaic of the school of P.Cavallini in the apse, a Madonna with St.Chrysogono and St.James.

S.Croce in Gerusalemme ('Basilica Sessoriana'; Piazza S.Croce in Gerusalemme): This, one of the 'seven churches' in Rome, contains relics of the Cross of Christ found by the Empress Helena, the mother of Constantine, in the Holy Land on 3

May 326, and brought to Rome. They were first housed in the Palatium Sessorianum, then in 1144 Pope Lucius II built a basilica for them within the walls of the 3C palace; this was redesigned in baroque style by D.Gregorini in 1743–50. The brick tower with coloured insets was part of the Romanesque building, but the lavishly articulated façade with an oval portico topped with the sculpture 'Apotheosis of the Cross' has rococo traits. The plain interior with a single aisle still has a Cosmati-work floor and 8 ancient columns from the earlier Romanesque building. Apse fresco 'St.Helena finds the Cross' (c.1500, by A.Romano). Under the high altar are relics of the martyrs Caesarius and Anastasius. Reliquary chapel with particles of the Cross. Chapel of St.Helena in the crypt, built on earth from Mount Golgotha.

S.Francesca Romana (opposite the Colosseum): A new church was built in 1216–27 on the site of an oratory for St.Peter and St.Paul, the 9C church of S.Maria Nova; it was given its present name in the 15C and rede-

signed in the baroque style by C.Lombardi in 1600–15. The splendid bell tower was part of the Romanesque building, but the pilastered façade with triangular pediment topped with statues and side scrolls shows the influence of Palladio. The flat-ceilinged interior has a coloured marble confessio (1644–9, by Bernini) and the crypt a relief panel from the old high altar (c.1650, by E.Ferrata).

S.Francesco a Ripa (Piazza S.Francesco d'Assisi): The Franciscans built a monastery church in the years following 1231 on the site of a pilgrims' inn said once to have housed St.Francis of Assisi. The columned basilica with nave and two aisles was largely rebuilt by M.de'Rossi from 1682 onwards. The finest of the lavish side chapels is the Cappella di S.Anna, which contains the passionate statue of the Blessed Luisa Albertoni (d.1674), an excellent late work by Bernini.

Il Gesù (Piazza del Gesù): This is the Western prototype of the longitudinal domed church and was the model for

S.Giovanni in Laterano

numerous baroque churches. It is the mother church of the Jesuit Order, endowed by Cardinal Alessandro Farnese of Vignola; work started in 1568 and was completed in 1584. The pre-baroque pilastered façade rises towards the centre, and has a triangular pediment and side scrolls; it was designed by G.della Porta (*c*.1576). The interior was redesigned in the baroque style in the 17C. It is built on a Latin cross plan with tunnel-vaulted nave and transepts, semicircular apse and dominant crossing dome, on the model of S.Andrea in Mantua. The nave is designed for Jesuit-style mass and preaching, while the rows of interconnected side chapels are reserved for pastoral purposes. The management of light is an important feature; the principal sources are the nave vaults and the dome. The baroque decoration gives the originally austere room a festive look. Fresco in the nave vault: 'Triumph of the Name of Jesus' (by Baciccia).

S.Giovanni dei Fiorentini (Via Giulia): The church of the Florentines in Rome was started by J.Sanso-

vino as a centrally-planned building, and continued by A.da Sangallo the Younger as an academic and austere piered basilica with nave and two aisles, transept and crossing dome; this work was completed in 1564. Michelangelo submitted ambitious designs for a centrally-planned building in 1556, but they were rejected. The building was continued by G.della Porta in 1584–1614 (transept and choir), by C.Maderna from 1611–14 (octagonal crossing dome) and A.-Galilei in 1734 (façade). Furnishings: high altar (by Borromini), tombs. The crypt, a masterly oval space with a shallow dome designed by Borromini, was used as the tomb of the Falconieri.

S.Giovanni in Laterano and **Scala Santa** (Piazza S.Giovanni in Laterano): The palace of the Plautii Laterani came into the possession of the imperial family in the 3C through Fausta, the wife of Constantine. Constantine presented the buildings to Pope Melchiades, and it remained the papal residence until the time of the exile in Avignon. S.Giovanni in

S.Giovanni in Laterano, interior

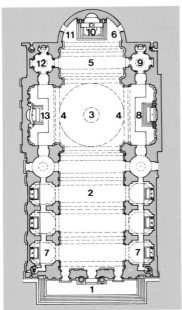

Il Gesù 1 Façade (by G.della Porta, *c.* 1580) **2** Nave **3** Crossing dome **4** Transept **5** Choir **6** Apse (**2–6**) with frescos by G.B.G.Baciccia, 1669–83) **7** Side chapels, extending the length of the nave to the transept, seating above them **8** Altar of St.Francis Xavier (by P.da Cortona, 1674–8; altar picture by C.Maratta) **9** Cappella del S.Cuore (attributed to G.della Porta. frescos by B.Croce, 1599) **10** High altar (by A.Sarti, 1834–43) **11** Bust at the memorial of St.Robert Bellarmin (by Bernini, 1622) **12** Cappella di S.Maria degli Astelli (by G.Valeriani, frescos by A.Pozzo) **13** Tomb altar of St.Ignatius (by A.Pozzo, 1696–1700) with silver statue (by P.Legros) and the marble groups of the Trinity, Faith and Religion

Laterano is still the titular church of the Bishop of Rome, and thus the highest-ranking church in Catholic Christendom, the first of the 4 basilicae maiores and actual papal church. Basilica and palace are extra-territorial Vatican possessions. Originally dedicated to the Salvator (Redeemer), the church later came under the patronage of St.John the Baptist and St.John the Evangelist. It was the first monumental building in Christendom, and built with imperial funds; it is a columned basilica with nave and four aisles, transept and apse, formerly with a massive atrium. It was rebuilt after an earthquake in 905 under Pope Sergius III, and very lavishly decorated. After several fires the building fell into disrepair during the the Popes' exile in Avignon. Later restoration altered the appearance of the original basilica: in 1585 Domenico Fontana added a portico to the transept, and the church was redesigned in the baroque style by Borromini from 1650; A.Galilei added the façade in 1733–6 and the choir was enlarged in 1886. Beyond the façade, articulated with colossal pilasters, is Borromini's nave, which preserved the basilican character of the building. The arch-piers have been joined together to form pier blocks articulated with pilasters, giving movement to the nave. The vigorous niches contain figures of the Apostles. The *cloister*, completed in 1230, is similar to that of S.Paolo fuori le mura. The *Lateran baptistery, S.Giovanni in Fonte*, was built to a circular design by Constantine the Great on the foundations and rooms of the Laterani palace. It is the oldest Christian baptismal church, and was redesigned as an octagon under Pope Sixtus III (432–440). It was altered in the early 16C and in the 17C. In the Cappella della S.Seconda e S.Rufina, the old entrance to the baptistery, a small 5C apse mosaic has survived. The important 7C mosaic in the Cappella di S.Veneziano depicts among other things symbols of the Evangelists, Jerusalem and Bethlehem, Christ and Mary and Popes John IV and Theodore. The bronze door of the Cappella di S.Giovanni Evangelista dates from 1190, the alabaster altar is early baroque. The *Lateran Palace* in its present form was built in 1586 under Sixtus V by D.Fontana. The building is an extension of the basilica, and is built around three sides of a courtyard. Sixtus V also had the columns from

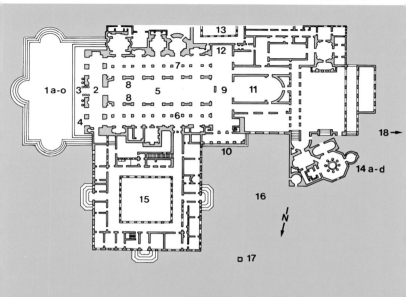

S.Giovanni in Laterano 1 Main façade (by A.-Galilei, 1733–6) with main and side portals, benediction loggia and attica figures (from left to right): **a** Eusebius **b** Thomas Aquinas **c** Basil **d** John Chrysostom **e** Ambrose **f** Gregory the Great **g** John the Baptist **h** Christ **i** John the Evangelist **j** Jerome **k** Augustine **l** Athanasius **m** Gregory of Nazianzus **n** Bernard of Clairvaux **o** Bonaventure **2** Main façade portico **3** Ancient bronze door of the Curia in the Forum Romanum **4** Porta Sancta **5** Nave (rebuilt in 1650 by Borromini) **6** right-hand double aisle with numerous tombs of popes, cardinals and wealthy Roman citizens **7** left-hand double aisle with Cappella Corsini (by A.Galilei, c. 1734) **8** Columned tabernacle and monumental niche figures of the Apostles (1703–19) **9** Transept (by G.della Porta) **10** N. portico (by D.Fontana, 1585) **11** Choir (19C) with papal throne (attributed to G.di Stefano, 1367; rebuilt 1851, relics of the heads of Peter and Paul) and bronze tomb slab (by S.di Giovanni Ghini, 1432) **12** Sacramental altar (by P.P.Olivieri, 16C) **13** Cloister (by father and son Vassalletto, c. 1240) with numerous spoils from the old basilica **14** Baptistery S.Giovanni in Fonte (early Christian, 5C; altered in the 16C and the baroque period) with 5–7C side chapels: **a** Cappella del Battista **b** Cappella delle SS.Seconda e Rufina **c** Cappella di S.Venanzio **d** Cappella di S.Giovanni Evagelista **15** Lateran Palace (by D.Fontana, 1586) **16** Piazza S.Giovanni in Laterano **17** Egytian obelisk from the Circus Maximus **18** Ospedale di S.Giovanni (founded 1218, rebuilt c. 1650) on the remains of ancient buildings

the Circus Maximus set up in front of the palace. On the N. side of the church of S.Giovanni in Laterano is the *Ospedale di S.Giovanni*, founded in 1216 and rebuilt in the 17C. It is built on the remains of older buildings, including houses which may have belonged to Annius Verus and the Laterani family. NE of the Lateran Palace is the shrine of

SS.Salvatore della Scala Santa, built in 1585 by D.Fontana over the remains of the 4C papal palace. The building houses the *Sacred Ladder*, consisting of 28 marble steps clad in wood. It is said to have come from the house of Pilate, and to have been brought to Rome by Helena. In the upper storey is the former papal private chapel, decorated by Cosmati workers in the 13C. This *Capella Sancta Sanctorum* contains costly relics, including a picture of Christ set in silver (6&7C), which according to legend was not painted by human hand. There are remains of the dining room of the old Papal Palace on the E. exterior wall.

SS.Giovanni e Paolo (Piazza dei SS.Giovanni e Paolo): Tradition has it that the imperial officials John and Paul were executed during Julian the Apostate's persecution of the Christians in the Roman house over which the titular church was built in 401–417. It was rebuilt in the mid 12C, and the portico, with eight ancient columns in its arches, the campanile with its high lower storey and six upper ones, and the impressive dwarf gallery of the apse also date from this period. In the interior the basilica with nave and two aisles has maintained its former proportions under the baroque additions of 1718. The ceiling dates from 1598. There are frescos from various periods in the 2C AD *Roman house* under the church.

S.Giovanni a Porta Latina (Via S.Giovanni a Porta Latina): The original 5C building was replaced by a new building *c*.722, and this was completed in its present form in 1191. The exterior has a portico (12C, Langobard ornamental slabs), lavishly articulated Romanesque campanile and decorated outer choir (8C). The interior of the columned basilica with nave and two aisles has ancient columns, open ceiling and semicircular apse. In the nave is is the finest *fresco cycle* in Rome, created after 1200 with the earthy expressiveness of differing temperaments: 46 scenes from the Old and the New Testament (nave), Christ as Judge of the World (entrance) and the Apocalyptic Lamb (triumphal arch).

S.Ignazio (Piazza S.Ignazio): This building in honour of St.Ignatius Loyola created by Orazio Grassi in association with the Jesuit College in 1626–85 is the most important Jesuit church in Rome after Il Gesù. The broad, pedimented, pilastered façade with side scrolls has an emphatic central portal which extends into the upper storey. The interior is a roomy, well-proportioned cruciform space with aisle-like side chapels. The crossing dome was never built. Andrea Pozzo's trompe l'oeil paintings in the nave and apse are of great artistic significance. The 'Apotheosis of St.Ignatius' and the 'Triumph of Faith' are presented in front of the open heavens, and the whole design is framed with fantastic trompe l'oeil architecture in which paint and the real building mingle. A marble slab marks the ideal point from which it should be viewed. In the right transept is the tomb of St.Aloysius with altar and relief of the 'Triumph of Aloysius Gonzaga' (1699, by P. Legros). In the left transept 'Annunciation' (1750, by Valle). In the right side chapel is the monumental tomb of Pope Gregory XV (by Legros).

S.Ivo alla Sapienzia (Corso del Rinascimento): This church, built by Francesco Borromini in 1642–60, forms an atrium-like courtyard with the two wings of the Palazzo della Sapienza (1587, by G.della Porta, former university); the courtyard is surrounded by two-storey arches, also on the entrance side, which is otherwise free of buildings. The two-storey, concave façade of the church is articulated with pilasters and has round-arched windows, with a portal and larger windows in the centre. The attica is set at the level of the palace and has small side protrusions thought to be 'monti', the heraldic mountains from the arms of Pope Alexander VII Chigi (1655–67).The billowing tall walls of the building are set back, and seem to hover above the façade; at the top is a lantern with many indentations, concluding in a spiral campanile. The staggered arrangement of the building, the

S.Giovanni in Laterano, mosaic in the apse dome

rhythmically alternating indentations and the contrast with the austere palace are deliberate architectural devices by Borromini. The building is centrally planned on a circular design and is alternately surrounded by three semicircles and three trapeziums, which interconnect to form triangles, symbolic of the Trinity. The resultant ground plan is not unlike a bee, thought to be a play on the heraldic device of Pope Urban VIII Barberini (1623–44). The walls are articulated with pilasters and are broken by openings and conclude in a cornice like a garland. High altar picture (1661, by P.da Cortona).

S.Lorenzo fuori le mura (Piazza S.Lorenzo): This massive church is one of the seven pilgrimage churches of Rome and a Patriarchal basilica; it grew from two churches, which were joined in the early 13C: one was the late-6C Pelagius basilica, which developed from the basilica with nave and two aisles built *c*.330 by the Emperor Constantine over the grave of St.Laurentius, and from the church of the Madonna to the W., also a basilica with nave and two aisles (possibly a 5C basilica maior). It was largely rebuilt in 1864–70, and restored in the manner of the original in 1945–61 after being damaged in an air raid in 1943. The brick building has a campanile and portico with 7 entrances (*c*.1220, by the Vassalletti). The nave is high, with narrow aisles, and the wall is made up of Ionic columns, entablature, and a plain upper wall with windows. The triumphal arch sweeps very low, and leads to the Pelagius basilica, which now serves as the sanctuary; the nave was raised in an ugly fashion in the 19C. The walls consist of Corinthian columns, entablature, round-arched galleries and upper wall with windows. The side aisle leads to the former portico, furnished as a funerary chapel for Pope Pius IX in 1878. Furnishings: triumphal arch mosaics: Christ on the globe between Peter and Paul, Pope Pelagius as endower of the church with St.Laurence, saints and representations of church history; Cosmatiwork floor (12C), marble ciborium (1148), bishop's throne (13C, by the Cosmati), marble pulpits (13C), Easter chandelier (13C), tomb of Cardinal Fieschi (c.1265, destroyed 1943 and restored). Crypt with remains of the patrons of the city of Rome, Laurence and and Stephen. Cloister with upper storey (12C) leading to the catacomb of St.Cyricia with early Christian frescos and columbarium.

SS.Luca e Martina (Via del Foro Romano): This is one of the finest baroque churches in Rome, built in 1634–50 by Pietro da Cortona on the foundations of an ancient building and a 6C church. The façade is important in the history of architecture; it is articulated with pilasters and columns, has a convex central section and a dominant drum dome with lantern. The cruciform centrally-planned building has semicircular apses at the end of each arm. The interior walls are broken by pilastered and columned round niches. High altar with sculpture of St.Martina (c.1650, by N.Menghini). Tomb of Pietro da Cortona by the portal. The older lower church was simply refurbished by Cortona. Bronze altar with urns of St.Martina and another saint, relief (C.Fancelli), terracotta sculpture (A.Algardi), 4 sculptures of saints (C.Fancelli).

S.Luigi dei Francesi (Piazza S.Luigi dei Francesi): G.della Porta created the façade of the French national church, started in 1518. The broad façade, articulated with pilasters and cornices, has a central portal in the form of a columned aedicula, side portals, picture niches and windows. The well-proportioned Renaissance interior was redecorated in the 18C; it has a nave and two aisles and a dome above the choir. Furnishings: ceiling painting 'Death and Glorification of S.Luigi' (1756–64, by C.D.Natoire). In the second chapel on the right is a fresco cycle with scenes from the life of St.Cecilia (1616–17, by Domenichino). By the first pillar on the left is the tomb of the painter Claude Lorrain (1836, by P.Lemoyne). The church's most important possession is the picture cycle of the story of Matthew (1599–1602, by Caravaggio) in the Contarelli chapel, the tomb of Cardinal Mathieu Contrel.

S.Marco (Piazza Venezia): The church was founded in 833 under Pope Gregory IV on the site of an earlier building founded in 336 and dedicated to Mark the Evangelist. In 1464–71 it was integrated into the newly-built Palazzo Venezia. The church has a loggia façade (1466) and portico with round arches, which make it stand out against the walls of the palace; the brick campanile has triplet windows (12&13C). The 9C columned basilica is the core of the harmonious interior with nave and two aisles; it was redesigned in the baroque style in 1740–50. The important Carolingian frescos in the apse are from the old basilica: Christ with popes, saints and the patron of the church, Agnus Dei, accompanied by 12 Apostles in the symbolic form of lambs (827–44). There is a fine coffered ceiling (1471, by G. and M.de'-Dolci). In the sacristy, paintings of the patron saint (15C, by M. da Forli) and baldacchino altar (c.1475, by M.da Fiesole and G.Dalmata). Relics of martyrs in the Carolingian crypt.

S.Maria degli Angeli (Piazza della Republica): The first plans to establish a Carthusian monastery in the

S.Maria in Aracoeli, Anthony of Padua, 15C ▷

S.Maria in Aracoeli, detail of the ceiling

slowly deteriorating Baths of Diocletian date from 1100, but building did not start until 1563; the adaptation was designed on a Greek cross plan by Michelangelo. The church was much altered after Michelangelo's death in 1564 and practically rebuilt in the 18C by L.Vanvitelli, who turned it on its axis. Michelangelo used the former Tepidarium of the baths with its giant groin vaulting on 8 huge columns as the transept, and the narrow sequence of Frigidarium, rotunda and Caldarium as the long axis. A newly-built round apse completed the E. side, and the main portal was in the S. Vanvitelli broke off Michelangelo's apse and replaced it with the sanctuary, thus completing the turn of the axis. Vanvitelli was also responsible for the architectural decoration. Furnishings: 12 large altar pictures from St.Peter's (the gift of Pope Benedict XIV), high altar, flanked by the tombs of Pope Pius IV and Cardinal Serbelloni (designed by Michelangelo), between the rotunda and the transept sculpture of S.Bruno (1766, by J.-A.Houdon), meridian set in the floor in 1703 by Pope Clemens XI.

S.Maria dell'Anima (Via S.Maria dell'Anima): The church of the German Nation, meaning the Holy Roman Empire, was built by an unknown, presumably German architect at the behest of the Strasbourg prior Johannes Burkhard in 1501–23. It has a late-Gothic campanile and three-storey Renaissance façade with 3 portals, of which the central one is decorated with the marble sculpture of S.Maria dell'Anima. The fine Renaissance interior shows German influence and is an almost square hall with nave and two aisles; the narrow choir provides a focal point. Furnishings: on the high altar is a votive

S.Maria in Aracoeli 1 Staircase (1348, by L.di Simone Andreozzi) **2** Façade with main and side portals **3** Nave (13C) with wooden ceiling endowed in 1571 to commemorate the Battle of Lepanto **4** Aisles **5** Transept **6** Choir with baroque high altar and Byzantine Madonna (12C) **7** Choir choirs, on the right Cappella del Sacramento, on the left Cappella di S.Gregorio **8** Tomb of the Archdeacon Giovanni Crivelli (by Donatello, 1432–3) **9** Tomb of the Astronomer Ludovico Grato Margani **10** Cappella Bufalini or S.Bernardino with important frescos by Pinturicchio (*c.* 1485) **11** Cappella della Pietà **12** Cappella di S.Bonaventura **13** Cappella del Crocifisso **14** Cappella di S.Pietro d'Alcantar **16** Cappella di S.Diego **17** Side entrance **18** Cappella di S.Pasquale **19** Cappella di S.Francesco **20** Tomb of Pope Honorius IV **21** Tomb of Luca Savelli (*c.* 1287) **22** Cappella di S.Rosa with Madonna mosaic (late 13C) **23** Altar of St Charles Borromeo **24** Wedding altar **25** Cappella del S.Bambino with miraculous Christ Child of Aracoeli **26** Colossal staue of Leo X (by D.Aimo, 1514) **27** Tomb of Cardinal Matteo d'Acquasparta (d.1303, attributed to G.di Cosma) **28** Aedicule (1602) on the site of the Sybil's promise, with porphyry tub containing the bones of St.Helen, and altar said to have been endowed by Augustus Caesar **29** Ambones (by L. and G.Tebaldo, *c.* 1200) **30** Altar of S.Giovanni da Capistrano **31** Cappella della Madonna di Loreto **32** Cappella di S.Margherita **33** Cappella di S.Michele (architecture by C.Rainaldi) **34** Cappella dell'Ascensione **35** Cappella di S.Paolo **36** Cappella di S.Anna **37** Cappella di S.Antonio with altar fresco of the titular saint (by Benozzo Gozzoli, *c.* 1450) **38** Crib **39** Cappella dell'Immacolata

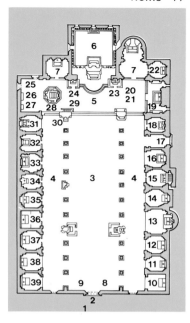

picture of the Holy Family (by G.Romano, originally intended for the Fugger chapel), in the choir tomb of Hadrian VI, the last German Pope (1532, by B.Peruzzi)), among other things in the nave tombs (17C, by F.Duquesnoy), on the inner entrance wall 2 cardinals' tombs (16C, by G.van den Vliete and G.Mangone). Chapels, on the right: 1. Altar picture of St.Benno (1618, by C.Saraceni); 2. Chapel of St.Anne, with frescos of the life of the saint (17C, by G.F.Grimaldi); 3. Chapel of St.Mark, endowed by Jakob Fugger for his brother Markus, who died in 1478; 4. Originally claimed by the Guelphs; on the left: 1. Endowed by the Lübeck patrician L.Ursinus de Vivariis (d.1619); 2. Chapel of St.Barbara with frescos from the life of the saint (*c.*1535, by M.Coxie); 3. Consecrated in 1510, endowed by Johann Albrecht of Brandenburg.

S.Maria in Aracoeli (by the Campidoglio): This is the place at which the Tiburtine Sybil is said to have prophesied the birth of Christ to the Emperor Augustus. In 1250 the 6C church in the style of the Mendicants was built over the remains of a Roman shrine to Juno. The monumental steps were built by L.di Simone Andreozzi in 1348 as a thanksgiving by the Romans for the end of the plague. It was the seat of the medieval Roman parliament, and the coffered ceiling is a memorial to the celebration of the victory of the Christian fleet at Lepanto, which was held here. The basilica with nave and two aisles has round arches over ancient columns, side chapels like aisles, a short transept, and main and side choirs. The brick façade is very plain. Lavish furnishings of a later period.

S.Maria in Campitelli (Piazza

Campitelli): The principal work of C.Rainaldi, commissioned by Pope Alexander VII and built in 1663–7 as a votive church to accommodate the 'Madonna in Portico'. The two-storey façade is lavishly articulated with 3 portals, broken pediments, columns and a moulded cornice. The hall-like interior has Corinthian columns, and consists of two sections associated in a rather complex way, side chapels, dome and semicircular apse. The most important feature of the furnishings is the high altar, blazing with light, on which is the miraculous image (13C original). The furnishings are otherwise 17&18C baroque.

S.Maria in Cosmedin (Piazza della Bocca della Verità): This is a basilica with typically medieval choir, three apses and a hall crypt. It was built in the 12C by the Forum Boarium over the Statio Annonae, a 4C market building of the late antique period. The plain brick building has a slender, richly articulated campanile and a portico with columned baldacchino. Anyone swearing an oath in medieval Rome had to put his hand in the mouth of truth, the Bocca della Verità, an ancient triton mask set in the wall of the portico. The rounded arches in the basilica with nave and two aisles and flat ceiling are supported in a pattern of three columns followed by one pier. Unified 12C furnishings with splendid Cosmati marble work: floor, schola cantorum, marble pulpits, episcopal throne; 13C paschal candlestick, ciborium. The political squabbles between the Emperor and the Pope are reflected in remains of early 12C frescos, in which Charlemagne is juxtaposed with Nebuchadnezzar. Sacristy with mosaic fragments of 706. The crypt is the first with a nave and two aisles in Rome.

S.Maria Maggiore (Piazza di S.Maria Maggiore): Pope Sixtus III (432–440) commisioned a new building on the site of a first basilica built by Pope Liberius (352–366) for this important pilgrim and patriarchal church; the original construction and furnishings have survived to a large extent. The transept and the present apse were added in the 13C, and the

S.Maria Maggiore

so-called Cappella Sistina and the Pauline Chapel date from 1586 and 1611.

The *exterior* is now dominated by the main façade created by F.Fugga from 1741 and C.Rainaldi's choir façade, started *c.*1670; Rainaldi's façade rises through two storeys, and has broad pilasters and balustrades. It is approached by the great staircase, and covers the transepts and the two chapels. In the *interior* the broad nave is divided from the aisles by long, narrow rows of Ionic columns with architrave. The upper walls of the nave are articulated with pilasters, each with two small adjacent twisted columns to frame the windows and mosaics. The coffered ceiling is probably by G.da Sagnallo, in 1493–8. The 5C *mosaics* on the upper walls of the nave and the triumphal arch are a unique and lavish cycle of Old Testament scenes, and the glorification of Mary, who from the time of the Council of Ephesus in 431 was recognised as the Mother of God, not just as the Mother of Christ. The apse mosaic is by the Franciscan J.Torriti; it dates from 1292–5, and harmonises

well with the old mosaics. In the centre of the hemisphere is the Coronation of Mary, surrounded by saints, with Pope Nicolas IV (who endowed the new apse) and Cardinal Jacopo Colonna. The *Cappella Sistina* is on a Greek Cross plan and has an octagonal dome; it was built by D.Fontana in 1584–90. Underneath it are the remains of the building constructed by A.di Cambio in the late 13C for the Bethlehem crib. The dome of the chapel has lavish Mannerist paintings; the space is dominated by Fontana's papal tombs. The canonized Pope Pius IV is enthroned on a columned wall, surrounded by detailed reliefs with scenes from his life, created by N.d'Arras and E.de Rivière. Pope Sixtus V is represented as a kneeling supplicant. Opposite is the *Cappella Paolina*, completed by F.Ponzio in 1611; the golden shrine on the magnificent altar with the venerated mid-13C picture of the Madonna is its central feature. Ponzio also designed the two *papal tombs*. The statue of Pope Paul V is the work of S.da Viggiù, also the statue of Clement III; the 5 reliefs are by C.Rus-

S.Maria Maggiore, interior

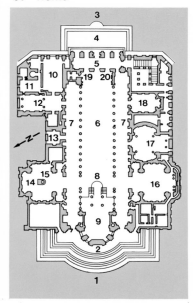

S.Maria Maggiore 1 Piazza Esquilino with obelisk from the mausoleum of Augustus (erected 1587) **2** Choir façade with staircase (c. 1670, by C.Rainaldi) **3** Piazza S.Maria Maggiore with cipoline column from the Basilica of Maxentius (erected in 1613 by C.Maderna), now Mary column (statue by G.Berthélot) **4** Main façade with 5 portals (by F.Fuga, 1741–50) and Romanesque campanile (rebuilt 1377) **5** Portico with benediction loggia (by F.Fuga, 1741–50 **6** Nave with gilded coffered ceiling (by G.da Sangallo, 1493–8) and lavish fresco decoration) (4&5C) with Old Testament scenes **7** Aisles **8** Triumphal arch with mosaics of the Childhood of Christ **9** Choir and apse with mosiacs (by J.Torriti, 1292–5), central Coronation of the Virgin **10** Sacristy (architecture by F.Ponzio, 1605) with frescos by D.C.Passignano **11** Cappella di S.Michele **12** Baptistery (by F.Ponzio, 1605) with relief of the Assumption (by P.Bernini, 1606–11) **13** Cappella delle Reliquie (by F.Fuga, 1750) **14** Cappella Sistina (by D.Fontana, 1584–90) with underground chapel containing relics from the crib at Bethlehem. Remains of an earlier building (13C, by A.di Cambio) with Christmas group **15** Monumental tombs of Popes Sixtus IV and Pius V **16** Cappella Paolina (by F.Ponzio, 1611) with venerated picture of Mary 'Salus Populi Romani' (c. 1250) and papal tombs of Paul V and Clement VIII (architecure F.Ponzio, sculpture S.da Viggi) **17** Cappella Sforza (by G.della Porta, 1564–73) with altar picture by G.S.Sermoneta **18** Cappella Cesi (by M.Lunghi the Elder, c. 1550) with altar picture by G.S.Sermoneta **19** Tomb of Pope Clement IX (by C.Rainaldi, 1671) **20** Tomb of Pope Nicholas IV (by Fontana, 1674)

coni and P.Bernini, the father of Lorenzo.

S.Maria sopra Minerva (Piazza della Minerva): The only large Gothic church in Rome, built on the remains of a temple of Isis wrongly associated with Minerva. It was begun c.1280 and completed c.1500. The Renaissance façade of 1453 was redesigned in the baroque style in the 17C, and the interior much restored in the mid 19C. The hall-like pillared basilica with nave and two aisles has 16&17C side chapels, and main and side choirs. The massive groin vaulting of the nave was the first large-scale post-antique vaulting in Rome. This church of the Mendicant Order was intended for popular worship and is lavishly decorated in the side chapels in particular (see plan).

S.Maria della Pace (Vicolo della Pace): Pope Sixtus IV commissioned this building, attributed to B.Pontelli, in 1482 to commemorate peace with Milan (hence 'della pace'). Bramante completed it in 1500–4 with a well-proportioned cloister, while the impressive façade was the work of P.da Cortona in 1656&7. The central section, shaped like a rotunda in the lower storey, is convex, while the body of the façade is concave; the upper part of the central section pulls back again, and is topped by a triangular pediment with a segmented arch. The interior consists of a nave with side chapels, octagonal dome and square choir. The dome was painted by B.Peruzzi and decorated with outstanding stucco by C.Maderna. The finest interior features are Raphael's paintings on the chapel arches, from left to right the Sybils of Cumae, Persica, Phrygia and Tiburtina. Cappella Cesi with altar paintings by A.da Sangallo the Younger. Cloister by Bramante with pillars, pilasters and columns articulating the harmonious double loggias.

S.Maria del Popolo (Piazza del

opolo): The tree in which demons associated with the soul of the emperor Nero were supposed to have lived once stood on the site of a chapel built in 1099 and a parish church for the people ('del popolo') completed in 227. The present pillared basilica followed in 1472–7. The plain façade has pilasters and a pediment; campanile, octagonal dome and domed Capella Cybo are the dominant features of the exterior. The building has a nave and two aisles with groin vaulting (altered in the 17C) and leads to a long monks' choir (1505, by Bramante) and is surrounded by side chapels. Furnishings: in the choir vault, frescos of the 'Coronation of the Virgin' (by Pinturicchio) and cardinals' tombs by Sforza and della Rovere (c.1507, by A.Sansovino). Dramatic chiaroscuro paintings of the Conversion of St.Paul' and 'Crucixion of St.Peter' (1600&1, by Caravaggio) in the Cappella Cesari in the left transept. In the sacristy altar tabernacle (15C, by A.Bregno). Side chapels in the nave, right hand side: 1. Cappella della Rovere with cardinals' tombs (second half of the 15C, by A.

Bregno), altar painting (Pinturicchio) and Madonna (M.da Fiesole); 2. Capella Cybo, funerary chapel of Cardinal A.Cybo, domed, cruciform centrally-planned building by C.Fonta; 3. with monument to Cardinal C.della Rovere (15C, by A.Bregno); left hand side: 3. Capella Chigi, cruciform domed building (1513–15, by Raphael) with dome mosaics (1516, by L.della Pace), altar picture (S. del Piombo) and 4 niche figures (Lorenzetto, Bernini).

S.Maria in Trastevere (Piazza S.Maria in Trastevere): The oldest church of Mary in Rome. The original building dates from the 3&4C, and was rebuilt as a hall-like old Christian basilica in the middle of the 12C. The church has a plain Romanesque campanile and a elegantly articulated apse; the façade has a baroque portico and a mosaic of the Madonna in the upper section (c.1200). The basilica with nave and two aisles, apse, choir chapels and transept has an architrave supported by antique columns, a Cosmati-work floor and a gilded ceiling. (1617, by

S.Maria sopra Minerva, F.Lippi: Thomas and the Heretics

S.Maria sopra Minerva 1 Piazza della Minerva with monument consisting of an elephant carrying an obelisk (by E.Ferrata, 1667, model by L.Bernini) **2** Renaissance façade (1453, redesigned in the baroque style in the 17C) **3** Nave **4** Aisles **5** Transept **6** Choir and apse **7** Baptismal chapel **8** Cappella Caffarelli **9** Cappella Colonna **10** Cappella Gabrieli **11** Former side portal **12** Chapel with Annunciation painting (by A.Romano, 15C) **13** Cappella Aldobrandini (by G.della Porta and C.Maderna, c. 1600) with Last Supper painting (by F.Barocci) and Aldobrandini tombs **14** Chapel with Judge of the World fresco (by M.da Forli) **15** Chapel of the Cross **16** Cappella Carafa (consecrated 1493) with splendid frescos by Filippino Lippi (life of St.Thomas Aquinas, Annunciation and Assumption, founder) and tomb of Pope Paul IV (design P.Ligorio) **17** Tomb of Bishop Guillaume Durand (d.1296, attributed to Giovanni di Cosma) **18** Cappella Altieri **19** Cappella Capranica **20** Statue of St.John the Baptist (1858, by G.Obici) **21** High altar with tomb of St.Catherine of Sienna (1347–80) **22** Tomb of Pope Leo X **23** Tomb of Pope Clement VII **24** Christ with the Cross, important work by Michelangelo (1519–21) **25** Left-hand side choir, now side exit, with tomb of the painter Fra Angelico da Fiesole (1387–1455) **26** Cappella Frangipane e Maddaleni-Capiferro **27** Sacristy **28** Room in which St.Catherine of Sienna died, with frescos by A.Romano **29** Room of the Popes **30** Cloister **31** Museum **32** Chapel of St.Dominic with tomb of Pope Benedict XIII (by Marchioni, 1724–30) **33** Chapel of St.Hyacinth **34** Chapel of Pope Pius V **35** Maria Raggi monument **36** Cappella Lante della Rovere **37** Pulpit **38** Cappella Giustiniani with Umbrian School picture of Christ **39** Tomb of Giovanni Vigevano **40** Cappella Grazioli **41** Chapel of St.John the Baptist **42** Tomb of Cesare Fabbreti **43** Chapel of the Sacred Heart **44** Tomb of Francesco Tornabuoni (by Mino da Fiesole, 1480)

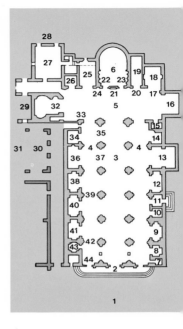

1

Domenichino). The important apse mosaics show in the upper panel (c.1140): Christ and Mary enthroned, for the first time almost equally ranked, with saints and Pope Innocent II with a model of the church, under that the Agnus Dei with the 12 Apocalyptic Lambs; in the lower panel (c.1291, by P.Cavallini): Madonna in gloriole and scenes from the life of the Virgin with landscapes and architectural perspectives. In the side chapels paintings by ⟨P.Cati (1589) and A.Gherardi (1680).

S.Maria in Vallicella (Piazza della Chiesa Nuova): M.da Città di Castello built the funerary church of St.Filippo Neri on the site of a ruined Romanesque church in 1575. This important baroque building has a large pilastered façade and is a cruciform pillared basilica with nave and two aisles and crossing dome. Important monumental frescos in the nave, dome and apse (early 17C, b. P.da Cortona). High altar pictures Madonna, surrounded by angels and saints (1608, by Rubens). To the left by the church *Oratorio dei Filippini* built in 1637–50 by Francesco Borromini with concave-convex, pilastered brick façade. 2 courtyards, sacristy and refectory of the Brotherhood of St.Filippo Neri are adjacent.

S.Maria della Vittoria (Piazza S.Bernardo): This building was started by C.Maderna in 1605, and received its present name in honour of a picture of the Virgin which the Catholic League believed to have brought them victory ('della Vittoria' at the battle of the White Mountain. The miraculous image was destroyed

S.Maria sopra Minerva, interior (left), Annunciation, by F.Lippi (right)

by fire in 1833. The pilastered façade was built by G.B.Soria in 1625&6. It has a heavy pediment and a portal framed with an aedicula. The nave has one aisle and tunnel vaulting, side chapels, short transept and a semicircular apse. It makes a festive impression because of its brightly-coloured marble and lavish decoration. Apse painting 'Madonna della Vittoria' (1855, by L.Serra). The dominant interior feature is the Cornaro chapel (fourth on the left), with the altar of St.Theresa, Bernini's principal architectural work, dating from the mid 17C. In the marble-clad niche is the marble sculpture of 'St.Theresa in Ecstasy'.

SS.Nereo e Achilleo (Piazzale Numa Pompilio): This is one of the first titular churches in Rome, and was originally called S.Fasciola; according to legend, St.Peter, fleeing from prison, lost the bandage from the wound made by his chains here. The church was rebuilt under Pope Leo III (795–816), and the exterior of the early Christian basilica dates from this time; the interior was radically altered in 1597. The mosaics on the triumphal arch, Transfiguration of Christ, Madonna with angel and Annunciation date from *c*.800.

S.Paolo fuori le mura (Via Ostiense): This church built over the tomb of St.Paul is one of the seven pilgrimage churches of Rome, also one of the five basilicae maiores; it belongs to the Vatican state. The Emperor Constantine had a memorial chapel built on the site where Paul was beheaded *c*.67. Roman emperors had the columned basilica with nave and four aisles and transept built *c*.386–410; in the 5C the poet Prudentius praised it as the 'Golden Cathedral'. The Benedictines were responsible for the monastery buildings(936) and the cloisters (1205–41). The frescos in the nave and the 13&14C façade mosaic are the work of P.Cavallini, the façade portico is by Galilei, 1750. The venerable basilica, the last Christian imperial basilica in Rome, was destroyed by fire in 1823. The rather unsuitable reconstruction of 1874 under L.Poletti only allows us to sense the character of the old basilica through an academic and historical disguise. The atrium is surrounded by a forest of columns, and has a memorial to St.Paul in the middle. The façade has a pediment mosaic with Christ Blessing with Apostle Princes. There is a campanile. A bronze door from the old basilica (c.1070) has survived in the Porta Sancta (right portal). The nave has 80 new monolithic columns; the transept includes the only surviving old sections of the building. The monumental triumphal arch has 5C mosaics (restored in the 18&19C): Christ in the gloriole with the Apostle princes. Apse mosaic (19C copy of the 1285 original): Pantocrator with 4 Apostles. Furnishings: ciborium above the papal altar in the Apostles' crypt (1285 by A.di Cambio). Right of the altar magnificent paschal candlestick with figures (c.1190, by P.Vassalletto and N.di Angelo). In the sacramental chapel wooden crucifix (c.1300). Baptistery, cruciform plan since the restoration of 1930. The magnificent cloisters (1205–41, by the Vassallettis) have double columns decorated with foliate capitals and mosaic intarsia work; the design is particularly lavish. The museum contains among other things the Carolingian Bible of Charles the Bald and remains of the portrait medallions of popes (5–9C), which once decorated the nave, and other parts of the church.

S.Pietro in Montorio (Via Garibaldi, Gianicolo): The church of the Franciscan monastery on the 'monte d'oro' was first mentioned in the 9C

and built c.1500 by B.Pontelli. It is famous for the tempietto added in 1502 by Bramante, an epoch-making High Renaissance building. This plain, single-aisled church has side chapels and transept-like exedrae, and ends in a monks' choir. Chapels, on the right: 1. Altar painting 'Scourging of Christ' (1519–25, by S.del Piombo); on the left: 2. Cappella Raimondi (c.1638, by Bernini). The Tempietto di Bramante was held to have been built at the point where Peter was crucified, but this has been disproved historically. The building is in the form of a cylinder on a three-tiered base and has a hemispherical dome with baroque lantern. The lower storey is surrounded by a ring of 16 Doric columns supporting a pediment with metopes; the upper storey only appears to be set back. There was a plan to surround the exterior of the building with columns as well, but fortunately this was never realized.

S.Pietro in Vincoli (Piazza di S.Pietro in Vincoli): This building was started by the priest Philippus in 431, with the aid of the Emperor, and consecrated by Pope Sixtus III between 438 and 440. The pillared portico was built under Pope Sixtus IV (1471–84); in the 16C the second storey with architrave windows was added. Inside the basilica the wide nave is separated from the two narrow aisles by 20 fine Doric columns supporting round arches; there is a transept with side apses. The groin vaulting in the aisles dates from the time of Pope Julius II (1503–13), the ceiling of the nave was built to F.Fontana's design in the first half of the 18C. The finest work of art in the church is the memorial to Julius II erected by Pope Paul III., with figures by Michelangelo of Moses, Rachel and Leah. The grandiose figure of Moses dates from 1513–16, but the statues of Leah and Rachel

S.Maria del Popolo, Immaculate Conception, by C.Maratta ▷

S.Maria del Popolo, Conversion of Paul (left), by Caravaggio, left-hand aisle (right)

were not started until 1542. The other figures are the work of R.da Montelupo (Sybil and prophet), M.del Bosco (recumbent figure of the Pope), among others. A fine Renaissance tabernacle under the altar contains the chains of St.Peter.

S.Prassede (Via S.Prassede): The original 5C building dedicated to St.Praxedis had a successor in 822, acquired by the Benedictines in 1198. The courtyard of the church is reached via a gateway and passageway with steps; the only distinctive feature of the plain façade is a Renaissance portal. The basilica with nave and two aisles has side chapels, narrow transept and a broad apse; the nave has a pattern of 2 columns and one pillar, and also diagonal flying buttresses. The most important 9C mosaic cycle in Rome: triumphal arch: New Jerusalem, Christ with Apostles, prophets and saints; apse arch: Apocalyptic Lamb and scenes from the Apocalypse; apse vault: Agnus Dei and the 12 Lambs of the Apocalypse (Apostles), saints, Pope Paschal as benefactor of the church. Lavish furnishings (see plan).

S.Prisca (Via di S.Prisca): According to legend this church, built *c.*499 stands on the site of the house of the Christian couple Aquilla and Prisca with whom St.Peter and St.Paul stayed. It was restored in 722 and altered in the 11C, and altered again in 1456 and in 1600 to its present form. The tunnel-vaulted *crypt* was built in Roman rooms in the form of three arms of a cross, and has early baroque wall paintings. The most remarkable of the excavated Roman rooms is the 3C *Mithraeum*, with wall

S.Paolo fuori le mura, apse mosaic

paintinga and a haut-relief of the god Mithras. A small museum has been set up to show the objects which have been found.

S.Pudenziana (Via Urbana): It appears that this church was established in the house of Senator Prudens, whose daughters Praxedis and Pudentiana are said to have been converted by St.Peter. The basilica was started in the late 4C and completed in 417; the present building is largely the result of medieval rebuilding in 1589; fragments of a Roman portal have survived, despite later alterations. The five-storey bell tower dates from the late 12C. In the interior an outstanding *apse mosaic* from the period *c*.400 has survived. A bearded Christ is enthroned in front of the buildings of the New Jerusalem, with Peter, Paul and the 12 Apostles. Peter and Paul are wreathed

with personifications of the Jewish and the heathen church (or St.Praxedis and St.Pudentiana?). The impressive *Cappella Caetani* by the left aisle was begun by F.Volterra and completed by C.Maderna in 1598; the coloured marble decoration was the work of G.B.della Porta, and the relief of the Adoration of the Magi by P.P.Olivieri. The *Oratorium Marianum*, reached by a staircase from the left aisle, may have been part of the 2C first church; 9&11C wall paintings have survived.

SS.Quattro Coronati (Via dei Querceti): The church was originally founded in the 4C in honour of 4 martyrs; it was replaced by a basilica with nave and two aisles in the middle of the 9C. After destruction by the Normans in 1084 it was rebuilt in the early 12C, using the old apse and the W. part of the nave. Striking exterior features are a gigantic Carolingian round apse, a medieval campanile and 2 atria. The galleried basilica has an alternating pattern of pillars and columns, and a wooden coffered ceiling in the nave (16C). There is a representation of the story of the Quattro Coronati in the apse (c.1630, by G.da S.Giovanni). In the Carolingian crypt are 4 sarcophaguses containing the relics of the martyrs. The 13C cloisters have alternating groups each of 5 double columns and 1 pillar, fountain in the courtyard (c.1100). Oratory of St.Silvester (by the left

atrium): This building was consecrated in 1246 and has fine ornamental painting in its tunnel vault. On the wall is a representation of the Last Judgement, below that a frieze with 8 incidents from the Constantine legend, culminating in a scene of the Roman Emperor handing power in Rome over to the Pope. Insistence on the Pope's claim to power over the Emperor shows unmistakably in these 13C works of art.

S.Sabina (Piazza Pietro d'Illiria): The present pillared church was built

S.Pietro in Vincoli 1 Renaissance façade **2** Portico (by B.Pontelli, 1471–83) with 16C upper section **3** Marble portal (15C) **4** Nave with ancient Roman columns and painted ceiling (designed by F.Fontana, first half of the 18C) **5** Aisles **6** Transept **7** Main apse **8** Side apses **9** Access to the excavations **10** Remains of the entrance (4C) **11** 'Miracle of the Chains' (by G.B.Parodi) **12** 'S.Agostino' (attributed to Il Guercino) **13** Memorial to Cardinal Margotti (by Il Domenichino) **14** 'Release of St.Peter' (copy after Il Domenichino) **15** Memorial to Cardinal Agucchia (by Il Domenichino) **16** Cenotaph of Pope Julius II, masterpiece by Michelangelo and colleagues, with famous statue of Moses (1513–16) **17** S.Margherita (by Il Guercino) **18** 5C Confessio; Altar of the Chains with bronze doors by Pollaiolo; behind, sarcophagus of the Maccabees

19 5C high altar with frescos by G.Coppi **20** Tomb of Don Giulio Gorio **21** Monument to P.M.Vecchiarelli (by P.Vechiarelli) **22** Mosaic of St.Sebastian (by a 7C Byzantine master) **23** Monument to C.Aldobrandini **24** 'Descent from the Cross' (by C.Roncalli, known as Il Pomarancio) **25** Tomb of Cardinal Nicholas of Cusa (d.1465, by A.Bregno). the famous theologian and philosopher, with relief slab 'Nicholas of Cusa before St.Peter' **26** Tomb of the important Florentine artists and brothers Antonio and Piero Pollaiulo (by L.Capponi, c. 1500). Above this 'Atonement Procession on the occasion of the plague of 1476' (anonymous, 15C) **27** Front sacristy with 'S.Agostino' (by P.F.Mola) and 'Release of St.Peter' (by Domenichino) **28** Sacristy **29** Cloister (by G.da Sangallo, late 15C)

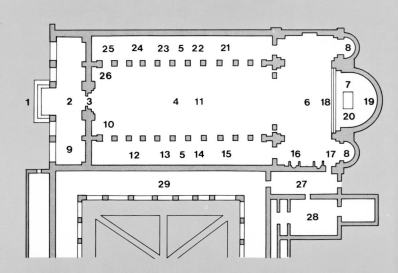

in 425–432 by Peter of Illyria on the foundations of an ancient titular church, probably sited in the house of the Roman matron Sabina. The church has been carefully restored to its original condition in the present century. The door in the central W. portal dates from c. 432, and is the oldest wooden door with figurative carving in Christian art; 18 of the 28 pictorial panels are extant, including the oldest surviving representation of the Crucifixion. The nave has a flat ceiling and 20 fluted Corinthian columns in Parian marble; the roof

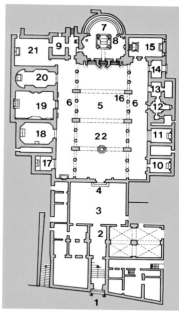

S.Prassede 1 Access portal **2** Stairs to atrium **3** Atrium **4** Renaissance portal **5** Nave **6** Aisles **7** Presbytry with 9C mosaic cycle; under this ambulatory crypt dating from 822 with Confessio above the tombs of the sainted sisters Praxedis and Pudentiana **8** High altar **9** Campanile **10** Rosary chapel **11** Cappella Cesi **12** Chapel of St.Zeno, commissioned by Pope Paschal I (817–24) as tomb for his mother Theodora; walls and vault with gold-ground mosaics; altar mosaic of S.Maria Liberatrice (13C); beside the chapel fragment of the column at which Christ was scourged, brought to Roma by Cardinal Colonna in 1223 **13** Room with tomb of Cardinal Alano **14** Side entrance **15** Chapel of Christ Crucified **16** Tomb of G.B.Santoni **17** Chapel of St.Peter **18** Chapel of St.Charles **19** Cappella Olgiati, built in 1590 as funeral chapel for Bernardo Olgiati, Man-

nerist painting (by G.Cesari, 1592–3) **20** Sacramental chapel **21** Sacristy **22** Well of the Blood of the Martyr

S.Paolo fuori le mura, nave

beams are exposed in the aisles. The apse fresco was painted by F. and T.Zuccaro in the 17C, following remnants of the original mosaic to a certain extent. The schola cantorum was restored from 8, 9 and 11C fragments; in front of it is the mosaic grave slab of the Dominican General Munoz de Zamora (d. 1300). The Madonna of the Rosary in the chapel of St.Catherine was painted by Sassoferrato in 1643. The wonderful *cloister* dates from 1212. The Dominican Order was founded in the adjacent *monastery*; it was here that St.Dominic met St.Francis, and St.Thomas Aquinas taught here.

S.Sebastiano ad Catacumbas (Via Appia Antica): This church, one of the seven pilgrimage churches of Rome, is in the dip of the Via Attica Antica formerly called 'ad catacumbas'; the word catacomb, applied to burial places in general, originated from the burial place here. Constantine the Great's basilica with nave and two aisles was restored in the 13C and finally rebuilt by F.Ponzio *c.* 1612 as a small-scale baroque building; façade and portico are by G.Vasanzio. The Cappella Albani for Pope Clement XI (1700–21) was built by C.Fontana and decorated by C.Maratta. In the nave is the altar of St.Sebastian, with recumbent marble figure by Bernini's pupil A.Giorgetti, opposite a wall with relics. Left of the façade of the church is access to three *Roman tombs* dating from approximately 160 AD; they were originally columbaria, later rebuilt as burial chambers, their interior walls lavishly decorated with stucco and frescos. The central feature of the Christian catacombs is the *crypt of St.Sebastian* with the bones of the martyr in a stone coffin. A bust of the saint, set on a fragment of a column, is said to be by Bernini. Inscriptions on the walls of the so-called *Triclia* invoke the support of the Apostles Peter and Paul (in the 3C the remains of the two saints were said to have lain in the catacombs for a

while). Above ground are parts of three 3C *Roman dwellings*; these were used as foundations for the *Basilica of Constantine*, apparently a building with nave and two aisles, with aisles and apses surrounded by arches. Foundations and floors of the semicircular tomb of St.Quirinus, the so-called *Platonia*, have been successfully excavated. There are remains of Roman frescos in the adjacent *Oratory of Pope Honorius III* (1216–27).

S.Stefano Rotondo (Via di S.Stefano Rotondo): In the 7C an apse was added to this rotunda built under Pope Simplicius (468–483) and an archway in the high central area in the 8C. The building was reduced in size in the 12C; the columns which originally separated the two ambulatories are now incorporated in the exterior wall. The arms of a Greek cross inscribed within a circle serve as entrance hall and chapels. In the chapel of St.Primus and St.Felicianus is a small 7C apse mosaic showing Christ above his cross, with two saints. The tomb in the chapel of St.Stephen of Hungary dates from the early 16C, the 34 early-17C frescos with scenes from the martyrdom of the saints are by C.Pomarancio and A.Tempesta.

S.Susanna (Piazza S.Bernardo): This church was founded *c.*290, rebuilt *c.* 800 and again in 1475; it is now the national church of the United States of America, with one of the finest baroque façades in Rome, created by C.Maderna in 1603. It is dynamically articulated with half-columns and pilasters, and has a striking pediment and aedicules. The baroque interior has side chapels and apse, and wall frescos with scenes from the life of the patron saint (*c.* 1600, by B.Croce).

SS. Trinità dei Monti (Piazza della Trinità dei Monti): The twin-towered

S.Paolo, triumphal arch of Galla Placidia ▷

S.Prassede, mosaic, Madonna

S.Prassede, mosaic of Christ

façade of this church, built 1495–1585 for Charles VIII of France, towers over the Spanish Steps. The pilastered façade shows Nordic influence and has a central portal framed by a columned aedicule. The single-aisled interior has side chapels and a rib-vaulted choir, and some worthwhile paintings; D.da Volterra's are outstanding: 'Descent from the Cross', (1541), 'Ascension of Mary' (mid 16C).

III. The Vatican

A. The Vatican State.

The Vatican did not become the permanent residence of the Popes until their return from exile in Avignon in 1377; the Lateran Palace fulfilled this function until then. The church state's possessions in central Italy go back to a gift from the Frankish King Pépin; they were taken over by the kingdom of Italy in 1870. The Lateran Treaty, concluded between the Pope and Mussolini in 1929, ended the quarrel between church and state caused by the seizure. The Pope became head of the new sovereign state, which was officially known as Stato della Città del Vaticano. It has an area of 0.44 square kilometres, and about 1,000 citizens, making it the smallest state in the world; it has the largest palace, however, and the mightiest church in Christendom. It includes the Vatican City, with St.Peter's, St.Peter's Square, the Vatican Palace, museum buildings and the walled Vatican gardens, and also the extraterritorial areas of S.Giovanni in Laterano, S.Maria Maggiore, S.Paolo fuori le mura, the catacombs, various palaces and the summer residence in Castel Gandolfo. The state frontier is a white line at the edge of St.Peter's Square. The Holy Father, also supreme overlord of the Catholic Church, personally holds full legislative, executive and judicial

S.Pietro in Vincoli, Moses, by Michelangelo ▷

powers, and is head of the state administration (Governatorato). The Vatican is provided with all the essential institutions of a sovereign state: defence (Gendarmerie, Swiss Guard), its own economic enterprises, finance (coinage prerogative), post office (stamps, telephone, telegraph), transport, (own car park, station, helicopter pad), information (own printing facilities, daily paper 'Osservatore Romano', radio station 'Radio Vaticana') and territorial devices (flag, 'SCV' vehicle plates). Only St.Peter's Square, St.Peter's, the Vatican museums, the Camposanto Teutonico and the church of S.Anna may be visited without special permission.

B. St.Peter's/S.Pietro in Vaticano and St.Peter's Square/Piazza S.Pietro.

Church and square are on the site of one of the great cemeteries of ancient Rome. The Apostle-Prince Peter was also buried here after his martyrdom in the Circus of Nero on the left of the church c. 64. His grave rapidly became a place of worship for early Christians. Here Constantine the Great built the first St.Peter's; the slope was so steep that it was necessary to construct a huge substructure at one end and to cut away a great deal of ground at the other. Old St.Peter's, a basilica with nave and four aisles, huge atrium with columns, massive transept and apse was completed in 349. The building was lavishly furnished in the course of the centuries, but had become so dilapidated in the 15C that a replacement was considered. Work started on the choir and transept under B.Rosselino in 1452, but work on the church as a whole did not start until 1506, under Pope Julius II. It was originally intended by Bramante as a centrally-planned building with nave and two aisles on a cruciform ground plan, but by the time he died only part of the lower section of the dome and the S. transept had been completed. Raphael then took over the project, and from 1514 the plan was changed in favour of a longitudinally organized basilica with nave and two aisles with side chapels and transepts. Under his successors B.Perruzzi and A.da Sangallo sections of the transept were vaulted, and space was created for the Vatican grottoes by raising the floor. The final decision on how the building was to be completed was not made until Michelangelo (1546/57) simplified Bramante's centralized plan, and started work on it again, this time on a colossal scale. When he died, in 1564, the drum of the dome was complete. After this the building was completed by G.della Porta, G.B.Vignola and D.Fontana in 1590; its area was finally less than that of Old St.Peter's. The centrally-planned building, however, did not meet the liturgical requirements of the Council of Trent, with the result that Paul V commissioned Carlo Maderna to add a nave to the church. Extension work began in 1607, and the new building was consecrated by Urban VIII in 1626. Under Pope Alexander VII, Bernini realized the wonderful concept of St.Peters Square, the crowning glory of the group of buildings.

St.Peter's Square: The central and dominant position of the ancient obelisk from the former Circus of Nero erected under Pope Sixtus V by D.Fontana in 1586, the visibilty of the loggia for the papal blessing of the people, and harmony with the architecture of the palace were the essential design premises for the square. Bernini solved the problem by dividing the available area into two halves, the Piazza obliqua and the Piazza retta. The colonnades, consisting of four rows of monumental Doric columns, and pillars in the elliptical section of the square, form a clear division, without completely closing the square off from the outside world. The central obelisk and the fountains created by Maderna at the sides are

Raphael's Stanze: Borgo Fire, detail ▷

Vatican City, Plan

Viale Centrale del Bosco

17 Radio Vatican

Viale Vaticano

Viale de Osservatorio

15 Ad

16
Collegio Etiopico

Eliporto

17 Radio Vatican

School of Mos

13

18
Mura di Leone IV.

14 Sta

Viale Vaticano

Via Nicolo V.

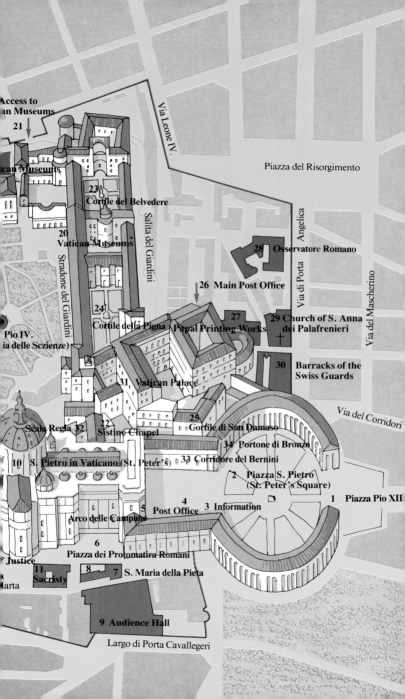

**Access to
an Museums**

21

Via Leone IV.

can Museums

Piazza del Risorgimento

23

Cortile del Belvedere

Salita del Giardini

**20
Vatican Museums**

28 Osservatore Romano

Stradone del Giardini

26 Main Post Office

24

27

**29 Church of S. Anna
dei Palafrenieri**

**Pio IV.
ia delle Sczienze)**

Cortile della Pigna Papal Printing Works

**30 Barracks of the
Swiss Guards**

31 Vatican Palace

Via del Corridori

25

**Scala Regia 32   22
Sistine Chapel**

Cortile di San Damaso

34 Portone di Bronzo

10 S. Pietro in Vaticano (St. Peter's)

33 Corridore del Bernini

**2   Piazza S. Pietro
(St. Peter's Square)**

1 Piazza Pio XII

5 Post Office   4

3 Information

Arco delle Campane

**6
Piazza dei Protomatira Romani**

Justice

**11
Sacristy**

8   7 S. Maria della Pieta

arta

9 Audience Hall

Largo di Porta Cavallegeri

the principal features. The second, trapezoid half of the square establishes the link with the church, and at the same time forms the entrance (on the right) to the Papal Palace, with bronze door and Scala Regia behind it. The square is framed by 140 monumental statues of saints on the colonnades. The steps in front of the church reduce the distance to the building by an optical trick, and stress the impression of height given by the façade.

St.Peter's Church: C.Maderna's façade has nine axes and three tiers, and is dominated by Michelangelo's powerful dome. Horizontal articulation on the ground floor is by round arches and rectangular portals, and also niches with figures, and in the upper storey by large loggia windows. Above this is a massive cornice with central triangular pediment and a huge attica rather like a mezzanine, surmounted by a balustrade and monumental sculpture. Vertical articulation is by means of a central section like a triumphal arch concealing the vestibule, and a stump of tower on each side. The overall impression is of a gigantic domed palace, with the middle of the 'piano nobile' occupied by the balcony on which the Pope appears to give his blessing 'urbi et orbi', and from which the name of a new Pope is proclaimed. The portico leads to the Porta Sancta, which is only opened in a Holy Year. The other portals lead into the interior of the cruciform basilica with nave and two aisles, transept with three aisles and monumental dome over the crossing supported by four pentagonal piers almost 79 ft. in diameter. Beyond the crossing are the choir and polygonal apse. The tunnel-vaulted nave is divided from the domed aisle bays with side chapels by four broad arches. St.Peter's has an area of 160,000 sq. ft. and can hold over 60,000 people, which makes it the largest church in Christendom. The theological and artistic focal point of the interior is the tomb of St.Peter, with Bernini's baldacchino

S.Pietro in Vaticano 1 St.Peter's Square (by Gian Lorenzo Bernini, 1656–67) **2** Façade (by C.Maderna) with benediction loggia and attica figures (Christ, John the Baptist, Apostles except Peter) **3** Portico with five portals **a** Porta della Morte (by G.Manzù) **b** Porta del Bene e del Male

St. Peter's

(by L.Minguzzi, 1977) **c** Main portal with double bronze door (by A.A.Filarete, 1433–5) **d** Porta dei Sacramenti (by V.Crocetti, 1965) **e** Porta Sancta with bronze door (by V.Consorti, 1950) **4** Nave (by C.Maderna, started 1607, consecrated 1626) **5** Dome (started by Bramante in 1506, continued by Michelangelo 1547–64, then under the direction of Vignola, P.Ligorio, G.della Porta and D.Fontana, completed by 1590 under G.della Porta and Fontana) **6** Papal altar above the tomb of St.Peter, Confessio in front of it, altar baldacchino above it (by Bernini, consecrated 1633) **7** Statue of St.Veronica (by F.Mocchi, c. 1627–43) **8** Statue of St.Helena (by A.Bolgi) **9** Statue of St.Longinus **10** Statue of the Apostle Andrew (by F.Duquesnoy) **11** Bronze of St.Peter Enthroned (by Arnolfo di Cambio?, 13C) **12** Choir apse with Cathedra Petri (by Bernini, 1656–66) **left** Tomb of Pope Paul III Farnese (principal work of G.della Porta 1549–75) **right** Tomb of Pope Urban VIII Barberini (by Bernini, 1628–47 **13** Tomb of Pope Clement X (d. 1676, architecture M.de'Rossi, sculpture Ercole Ferrata) **14** Cappella di S.Michele **15** Tomb of Pope Clement XIII (by Canova, 1748–92) **16** Tomb of Pope Benedict XIV (architecture P.Bracci, sculpture G.Sibilia, 1769) **17** Cappella Gregoriana (architecture G.della Porta, design Michelangelo, mosaics G.Muziano, 1581) with altar picture of the Virgin of Mercy (12C) and tomb of Pope Gregory XVI (d.1846, by L.Amici) **18** Tomb of Pope Gregory XIV (d.1591) **19** Tomb of Pope Gregory XIII (sculpture C.Rusconi) **20** Sacramental chapel with altar (by Bernini) and altar picture (by P.da Cortona) **21** Mausoleum of Countess Mathilda of Toscana **22** Tomb of Pope Innocent XII (by F.Valle, design F.Fuga) **23** Chapel of St.Sebastian with monuments to Pope Pius XI (1949) and Pius XII (1964) **24** Cenotaph of Queen Christina of Sweden (d.1689 in Rome, design C.Fontana)

and statue of Pope Leol XII (by G.de Fabris, 1836) **25** Cappella della Pietà with Michelangelo's famous masterpiece (1498–50, restored in 1972 after deliberate damage) **26** Baptismal chapel, font with bronze lid (by C.Fontana), mosaics with Christ's Baptism in the Jordan etc. **27** Memorial to Maria Clementina Sobieska (d.1735, architecture F.Bargioni, sculpture P.Bracci, mosaic P.P.de Cristofari) **28** Stewart monument (by A.Canova, 1817–21) **29** Cappella della Presentazione, in which Popes used to lie in state until their burial; papal monuments for Benedict XV and John XIII **30** Double tomb of Pope Innocent VIII (1498, by A.Pollaiulc) as living ruler and dead figure **31** Monument to Pope and Saint Pius X (d.1914) **32** Cappella del Coro with stucco by G.B.Ricci, Immaculata mosaic by P.Bianchi and tomb of Pope Clement XI (1700–21) **33** Tomb of Pope Innocent XI (by P.E.Monnot, c. 1700 **34** Tomb of Pope Leo XI Medici (by A.Algardi) **35** Cappella Clementina (architecture by G.della Porta) with tomb of Pope Pius VII (by B.Thorvaldsen) **36** Tomb of Pope Pius VIII (by P.Tenerani) **37** Tomb of Pope Alexander VII, masterly late work of Bernini and colleagues **38** Cappella della Colonna with altar picture of the Madonna from Old St.Peter's and Altar of Pope Leo the Great with monumental marble relief 'Leo meets Attila the Hun in 452' **39** Tomb of Pope Alexander VIII (architecture A.di San Martino, sculpture A. de'Rossi, 1725) **40** Steps and lift to roof and Michangelo's dome **41** Access to sacristy and Museo Storico Artistico **42** Sacristy (by C.Marchionni, 1776–84 **a** Sagrestia Comune with dome and columns from the villa Adriana near Tivoli **b** Sagrestia dei Cononici with paintings by F.Zuccaro, F.Penni, G.Romano and A.Calvucci **c** Chapterhouse with paintings by A.Sacchi **43** Museo Storico Artistico with Tesoro di S.Pietro **44** Access to Vatican grottoes

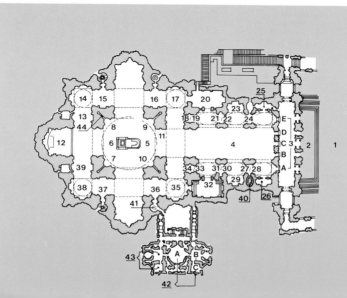

Popes

The years indicate the duration of the pontificate.
Antipopes in italics.

Peter (Palestine)	d. 64 or 67
Linus (Tuscia, Italy)	67–76
Anacletus (Rome)	76–88
Clement I (Rome)	88–97
Evaristus I (Greece)	97–105
Alexander I (Roman)	105–115
Sixtus I (Roman)	115–125
Telesphorus (Greece)	125–136
Iginus (Greece)	136–140
Pius I (Italy)	140–155
Anicetus (Syria)	155–166
Soter (Italy)	166–175
Eleutherius (Greece)	175–189
Victor I (Africa)	189–199
Zephyrinus (Rome)	199–217
Calixtus I (Rome)	217–222
Hippolytus	*217–235*
Urban I (Rome)	222–230
Pontianus (Rome)	230–235
Anterus (Greece)	235–236
Fabian (Rome)	236–250
Cornelius (Rome)	251–253
Novatian	*251*
Lucius I (Rome)	253–254
Stephen I (Rome)	254–257
Sixtus II (Greece)	257–258
Dionysius (unknown)	259–268
Felix I (Rome)	269–274
Eutychianus (Italy)	257–283
Caius (Dalmatia)	283–296
Marcellinus I (Rome)	296–304
Marcellus I (Rome)	308–309
Eusebius (Greek)	309–311
Melchiades (Africa)	311–314
Sylvester I (Rome)	314–335
Mark (Rome)	335–336
Julius I (Rome)	337–352
Liberius (Rome)	352–366
Felix II	*355–365*
Damasus I (Spain)	366–384
Ursinus	*366–367*
Siricius (Rome)	384–399
Anastasius I (Rome)	399–401
Innocent I (Italy)	401–417
Zosimos (Greece)	417–418
Boniface I (Rome)	418–422
Eulalius	*418–419*
Celestine I (Italy)	422–432
Sixtus III (Rome)	432–440
Leo I (Italy)	440–461
Hilary (Sardinia)	461–468
Simplicius (Italy)	468–483
Felix III (II) (Rome)	483–492
Gelasius I (Africa)	492–496
Anastasius II (Rome)	496–498
Symmachus (Sardinia)	498–514
Laurentius	*498–505*
Hormisdas (Italy)	514–523
John I (Italy)	523–526
Felix IV (III) (Italy)	526–530
Boniface II (Rome)	530–532
Dioscurus	*530*
John II (Rome)	533–535
Agapetus I (Rome)	535–536

Silverius (Italy)	536–537
Vigilius (Rome)	537–555
Pelagius I (Rome)	556–561
John III (Rome)	561–574
Benedict I (Rome)	575–579
Pelagius II (Rome)	579–590
Gregory I (Italy)	590–604
Sabinianus (Italy)	604–606
Boniface III (Rome)	606–607
Boniface IV (Italy)	608–615
Deodatus I (Rome)	615–618
Boniface V (Italy)	619–625
Honorius I (Italy)	625–638
Severinus (Rome)	638–640
John IV (Dalmatia)	640–642
Theodore I (Greece)	642–649
Martin I (Italy)	649–655
Eugenius I (Rome)	654–657
Vitalian (Italy)	657–672
Deodatus II (Rome)	672–676
Donus (Rome)	676–678
Agatho (Sicily)	678–681
Leo II (Sicily)	682–683
Benedict II (Rome)	684–685
John V (Antioch)	685–686
Conon (Thrace)	686–687
Theodore II	*687*
Paschal I	*687–692*
Sergius I (Syria)	687–701
John VI (Greece)	701–705
John VII (Greece)	705–707
Sisinnius (Syria)	707–708
Constantine (Syria)	708–715
Gregory II (Rome)	715–731
Gregory III (Syria)	731–741
Zacharias (Greece)	741–752
Stephen II (Rome)	752
Stephen III (Rome)	752–757
Paul I (Rome)	757–767
Constantine II	*767–768*
Philip	768
Stephen IV (Sicily)	768–772
Hadrian I (Rome)	772–795
Leo III (Rome)	795–816
Stephen V (Rome)	816–817
Paschal I (Rome)	817–824
Eugenius II (Rome)	824–827
Valentine (Rome)	827
Gregory IV (Rome)	827–844
John VIII	*844*
Sergius II (Rome)	844–847
Leo IV (Rome)	847–855
Anastasius III	*855*
Benedict III (Rome)	855–858
Nicholas I (Rome)	858–867
Hadrian II (Rome)	867–872
Stephen VI (Rome)	885–891
Formosus (Italy)	891–896
Boniface VI (Rome)	896
Stephen VII (Rome)	896–897
Romanus (Italy)	897
Theodore II (Rome)	897
John IX (Italy)	898–900
Benedict IV (Rome)	900–903
Leo V (Italy)	903
Chistophorus	*903–904*
Sergius III (Rome)	904–911
Anastasius III (Rome)	911–913
Landonius (Italy)	913–914
John X (Italy)	914–928
Leo VI (Rome)	928
Stephen VIII (Rome)	928–931

John XI (Rome)	931–935
Leo VII (Rome)	936–939
Stephen IX (Rome)	939–942
Marinus II (Rome)	942–946
Agapetus II (Rome)	946–955
John XII (Italy)	955–964
Leo VIII (Rome)	963–965
Benedict V (Rome)	964–966
John XIII (Rome)	965–972
Benedict VI (Rome)	973–974
Boniface VII	*974*
Benedict VII (Rome)	974–983
John XIV (Italy)	983–984
John XV (Rome)	985–996
Gregory V (Germany)	996–999
John XVI	*997–998*
Sylvester II (Italy)	999–1003
John XVII (Rome)	1003
John XVIII (Rome)	1004–1009
Sergius IV (Rome)	1009–1012
Benedict VIII (Italy)	1012–1024
Gregory VI	*1012*
John XIX (Rome)	1024–1032
Benedict IX (Italy)	1032–1044
Sylvester III (Italy)	1045
Benedict IX (a second time)	1045
Gregory VI (Rome)	1045–1046
Clement II (Germany)	1046–1047
Benedict IX (a third time)	1047–1048
Damasus II (Germany)	1048
Leo IX (Germany)	1049–1054
Victor II (Germany)	1055–1057
Stephen X (Lorraine)	1057–1058
Benedict X	*1058–1059*
Nicholas II (France)	1059–1061
Alexander II (Italy)	1061–1073
Honorius II	*1061–1072*
Gregory VII (Italy)	1073–1085
Clement III	*1080–1100*
Victor III (Italy)	1086–1087
Urban II (France)	1088–1099
Paschal II (Italy)	1099–1118
Theoderic	*1100–1102*
Albert	*1102*
Sylvester IV	*1105–1111*
Gelasius II (Italy)	1118–1119
Gregory VIII	*1118–1121*
Calixtus II (France)	1119–1124
Celestine II	*1124*
Honorius II (Italy)	1124–1130
Innocent II (Rome)	1130–1143
Anacletus II	*1130–1138*
Victor IV	*1138*
Celestine II (Italy)	1143–1144
Lucius II (Italy)	1144–1145
Eugenius III (Italy)	1145–1153
Anastasius IV (Rome)	1153–1154
Adrian IV (England)	1154–1159
Alexander III (Italy)	1159–1181
Victor IV	*1159–1164*
Paschal III	*1164–1168*
Calixtus III	*1168–1178*
Innocent III	*1179–1180*
Lucius III (Italy)	1181–1185
Urban III (Italy)	1185–1187
Gregory VIII	1187
Clement III (Rome)	1187–1191
Celestine III (Rome)	1191–1198
Innocent III (Italy)	1198–1216
Honorius III (Rome)	1216–1227
Gregory IX (Italy)	1227–1241
Celestine IV (Italy)	1241

1503–1513
JULIUS II
DELLA ROVERE

1513–1521
LEO X
MEDICI

1534–1549
PAUL III
FARNESE

1585–1590
SIXTUS V
PERETTI

1592–1605
CLEMENT VIII
ALDOBRANDINI

1605–1621
PAUL V
BORGHESE

1623–1644
URBAN VIII
BARBERINI

1644–1655
INNOCENT X
PAMPHILI

1655–1667
ALEXANDER VII
CHIGI

Innocent IV (Italy)	1243–1254
Alexander IV (Italy)	1254–1261
Urban IV (France)	1261–1264
Clement IV (France)	1265–1268
Gregory X (Italy)	1271–1276
Innocent V (Savoy)	1276
Hadrian V (Italy)	1276
John XXI (Portugal)	1276–1277
Nicholas III (Rome)	1277–1280
Martin IV (France)	1281–1285
Honorius IV (Rome)	1285–1287
Nicholas IV (Italy)	1288–1292
Celestine V (Italy)	1294
Boniface VIII (Italy)	1294–1303
Benedict XI (Italy)	1303–1304
Clement V (France)	1305–1314
John XXII (France)	1316–1334
Nicholas V	*1328–1330*
Benedict XII (France)	1334–1342
Clement VI (France)	1342–1352
Innocent VI (France)	1352–1362
Urban V (France)	1362–1370
Gregory XI (France)	1370–1378
Urban VI (Italy)	1378–1389
Boniface IX (Italy)	1389–1404
Innocent VII (Italy)	1404–1406
Gregory XII (Italy)	1406–1415
Popes in Avignon:	
Clement VII	*1378–1394*
Benedict XIII	*1394–1423*
Clement VIII	*1423–1429*
Benedict XIV	*1425–1430*
Popes in Pisa:	
Alexander V	*1409–1410*
John XXIII	*1410–1415*
Martin V (Rome)	1417–1431
Eugenius IV (Italy)	1431–1447
Felix V	*1439–1449*
Nicholas V (Italy)	1447–1455
Calixtus III (Spain)	1455–1458
Pius II (Italy)	1458–1464
Paul II (Italy)	1464–1471
Sixtus IV (Italy)	1471–1484
Innocent VIII (Italy)	1484–1492
Alexander VI Spain)	1492–1503
Pius III (Italy)	1503

Julius II (Italy)	1503–1513
Leo X (Italy)	1513–1521
Hadrian VI (Holland)	1522–1523
Clement VII (Italy)	1523–1524
Paul III (Rome)	1534–1549
Julius III (Rome)	1550–1555
Marcellus II (Italy)	1555
Paul IV (Italy)	1555–1559
Pius V (Italy)	1566–1572
Gregory XIII (Italy)	1572–1585
Sixtus V (Italy)	1585–1590
Urban VII (Rome)	1590
Gregory XIV (Italy)	1590–1591
Innocent IX (Italy)	1591
Clement VIII (Italy)	1592–1605
Leo XI (Italy)	1605
Paul V (Rome)	1605–1621
Gregory XV (Italy)	1621–1623
Urban VIII (Italy)	1623–1644
Innocent X (Rome)	1644–1655
Alexander VII (Italy)	1655–1667
Clement IX (Italy)	1667–1669
Clement X (Rome)	1670–1676
Innocent XI (Italy)	1676–1689
Alexander VIII (Italy)	1689–1691
Innocent XII (Italy)	1691–1700
Clement XI (Italy)	1700–1721
Innocent XIII (Rome)	1721–1724
Benedict XIII (Rome)	1724–1730
Clement XII (Italy)	1730–1740
Benedict XIV (Italy)	1740–1758
Clement XIII (Italy)	1758–1769
Clement XIV (Italy)	1769–1774
Pius VI (Italy)	1775–1799
Pius VII (Italy)	1800–1823
Leo XII (Italy)	1823–1829
Pius VIII (Italy)	1829–1830
Gregory XVI (Italy)	1831–1846
Pius IX (Italy)	1846–1878
Leo XII (Italy)	1878–1903
Pius X (Italy)	1903–1914
Benedict XV (Italy)	1914–1922
Pius XI (Italy)	1922–1939
Pius XII (Rome)	1939–1958
John XXIII	1958–1963
Paul VI	1963–1978
John Paul I	1978
John Paul II	1978

and the papal altar above it. See plan for additional details. *Sacristy:* built in 1776–84 by C.Marchionni. *Museo Storico Artistico:* This grew up around the old treasury, the Tesoro di S.Pietro. The following exhibits are particularly worth seeing: copy of the Throne of Peter, a gift of Charles the Bald on the occasion of his coronation as emperor in 875, found in 1970 in Bernini's Cattedra Petri; Room II. Magnificent marble ciborium (*c.* 1433, by Donatello) with the Madonna della Febre (by L.Memmi);

Room III. Sepulchre of Pope Sixtus IV della Rovere (1489–93, by A.Pollaiuolo); Room IV. Marble sarcophagus of Junius Bassus (mid 4C); Room IX. *Vatican Grottoes:* Access to the grottoes under St.Peter's with their various tombs is by the dome pier of St.Helen. Some of the rooms may only be visited by special permission of the Reverenda Fabbrica di San Pietro. In the so-called New Grottoes are the tomb of Pope Paul II (d. 1471, by M.da Fiesole among others, in the largest chapel on the N. side), relief from the old high altar of St.Peter's (15C, by M.Pollaiuolo, on the left of the ambulatory), chapel of St.Peter with altar by the tomb of Peter (6C). Czech chapel with wall picture of the Madonna della Bocciata, Madonna chapel with the Madonna delle Partorienti (attributed to M.da Forli). The so-called Old Grottoes are a hall crypt with three aisles, in which parts of Old St.Peter's have survived. They contain tombs of Popes and cardinals, emperors and kings, and also altars from Old St.Peter's. The 'Madonna degli Orsini' altar relief in the left aisle is striking (15C, by I.da Pisa), as is the 3C marble sculpture of Peter by the exit. *Necropolis* (may only be visited by permission of the Reverenda Fabbrica di San Pietro): Pope Pius XII (1939–58) commissioned excavation of the cemetery presumed to be under St.Peter's, and 22 mausoleums and 2 tombs were discovered. One of the simple tombs under the Confessio has been identified with some certainty as being St.Peter's. It is known to have been venerated for years; it was furnished as a memorial *c.* AD 160; the ciborium was added by Constantine the Great. The floor was raised in the 9C in order to make the martyr's grave part of the high altar of St.Peter.

Campo Santo Teutonico and Church of S.Maria della Pietà: The German foundation was established by the Scola Francorum, first mentioned in 799, and in 1461 was taken over by the 'Arch-Brotherhood of Our Lady on the Campo Santo Teutonico by St.Peter's in Rome'. The church is a cruciform hall with nave, two aisles and two side choirs, built in 1475–1501. The bronze portal (by E.Hillebrandt) and the windows (G.Meistermann) were endowed by German Federal Presidents. Research into antiquity is conducted in the Priests' College, founded in 1876. Vatican Palace: only the rooms which are part of the Vatican Museum may be visited. Nicholas III (1277–80) made the Vatican the papal residence. In subsequent years various Popes developed the site, which has some magnificent individual features, but is not always easy to take in as a whole. The most important building phases were: under Nicholas II, opening up

Sistine Chapel, detail of Michelangelo's ceiling

of the present Belvedere Court; Nicholas V: palace around the Cortile dei Pappagalli (*c.* 1450); Sixtus IV: Sistine Chapel (1473); Alexander VI: (1492–1503) Appartamento Borgia and Borgia Tower; Julius II: galleries around the Belvedere Court (1503–15, by Bramante, A.da Sangallo the Younger, B.Peruzzi, G.Romano and others); Leo X: Raphael's Stanze and Loggias; Paul III (1534–49): Scala Regia and Cappella Paolina (by A. da) Sangallo); Pius IV (1559–65): Casino di Pio IV (by P.di Ligorio); Pius V (1566–72) and Sixtus V (1585–90) palace building on St.Peter's Square (by D.Fontana); Alexander VII: Scala Regia (1659, by Bernini). For further details, see Vatican Museum.

Also worth seeing: *Audience Hall (Sala delle Udienze Pontificie)*, hall built in 1964–71 by P.L.Nervi for papal audiences, able to accommodate 18,000 people. *S.Anna dei Palafrenieri* (by the Porta S.Anna): oval building dating from 1573 by Vignola with fine lunette frescos (early 18C, by I.Stern), parish and funerary church of the Vatican, under the aegis of the Confraternità dei Palafrenieri della Corte Papale.

C. Vatican Museums (entrance in the Viale Vaticano).
The history of the Vatican collections began in 1603, when Julius II put the statue of Apollo on show, followed in 1506 by the Laocoön group. They were exhibited next to each other in the statue court of the Belvedere, the summer residence of Pope Innocent VIII (1484–92), hence the name Apollo Belvedere. The Laocoön group in particular was soon to achieve great fame and even political significance. In the mid 16C the library was added, providing accommodation for the Museo Sacro, created by Benedict XV in 1756, and the Museo Profano, founded in 1767. When Clement XIV acquired various collections of antiquities in 1770 the Vatican Museum was systematically extended, starting at the Statue Court of the Belvedere, and connecting the library's art collections with the Museo Pio Clementino. The Pope was forced by the Treaty of Tolentino (1797) to restore many valuable works

Interior of St.Peter's

to Napoleonic France (return 1816). At the same time the Museo Chiaramonti and the Galleria Lapidaria came into being under Pius VII (1800–23). Then came the Braccio Nuovo (1822, by R.Stern), under Gregory XVI (1831–46) the Museo Gregoriano Egizio and the Museo Gregoriano Profano (like the two following institutions originally in the Lateran Palace, in the Vatican from 1962), under Pius IX the Museo Pio Cristiano and in 1927 the Museo Missionario-Etnologico. The Lateran Treaties (1929) obliged the Popes to open their collections to the public. Under Pius XI the present museum entrance and the Pinacoteca (1923, by L.Beltrami) were added. Finally came the Salette degli Originali Greci (1960), the transfer of the three Lateran museums to the Vatican, (from 1962), the Museo Storico (1973) and the Collezione d'Arte religiosa moderna. Fixed routes through the museums are prescribed for visitors, with a total length of over 7 km., past almost 50,000 exhibits and through a part of the Vatican Palace (Stanze and Loggia of Raphael, Sistine Chapel, Papal chapels, Scala Bramante, Appartemento Borgia, library etc.).

Museo Gregoriano Egizio: The Egyptian section was opened in 1839 under Gregory XVI, and shows numerous finds from Rome and Tivoli in ten rooms. Room V: monumental sculpture of Queen Tuaa (mother of Rameses I), *c.* 1300 BC, 19th dynasty of the New Empire.

Museo Chiaramonti: This corridor with 59 sections and about 1,000 extremely varied ancient pieces was turned into a museum by A.Canova. Adjacent is the Galleria Lapidaria (inscription gallery), which may only be visited with the permission of the directors of the museum.

Museo Pio Clementino: This museum built between 1770 and 1784 under Clement XIV and Pius VI houses well-known antiquities. Gabinetto dell' Apoxyomenos; sculpture of Apoxyomenos ('The Scraper', *c.* 320 BC by Lysippos; Roman copy of Greek original). Cortile Ottagono:

Laocoön, Vatican Museums

marble statue of 'Apolloe Belvedere' (Roman copy *c*. AD 130, from a Greek bronze original, *c*. 330 BC, by Leochares). The famous Laocoön group (*c*. 50 BC, by the Rhodian sculptor Agesandros and his sons). Gabinetto delle Maschere: Venus of Knidos (replica of the original by Praxitiles). Sala delle Muse: marble seated figure of the 'Belvedere Torso', by the Athenian sculptor Apollonius).

Museo Gregoriano Etrusco: The Etruscan collection was founded in 1837 by Gregory XVI, and houses mainly finds from South Etruscan necropolises which were once owned

Vatican Museums 1 Museo Gregoriano Egizio 2 Museo Chiaramonti 3 Galleria Lapidaria 4 Museo Pio Clementino 5 Museo Gregoriano Etrusco 6 Scala Bramante 7 Salette degli Originali Greci 8 Scala dei Relievi Assiri 9 Collection of ancient vases 10 Scala della Biga 11 Galleria dei Candelabri 12 Galleria degli Arazzi 13 Galleria delle Carte Geografiche 14 Appartamento del S.Pio V 15 Sala del Sobieski 16 Sala dell'Immacolata 17 Chapel of Urban VIII 18 Raphael's Stanze 19 Loggia di Raffaelo 20 Sala dei Chiaroscuri 21 Cappella Niccolina 22 Appartamento Borgia 23 Collection of Modern Religious Art 24 Sistine Chapel 25 Biblioteca Apostolica Vaticana 26 Braccio Nuovo 27 Pinacoteca 28 Museo Gregoriano Profano 29 Museo Pio Cristiano 30 Museo Missionario-Etnologico 31 Museo Storico

by the church state. The 18 rooms also accommodate the Scala Bramante (X), Roman (VIII), Greek (XII), Assyrian (XIII) antiquities and the collection of ancient vases (XIV–XVIII). II: Sala della Tomba Regolini-Galasi: the burial chamber of the same name, called after the excavators, from the Sorbo necropolis S. of Cervéteri was the source of the items exhibited here. III: Sala dei Bronzi: large bronze of 'Mars of Todi'. X: Scala Bramante: the famous spiral staircase built after 1400 by Bramante for Julius II. which it was possible to ascend on horseback. XII: Salette degli Originali Greci: sculptural fragments from the Parthenon (447–432 BC), especially the famous horse's head from Athena's team on the W. pediment. Grave of a youth (*c*. 450 BC). Ancient vase collection. XVI: Lower hemicycle: amphora of Exekias (Attic, black-figured, *c*. 525 BC, by Exekias). Upper hemicycle: amphora of Achilleus (Attic red-figured, *c*. 450 BC, signed 'Achilleus').

Sala della Biga: This domed rotunda was built for Pius VI (1775–

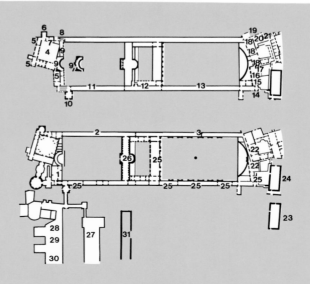

99) by G. Camporese. It contains the Biga (two-horsed chariot); only the chariot itself is ancient.

Galleria dei Candelabri: This former loggia was named after the richly-decorated Roman chandeliers (1/2C AD, placed here in 1792).

Galleria degli Arazzi: Tapestry gallery, named after the Flemish town of Arras (centre of the tapestry-makers' art).

Galleria delle Carte Geografiche: Maps and vedutas (1580–3, by I. Danti). There is a view of the Bramante's Belvedere Court to the left and the Vatican Gardens with the Casino Pio IV to the right.

Chapel of Pius V: Wall (G.Vasari) and ceiling painting (F.Zuccaro).

Sala Sobieski: Monumental historical painting 'Battle at the Kahlenberg', near Vienna (1683) with John III Sobieski as conqueror of the Turks (presumed to date from 1883, by J.Mateiko).

Sala dell'Immacolata: Named after the fresco of the 'Immaculate Conception' (*c.* 1854, by F.Podestis). Model of the dome of St.Peter's (1558–60, by Michelangelo).

Stanze of Raphael: Raphael was commissioned to paint the rooms by Julius II in 1508. Stanza dell'Incendio di Borgo: ceiling painting (by Perugino) and wall paintings (1514–17, by Raphael and his pupils). 'Fire of Borgo in 847', 'Charlemagne Crowned Emperor by Leo III in 800', 'Victory of Leo IV over the Saracens near Ostia in 849', 'Oath of Leo III'. Stanza della Segnatura ('Signature Room', so called because the Pope signed his bulls here): Magnificent High Renaissance frescos (1508–11, principal work of Raphael). 'Disputà del Sacramento' (Transfiguration of the altar sacrament), 'The School of Athens' with Plato and Aristotle at the centre, 'Parnassus' and 'Administration of Sacred and Profane Justice'. Stanza d'Eliodoro: ceiling paintings (by Peruzzi) and wall paintings (1512–14, by Raphael). 'Driving of Heliodor from the Temple', 'The

Museo Gregoriano Egizio, Egyptian head

Mass at Bolsena', 'Leo I drives out Attila' and 'Peter Liberated from his Prison'. Sala di Costantino: painted after 1520 (death of Raphael) by his pupils G.Romano, F.Penni and R.del Colle. The central feature is 'The Victory of Constantine over Maxentius' and other scenes featuring Constantine, and papal virtues.

Loggias of Raphael: This gallery was begun by Bramante in 1513–18 and painted by Raphael. The socalled Bible of Raphael shows 52 scenes from the Old and New Testaments in 13 vaulted bays. The walls are decorated with fine grotesques. There is a view from the loggia of the courtyard of the Vatican Palace.

Chapel of Nicholas V: Splendid frescos with representations of the lives of St.Laurence and St.Stephen (1455, by Fra Angelico da Fiesole and assistants).

Chapel of Urban VIII: Painted by P.da Cortona.

Appartamento Borgia: Painted by Pinturicchio and assistants in 1492–5 for Alexander VI. The finest of the six rooms is the Sala della Vita dei Santi; the frescos are Pinturicchio's masterpiece.

Collezione d'Arte religiosa moderna: The collection of modern religious art was started by Paul VI in 1973, and has 54 rooms containing works by the most celebrated contemporary artists.

Cappella Sistina/Sistine Chapel: Scene of the papal election and private papal services. Thanks to its unique frescos the architecturally plain room (1473–84, by G. de Dolci) is a major work of Renaissance art. Ceiling paintings (1508–12, by Michelangelo): 'God Separates Light and Darkness', 'God Creates Sun, Moon and Stars', 'Separation of Water and Land', 'Creation of Adam', 'Creation of Eve', 'Fall of Man and Expulsion from Paradise', 'Noah's Thanks-Offering', 'Flood', 'Noah's Drunkenness'. The scenes are presented with solemn drama and great dynamism of gesture. Corner panels of ceiling: 'Esther', 'Bronze Snake', 'Judith', 'David and Goliath', further Sybils and prophets. 20 years later Michelangelo created the powerful fresco of the 'Last Judgement' on the altar wall (1534–41). It contains a total of 391 figures, originally naked, reflecting Michelangelo's idealism and humanism, and to an extent his political and religious views; some of them had to be dressed at a later date by D.da Volterra. The central figure is the Judge of the World, with Madonna, Apostles and Saints, and on the left those permitted to enter Heaven, and on the right those condemned to Hell. Wall paintings: on the left: 'Circumcision of Moses' (Perugino and Pinturicchio), 'Youth of Moses', (Botticelli), 'The Crossing of the Red Sea', (school of Ghirlandaio), 'Moses Receiving the Tablets of the Law' (C.Roselli et al.), 'Punishment of Korah' (Botticelli), 'Death of Moses' (Signorelli); on the right: 'Baptism of Christ' (Perugino), 'Healing of the Leper' (Botticelli), 'Call of Peter and Andrew' (Ghirlandaio), 'Sermon on the Mount and Healing of the Leper' (C.Rosselli), 'Christ Hands over the Keys to Peter', (Perugino), 'Last Supper' (C.Rosselli).

Art Collection in the Biblioteca Apostolica: Applied art collection in two rooms and the Chapel of S.Pio V (1566–72, painted by J.Zucchi to a design by Vasari).

Sala delle Nozze Aldobrandine: This room was built in 1611 and the ancient wall paintings were placed here in 1838. In the centre is the 'Aldobrandine Wedding' (Augustan,

Raphael: Coronation of the Virgin (Vatican Museums) ▷

named after Cardinal P.Aldobrandini). Sala dei Papiri, established *c.* 1770 to house the 'Ravenna Papyri' (6–9C).

Museo Sacro: Established in 1756 to accommodate minor works of early Christian art, wax mosaic of St.Theodore (12/13C). Galleria di Urbano VIII, established to accommodate the Biblioteca Palatina.

Salone Sistino: This fine Mannerist library was built in 1587 by D.Fontana on the second floor of the Vatican Library; it is a hall with two aisles and groin vaulting. The building cuts through the Belvedere Courtyard, destroying what used to be the most beautiful of the Renaissance garden courts, designed by Bramante, with steps and exedra. Splendid wall paintings in the Sistine Hall (*c.* 1587, presumably by P.Orsini et al.). Two sequences of pictures: 'The Councils General' and the 'Great Libraries'.

Braccio Nuovo (New Museum Section): Ancient works are housed in the early-19C historicist hall which cuts through the the Belvedere Courtyard parallel to the library. Sculpture of Doryphoros, the spear carrier (Roman copy after a Greek original by Polykletes, *c.* 440 BC) which even in ancient times was considered to be ideally proportioned. Statue of Augustus from the Prima Porta (Roman, *c.* 20 BC).

Pinacoteca: Predominantly panel paintings by 14–19C Italian masters in fifteen rooms set up in 1932.

Museo Gregorio Profano: Collection of antiquities with finds from the former church state. Athena-Marsyas group (marble copy of a bronze original by Myron, 450 BC). Sculpture of Sophocles (after a bronze original by Lykurgos, *c.* 340 BC) and other portraits of famous Greeks. Cancelleria reliefs of the Adventus of the Emperor Vespasian and the Profectio of the Emperor Domitian (historical representations *c.* AD 90).

Museo Pio Cristiano: Collection of early Christian sarcophaguses and inscriptions arranged by subject.

Museo Gregoriano Egizio, Egyptian censor

Sculpture of the Good Shepherd (3C AD) 'Dogmatic Sarcophagus' (*c.* 350 AD) and other sarcophaguses with Biblical scenes.

Museo Missionario-Etnologico: Ethnological museum which grew out of the Mission Exhibition of 1925, with cult-historical exhibits from Asia, Africa, Australia, Oceania and America in 24 departments.

Museo Storico: Historic papal vehicles and uniforms in two departments.

IV. Secular Buildings

1. Streets and Squares

Streets

Via della Conciliazione: 'Street of Reconciliation', between Castel Sant'Angelo and St.Peter's Square. A street of this kind was planned by Bernini and Valadier, but it was not built until after the conclusion of the Lateran Treaties (1929) in 1936–9, by pulling down the so-called *Spina di Roma*. The street has a mixture of old and new buildings.

Via del Corso (Piazza Venezia-Piazza del Popolo): Main street in the 18C, named after medieval Jewish races for the diversion of the people; contains numerous palaces.

Other streets worth seeing: The twisted, narrow streets of the old town on the *Campus Martius* (bend in the Tiber E. of the river) are of general interest, and offer an opportunity to experience everyday life in Rome (crafts, street markets etc.). *Via Condotti* (Via del Corso-Spanish Steps), today the city's most elegant shopping street. *Via Veneto* (Piazza Barberini-Villa Borghese), with luxury hotels and expensive street cafés; little has survived of its cosmopolitan feel.

Squares

Campo de'Fiori: One of the liveliest markets in the city: behind the remains of the 1C BC theatre of Pompey, now surrounded by blocks of flats; in the past it was the place of execution for heretics (see Giordano Bruno Monument).

Piazza di Campodiglio (Capitoline): In the dip between the two high points of the city's ancient fortress hill; redesigned by Michelangelo (including the siting of the ancient equestrian statue of Marcus Aurelius in the centre of an ornamental circle); the statue has been under restoration since 1981. On the long sides Palazzo dei Conservatori and Palazzo Nuovo, built on the remains of the ancient tabularium of the Senators' Palace.

Piazza Garibaldi (on the Gianicolo): This has one of the finest views of the city and surrounding hills; by the Garibaldi memorial busts of heroes of the Risorgimento.

Piazza Navona: One of the homeliest parts of the city on the site of the ancient Stadium of Domitian (1C AD; remains of the substructure visible from outside to the N). 17C fountains by Bernini and others. The square is dominated by the façade of S.Agnese in Agone. As recently as the last century the square was flooded for the amusement of the populace.

Piazza del Popolo: At the point where the main roads from Cassia and Flaminia meet (see Porta del Popolo). In the centre is an ancient Egyptian obelisk; the Via del Corso begins between the churches of S.Maria dei Miracoli and S.Maria in Monte Santo (both 17C). Neoclassical design by Valadier over the square of *Monte Pincio* in 1809–14; there is a famous view of St.Peter's from the Piazzale Napoleone, at its best at sunset.

Piazza del Quirinale: Decorated with an ancient Egyptian obelisk which was combined with an antique statue of the Dioskuri from the Baths of Constantine. There is also a fine view over the roofs of the old town to the dome of St.Peter's.

Piazza della Rotonda:In front of the Pantheon, now a meeting-place of young people until late at night. On the E. side is the 'Albergo del Sole', one of the oldest inns in the city.

Piazza di Spagna: One of the 'Romantic' centres of the town; named after the Spanish delegation to the Vatican (accommodated in the nearby Palazzo di Spagna since the 17C). The magnificent *Spanish Steps* are the central feature, built in 1723–5 by F.de Sanctis; the design is essentially asymmetrical; above them is the façade of SS. Trinità dei Monti, which dominates the entire area. The ancient Egyptian obelisk was placed in front of it in 1789.

Piazza Venezia: Focal point of the city's traffic; dominated by the gigantic National Monument and the Palazzo Venezia.

Also worth seeing: *Piazza Cavalieri*

Spanish Steps and Trinità dei Monti

di Malta (on the Aventine) with a famous view through the keyhole of the portal to the park of the Maltese Priory, and of the dome of St.Peter's. *Isola Tiberina* (Tiber island), a centre of care for the sick since ancient times (Temple of Aesclepius, god of healing; now a hospital); on the E. bank downstream is an ancient relief in the form of a ship; Piazza della Bocca della Verità, on the bank of the Tiber on the site of the ancient Roman cattle market (S.Maria in Cosmedin is worth seeing, and the two Roman temples). *Piazza Borghese*, dominated by the Palazzo Borghese; daily antiques market in the square (specializes in books and engravings). *Piazza Colonna*, a centre even in ancient times (the 2C AD Marcus Aurelius column has survived). *Piazza Farnese* in front of the imposing Palazzo Farnese, particularly impressive on summer evenings. *Piazza Montecitorio* in front of the Italian Parliament Building. *Piazza S.Bernado*, framed with fine Renaissance and baroque buildings. *Piazze S.Maria in Trastevere* in the centre of the 'Trans Tiberim' area, a suburb of the city from ancient times.

2. Palaces, Villas and Gardens

Palazzo Barberini (Via delle Quattro Fontane): Most important high baroque palace in Rome. Built 1625–33 by Maderna, Bernini and Borromini; model for Upper Italian villas (wings set forward). Threefold order of columns on the façade in classical sequence (Doric, Ionian, Corinthian). In the interior, main staircase by Bernini; spiral staircase in the right wing by Borromini; trompe l'oeil painting on the ceiling of the salon by P. da Cortona (1632–9). Gallery of ancient art now housed in the palace.

Palazzo Borghese (Piazza Borghese): Started *c.* 1590 by M.Lunghi, extended after 1600 by F.Ponzio. Irregular ground plan; main façade (longest in Rome) is curved, hence popularly known as 'il cembalo'. Atmospheric courtyard with ancient statues; access from here to garden court in the style of a rural villa.

Palazzo della Cancelleria (Piazza della Cancelleria): One of the finest Renaissance palaces in the city. Built 1483–1511; architect unknown. Three-tier main façade in Travertine marble. Pilasters on the first and second levels arranged in accordance with the golden mean. Finest feature of the interior is the 'Sala di Cento Giorni' with frescos by Vasari dating from 1546. It has been the seat of the Apostolic Chancellery and a possession of the Vatican since 1870.

Palazzo Farnese (Piazza Farnese): Most important palace in the city. A.da Sangallo began to build in 1514, Michelangelo took over direction of the work from 1546 (he was responsible for the cornice and the upper storey in the courtyard). Magnificent yellow-brick Renaissance façade; the courtyard has columns of the three ancient orders. There are fine frescos by A.Caracci on the first floor.

Fontana di Trevi

Palazzo Massimo alle Colonne (Corso Vittorio Emanuele): B.Peruzzi reconstructed an earlier building in the style of an old Roman residence, in 1534–6. In the lower storey is a portico with six columns, and above three rows of windows which are almost Mannerist in style. Two court-yards (each with a nymphaeum, dating from 1620 and 1627 respectively). The 16C interior decoration has survived in very good condition.

Palazzo Spada (Piazza Capo di Ferro): Built after 1540, architect uncertain; restored by Borromini in 1632. Now seat of the upper house of the Italian Parliament. The main façade has aedicules with statues of Roman heroes and emperors, court-yard with pillared arcades. In the left-hand rear courtyard is a corridor almost 30 ft. long designed by Borromini, which by trompe-l'oeil gives the effect of an arcade. In the interior is the 'Salone del Trono' with an ancient statue of Pompey (said to be the one under which Julius Caesar was assassinated).

Palazzo Venezia (Piazza Venezia): Built in the 15C by unknown masters; from 1564–1797 property of the Republic of Venice, hence the name; to 1943 official residence of Mussolini. Above the façade is a castellated wall passage with massive corner tower, above the central portal a balcony from which Mussolini made many of his speeches. The interior includes a vestibule with fine Renaissance coffered ceiling and the gigantic Sala Regia. To the S. is the *Palazetto Venezia* with a fine courtyard.

Villa Ada (N. of the centre): Originally Villa Savoia, privately owned by the Italian royal family; extensive grounds. It was in this villa that Mussolini was arrested on the orders of King Victor Emmanuel III on 25 July 1943. Now seat of the Egyptian Embassy.

Villa Borghese: Commissioned by Cardinal Scipione Borghese and built 1613–16; extended in the neoclassical style by Camillo Borghese, the brother-in-law of Napoleon I. It encloses roughly 6 square kilometres. Particularly striking features include the *Giardino del Lago*, the *equestrian amphitheatre* on the Piazza di Siena and the *Fontana dei Cavalli Marini* of 1770. The *Casino Borghese* now houses the Galleria Borghese.

Villa Celimontana (or Villa Mattei; S. of the Colosseum): Named after the ancient Mons Caelius, which was settled in the earliest Roman period; park arranged in terraces. Particularly fine view to the S. over the Baths of Caracalla to the Alban Hills. The Casino is the seat of the Geographical Society and the International Society for the Study of Mediterranean Archaeology.

Villa Doria Pamphili (W. of the Gianicolo): Largest park in the city (9 square km.), designed in 1644. Access is through a triumphal arch on the site of a casino destroyed during Garibal-

di's conflict with the French. The E section is decorated with statues arches and fountains. The villa palace in the Palladian style is worth seeing.

Villa Giulia (Viale delle Belle Arti) Built by Vignola 1551–3 for Pope Julius III, designed in the style of 'Villa Suburbana'. Two-tier façade two courtyards behind it (the ground plan is a mixture of rectangle and semicircle). The Etruscan Museum of the same name has been housed here since 1880.

Villa Madama (Monte Mario) Started in 1516 to plans by Raphael based on antique models, taken over by A. da Sangallo; named after Margaret of Parma ('la Madama'), the daughter of Charles V. The villa is the first building of its kind in the city The site is terraced, and set on a hillside; at the top is a theatre, in the middle the central Casino; the stucco decorations in the loggia are particularly worth seeing; they are by G.Romano and G.da Udine, and based on ancient models.

Also worth seeing: *Casa dei Crescenzi* (Via del Teatro di Marcello) defensive building constructed from Roman spoils (inscription over the portal). *Collegio Romano* (Piazza del Collegio Romano), built in the 16C as a Jesuit College. *Farnese Gardens* (on the Palatine), designed by Vignola in the 16C. *Palazzo Braschi* (Corso Vittorio Emanuele), built in 1792, the last building of its kind in Rome; the staircase constructed from ancient columns is particularly worth seeing *Palazzo Capranica* (Piazza Capranica), fine early Renaissance building *Palazzo Chigi* (Via del Corso) dating from the 16C, now residence of the Italian Prime Minister. *Palazzo Colonna (Via della Pilotta)*, started in the 15C, residence of the family of the same name, who have continually extended it. Across the Via della Pilotta is the *Villa Colonna*, which belongs to the palace (access via Vi

XXV Maggio). *Palazzo della Con-sulta* (Piazza del Quirinale), built in the 18C as Papal court of justice, now seat of the Italian constitutional court. *Palazzo Corsini* (Via della Lungara), built in the 18C by F.Fuga. *Palazzo Doria* (Via del Corso), largest palace in Rome with fine façade dating from 1734. *Palazzo Giustianini* (Via della Dogana Vecchia), completed by Borromini in 1651, seat of the President of the Italian Senate. *Palazzo del Governo Vecchio* (Via del Governo Vecchio) with fine 15C portal. *Palazzo Madama* (Corso del Rinascimento), built in the 16C as a palace for the Medici, seat of the Italian Senate since 1871. *Palazzo Mattei* (Piazza Mattei), built in the 16&17C; fine courtyard in the Palazzo Mattei di Giove). *Palazzo Montecitorio* (Piazza Montecitorio), built 1650–94 by Bernini and Fontana, seat of the Italian Parliament since 1871. *Palazzo Pallavicini Rospigliosi* (Via XXV Maggio), built by Maderna in the 17C; G.Reni's 'Aurora' fresco is in the garden Casino. *Palazzo Quirinale* (Piazza del Quirinale), summer residence of the Popes from the 16C, seat of the Kings of Italy until 1946, now residence of the Italian State President; fine early baroque façade and extensive gardens laid out by Maderna. *Palazzo Regis* (Corso Vittorio Emanuele), built in 1523 by A.da Sangallo, a model of economical yet masterly architecture. *Palazzo Ruspoli* (Via del Corso), dating from 1556, fine staircase by M.Lunghi the Younger. *Palazzo Vidoni Caffarelli* (Corso Vittorio Emanuele), originally designed by Raphael in 1515. *Palazzo Wedekind* (Piazza Colonna), built in 1838; 16 ancient columns from Veii in the portico. *Parco di Colle Oppio* (NE of the Colosseum) on the site of the ancient Baths of Trajan (surviving ruins); fine view of the Colosseum. *Torre dei Conti* (Via Cavour/Via dei Fori Imperiali), built in the 13C and altered later. *Torre dei Milizie* (Via IV Novembre), one of the oldest towers in Rome; it dates from the 13C, but legend has it that it was from here that Nero watched Rome burning. *Villa Farnesina* (Via Lungara), 16C, lavishly decorated with frescos; now seat of the Italian Academy of Science. *Villa Medici* (Viale della Tri-

Monument to Victor Emmanuel II (Piazza Venezia)

nità dei Monti), 16C, with lavish façade on the garden side. *Villa Sciarra* (S. of the Gianicolo). *Villa Torlonia* (Via Nomentana), rebuilt in the 19C, Mussolini's private residence for a time.

3. Bridges and Gates

Bridges

The surviving ancient Roman bridges are described in detail under 'II.Ancient Monuments'; summarized in brief, working upstream: *Ponte Milvio* ('Ponte Molle'), *Ponte Fabricio*, *Ponte Rotto* (formerly Pons Aemilius).

More recent bridges

Ponte Flaminio, built under Mussolini in typically Fascist style; it carries the arterial road to the Via Cassia (to Florence) and the Via Flaminia (to Terni).

Ponte S.Angelo (leads to the Castel Sant'Angelo): Built in AD 134 to connect the Mausoleum of Hadrian (Castel Sant'Angelo) with the Campus Martius; the three central arches from the ancient bridge have survived. It was decorated in 1669–71 by Bernini and his studio with ten statues of angels (bearing the attributes of Christ's suffering); the two statues created by Bernini himself (one holding the inscription from the Cross, the other the Crown of Thorns) are now in S.Andrea delle Fratte.

Ponte Cestio (leads to the Tiber island): The original Pons Cestius, dating from the 1C BC, was pulled down in 1889 to broaden the right arm of the Tiber; the present bridge was completed in 1892; the central arch was built from ancient material. There is an ancient inscription built into the right balustrade (renewal of the bridge in AD 370 by the Emperors Valentinian, Valens and Gratianus).

Ponte Sublicio, the ancient Pons Sublicius. Historically the oldest bridge in the city, but the structure is

later (Horatius Cocles held the bridge against the Etruscans under King Porsenna).

Gates

The *ancient city gates* surviving from the *Aurelian Wall* are described in detail under 'Ancient Monuments'.
City gates (clockwise, beginning in the N. of the inner town):

Porta del Popolo: The traditional N. entrance, known in ancient times as the Porta Flaminia, and in the Middle Ages as Porta S.Valentino, later fell into disrepair. The exterior face was rebuilt 1561–3 by Nanni di Baccio Bigio to a design by Michelangelo (one arch, modelled on the Roman triumphal arch), using some ancient columns. Statues of Peter and Paul by F.Mochi. Face on the Piazza del Popolo side 1655 by Bernini on the occasion of the visit of Queen Christina of Sweden (inscription on the Attica); above this arms of Chigi Pope Alexander VII (1655–67). In 1879 the two towers on either side of the door were pulled down to allow the side portals to be installed.

Porta Salaria (Plan of the ancient gate on the surface of the modern street).

Porta Pia (Via XX Settembre/Via Nomentana): Built 1561–5 by Pope Pius IV to a design by Michelangelo. Original interior face (splendid portal, with pilasters and cornice); exterior face rebuilt 1864 (pediment, statues of St.Agnes and St.Alexander). The Bersaglieri Museum is now housed in the outer sections. To the right of the gate is the point at which Nationalist troops forced their way into the town through a breach in the wall on 20 September 1870 (memorial stone).

Porta Maggiore (also known as Porta Praenestina or Labicana).

Porta S.Giovanni, built in 1574 to replace the Porta Asinaria.

Porta Metronia (also known as 'Metrovia') rebuilt in 1157 (inscription on one tower).

Porta S.Sebastiano (formerly Porta Appia): Represents the beginning of the *Bastione Sangallo*, built under Pope Paul III in 1534 by Antonio da Sangallo to fortify the city wall; it continues via the **Porta Ardeatina** to the **Porta S.Paolo**.

Porta Portese: The old Porta Portuensis was destroyed by Pope Urban VIII in 1643; it was sited *c.* 500 yards S. of the present gate; the gate was rebuilt in 1644&5 under Pope Innocent X by Marcantonio de Rossi. The façade is decorated with columns and niches, and the coat of arms of the Pamphili Pope.

Porta S.Pancrazio (on the Gianicolo): The original Porta Aurelia was replaced by Pope Urban VIII in 1642; this was so badly damaged in the fighting between Garibaldi and the French in 1849 that Pope Pius IX commissioned the present building in 1854.

4. Fountains and Monuments

Fountains

Fontana dell'Acque Felice (Piazza S.Bernado): Commissioned from D.Fontana by Pope Sixtus V, and built 1585–7. It is the first important baroque fountain in the city; the water comes from the Alban Hills in an aqueduct which still has some ancient sections. It is articulated with half columns; in the two side niches are statues of river gods (by F.Vacca and G.B.della Porta); in the centre Moses (by P.da Brescia). The four lions are copies of Egyptian originals (Vatican).

Fontana dell'Acqua Paola (in the Gianicolo): End of an ancient aqueduct from Lake Braccia; the fountain was completed in 1612 in archaistic style by F.Ponzio. In the centre are three round arches, each flanked with a small arch. Pope Paul V's inscription in celebration of the building is on the attica.

Fontana dei Fiumi (Piazza Navona): Built in 1647–52 by L.Ber-

Palazzetto dello Sport

nini. Lower section is a rocky landscape, above it an obelisk from the stadium of Domitian, which stood on the site in ancient times. On and in front of the rock are the gods of the then most important rivers of the four quarters of the globe: in the N. the Nile (by A.Brancelli) and the River Plate (by F.Baratta), in the S., the Danube (by A.Lombardo) and the Ganges (by C.Adam). Above the rock are plants and animals typical of the quarter of the globe concerned. The god of the Nile has his hands over his eyes to show that at the time the sources of the Nile had not been discovered.

Fontana del Moro (Piazza Navona): Built by G.A.Mari, a pupil of Bernini, to designs by his master. It represents a Moor fighting a dolphin; the four tritons are copies of originals in the Villa Borghese.

Fontana della Navicella (Piazza della Navicella): Built under Pope Leo X (1513–21); the little marble ship in the centre seems to be based on ancient Roman models.

Fontana delle Tartarughe (Piazza Mattei): Built in 1581–4 by G.della Porta and T.Landini; the tortoises from which it takes its name were added in the 17C. The round bowl is set on a quatrefoil decorated with shells at the corners; in front are four lively, playful figures of boys helping the tortoises over the edge.

Fontana di Trevi (Piazza di Trevi): The most famous fountain in Rome, completed in 1762 after the death of the architect N.Salvi; it is set at the end of the ancient Acqua Vergine. The background is in the form of a Roman arch with three openings; attica above the massive columns, to the sides rectangular niches. In the centre is the figure of Oceanus, at his feet sea-horses, tritons and shells (by P.Bracci); in the left-hand niche is a figure of Abundance, on the right Health (both by F.Valle); over the right niche is a relief explaining the name 'Acqua Vergine' (a virgin showing the spring to Roman soldiers).

Fontana dei Tritoni (Piazza Barberini): Built *c.* 1640–4 by Bernini.

Villa Borghese, lake

Four dolphins supporting shells on their tails, a triton blowing a a powerful jet of water from a shell. The fountain bears the arms of the Barberini family. At the point where the square joins the Via Veneto is the **Fontana delle Api** (Bee Fountain): two worker bees drinking, and the queen bee taking flight (a reference to the Barberini family, whose coat of arms features three bees).

Other fountains worth seeing (arranged according to site): *Piazza Bocca della Verità. Piazza della Repubblica (Naiad Fountain). Piazza di Spagna (Fontana della Barcaccia* by L.Bernini). *Piazza Farnese* (granite bowl from the Baths of Caracalla). *Piazza S.Maria in Trastevere. Villa Borghese (Via Pinciana).* Junction of the *Via Quattro Fontane/Via Nazionale. Villa Medici.*

Memorials and monuments
Cola-di-Rienzo-Monument (Capitol): Halfway up on the left of the stairs to the Capitol designed by Michelangelo, in memory of Cola di Rienzo (1313–54), who as tribune of the people renewed the old Roman Republic for a short time in 1347; an early fighter for Italian national unity.

Elephant Monument (Piazza della Minerva): An elephant made in 1667 after a model by Bernini carries an ancient Egyptian obelisk (6C BC). The inscription (written by Pope Urban VIII) asks for strength from he who bears wisdom.

Fosse Ardeatine (Via Ardeatina): Memorial to the hostages shot by the SS in March 1944 (in retaliation for a partisan attack on German soldiers; 335 victims, including many Jews). The memorial is in the tufa caves in which the shooting took place, with the sarcophaguses of the victims in an adjacent hall; there is a small museum a little higher up.

Garibaldi Monument (on the Gianicolo): Built by Gallori in 1895 in honour of the Italian national hero Giuseppe Garibaldi (Garibaldi defended himself against the French General Oudinot in the Gianicolo in 1849). To the N. is a monument to

Galleria Borghese (Villa Borghese), Paolina Borghese by Canova

Galleria Borghese, Rape of Proserpina, by Bernini

the *Piazza Navona*; in the *Piazza del Popolo*; above the *Spanish Steps*; in front of the *Quirinal Palace*; in front of *S.Giovanni in Laterano* (the highest in Rome (*c.* 105 ft.) and the oldest (*c.* 3,500 years old); in front of *S.Maria Maggiore*; in the *Villa Celimontana*; in the *Pincio*; in front of the *Stazione di Termini*.

Also worth seeing: *Giordano Bruno Monument* (Campo di Fiori) in memory of the philosopher burnt for heresy here in 1600. *Goethe Memorial* (Villa Borghese, Viale Goethe). *Column of Mary* (in front of S.Maria Maggiore), only surviving column from the Basilica of Maxentius. *Pasquino Statue* (NE corner of the Palazzo Braschi/near Piazza Navona), an ancient torso on which malicious and mocking verses were written at the time of the papal domination.

V. Rome in the 19&20C

There were three important phases in the development of the city in these centuries: the *period after 1870*, when Rome became the capital of Italy again, the *Fascist period* (1922–43) and the *period after the Second World War*.

Period after 1870

Many areas which previously had been sites for parks and villas were built on because of the rapidly increasing need for residential and office accommodation; the Prati area of the city (N. of the Vatican) with its streets laid out at right angles and neo-classical residential blocks is typical of the period. At the same time lavish new streets were driven through the old town (e.g. the Corso Vittorio Emanuele). The old town was protected from disastrous floods by the building of a barrier on both sides of the Tiber; broad roads were also built along the river, sweeping away the old Tiber docks ('Ripetta').

Individual buildings worth see

Garibaldi's wife and fellow fighter Anita.

National Monument (Piazza Venezia): Built in 1885–1911 to plans by G.Sacconi in memory of the founder of modern Italy Victor Emmanuel II; since 1921 it has also contained the Tomb of the Unknown Soldier. On the first step is the 'Altar of the Fatherland'. Archaistic style, built in extremely durable white Lombardy marble. The monument is decorated with numerous bronze statues, some of them gilded; the central feature is a 52 ft. equestrian statue of the king.

Obelisks: There are 13 obelisks still standing in the city: in *St.Peter's Square* (the only monolith of this size); in front of the *Pantheon*; in front of the *Parliament Building*; in front of *S.Maria sopra Minerva*; in

ing: *Palace of Justice* (Lungotevere Prati), built 1889–1900, one of the masterpieces of Italian architecture of the period. *Monument to Victor Emmanuel II* (Piazza Venezia), also known as 'Rome's dentures' (see under 'Fountains and Monuments'). *Palazzo dei Esposizioni* (Via Nazionale).

Fascist period

The architecture of Italian Fascism, typically for a political system of this kind, is characterized by uniformity and lack of individuality; it is intended to be functional and to represent the power of the state. An additional characteristic of Italian Fascism (in accordance with the aim for renewal of the old Roman world empire) is the adoption of features of the architecture of Imperial Rome.

In the Foro Italico there is still an obelisk with inscription erected to the 'Duce' by the Balilla, the Fascist State Youth Movement in 1932, showing how much the Romans and indeed all the Italians see the architectural remains of Fascism as a kind of historical document, and not as surviving items from a criminal system which must be removed at all costs.

Foro Italico (Lungotevere Diaz): Built as a sports stadium from 1928. The focal point is the *Stadio dei Marmi*, topped by 60 statues, each representing an Italian province and a particular sport. N. of this is the Italian Foreign Office building, also dating from the Fascist period. The complex was extended for the Summer Olympics in 1960 (including extension of the Olympic Stadium, swimming baths).

Piazza Augusto Imperatore (between the Corso and the Tiber): Built as a setting for the ancient Mausoleum of Augustus. The façades of adjacent buildings still show original

Galleria Borghese, Apollo and Daphne, by Bernini ▷

relief decoration with nationalistic inscriptions from the Mussolini era.

EUR (to the S., Ostia direction): Built for a 'World Fair' ('Esposizione Universale di Roma') planned for 1942, but cancelled because of the war; it was not completed in the Fascist period. The principal building from this epoch is the 'Palazzo dei Eroi'. Extended after the Second World War to designs in keeping with that period (see below).

Other notable buildings from the Fascist period: *side sections of the Stazione di Termini. Post Office* (Piazza di Porta Capena). *Via della Concilazione*, the 'Street of Reconciliation' between the Castel Sant'Angelo and the Vatican built after the Lateran Treaty of 1929.

Period after the Second World War

As Rome is not the economic centre of Italy the city skyline has largely been kept free of high-rise buildings (the only exception within a limited area is the EUR complex). The best example

Boy Removing Thorn, Musei Capitolini

of modern architecture in Rome is the sports centre for the 1960 Summer Olympics.

Palazzetto dello Sport (Viale Tiziano): Built by Pier Luigi Nervi in 1957, also for the Olympic Games; it can accommodate *c.* 5,000 spectators. Circular plan with a rectangular field within it. The overall concept of the building is based on two bowls one inside the other (lower bowl spectators and field, upper bowl a dome). The exterior is articulated by the 36 Y-shaped concrete supports for the dome.

Palazzo dello Sport (EUR, Via Cristoforo Colombo): Built in 1960 as the last masterpiece of the great Italian architect Pier Luigi Nervi over an artifical lake. Capacity *c.* 15,000 spectators. Round building with dome (*c.* 328 ft. in diameter, consisting of wave-shaped units); the circular arena is set below ground level with three tiers of spectators above it; it is also used for non-sporting purposes today.

Stadio Flaminio (Viale Stadio): Football stadium seating *c.* 45,000 spectators built for the Olympic Games by Pier Luigi Nervi on the site of the old National Stadium.

Other modern sporting facilities which are worth seeing: *Olympic Stadium* (in the Foro Italico). Olympic *Cycle Racing Stadium* (in the EUR complex, Viale dell'Oceano Pacifico).

Stazione Termini (Piazza di Cinquecento): Started in 1938, not completed until 1950. Side sections in the Fascist pseudo-Roman style, main building modern. Concourse with upswept roof in front of the ten-storey administrative building; the main building is clad in Travertine marble. An unfortunate aspect of the unchecked growth of the city of Rome in recent decades is a circle of suburbs, the so-called *subure*, many of which are extremely ugly; they show a complete lack of any sense of overall design, and are eating more and more deeply into the Campagna.

VI. Theatres, Concert Halls and Libraries

Theatre and Opera
The Roman theatre is served by a mixture of resident companies ('teatro stabile') and visiting ensembles. For all practical purposes tickets are only available at the box-office of the theatre concerned. The season lasts from October to June. There are a large number of open-air performances in the summer as part of the 'Estate Romana'.

Teatro Argentina (Lago Argentina): Roman municipal theatre; usually presents classical Italian plays.

Teatro Eliseo (183 Via Nazionale) with a large and a small auditorium.

Teatro Rossini (14 Piazza S.Chiara): The Roman folk theatre.

Dying Gallian, Musei Capitolini

Teatro Sistina (129 Via Sistina): The oldest and best-known light theatre in the town.

Teatro Sala Umberto (50 Via delle Mercede): better-quality musicals.

Other theatres: *Teatro Centrale* (6 Via Celsa). *Convento occupato* (61 Via del Colosseo), left-wing avant-garde theatre. *Teatro dei Satiri* (19 Via di Grotta Pinta). *Teatro dei Servi* (22 Via del Mortaro). *Teatro delle Muse* (43 Via Forli). *Teatro Goldoni* (4 Vicolo de Soldati). *Teatro la Maddalena* (18 Via della Selletta): feminist plays. *Teatro Parioli* (20 Via Giosuè Borri). *Teatro Quirino* (1 Via Marco Minghetti). *Teatro Piramide* (Via G.Benzoni), avant-garde. *Teatro Spazio Uno* (3 Vicolo dei Panieri), avant-garde. *Teatro Tenda* (Piazza Mancini). *Teatro in Trastevere* (3 Vicolo Moroni) intellectual. *Teatro Valle* (23 Via del Teatro Valle).

Opera: *Teatro del Opera* (72 Via Firenze). *Baths of Caracalla:* Performances of classical opera and ballet as part of the 'Estate Romana'.

Concerts

Rome itself has only the RAI symphony orchestra and the famous choir of the Conservatoire of S.Cecilia.

Concert halls (programme information from newspapers and posters): *Auditorio del Foro Italico* (26 Lungotevere Diaz). *Auditorio del Gonfalone* (32a Via del Gonfalone). *Auditorio Pio* (4 Via della Conciliazione). *Auditorio del S.Leone Magno* (38 Via Bolzano). *Aula Borrominiana dell' Oratorio di S.Filippo Neri* (18 Piazza della Chiesa Nuova). *Basilica di Massenzio* (Via dei Fori Imperiali) for open-air concerts in the summer. *Sala dell'Accademia di S.Cecilia* (18 Via dei Greci). *Teatro di Castel Sant'Angelo* (Lungotevere Castello) for chamber concerts. *Teatro Olimpico* (17 Piazza Gentile da Fabriano).

Libraries

There are numerous academic libraries (in each of the foreign academies, for example), and only those important for the visitor interested in art and history are listed. *Biblioteca Alessandrina Universitaria* (Città Universitaria). *Archivio di Stato di Roma* (40 Corso Rinascimento). *Archivio Storico Capitolino* (18 Piazza della Chiesa Nova). *Biblioteca della Civiltà Cattolica* (1 Via Porta Pinciana). *Biblioteca di Conservatorio di Musica di S.Cecilia)* (18 Via dei Greci). *German Library* (267 Via del Corso). *Library of the German Archaeological Institute* (79 Via Sardegna). *Fototeca di Architettura e Topografia dell'Italia Antica* (5 Via Masina). *Biblioteca Hertziana* (28 Via Gregoriana). *Istituto per Archeologia e Storia dell'Arte* (3 Piazza Venezia). *Istituto Storico Italiano* (4 Piazza del Orologio). *Biblioteca Nazionale Centrale* (Via Castro Pretorio). *Biblioteca della Storia Moderna e Contemporanea* (32 Via Caetani).

VII. Museums

There are about 60 museums and art collections in Rome which are open to the public. Museums are closed on Mondays, and also at New Year,

Cupid and Psyche, Musei Capitolini

Capitoline Venus, Musei Capitolini

Easter, and on 1 May, 15 August and 25 December.

Galleria Borghese (Villa Borghese; Via Pinciana): Art collection of 17C Cardinal Scipione Borghese; it consists of ancient works and numerous sculptures by Bernini and Canova, paintings by Raphael, Antonello da Messina and Caravaggio.

Galleria Nazionale d'Arte Moderna (Villa Borghese; 131 Viale delle Belle Arti): Most important collection of 19&20C Italian sculpture and painting.

Musei Capitolini (Piazza del Campidoglio): One of the most important collections of antiquities in the world, shown in the *Palazzo Nuovo* (on the left), the Palazzo dei Conservatori (on the right) and the Palazzo Caffarelli (behind the Palazzo dei Conservatori). There is a *pinacoteca* on the second floor of the Palazzo dei Conservatori. One of the most important ancient pieces is the Italian/Etruscan 'Capitoline She-Wolf' (5C BC).

Museo Barracco (168 Corso Vittorio Emanuele II): Collection of antiquities with classical Greek art as its central feature.

Museo della Civiltà Romana (EUR, Piazza G.Agnelli): Collection of models, casts and reconstructions of important objects of the Imperial Roman period. The model of Rome under the emperors is particularly impressive.

Museo di Castel Sant'Angelo (Lungotevere Castello): The visit includes the Popes' residential rooms, decorated with frescos in the Renaissance period, some with original furnishings; there is also a wide-ranging collection of weapons from ancient times to the present day.

Museo Nazionale Romano (Viale delle Terme): Housed in the ancient Baths of Diocletian; this is also one of the world's most important collections of antiquities. Major exhibits include the 'Venus of Cyrene' and the 'Ludovisi Throne'.

Hermes, copy after Praxiteles (4C BC)

Amazon, copy after Phidias, Vatican

Museo Nazionale di Villa Giulia (Villa Borghese; Piazzale Villa Giulia): One of the most important collections of items excavated in southern Etruria (including Caere, Tarquinia, Veii, Vulci). The 'Veii Apollo' in Room 7 is particularly worth seeing and also the Etruscan gold jewellery from the Castellani collection.

Museo di Palazzo Venezia (Piazza Venezia/Via del Plebiscito): Lavish collection of medieval and Renaissance Italian applied art (including paintings by Benozzo and Gozzoli, and sculpture by Mino da Fiesole).

Museo della Preistoria e Protostoria del Lazio 'Luigi Pigorini' (EUR, Viale Lincoln): The museum is arranged geographically and covers the pre- and early history of the region (flora, fauna, effect of man on the environment).

Museo di Roma (Palazzo Braschi, 10 Piazza S.Pantaleo): Lavish collection of documentation on Roman life in the Middle Ages and the modern period.

Other important museums: *Galleria Colonna* (17 Via della Pilotta), with wide-ranging collection of paintings (including Veronese, Tintoretto). *Galleriaë Doria* (1a Piazza del Collegio Romano), picture galley with works by Lippi, Titian, Velasquez among others. *Goethe Museum* (18 Via del Corso) in the house in which Goethe lived from 1786–88; documentation of his Italian journey. *Historical Museum* on the liberation of Rome from Fascism (145 Via Tasso). *Keats and Shelley Memorial House* (25 Piazza di Spagna), with memorabilia of these two great poets who died in Italy. *Crib Museum* (31a Via Tor Conti), open daily in the Christmas period, otherwise on Saturdays. *Cabinet of Engravings* (5 Via della Stamperia), Italian engraving (particularly Piranesi). *Museum of the Walls of Rome* (18 Porta S.Sebastiano), covers

the development of the city walls. *Museum in the Villa Albani* (Via Salaria/Via Villa Albani), remains of Cardinal Albani's collection of antiquities, built up by Winckelmann from 1758 (access only by special permission of the administration). *Museum of Oriental Art* (248 Via Merulana). *Napoleonic Museum* (1 Via Zanardelli) with various memorabilia of the Bonaparte family. *Museum of Folk Art* (EUR, 10 Piazza Marconi) with lavish collections on the daily life and customs of the Italian people. *Central Museum of the Risorgimento* (Via S.Pietro in Carcere), covering the 19C Italian unification movement.

VIII. Festivals and Traditions

So-called **Bevana** (derived from 'Epiphany') on 6 January in the Piazza Navona, with a large toy market (the climax of the feast is on the preceding night).

On 19 March **Feast of St.Joseph**, celebrated above all in Trionfale, the part of the city NW of the Vatican: special 'Bignè' and doughnuts baked in the streets.

On Easter Sunday in a festive service the Pope gives his **Apostolic blessing** to the city and the world ('urbi et orbi'). On Easter Monday it is customary for citizens of Rome to make trips out into the area around the city.

April: **Spring Festival** with lavish floral decoration on the Spanish Steps.

On the night of 23&24 June the **Feast of St.John** is celebrated in the suburb of the town known as S.Giovanni; there are games and singing competitions; snails and sucking pigs are eaten, and 'Castelli Romani' wine is drunk.

The **Festa de Noantri** in honour of

David, Galleria Borghese ▷

LXXVII

Eritrean Sybil (left), Delphic Sybil (right) by Michelangelo in the Sistine Chapel

the 'Madonna dei Carmine' takes place in mid July in the Trastevere.

15 August, **Ferragosto** (Assumption of the Blessed Virgin) is a principal feast day in Rome; anybody who is 'mobile' leaves the town for a day out.

On 8 December **(Conception of the Virgin)** the statue of the Virgin in the Piazza di Spagna is decorated with a garland; the people bring floral tributes throughout the day, the Pope pays his respects to Mary in person.

At **Christmas** fine cribs are set up in many of the churches; the one in the church of S.Maria in Aracoeli is famous; traditionally many Romans have their children recite poetry for the 'Santo Bambino'.

Other recurrent functions: In Spring and Autumn *art fair* in the Via Margutta. In May *antique furniture week* in the Via dei Coronari. In May/June *rose show* in the rose garden in the Via di Valle Murcia (near the Circus Maximus). In June/July on the banks of the Tiber the *Tevere Expo*, an exhibition from the Italian regions. In July/August *Estate Romana* ('Summer in Rome') throughout the central area, with interesting artistic and folk presentations.

Latium

02011 Accumoli

Rieti   p.321☐F 1

This town near the site of the abandoned ancient settlement of *Summata* grew up in the 13C on the *Via Salaria* (salt road) from Rome to the NE Adriatic coast, which had existed since Roman times; because of its position it was often involved in minor wars.

S.Maria della Misericordia (Via Roma): Baroque high altar. Painting on the left side altar (18C), probably by Alessandro Turchi, known as Orbetto (17C).

Via Tommasi: There are fine buildings from various periods on both sides of the main street: they include the *Palazzo Guasto* (No. 35), an attractive Renaissance building (16C) with reliefs around the windows. The *Palazzo del Podestà* dates from between 1220 and 1300; the adjacent *tower* is of similar date. 17C *Palazzo Moroni* (No. 54). The baroque *Palazzo Tommasi* is strikingly massive (17C).

01021 Acquapendente

Viterbo   p.230☐B 1

This little town was originally founded by the Faliscans, an old Italic tribe. In Roman times it was an insignificant settlement, in the 8C AD it was an Ottonian and Hohenstaufen fortress and was presented to the Papal States *c.* 1079 as part of the large central Italian possessions of Mathilda Countess of Tuscany. Towards the end of the 14C the town was subject first of all to Sienna, and then to the Sforza family; it was granted its charter by Pope Nicholas V *c.* 1450. It took over from Castro as bishopric when the latter town was destroyed in 1649.

Acquapendente is the birthplace of the medical scholar Girolamo Fabrici (1533–1619), who described the valves of the veins, and also of Giovanni Battista Casti (1724–1803), who

Acquapendente, S.Sepulcro cathedral

was famous particularly for his operatic libretti and political satires.

Traditional mid-May festival *(Festa di Mezzo Maggio)* for the Madonna del Fiore with pictures made with plants and flowers.

S.Maria (also **S.Francesco;** Piazza S.Maria): Gothic hall church with partially baroque interior: in the choir 17&18C frescos; carved figures of the Twelve Apostles above the altar (17C). Painting of the Nativity (second half of the 15C) by Jacopo del Sellaio (first altar on the right); 13C crucifix (second altar on the right); S. Bernardino by the 15C Siennese painter Sano di Pietro (on the left by the high altar).

S.Sepulcro cathedral: This building with its majestic twin-towered façade was partially redesigned in the baroque style in the mid 18C, but after damage by bombing in 1944 it was restored in accordance with its original Romanesque design; original central apse. Fragments of the original building are exhibited in the columned aisle on the S. side. In front of the high altar there are visible remains of the Romanesque building; the first pier on the right and the first two capitals on the right also originate from this building. On either side of the stairs to the presbytery are 15C reliefs by Agostino di Duccio (Victory of St.Michael over the Dragon, Tobias and the Archangel Raphael). S. transept: near the stairs portrait bust of Pope Innocent X by Alessandro Algardi (mid 17C); valuable *sacramental altar* with the Adoration of the Angel by Jacopo Beneventano (1522; the Last Supper was added by Giovanni Battista Troiani in 1881). Magnificent *baroque stalls* in the choir. By the steps to the N. transept

Acquapendente, Torre Barbarossa

Alatri, S.Paolo

painted 18C bust of saint and *Pietà* by
Girolamo Beneventano (*c.* 1500).
Splendid 9C *hall crypt* divided by columns with decorated Romanesque
capitals into nine aisles. 13C wall
paintings. On an altar on the left (with
base made of antique hewn stone) is a
relic from the Column of the Scourging. In a chapel on a lower level is a
relic from the hall of the Praetorium
in Jerusalem where pilgrims and cru-
aders assembled (Acquapendente
was involved in the Crusades as the
seat of the Abbey of S.Sepulcro).

Also worth seeing: Medieval town
wall with towers. *Palazzo Viscontini*
(Via Battista), majestic Renaissance
building dating from 1582 with a very
fine portal. *Palazzo Communale*
(Piazza Communale): neoclassical
building from the first half of the 19C;
monument to G.Fabrici by Tito Sar-
cchi (second half of the 19C). *Torre
dell' Orologio* (near the cathedral):
clock tower.

Environs: Ponte Gregoriano (*c.* 4
km. N.): The central arch of the
bridge over the Paglia was built *c.*
1580 to a design by Domenico Fontana during the pontificate of Gregory
XIII.
Proceno (9 km. NW): This
picturesque village is traditionally
held to have been founded in the late
6C BC by the Etruscan king Porsenna;
Etruscan tombs were discovered *c.*
2km. outside the town. Of the
churches *S.Agnese* in the upper part
of the town is particularly worth mentioning; it is said to have been built on
the site of one of the late 3C Roman
martyr's houses. Impressive medieval
castle with a main and three side
towers. *Palazzo Sforza:* splendid
Renaissance building dating from
1535.

Torre Alfina (11 km. E.): The boldly-sited medieval castle has been largely rebuilt.

03011 Alatri

Frosinone   p.323☐G 4

The town is presumed to have been founded in the 6C BC (a centre for the Hernici, who lived in and around the Sacco valley) and it became a Roman colony in the 4C BC ('ala' = wing in Latin, which led to the element of a winged fortress tower in the coat of arms, still present today) and shortly afterwards an important town with the status of municipium; its inhabitants were freemen, and had all the privileges of Roman citizens. The *acropolis* built in the 4C BC and the *town wall* with its massive stone blocks are first-class architectural features: the finest surviving set of buildings of their kind in Italy. In the mid 6C AD Alatri was destroyed in the campaign of the Ostrogoth King Totila against the Byzantine rulers and a little later was rebuilt as Civita-

nóva (new town) within the ancien fortifying walls.

Other essential elements in this ver interesting town are the medieva streets (e.g. *Corso Vittorio Emanue II* and *Via Matteotti*); the houses hav characteristic simple, straigh Romanesque doors (mostly in the sid streets) or 14C Gothic arche (particularly in the main streets which gives them considerable unity The medieval quarter known as *L Piagge* has survived almost intac Famous Good Friday procession wit Passion play.

S.Francesco (Corso Vittorio Ema nuele II): There is a fine *rosette* in th 13C façade of the church; its tracery i modelled on S.Maria Maggiore an forms a square in the centre. Th interior was redesigned in the baro que style in the 18C and there ar striking remains of 14&15C wa paintings.

S.Maria Maggiore (Piazza S.Mari Maggiore): The church was built i the 13C in the period of transitio

Alatri, S.Maria Maggiore, interior (left), lectern (right)

from Romanesque to Gothic, and combines elements of both styles. The façade has three portals (remains of 15C frescos in the lunettes) and a large rose window with central square). On the S. side of the campanile is a 15C Madonna fresco (likewise formerly the decoration in the lunette of a door which was later walled up). The interior has a nave and two aisles, but its symmetry was destroyed with the extension of the left-hand aisle in the 18C. The most valuable work of art in the church (first chapel on the left) is the Romanesque 'Constantinople Madonna', with the Christ Child on her lap (second half of the 13C).

S.Maria dei Padri Scolopi (Piazza S.Maria Maggiore): Stylistically coherent building dating from the second half of the 17C; its harmoniously proportioned and decorated interior adopts some rhythmic elements developed by Francesco Borromini. Next to it is the long façade of the *Palazzo del Collegio Gentili e del Liceo,* an originally medieval building which has been much altered, with

Gothic portal and Renaissance windows (*c.* 1530). Opposite is the elegant *Fonte Pia*, endowed by Pope Pius IX in 1870.

Cathedral of **S.Paolo** (on the former acropolis): Plain building with nave and two aisles and imposing 17C façade. In the chapel on the left by the high altar is the tomb of the early Christian Pope Sixtus I (*c.* 115–125), whose remains were brought to Alatri in 1132. The *bishop's palace* is next to the campanile. The *sexton's house* to the right of the church is based on an ancient section of wall, perhaps from the altar precinct of a shrine.

Acropolis and **town wall:** The ring wall is about 2 km. long and up to 10 ft. high, and consists of the 4C BC *cyclopean wall* with medieval additions (one of the two corner towers was rebuilt as a residence. There are fourteen massive piers in the SE corner. The largest of the five gates, the *Porta di Civita*, which is reached by steps (almost 15 ft. high, 9 ft. wide; the door lintel is a monolith almost 12 ft. long) forms the main entrance to the trape-

Alatri, San Maria Maggiore, Madonna and Child (left), Constantinople Madonna (right)

Alatri, S.Maria Maggiore, altar

Albano Laziale, S.Maria della Rotunda

zoid acropolis and the spacious square in which the cathedral stands. There is a splendid panoramic view from this point.

Museo Civico (Palazzo Casegrandi, Corso Vittorio Emanuele II): The Municipal Museum, consisting of the large 13C Gothic building and the adjacent Romanesque defensive tower, contains Roman finds and mainly sacred works of the Gothic period, including pictures by the painter Antonio of Alatri (15C).

Also worth seeing: *S.Silvestro* (Via S.Silvestro): Frescos from the time at which the church was built have been revealed under the Renaissance painting in the interior of this 13C church. The wall paintings in the crypt have survived only as fragments. *S.Stefano* (Piazza S.Stefano): Late-13C Gothic

church with central portal dated 128 and interior decorated in the barqou style in the 18C.

Environs: Chiesa della Dodic Marie (*c.* 2 km. W.): There are 15C frescos in the interior of this churc dedicated to the Twelve Marys: Ou Lady of Loretto and the Madonn with St.Laurence are attributed t Antonio of Alatri.
Chiesa della Maddalena (*c.* 1.5 km S.): The wall paintings in the churc which goes back to the early 13C, ar the work of Antonio of Alatri and hi studio (15C).
Fumone (8 km. NW): Characteristi and picturesque medieval village on cone-shaped hill; it seems to becom increasingly bleak outside the mai tourist season. The *castle* is docu mented from the 11C, and set in strategically important position (once

Albano Laziale, S.Pietro

Porta Pretoria

a papal bastion against the Normans and Saracens) was rebuilt in the 18C as a splendid residence, making use of much of the original structure and building materials; it is well worth seeing as an example of this kind of building (privately owned). It achieved a place in ecclesiastical history when in 1125 the Antipope Gregory VIII, the French Cluniac Mauritius Burdinus, was held prisoner here by Calixtus II, and again in 1296, when Celestine V, arrested by Calixtus' successor Boniface VIII, died here. *Collegiate church:* Homogeneous 18C baroque building on the site of the first church, mentioned in the 11C.
Tempio d'Alatri (1 km. N, on the left of S.S. 155): What remains of the foundations of this 4–3C BC temple suggests that it had colonnades on its two shorter sides.

00041 Albano Laziale
Roma   p.321 □ D 4

Albano, near the Lago di Alba on the Appian way, derives its name from the fertile area of *Albanus ager* on the S. edge of the lake, which was originally part of nearby *Alba Longa*. The settlement of Albano dates back to a military camp known as *Castra Albana*, established by the Emperor Septimius Severus for his II legion 'Parthica' in the grounds of the Emperor Domitian's villa. Albano was a bishopric from 460, and suffered in the church conflicts of the 13C; by the end of the century it was in the hands of the Savelli family of Ariccia, who built the *Castello Sevelli* on the remains of a Roman watch-tower to the W. of Albano. When the family fell from power in 1697 Albano returned to the Popes. Like nearby Ariccia it is today one of the towns of the 'Castelli Romani'.

Porta Pretoria (Via del Plebiscito): The main gate of the legionary camp of *Castra Albana* was revealed by an air raid in 1944. The gatehouse was 118 ft. long and almost 43 ft. high, and had three gateways and two side towers; it faced the Appian Way, the main road from Albano Laziale to Rome.

Cisternone (86 Via A.Saffa): Septimius Severus had an underground reservoir cut in the rock to provide water for his camp. Three rows of columns divided the trapezoid space into five vaulted aisles. The cistern has survived in good condition and can hold c. 10,000 cubic metres of water; it is one of the finest examples of Roman engineering.

Tomb of the Horatii and Curatii (Via Appia, Borgo Garibaldi): The ruins of the tomb are complex, and show it to have been of the Etruscan type with a rhomboid *burial chamber* surrounded by conical columns on short piers. Tradition insists that this is the tomb of the Horatii from Rome and the Curatii from Alba Longa, two pairs of triplets who fell c. 600 BC in combat over the supremacy of their home towns. It is clear, however, that the tomb was not built until the late Republican period.

Cathedral of S.Giovanni Battista (Piazza Sabatini): The cathedral was consecrated in the 4C by Emperor Constantine the Great. It has been much altered, and is now predominantly baroque. The plain interior columns (4C) from the original basilica have survived (Palazzina Ferraioli/Viale Risorgimento).

S..Maria della Rotonda (N. of the Porta Pretoria): Originally a nymphaeum from Domitian's villa, the little round building was extended by four niches and turned into a Christian church; the dome was a 16C addition. Further additions are the portico and the 13C Romanesque *campanile* The 16C alterations to the building were removed in the course of restoration in 1937 and the former appearance of the church largely restored.

S.Pietro (Corso Matteotti): The church of S.Pietro was built in the 6C over the remains of Roman bath opposite the Municipio. Roman bricks and other materials were used in the façade and portal. The notable *campanile* is articulated with sets of twin windows. In the single-aisled interior the *two tombs* of the Savelli family are worth seeing.

Museo Archeologico di Albano e della Latinità: The archaeologica museum has a collection of pre- and early historical finds, a *lapidarium* and a particularly large number of Roman architectural fragments and two interesting Etruscan *sarcophaguse*s.

Also worth seeing: The *amphitheatre* (Via Anfiteatro Romano) wa built by Septimius Severus in the 3C BC for c. 15,000 spectators; it is elliptical in plan. Near the church of S.Pietro the ruins of the Roman *baths* almost 100 ft. high in places and rising through three storeys, are impressive.

Environs: Ariccia (2 km. SE): In ancient times *Aricia* was one of the leading towns of Latium. It was supported by Aristodemos of Cumae in its fight against Porsenna's Etruscans and took part in all the attacks by the leagued of Latin cities against the hegemony of Rome. It was a papal possession from 1223, later passed to the Savellis, and in 1661 to the Chigis Gian Lorenzo Bernini designed the *Piazza della Repubblica* with its two decorative fountains in 1662–5.

S.Maria di Galloro (3 km. SE): The vigorous façade of this pilgrimage church built in 1624 was also designed by Gian Lorenzo Bernini (1661). It remains a popular place of pilgrimage.

03041 Alvito
Frosinone   p.323□H 4

This is one of the places which, because of its ancient ruins, is said to have been the Samnite city of *Cominum*, the site of which has never been exactly determined. It has been historically documented since the Middle Ages as the possession of various overlords (including the Abbey of Montecassino and Cesare Borgia), and, for a time, as the most important settlement in the Comino valley.

Parish church of **S.Simeone:** The lower part of the campanile has survived from the earlier Romanesque building. 18C baroque interior with magnificent *ceiling.* In the chapel on the left Temptation of Mary (late 16C); in the sacristy painting of the Crucifixion by Giuseppe Cesari, known as Cavalier d'Arpino (early 17C).

S.Maria del Campo (Cemetery): Rebuilt in the 15C with contemporary frescos. Ancient ruins nearby.

S.Nicola with fine baroque furnishings (18C). The former convent buildings were rebuilt in 1934 after serious earthquake damage.

Palazzo Ducale (now a local government building): Ducal Renaissance palace (with 18C baroque accretions), built *c.* 1580 by Cardinal Bartolomeo Gallio, rector of the Papal States province of Campagna-Marittima.

Environs: Castello/Castle (4 km. NW): 1220 ft. above Alvino is the imposing ruin of the castle founded by the counts of Alvino in 1094; it was extended on a massive scale by the Cantelmi family, into whose

Amaseno, S.Maria

possession it came after the earthquake of 1349. Although it was used as a quarry after destruction in the 16C, the remains still give an impression of the power of this once famous masterpiece of medieval fortress architecture.

Vicalvi (4 km. SW): The settlement goes back to the Roman *Vicus Albae* (remains of the megalith wall and a Roman Temple of Hercules). At the top of the hill are the impressive ruins of a massive 12C *round castle* with square towers.

03029 Amaseno
Frosinone   p.323□G 5

The town was founded in the 9C and renamed in 1872. It took its name originally from the church of *S.Lorenzo* (now called *S.Maria*), which was built in the second half of the 13C by Giacomo Gulinari and his sons. It displays many of the characteristics of Italian Cistercian Gothic: nave and two aisles, square choir and central rose window.

Environs: Madonna dell'Auricola (3.5 km. SE): Charmingly sited early-13C church with later accretions.

02012 Amatrice
Rieti   p.321☐F 2

A key date in the extraordinarily eventful history of this little town based on an ancient settlement is 1529: Amatrice, because it sided with the French King Francis I, was plundered and destroyed by Charles V's troops in the course of the struggle for power in Italy between France and Spain. It was rebuilt to a plan made in 1530 and generally attributed to the local painter and architect Nicola Filotesio, known as Cola dell'Amatrice (monument (1915) in the municipal gardens). The network of straight streets meeting at right angles, still discernible today, is a striking demonstration of Renaissance town planning.

S.Agostino (N. edge of the town): Gothic church with side walls articulated with tall arches with pilaster strips. Lavishly carved main portal dating from 1428 with sculpture of the Annunciation in the lunette; the rose window is a later addition. The interior was redesigned in the baroque style in the 18C; there are frescos of the Annunciation and the Madonna with Angels (1491&2) by the so-called Master of the Madonna della Misericordia. On the S. side of the church is a gate from the 14C city wall.

S.Francesco (Via Madonna della Porta): This large, austere church was built in the second half of the 14C, and has architectural features typical of the transition from Romanesque to Gothic which were out of date even then. The horizontally articulated façade (of the pattern developed in the Abruzzi) has a Gothic *portal*, and a Madonna between two angels made of coloured terracotta in the lunette. The interior has a nave and two aisles with a Renaissance vestibule, and numerous 15C frescos; the wall paintings in the apse are 15&16C (the Stem of Jesse is reminiscent of the school of Rimini). The cornice in the apse is partially supported by gargoyle-like corbels. Splendid baroque *carved altar* of the Madonna della Filetta by Giovanni Battista Gigli (17C); the reliquary in the form of a small temple (1492, by Pietro Vannini) which was once kept here is now in the priest's house. Above the altar is a fresco of the Last Judgement (late 14C). In a wall niche is a marble bust of Camillo Orsini, General Governor of the Vatican State under Paul IV, by Alessandro Leopardi (16C). Finely-carved baroque pulpit.

S.Maria Lauretana (also *S.Emidio*; Via Cola di Rienzo): The columns and early Gothic arches from an earlier building were retained when this originally Romanesque church was rebuilt in the 15C. The surviving frescos in the apse are the work of Dionisio Cappelli and his pupil Cola dell'Amatrice (*c.* 1510).

Also worth seeing: *Chiesa della Resurezione* (outside the town, near S.Agostino) by Vittorio Paron (1936) with apse fresco by Ferruccio Ferrazzi (1955) and sculpture by Venanzio Crocetti, Alessandro Monteleone and Francesco Nagni. *Torre Civica* (Via Umberto I): The 13C tower in the centre (opposite the Palazzo Municipale) sways about 8 inches when the bell rings.

Environs: Cornillo Nuovo (6 km. SE): Parish church of *S.Antonio Abate:* Altar niche and rear wall painted by D.Cappelli in 1511 (signed and dated) with scenes from the life of the church patron.

Filetta (5 km. N.): *S.Maria*: This pilgrimage church dates from the second half of the 15C and contains interesting frescos in various states of preservation on the choir arch and in the apse; they are the work of Pier Paolo da Fermo (1480) among others, showing the building of the church and the procession in which the miraculous image of Mary, found on this spot by a shepherdess, was brought here from Amatrice.

Prato (3 km. N.): In the parish church are three carved baroque altars by Giovanni Battista Gigli (17C), who is also buried here. Outside the town is the chapel of the *Iconetta di S.Appollonia* with 16C Renaissance frescos.

Retrosi (6 km. NE): The pilgrimage church of *S.Maria delle Grazie* (also *Icona Passatora*) was built in the 15C and has fine wall paintings (*c.* 1500). The fine Madonna della Misericordia of 1491 gave its name to the otherwise anonymous artist who also did a lot of work in S.Agostino (Amatrice); the same artist was also responsible for

the Madonna Enthroned with St.Anthony and St.Lucia (1490) and Christ Crucified. The other frescos are signed and dated by D.Cappelli (1508–10).

Scai (*c.* 16 km. SW): *S.Maria delle Grazie* (*c.* 2 km. outside the town): This outwardly plain late-16C church is worth seeing for its excellent *baroque interior*. Five splendid altars (17C) with outstanding paintings or sculpture.

03012 Anagni

Frosine   p.323☐F 4

This so-called *City of the Popes* is impressively medieval in appearance. Ancient *Anagnia* is presumed to have been founded by the Hernici in the 6C BC; shortly after it was conquered by the Romans in 306 BC it gained significance again as a municipium. As a result of the gift of Pépin of AD 756 Anagni left the sphere of influence of Byzantium and Ravenna and was handed over to the church and later came under the rule of the

Anagni, S.Maria cathedral, campanile (left), interior (right)

Anagni, S.Maria cathedral, crypt

Caetani. It was the birthplace and residence away from Rome of the late 12C to early 14C Popes Innocent III, Gregory IX, Alexander IV and Boniface VIII; the town, which had been a bishopric since the 5C, thus flourished in the high Middle Ages, and there are still fine individual buildings, groups of houses and streets of the period, despite much plundering and earthquake damage. The *Corso Vittorio Emanuele II* (between the Piazza Cavour and Piazza Innocenzo III) and its immediate surroundings give an outstanding impression of a 14C residential area; also the *Piazza Bonifacio VIII* and the *Via Dante* and parts of the ancient and medieval *town wall* around the Porta S.Maria. Substantial sections of the pre-Roman and Roman wall have survived in the Via Dante, the Via Piscina (Arcazzi di Piscina) and by the S. road round the town (Via Sottobagno).

There is a carnival famous for its procession and other events.

S.Andrea (Corso Vittorio Emanuele II): The oldest part of the church is the campanile of the original Romanesque building with a Gothic arch which was pierced later. The nave is 18C baroque. In the last side chapel on the right are parts of a fine *triptych* (early 14C).

Cathedral of **S.Maria** (Piazza Innocenzo III): This church on the site of the ancient acropolis is one of the most important Italian Romanesque buildings, both for its architecture and its interior decoration. There are a few Gothic alterations. It was here that Alexander III excommunicated Frederick Barbarossa, who refused to recognize him, and Innocent IV was crowned here in 1243. The church was built 1077–1104 and the transept

Anagni, cathedral, Apotheosis of the Lamb, 13C

was added c. 1200. The crypt is known to have existed from the early 2C; the relics of St.Magnus were interred here in 1130, and it was extended to form the present hall crypt in the early 13C; the splendid painting dates from the same period. The crypt was consecrated in 1255 by Alexander IV. The façade has three portals, which have lost all their decoration with the exception of traces in the lunettes and lower masonry. The *campanile* is beautifully articulated. In front of the W. side are (from W. to E.) the partially circular *baptismal chapel*, a double arch with terrace and above it a niche with austerely gloomy monumental figure of Boniface VIII (1295) and adjacent to this the *Caetani chapel* with Gothic arch. The high *main apse* is joined directly to the transept on the pattern of 4C Constantine basilicas, without a linking choir. The most striking exterior feature is the massive solidity of the walls and the smallness of the windows, despite the subtlety of the articulation. The interior is essentially Romanesque, and divided into a nave and two aisles by alternate columns and piers; the nave has the beamed ceiling and pointed arches characteristic of early Italian Gothic. The aisles have simple groin vaulting. The *mosaic floor* dating from 1227 (restored in 1880) is a magnificent piece of work by the group of artists known as the Cosmati, famous for virtuosity of technique and the way in which they related their compositions to the space in question. The *altar screen* is the work of the same craftsmen. On the altar is a vigorously articulated Romanesque *ciborium*. In the *Caetani chapel* (third side chapel) is the Cosmati-work tomb of this politically and intellectually influential family, which also produced Boniface VIII.

Anagni, cathedral, Galen and Hippocrates, 13C

The three-aisled *hall crypt of S.Magno* has fascinating *frescos* and a Cosmati-work floor dating from 1231 in unusually good condition. The pictorial cycles are of great iconographic interest; they were painted by three different anonymous artists between 1231 and 1255; their work can be distinguished by differences in style and quality. A passage leads to the adjacent *chapel of St.Thomas à Becket*, which was probably a Roman mithraeum. The wall paintings here are also Romanesque (events from the Old Testament, metaphors from the gospel, saints) and are in a folk style. *Treasury*: Lavish collection of medieval paraments and antepedia; masterpieces of medieval gold and silver work in particular; liturgical vessels and furnishings mainly from the Romanesque and Gothic periods. *Museum*: Collection includes marble and ancient and medieval inscriptions.

Casa Barnekow (81-83 Corso Vittorio Emanuele II): Good example of a medieval residence (14C) with a rebuilt roofed outer staircase. Façade painting by the Swedish painter Baron Albert von Barnekow (second half of the 19C).

Palazzo Bonifacio VIII (Vicolo S.Michele): Part of what was once a massive 13C building which still looks solid and threatening. In 1303 the Pope was for a short time held prisoner here by Sciarra Colonna and the ambassadors of Philip the Fair; the Colonnas were bitterly opposed to the disputed papal election of 1294 (Boniface had been in favour of the abdication of his predecessor Celestine V) and sided with the king in the

Anagni, cathedral, Samuel Blessing the Hebrews (left), Abraham and Melchisedech (right)

quarrel concerning the Pope's supremacy over secular power. A few decades later Dante was to condemn this illegal acquisition of the papal throne, but defended Boniface against the assault on his papal dignity (Purgatorio XX, 86-93).

Palazzo Communale (Corso Vittorio Emanuele II/Piazza Cavour): The Town Hall is a rather clumsy-looking 13C building with an unusually large arcade; the façade on the little Piazza dei Carceri is livelier, and has Romanesque double-arched windows, a small loggia and two elegant Gothic tripartite windows.

Also worth seeing: *Convitto Regina Margherita* (Viale Regina Margherita): This large complex goes back to a Dominican monastery, later much rebuilt and extended; tradition has it that the scholasticist and Dominican Albertus Magnus stayed here in 1256.

02013 Antrodoco
Rieti   p.321☐F 2

In the Middle Ages this was the heavily fortified residence of the dukes of Spoleto; it was known to the ancient geographer Strabon as *Vicus Interocrea* in the 1C BC. Antrodoco was destroyed on numerous occasions in the 13–15C because of its strategically important position at the point where two valleys carrying important trade and military roads met, and because of its resistance to Aragon rule in particular. After a period of relative peace its citizens once more (unsuccessfully) involved themselves in political events; in 1799 in the

Antrodoco, S.Maria 'extra moenia', campanile (left), portal (right)

struggle against revolutionary French troops, and in 1821 against the Austrians hastening to the aid of the Bourbons, who were under threat from revolts in Naples.

S.Maria 'extra moenia': This church was founded in the 5C beyond the S. edge of the town, probably beside a Christian cemetery; it was enlarged on several occasions and in its present form is an important 12C Romanesque building; the *campanile* was completed in the 13C. The interior has a nave and two aisles, separated on the left by columns and on the right by piers. One of the finest of the 13–15C wall paintings is a representation of St.Catherine of Alexandria (attributed to Pietro Colberti, first half to the 15C). On the high altar is a *Pietà* by a potter from the Abruzzi.

Opposite is the hexagonal baptistery of **S.Giovanni**, probably a medieval rebuilding of an early Christian baptismal chapel.

Parish church of **S.Maria Assunta** (Piazza Umberto I): Striking baroque building of 1712 on the site of an earlier medieval church; Romanesque portal from S.Maria 'extra moenia'.

Environs: Borgo Velino: (1.5 km. SW): There are remarkable 15&16C houses in the square of this village, which is documented from ancient times. The early-13C church of *SS.Dionisio, Rustico ed Eleuterio* (also *S.Antonio*) is half in ruins; it contains sections of an earlier 7&8C building. The 15C frescos by Dionisio Cappelli, once in the apse, are now in the Bishop's Palace in Rieti.

Castel S.Angelo (7 km. SW): A

village well worth seeing, occupied since the high Middle Ages and surrounded by a ring wall which has survived in part in good condition. The buildings are almost all 14&15C, which has preserved the historical character of the place.

Gole di Antrodoco (2 km. E.): Deep, wild gorge (almost 1.5 km. long) between Monte Giano (5991 ft.) in the N. and Monte Serrone (3425 ft.) in the S., where in 1799 the inhabitants of Antrodoco defeated French soldiers unfamiliar with the area and weighed down with armaments and baggage; in 1821 Gugliemo Pepe and his Carbonari army, opposed to Neapolitan Bourbon rule, were defeated here by the Austrians.

Gole del Velino are: About 3 km. N. of Antroduco (opposite the turning to Micigliano) are the ruins of the Abbey of SS.Quirico e Giulitta, probably dissolved in the 17C. Further N. (near the power station) are remains of the Roman *Via Salaria*, built in the Augustan period (supporting wall and an unusually high milestone marking the halfway point between Rome and the end of the road in what is now Porto d'Ascoli). Roman masons also worked on the nearby *bear rock*, 164 ft. high.

00042 Anzio

Roma   p.322□D 5

The fortress of *Antium* was established by the Volsci *(c. 500 BC)* on the flat coastal plain S. of Rome which had been settled since the Iron Age. The Romans made it into a colony in 338 BC and built summer villas, including those of Cicero and Nero, as well as harbour installations and two temples of Fortuna. The emperors Nero and Caligula were born in Anzio. From the 6C it was practically uninhabited, and laid waste by the Saracens, but it flourished in the 17&18C thanks to a new harbour built in 1698, commissioned by Innocent

XII. Anzio and neighbouring Nettuno were the scene of the Ango-American landing in central Italy on 22 January 1944.

Grotte di Nerone (Riviera di Ponente): Remains of the ancient *harbour wall* of Nero's silted-up port can still be seen under water W. of the present harbour mole. It is possible that the so-called grottoes of Nero were *harbour storehouses*; they are rectangular corridor-like brick-built rooms on the W. bank of the beach of Riviera di Ponente.

Villa di Nerone (Via Fanciulla d'Anzio): Remains of a large *imperial villa* have survived near the lighthouse. The ruined walls are in opus reticulatum, and ambulatories, terraces and a *communal room* restored under Hadrian can be discerned. Finds here *c.* 1500 included the *Apollo Belvedere*, the sculpture put on show by Pope Julius II, thus establishing the Vatican collections.

Also worth seeing: Parts of a Hellenistic/Roman *necropolis* were also excavated near the villa. NW of the villa on the cliffs the so-called *Arco Muto* can be seen, an artificial passage through the rocks pierced in Roman times; it is presumed that one of the temples of Fortuna was sited above it. At the beginning of the harbour mole is the much-restored medieval *citadel*, which acquired its present appearance as the result of a commission from Pope Pius VII. On a rise above the town are interesting remains of a *Roman villa* and *theatre* next to the Villa Spigarelli. On the E. edge of the town is the *Villa Borghese* (1660) with its spacious grounds.

Environs: Nettuno (3 km. E.):This little town, still walled, was probably founded by the Saracens; it came into the possession of the monastery of Grottaferrata in 1163, and later was passed on to the Frangipane, Colonna and Borghese families (1831).

Torre Astura (17 km. SE): The lonely, pentagonal *fortress* dating from 1193 is surrounded by water, and reached from the mainland by a bridge. The Hohenstaufen Konradin sought refuge here with counts Friedrich von Badenberg, Gerhard von Donoratico and Galvano Lancia after his defeat at Tagliacozzo, but was handed over to Charles of Anjou by the owner, Giovanni Frangipane.

03031 Aquino
Frosinone   p.323□H 5

Interesting medieval town with notable individual buildings. The Volscian town of *Aquinum* on the Via Latina was first mentioned in the late 3C BC; it became important commercially in the imperial Roman period and was famous for its purple dye works. Impressive ruins outside modern Aquino show that it must have been a flourishing town. Its walls were largely razed *c.* AD 552 by the Ostrogoth King Totila in his struggle against Byzantium; *c.* 577 the town

Aquino, S.Maria della Libera, portal

was completely destroyed by the Lombards. The new settlement was founded nearby in the 7C; in the early 8C it became an outpost of the Lombard duchy of Benevent against the Byzantine duchy of Gaeta and finally, in the mid 10C, the seat of the counts of Aquino. The territory changed hands frequently from the mid 15C, and was sold to the King of the Two Sicilies in 1796. The diocese had existed since the 5C and was joined to Pontecorvo and Sora (bishopric) in 1818. Aquino was the birthplace of the Roman orator and satirist Decimus Junius Juvenalis (Juvenal, *c.* AD 65–130) and of Pescennius Niger, in 193&194 Roman co-emperor with Septimius Severus.

S.Maria della Libera: The cathedral was completed in 1125; it was built using ancient materials (clearly visible in the campanile, for example) on the ruins of the Roman temple of Hercules Liberator (restored after bomb damage in 1944). The main portal is framed with fragments from the frieze of the Roman temple, with Romanesque ornamentation above it. In the lunette is a mosaic of the Madonna (12C), between representations of the countess-founders of the church Ottolinda and Maria, at rest in their coffins. Plain interior with three apses. To the left of the church, half submerged in a canal, is a *Roman arch*, said to be a memorial to Mark Antony (mid 1C BC).

Piazza S. Tomaso: The remains of the earlier medieval building destroyed in 1944 are alongside the modern church of S.Tomaso. The massive medieval tower on a lozenge-shaped plan, like the round tower by the road to the stream Le Forme d'Aquino, was part of the fortifications of the counts' castle; all that has survived of the latter are the remains in the Gothic Casa Quagliozzi.

Roman ruins of the ancient town: The street which leads across the stream from S.Maria della Libera rises past a fragment of the *Via Latina*, paved with tufa, and the little church of S.Tomaso with remains of a *Roman temple* (including a fine relief left of the entrance) to the *Roman gate*, *Porta di S.Lorenzo*; on the left is a section of the *town wall*, built of huge ashlar blocks. On the right at the next junction is the apse of the *Roman basilica* and later church of St.Philip and St.James. Near the road are ruins of the *amphitheatre*. A short distance from another section of the town wall are two large walls, probably from the temple of Ceres Helvina.

03032 Arce

Frosinone   p.323□G 5

Fine medieval centre. Traditional passion play on Good Friday.

SS.Pietro e Paolo (Main square): Built in the 17C on a Greek Cross plan with a twin-towered façade unusual in a country church.

Environs: Rocca d'Arce (2.7 km. E.): The village is spectacularly sited on a steep hill (1654 ft.), and is said to date back to the Volsci settlement of *Arx Volscorum* (Volsci fortress town), founded by Saturn, according to legend, and taken by the Romans in the 4C BC; the claim is supported by the remains of a megalith wall. The town was of strategic importance in later centuries as well; it was destroyed in Saracen raids in the 9C and much fought over by imperial and papal troops in the 12&13C. The *castle* also dates from this period.

00040 Ardea

Roma   p.322□D 5

Manzù Museum: This fine museum, beautifully executed by Tommaso Porn for the *Raccolta*

Amici di Manzù, was founded on the initiative of the friends of the sculptor Giacomo Manzù (b. 1908) in 1969. The collection includes 60 large sculptures, models and drawings, and together with the archives it provides a documentary record of the life and artistic activity of the sculptor. Thanks to Manzù's gift in 1981 the museum is now a branch of the state-owned Galleria d'Arte Moderna (q.v.) in Rome.

Environs: Lavinium (19 km. NE): The ancient town of *Laurentum* or *Lavinium* is being excavated near the modern town of *Pràtica di Mare*. Legend has it that Aeneas landed on the nearby coast and founded the settlement, named after his wife Lavinia. So far remains of walls, a necropolis, a tomb known as the *Heroon of Aeneas* and extensive baths have come to light; there are also thirteen altars from shrines dedicated to the gods of antiquity worshipped here, including Venus, Jupiter, Juno and Vesta, and also numerous terracotta statues, which are to be exhibited in an antiquarium.

03033 Arpino

Frosinone   p.323□G 5

The foundation date of this very old town with interesting ancient ruins cannot be determined exactly; like Alatri, Anagni, Rocca d'Arce and Atina it is held to have been founded by Saturn. The single kilometer of the original three of the *megalith wall* which has survived is the largest example of its kind in Italy, and is evidence of the once important Volscian town of *Arpinum*, conquered by the Romans in the second Samnite war in the late 4C BC. The ruins of the *acropolis* are on the E. hill (**Civitavécchia**), along with parts of the fortified medieval town. The territory of Roman Arpinum was the home of numerous important personalities:

Arpino, S.Michele (left), Pelasgian megalith wall (right)

the consul and army commander Gaius Marius (156–86 BC) was born into the rural aristocracy of Cereatae Marinae (probably on the site of modern Casamari); the orator and statesman Marcus Tullius Cicero (106–43 BC) was born near the modern Isola del Liri and liked to call himself a son of Arpinum; it is uncertain whether the commander and statesman Marcus Vespasianus Agrippa (63–12 BC) came from here or not. Arpino was prey to the devastating struggles for supremacy in Italy from the 7C to the 13C, and was destroyed successively by the Lombards, Franks, Saracens, Hungarians and Hohenstaufens; it became part of the Papal States in the late 13C, which saved it from further devastation. The painter Giuseppe Cesari (1568–1640) was called Il Cavalier d'Arpino after his birthplace: there are many of his works in local churches.

S.Andrea (Via del Colle): This church was founded in the 13C and rebuilt in Renaissance style in the first half of the 16C, then redesigned in the baroque style in the 18C. High altar painting by Giuseppe Cesari. Benedictine convent near the church.

S.Michele (Piazza del Municipio): Baroque version (18C) of a church which is thought to have been founded on the site of a Roman Temple of the Muses. The panels of the high altar and the right-hand section of the left-hand side altar are the work of Cesari. In a semicircle behind the high altar fragments of ancient wall paintings and nine niches, presumed to have contained statues of the Muses.

Piazza del Municipio: Probably on the site of the ancient forum. Bronze monuments to Marius and Cicero

Convitto Tulliano: Busts of Marius, Cicero and Agrippa on the façade of his institution founded in the second half of the 17C. On the left behind the Town Hall is the baroque church of *S.Carlo e Filippo* (18C).

Also worth seeing: *Castello* (Via Ciccodicola): Presumed to have been founded by the Neapolitan King Ladislaus in 1409, later much rebuilt (now a school); its chapel is in a medieval tower. *Fountain* (Piazzetta dell'Aquila) with the motif from the coat of arms of the town, two towers surmounted by an eagle. *War memorial* by local sculptor Domenico Mastroianni.

Environs: Civitavécchia (3 km. S.): This unique historic complex consists of the impressive ruins of the Volsci acropolis and the medieval castle. The *pointed gate* of the fortifying wall, unique in Italy both in size and the excellence of its condition, is the most remarkable feature. The arch is not, as is usual in the case of dry-stone building, constructed of wedge-shaped stones, but of ashlar blocks, piled one on top of the other and cut diagonally on the inside. **Mantopadre** (8.4 km. S.): Parts of the medieval ring wall of this town which has been settled since Roman times have survived.

3042 Atina

Frosinone   p.323☐H 5

This Volscian town, founded according to legend by Saturn (like Alatri, Anagni, Rocca d'Arce and Arpino) was conquered by the Romans in 293 BC, in the course of the third Samnite War. According to the poet Vergil it developed into a powerful town from the 2C BC, but it was completely destroyed in the 5C AD at the time of the decline of the Roman Empire. The oldest buildings in modern Atina date largely from the rebuilding of the town, which has been continuously occupied, after an earthquake in the late 14C.

S.Maria Assunta (Piazza Marconi): Baroque church built in 1725–46 with twin-towered façade. The interior decoration is contemporary with the building; there is a fine wooden *font* and a painting by Aloisio Volpi.

Palazzo Ducale (Piazza Saturno): The Cantelmi set an elegant memorial to themselves with their residence built in the second half of the 14C; they were one of the many families or institutions which ruled in Atina, including the dukes of Benevent, the abbey of Montecassino and the counts of Aquino.

Environs: Belmonte Castello (6.5 km. S.): Picturesque little village of charming medieval appearance. Tradition maintains that it came into being after the destruction in 293 BC by the Samnites of the Volscian settlement of *Cominium*, which has never been exactly located, but there is no historical evidence for this. 14C Gothic frescos in *S.Nicola*.
Casaláttico (8 km. SW): The name is traditionally derived from the villa of Titus Pomponius Atticus (friend and publisher of Cicero), which was converted into a castle in the Middle Ages. Parish church of *S.Barbato:* Picture of the saint of the school of the Neapolitan Santafede family (16C) and a fine Madonna of Mount Carmel by the Polish baroque painter Taddeusz Kuntz (18C).
Picinisco (12 km. NE): Popular resort with well-preserved medieval centre and 11&12C castle on the S. edge of the Parco Nazionale d'Abruzzo. Home of the writer Giustino Ferri (1857–1913).
S.Biagio Saracisino (16 km. NE): The name of this very striking village goes back to a Saracen settlement which sprang up here in the 9C AD.
S.Donato Val di Comino (10 km. N.): One of the best-known holiday

resorts in the province. Remains of a *cyclopean wall* found in the grounds of S.Fedele make this another possible site of the lost Volsci settlement of *Cominium*.

Settefrati (13 km. NE): Coins, clay goods and other utensils and statuettes of gods found in the area in 1958, some of which are 4C, suggest an ancient settlement which is otherwise unknown. *S.Maria delle Grazie* with lavishly decorated coffered ceiling and paintings by Marco di Sangermano. Pilgrimage church of *Madonna di Canneto*.

03040 Ausonia

Frosinone   p.323□H 5

This Ausonian town lost its political significance when the Oscan tribe was conquered by the Romans in the second Samnite war in the late 4C BC. The present town is based on a medieval settlement set a little higher on the hill NE of the ancient centre, of which some ruins have survived.

S.Michele Arcangelo: Gothic church built in the 14C over the remains of an temple of Hercules. The piers contain ancient temple columns. In the nave are two Roman altars (1&3C AD); pictures on the right-hand altar include a representation of the myth of Leda. Impressive ruins of the 11C *castle*. The village has some medieval houses, and modern buildings incorporating sections of older ones.

Environs: Castelnuovo Parano (2.5 km. N.): Picturesque, largely medieval village. Ruins of the *castle* built in the mid 12C by Abbot Desiderius of Montecassino (some sections have been adapted for residential purposes). In the little church nearby are fragments of several 12–14C *frescos* which are worth seeing.

Coreno Ausonio (3.2 km. SE): Village on the W. side of Monte Maio (3084 ft.), which was much fought over in the Second World War; Coreno Ausonio is known for its medieval quarries.

S.Maria a Coriano (*c.* 6 km. SW): The church was built on the site of a temple, the lower part of which, with columns and an inscription (2C AD) survived. In front of it are substantial remains of an *ancient wall*.

S.Mario del Piano (1.2 km. SW): Church built in the 15C within the ancient centre on the site of an earlier Romanesque building, with an extraordinary loggia above the vestibule inscription with completion date (1448) on the right corner pier. Interior redesigned in the baroque style in the 18C. *Renaissance sarcophagus* of the poet Elisio Calenzo (1521) in the nave. On the high altar, in the triptych signed by Giovanni of Gaeta (16C), is the carved image of the Madonna which is said to have arrived here in a miraculous fashion from Castro dei Volsci in 1100.

01022 Bagnoregio

Viterbo   p.320□C

This picturesque little town dates back to *Balneum Regis* (king's bath built in the 8C by the Lombard King Desiderius on the site of the ancient

Bagnoreggio, S.Agostino (left), S.Nicola cathedral (right)

settlement (Civita, see below), which had been destroyed. Birthplace of St.Bonaventure (*c.* 1221–1271). Traditional Good Friday procession representing the Passion on Golgotha.

S.Agostino (Piazza Plebiscito): The original 11C Romanesque church was replaced by the present Gothic building in the 14C. Numerous 14&15C frescos in the interior. On the N. wall important *panel pictures* (15C) by the Siennese Martino di Bartolomeo (St.Augustine and Nicholas of Tolentino) and Giovanni di Paolo (St.Clare and St.Scholastica); 15C wooden crucifix. Monument to St.Bonaventure by Cesare Aureli (1897) in the square.

Cathedral of **S.Nicola** (Piazza Cavour): This splendidly decorated baroque building was consecrated as cathedral instead of S.Donato in Civita in 1699. Bagnoregio's status as

a bishopric is documented from the 6C.

Environs: Castiglione in Teverina (14 km. E.): Wine-growing village above the valley of the Tiber founded in 1351. The remainder of the medieval centre of the village and the castle can be seen near the main square. There is a 15C painting of the Assumption in *SS.Filippo e Giacomo*.
Celleno (13 km. S.): Village mentioned from 1172 on the site of an Etruscan-Roman settlement, perhaps established by refugees from Férento, which was destroyed in the same year. The impressive *residence* of the Orsinis (16C) is in the upper, half-ruined part of the village.
Cívita (*c.* 0.8 km. E.): The 'dying town'. Until a few centuries ago the settlement was connected with Bagnoregio by an extension of the rocky spur which has now been destroyed

Civita (Bagnoregio), the 'dying town'

by erosion. This was the site of the Etrusco-Roman settlement documented by numerous archaeological finds and tombs. Continuous erosion has caused the collapse of the hill's extremities and swept away the houses in the village, which is anyway almost deserted. Civita gives an outstanding view of the eroded landscape with its tufa-brown and clay-grey tones, down to the valley of the Tiber. The interesting little town has mainly Gothic and Renaissance buildings, some of which are constructed from ancient materials. At the highest point is the Piazza S.Donato, presumably on the site of the Roman forum. Medieval parish church of *S.Donato* (cathedral of Bagnoregio until 1699); the original 8–11C building was much altered later. In the interior is an expressive crucifix of the school of Donatello (mid 15C).

01010 Barbarano Romano
Viterbo   p.322☐L 3

The village within the partially surviving walls still looks medieval. The holes and caves hewn in the rock (now stables and storerooms) were probably ancient burial places.

Antiquarium (In the Municipio/ Town Hall): Interesting archaeological collection with objects from the period of Villanova culture (*c.* 10–7C BC) and the Etruscan period (*c.* 6–2C BC); red- and black-figured Greek vases.

Environs: S.Giuliano (2 km. NE): The remains of a settlement excavated by Swedish scholars are considered to be part of the lost Etruscan town of **Marturanum**, mentioned by the

Roman historian Livy in the late 1C BC. There are also ruins of the medieval church of S.Giuliano and the castle. *Necropolises* with widely distributed individual tombs. The typological range of the Etruscan tombs between the archaic and Hellenistic periods (7–3C BC) is the important feature of the complex. Particularly remarkable and in relatively good condition are among others the *Tomba Costa* (4C BC); *Tomba Cima* (tumulus; 6C BC); *Tomba di Cervo* (tomb of the stag; cubic; 5C BC); *Tomba della Regina* (queen's grave; cubic). SE is the small *Villanova-Necropolis Chiusa Cima* (8–7C BC) with its characteristic Pozzo tombs (well-like shafts to contain urns) and fossa tombs (trenches for burying corpses, widespread from the 7C BC).

Necropolis **Valle Cappellana** (*c.* 6 km. N.): This Etruscan grave chamber known as *Tomba delle Colonne* (tomb of the columns) was named after the columns which are a feature of this carefully-designed complex.

01010 Blera

Viterbo   p.322□C 3

This little town is atmospheric and historical in character and goes back to the Etruscan settlement of *Bleva*, a provincial town in the territory of the Etruscan centre of Tarquinia, set at an important junction in the ancient road network; the surviving Roman bridges were also part of this (probably rebuilt by the Etruscans): the impressive almost 70 ft. long Ponte del Diavolo over the Biedano (a little upstream near the modern road bridge) and the Ponte della Rocca over the Rio Canale, NW of Blera. Both the large necropolises in the area (the settlement once extended further to the W.) and the drainage of the tufa layer by means of a network of channels meeting in a basin in the present Piazza S.Maria are evidence of the one-time prosperity of the town, especially in the 7–6C BC. Blera was no longer of economic importance in Roman times; it became a bishopric in the 5C (incorporated into Viterbo in the 12C), evidence of its subsequent revival; even after it had been destroyed by the Lombards in the second half of the 8C it developed as a centre of agriculture. The town is generally interesting in appearance; the buildings date largely from the 15&16C, and have the external staircases typical of the domestic architecture of the time.

Parish church of **S.Maria** (Piazza S.Maria): Former cathedral with nave and two aisles and Renaissance portal (1507). In the interior is a fine Roman *sarcophagus*. Etruscan and Roman inscriptions and fragments of reliefs are built into the walls of a former church (45a Via Roma).

Necropolises: Of the Etruscan burial places in the area the W. necropolis *Pian del Vescovo* (*c.* 1 km. away) beyond the Ponte della Rocca is most interesting because of its range of 7–6C cubic tombs, niche tombs, tumuli with shored-up mounds and a long house tomb.

Environs: Civitella Cesi (9 km. S.): Picturesque little village with a *castle* built in the 12&13C and altered in the mid 16C under Cardinal Federico Cesi (privately owned).
Grotta Porcia (4 km. NW): Etruscan grave mound and cult monument.
Luni sul Mignone: See Tarquinia, Environs: Monte Romano.
S.Giovenale (*c.* 8 km. NW): Unoccupied archaeological zone on the site of an ancient settlement which has been under investigation by the Swedish Institute in Rome since 1956. Remains of residences from pre-Etruscan cultures have been discovered (from roughly the 12C BC to the Villanova period around the 8C BC); they contained everyday objects and also fragments of Mycenean cera-

Bolsena, castle and Palazzo del Drago

mics dating from the 13–12C BC. The **grave chambers** hewn in the rocks in the surrounding area also date from this period (7–5C BC, including the *Grotta Tufarina*, untouched until its discovery and with a variety of grave goods); the imported Greek vases suggest that this Etruscan town, the name of which has so far not been discovered, was a prosperous community with flourishing trade connections. It was clearly abandoned in the 3C BC. There are no traces of Roman settlement, other than a few simple tombs. It was not until the mid 12C or the 13C that a place known as S.Giovenale, the name of which is derived from an early medieval chapel and which had a castle, appeared in historical records; the castle ruins still exist, along with a section of the Etruscane town wall. The medieval settlement was abandoned in the middle of the 15C.

01023 Bolsena

Viterbo   p.320☐B 2

This little town on the NE bank of the lake of the same name has many historic buildings in good condition; it is set in the foothills of the Monti Volsini, and also has a modern quarter. It probably dates back to *Velsna*, N. of Bolsena, one of the twelve main cities of the Etruscan alliance. Some scholars contend that this must have been the seat of the national shrine (now completely lost) of the patron goddess Voltumna; other possible sites of the temple, also the place of assembly of the Etruscan alliance, include Montefiascone. The town was conquered by the Romans in 280 BC, destroyed after a revolt and moved to the site of modern Bolsena with the latinized name Volsinii; Roman charter from 90 BC. A Christian community can be proved to have existed from the late 4C (seat of a bishop until the late 7C). The town was frequently destroyed in the troubled period around the fall of the Roman Empire, and in the 8C passed from the Lombards to the Pope, to whom it belonged with a few interruptions, and not always willingly, until the Papal States finally became part of the Kingdom of Italy in 1870. The walls were razed on the orders of Pope Gregory XI after the town rebelled against the church in 1377.

Evidence of the Etruscan and Roman past: Near the castle (on the road to Orvieto) is a section of the 4C BC town wall, once four km. long, which is particularly striking for the building techniques used. Piazza del Mercatello: Ruins of a *temple* which was probably dedicated to the Etruscan goddess of fate Nortia, even in Roman times; her principal cult site was Velsna. There are also substantial remains of a *bathhouse*, of the *amphitheatre* and of several houses. *Poggio Mozzetta* (1.5 km. NE): Specialists suspect that this set of buildings excavated *c*. 1950 includes the *acropolis* of the Etruscan city. Etruscan necropolises and individual grave chambers have been discovered in the area around Bolsena (Poggio Pesce, Poggio Sala, Poggio Vietana).

Collegiate church of S.Cristina (Piazza S.Cristina): The elegant *façade*, endowed by Cardinal Giovanni de'Medici (later Pope Leo X) was added in 1492–4 to the Romanesque church dating from the 11C. In the lunette of the central portal is a glazed terracotta *relief* showing Our Lady with St.Cristina and St.George, the work of the della Robbia family. 14C *campanile*. The interior has maintained its Romanesque character. The five-part altarpiece is probably the work of Sano di Pietro (15C). In the *Cappella di S.Lucia* (right apse) and the Gothic *rosary chapel* (middle of the right aisle) are

Bolsena, S.Cristina

frescos which are also of the 15C Sienna school. Above the 16C crucifix is an arch of heaven with angels' heads by the della Robbias. The *Cappella del Miracolo* is reached from the left aisle through a lavishly decorated Romanesque portal (lintel relief of the Wise Virgins and the Adoration of the Magi); it is a centrally-planned building dating from 1693: the high altar picture by Francesco Trevisani depicts the Miracle of the Blood, and the slabs on which the blood from the host was spilled form part of the altar. On the left is access to the *Grotta di S.Cristina*: the antechamber is hewn out of the rock—probably the cave once dedicated to Apollo—and leads to the catacombs; it contains the altar of the saint with a 9C *ciborium*; in 292 she was ordered by her father, the Roman prefect Urbanus, to be drowned in the lake as a Christian, but by a miracle the stone fastened to

her did not drag her to the bottom of the lake, but back to the bank. On the right near the entrance to the grotto is the *chapel of St.Michael*; altar picture by Giovanni della Robbia.
To the right of the church is a 15C *oratory* (now sacristy); the portal lunette contains a terracotta composition by the della Robbias.

S.Francesco (Piazza Matteotti): 13C Gothic church; later accretions were stripped from the plain design during restoration after bomb damage in 1944. A fine portal gives access to the interior; fragments of Gothic wall painting. A gate dated 1548 near the church leads to the medieval quarter.

Castle/Castello: This impressive building dates from the 13&14C, and was constructed under Orvieto rule. Though since restored, it was destroyed by the people in 1815 to avoid its being handed over to Lucien Bonaparte. It accommodates the *Museo Communale*/Municipal Museum, in which archaic, Etruscan and Roman archaeological finds from the region and 13–16C ceramics are displayed.

Museo Communale / Municipal Museum: See Castle/Castello.

Also worth seeing: *Palazzo del Drago* (below the castle, elegant 16C Renaissance building), once seat of the Papal Legate. *Palazzo Ranieri* (Piazza S.Cristina), plain Gothic building dating from 1299; Pius VII stayed here in 1815.

02021 Borgorose
Rieti   p.323☐F 3

In the Middle Ages the little town belonged first to the counts of Mareri, and then changed hands on numerous occasions; until 1960 it was known as *Borgocollefégato*.

S.Anastasia: The parish church was

built in the 18C on the site of an earlier medieval building, using heterogeneous but strikingly massive old masonry. Plain, rather crude rose window and a portal made up of ancient and Romanesque fragments. In the interior are several notable 15C frescos and 16&17C panel pictures.

Environs: Civitella (5 km. W.): The remarkable remains of the megalith wall are among the numerous archaeologically relevant traces of the Sabino-Roman past found principally in the area of the Salto reservoir known as 'Cicolano'.
Corvaro (3 km. NE): Since remains of a Latin temple (among other things) have been found there has been general agreement that this is the site of the Sabine town of *Orvinium*, mentioned by the Roman scholar Marcus Terentius Varro in the 1C BC, but never definitively identified (the assumption that it was sited at Orvinio, which was named for that reason, is considered inaccurate).
S.Giovanni in Leopardo (c. 1.5 km. SE): Ruins of the former Benedictine Abbey. It was first mentioned in 1153, and is completely in ruins. Surviving sections of the monastery church are parts of the outer walls, the choir and above all the five-aisled crypt, with capitals (second half of the 13C) decorated with a variety of plant and animal motifs.

02020 Borgo S.Pietro
Rieti   p.323☐F 3

This village was established in 1938 to replace the medieval village of the same name submerged in the reservoir, which is about 10 km. long. The *Clarissine Convent* founded in 1228 by St.Filippa, a member of the Mareri family, which ruled the area, also had to move. The old chapel, in which the relics of the saint were worshipped,

Bolsena, S.Cristina, fresco, 15C ▷

was transferred to the modern church: it contains frescos with a representation of the death of Mary (15C) and a late-16C wall painting attributed to Panfilo Carnassali of Rieti. The interesting *monastery museum* contains exhibits which include magnificent goldsmiths' work, liturgical garments, paintings and sculptures of various periods.

Environs: Concerviano (18 km. NW): Little village very charmingly sited above the Salto valley. The parish church has a 14C silver-plated cross and various 17&18C baroque paintings.
Rocca Ranieri (20 km. NW): Village which still makes a medieval impression. *S.Giovanni Battista:* Notable 16C frescos in the choir: they include the Annunciation, Coronation of Mary and scenes from the life of the saint.

03022 Boville Ernica

Frosinone   p.323☐G 5

This little town has existed since the 11C; it still has its triple medieval walls with 3 gates and 18 watch towers. Many of the buildings are medieval, Renaissance and baroque, and in a pleasing and attractive condition. The town was originally founded by the Hernici in the pre-Roman period, and remains of this setlement, parts of the cyclopean wall, and other buildings, have survived on the Monte de Fico 1 km. SE of the present town, which was sacked by the Saracens in the 9C AD and abandoned after destruction by the Hungarians in 939.

Castello Filonardi: Medieval building with dominant 16C alterations, including the outstanding *Renaissance portal* in the courtyard. In the rampart is a memorial to 28 January 1861, when the Piedmontese under Garibaldi met the Bourbon troops of the

King of Naples during the War of Italian Unification.

Environs: Monte S.Giovanni Campano (8 km. E.): This town, once under the counts of Aquino, was rebuilt after it was destroyed in 1495 by Charles VIII. It is said that Thomas Aquinas' family held him prisoner in the older part of the massive *Palazzo Baronale*, once a fortress with massive towers, to prevent him entering a monastery. Parish church of *S.Maria della Valle:* Bronze door (Porta Mirabile) by the contemporary sculptor Tommaso Gismondi.

00062 Bracciano

Roma   p.320☐C 3

Although it may be that there was an Etruscan settlement on the trachyte ridge above the SW bank of the crater lake *Lago di Bracciano*, the history of the little town which is sited there now does not begin until 1234, when the castle of the prefects of Vico and a settlement around it were mentioned for the first time. In 1419, the town was taken over by the Orsinis, and in 1696 by the Odescalchis.

S.Maria Novella: This late baroque church near the Augustinian monastery contains a number of important works by the Polish painter and honorary Roman Tadeusz Kuntze (Konicz), including the vast *apse fresco* (Ascension, *c.* 1764) and two altar paintings: a Pietà in the sacristy and a 'Transfiguration of S.Chiara' above the first side altar on the left.

S.Stefano: The *Salvator triptych* signed by Gregorio and Donato of Arezzo on the second side altar (1315) on the right and a 17C painting attributed to Domenichino with saints and members of the Orsini family are interesting features in the left arm of the transept of the Catholic parish church. The triptych depicts the

Bracciano, Castello Orsini

Redeemer with John the Baptist and S.Nicola of Bari on the front and on the back a Madonna in the Mandorla with St.Stephen and St.Laurence.

Castello Orsini: Napoleone Orsini began to build the present castle after he had taken the old prefectorial castle . 1470, and it was completed by his son Gentile Virginio c. 1485. The French King Charles VIII waited for reinforcements here against Pope Alexander VI, who unsuccessfully laid siege to this masterpiece of medieval fortress architecture. The building has survived in good condition; it is built as an irregular pentagon with a protruding entrance. The plain outer walls with rectangular windows and the six tall corner towers are all battlemented. The courtyard is trapezoid with loggia and colonnade, a fine columned exterior staircase and three residential wings.

The 17 lavishly furnished rooms in the lower and upper storeys are open to the public. The *library* (Room I) with its stucco on a gold background and the *Studiolo* (Room II) are decorated with frescos by Taddeo Zuccaro. The Italian King slept in the *Chamber of Umberto I* (Room II) in 1900; it has a painted wooden ceiling by Antoniazzo Romano and a 15C four-poster bed. The *Sala del Trittico* (Room IV) has a fine fireplace (16C); the room is named after the triptych of the Umbrian school which is kept here (Annunciation, Crucifixion, St.Mary and St.John) dating from the 15C, the *Sala di Pisanello*, (Room V) so-called because there are frescos of his school (scenes of country life, hunting and the legend of the spring). The *Hunting Trophy Chamber* (Room VI), with access to the courtyard, originally extended through two storeys and was almost 50 ft. high. Another room

(Room XIII) was created above it by the insertion of a ceiling in 1906. There are surviving frescos (1491) by Antoniazzo Romano and his school. On the walls of the *Sala Orsini* (Room VII) are family portraits and two marble busts (Paolo Giordano Orsini and his wife Isabella de'Medici, whom he later strangled) by Gian Lorenzo Bernini. The *Sala di Isabella* (Room IX) has coats of arms of the Orsinis and a painted wooden ceiling, the first in the castle, by Antonazzio Romano and his pupils; this room is reached via the *Sala del Leone* (Room VIII) with 15C paintings of the Venetian school (St.Anthony of Padua with bishop saint). The rooms in the upper storey are reached by a spiral staircase; the most important are the *Sala d'Armi* (Room XIII) with Italian and German tournament armour (15&16C), the *Sala Siciliana* (Room XV) with a large Sicilian wrought-iron bed (16C) and the *Sala Etrusca* (Room XVI) with an interesting collection of Etruscan finds from Cerveteri and Palo (qq.v.).

Environs: Manziana (6 km. NW) Interesting features in the tree-lined *Piazza Tittoni* are the palazzo of the same name by Ottaviano Mascherini, 16C houses and the fountain (1733).
Trevignano Romano (12 km. N.) Lavish furnishings in the church of *S.Maria Assunta*, including choir frescos reminiscent of Raphael dating from 1517 (Coronation of Mary). The church of *S.Caterina* is based on a Roman building.
The Town Hall houses an interesting antiquarium with finds from the ancient necropolis of *Sabatia*.

01011 Canino

Viterbo   p.320☐B 2

This little country town has a historic centre still surrounded by parts of the ring wall with towers; it is a former Etruscan settlement and takes its name from the Canini tribe which lived here in the Roman period. Canino was part of the Papal States from the 11C, with the exception of temporary subjugation to Viterbo in the 13C and the Farnese duchy of Castro in the 16&17C. In 1808 Napoleon's brother Lucien Bonaparte acquired the fief from Pius VII. Lucien became Prince of Canino and Musignano, and lived here for a long time. The site was full of inestimably valuable archaeological treasures, especially the Etruscan necropolises at Vulci, and as their owner, after the accidental discovery of a grave chamber in 1828, he commissioned excavations which proved to be most fruitful: fine bronze sculptures, utensils, jewellery and countless Greek vases of the highest quality were discovered. But the fashionable interest in things Etruscan which resulted soon degenerated into an endless sequence of lucrative lootings, often detrimental to the objects found, through haste and ignorance; superficially less attractive finds were often left behind or even broken, and no account was taken of the exact point at which they were found. Canino is the birthplace of Alessandro Farnese (1468–1549), who later became Pope Paul III.

The olive feast ('Sagra dell'Olivo') takes place annually in early December (Canino olive oil is famous for its purity).

Collegiate church of **SS.Giovanni e Battista** (Piazza De Andreis): In the interior are a very fine painting of the Adoration (15C) and two circular pictures of Apostles of the 16C Tuscan school. On the right is the neoclassical Bonaparte chapel with a tomb relief of the school of Antonio Canova. In the square is a Vignola fountain dating from the second half of the 16C; the twelve-sided basin bears the coats of arms of the Farnese family and the town.

S.Francesco: In the interior are a painting of St.Anthony of Padua of the Viterbo school dated 1487 and a Madonna with Saints by Monaldo Trofi (early 16C).

Palazzo Bonaparte: Built in the early Renaissance by the Farneses and extended for the princes by Giuseppe Valadier.

Environs: Castellardo (*c.* 4 km. NW): Ruins of a medieval village abandoned after sacking.
Cellere (6 km. N.): Church of *S.Egidio*, built in the first half of the 16C by Antonio da Sangallo the Younger. Is on the N. edge of the village, which was a medieval area reached through a gate, and a modern area. The church has four chapels set at the points at which the arms of a Greek cross intersect. 15C former *castle* of the Farnese family, rebuilt for residential purposes.
Musignano (5 km. S.): The massive remains of the Roman Apollinaris baths are near the medicinal springs.

02014 Cantalice

In the Middle Ages this village on the

steep cliff on the W. flank of the Monti Reatini successfully resisted violent attacks from Rieti; in the 16C it came into the possession of the Farnese family. The defiant medieval castle, and also the grim exterior of the old houses, with only a very few small windows in the more vulnerable lower storeys, still show the legendary ease with which Cantalice could be defended.

S.Felice: 18C baroque church on an exposed site beneath the castle. The architectural decoration and campanile are striking features of the village. Another interesting item is the 16C *Renaissance loggia* of the Casa Ramacogi, a little lower down the hill.
Parish church of **S.Maria del Popolo:** *Renaissance portal* dating from 1548 in the otherwise plain exterior. On the high altar is a 16C painting of the Last Supper.

01010 Capodimonte

Capodimonte originally belonged to Orvieto, came into the possession of the Popes in 1296 and passed to the Farnese family in the 15C. Renaissance *Palazzo Farnese* (Piazza della Rocca), commissioned in the first half of the 16C by Pierluigi Farnese to designs by Antonio da Sangallo the Younger; it replaced the castle of 1254. The building is essentially defensive, but the octagonal shape set within the square walls of the earlier medieval building gives the palace elegance and rhythm.

Environs: Bisenzio (*c.* 4 km. NW): Ruins of various periods: *Bisentium* was probably founded in the 8C BC by the Etruscans, fell to the Romans in the 4C BC and was sacked by the Lombards in the 8C AD; the bishopric was transferred to Castro. There is evidence of resettlement from the 10C, but the little town was comple-

FRANCISCVS · GALLIARVM · REX · CAROLVM · V · AVGVSTVM
COMPRIMENDAE · DEFECTIONIS · CAVSA · IN · BELGAS · PROFICISCENTEM
ET · ALEXANDRVM · FARNESIVM · CARDINALEM · MAGNIS
DE · REBVS · LEGATVM · LVTETIAE · PARISIORVM
AMPLISSIMO · APPARATV · SVSCIPIT · ANNO · SALVTIS · ꝯↃDXL

tely destroyed again *c.* 1265 as a consequence of the murder of the Papal Governor at the bidding of Pope Urban IV (the ruins were intended to be used in part as building materials for the Papal castle in Marta). The subsequent rebuilding was undertaken under the counts of Bisenzio; in 1816 however it was finally abandoned, among other reasons because of malaria in the surrounding marshland. *Necropolises:* There are four early Etruscan necropolises, now scarcely recognizable, in the surrounding area. They date from the 8–6C BC, and from N. to S. are S.Bernardino, Bucacce, Olmo Bello and Polledrara; at the fork of the lake road and the road to Valentano is the Palazetta necropolis. Outstanding Etruscan artefacts were found in the Olmo Bello necropolis in particular (now largely in the Villa Giulia Museum in Rome or in the Viterbo Museum).

Isola Bisentina (3 km. N.; privately owned): Island in Lake Bolsena, 2297 ft. long and 1640 ft. wide, highest point is the 184 ft. Mount Tabor. The *Palazzo Farnese* (near the landing stage) is early 16C and is attributed to Antonio da Sangallo the Younger. Next to it is the church of *SS.Giacomo and Cristoforo*, probably by the same architect; the dome was completed by Vignola in the mid 16C; in the interior is the tomb (1449) of the Papal General Ranuccio Farnese, transferred from another church. On the S. tip of the island (La Rocchina) is a *chapel* by A. da Sangallo; it is a graceful Renaissance design: circular interior within octagonal exterior walls. Etruscan graves were discovered in the same area. On the path to Mount Tabor (N. peak) there are five *chapels* built *c.* 1450; notable features of their interiors are the wall paintings (late 15C) by a follower of

◁ *Caprarola, Charles V and Cardinal Alessandro Farnese, painting by Zuccari*

the Florentine Benozzo Gozzoli (first chapel) and a stylistically similar representation of the Transfiguration of Christ (third chapel).

01032 Caprarola

Viterbo   p.320□C 2

This little place became famous through the magnificent *Farnese Palace*, one of the finest princely residences in Europe and a masterpiece of Mannerist architecture and interior decoration at the point of transition between Renaissance and baroque. In 1537 the village became part of the newly-established duchy of Castro di Farnese, but after two Castro wars between the Farneses and the victorious Pope it fell to the church, with the exception of the Palazzo Farnese and its beautifully designed park, which contains the *Villa Farnese*, the summer residence of the Italian President (the grounds are not open to the public). In the 18C the palace fell to the Spanish Bourbons, and consequently to the Kingdom of the Two Sicilies. On the last Sunday in August the 'Sagra delle Nocciole' (Feast of the Hazelnuts) is celebrated.

Palazzo Farnese: The massive ground floor was originally the complete lower storey of a pentagonal castle for Pierluigi Farnese by Antonio da Sangallo the Younger. Instead of continuing with this after the death of Pierluigi, his son Cardinal Alessandro commissioned a summer residence from Vignola, using the existing building (1559–75); his brief was to produce a building representative of the might of the princely house, but which was also to catch the intellectual dynamism of an age of transition. The lavish *fresco decoration* is an art-historical treasure, and in contrast with the furnishings it has largely survived in good condition. It is a feature of most of the rooms, and is the work of notable artists, in

Caprarola, panorama

particular the brothers Federico and Taddeo Zuccaro, during and after the period of completion of the building.

Ground floor: F.Zuccaro's frescos (1567–9) on the left of the *entrance hall* show views of the palaces, towns and villages belonging to the Farnese family (including the Caprarola residence itself). *Jupiter room*/Salone di Giove (2) with perspective architectural painting by Vignola and incorporated pictorial scenes, probably by T.Zuccaro (1560–1). The round *courtyard* within the pentagonal building is very beautiful, and reaches an architectural climax in the piano nobile. Under this is the circular *cellar*, hewn into the tufa (3a) with a hollow central column used both to support the vaulting and for the storage of water. The monumental *spiral staircase*/Scala Regia (4) is one of Vignola's most interesting crea-

tions: it is supported by thirty pairs of massive Doric columns; the *dome* and the lively painting of grotesques and landscapes by Antonio Tempesta and Paul Bril (1580–3) lead the eye upwards.

First floor: The Farnese possessions are the theme of F.Zuccaro's frescos in the *Hercules room*/Salone Regio (5). On the ceiling is the myth of the origin of Lake Vico (q.v.). The *round chapel* (6) is beautifully decorated with stucco and painting by the Zuccari. It is thought that the figures of the Apostles Thaddeus and James the Elder are portraits of T.Zuccaro and Vignola. The pictures by T.Zuccaro in the next room *(Salone dei Fasti Farnesiani* (7) are devoted to the great deeds of the House of Farnese. T.Zuccaro's wall paintings in the adjacent room, the Sala del Concilio di Trento (8) glorify Pope Paul III

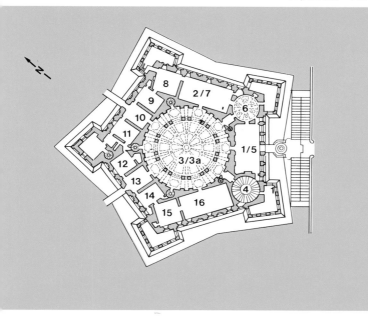

Caprarola, Palazzo Farnese Ground floor **1–4,
1** Entrance hall **2** Hall of Jupiter (Salone di
Giove) **3** Courtyard **3a** Cellar **4** Spiral staircase
(Scala Regia) Piano Nobile **5–16, 5** Hall of Her-
cules (Salone Regio) **6** Chapel **7** Chamber of the
Great Deeds and Events of the Farnese Family
(Salone dei Fasti Farnesiani) **8** Chamber of the
Council of Trent (Sala del Concilio di Trento) **9–
11** Summer Apartment (**9** 'Morning' bedroom **10**
Dressing room 'of the wool weavers' **11** Work-
room 'of the philosopher') **12–14** Winter Apart-
ment (**12** Room 'of Atonement' **13** Room 'of the
Pronouncement of Justice' **14** Room 'of Dreams')
15 Hall of Angels **16** Hall of the Map of the World

Alessandro Farnese), who sum-
moned the first Council of Trent for
the renewal of the Catholic church in
1545. The suites of the *Summer apartments*/Appartamento Estivo (9-11)
and the *Winter apartments*/Apparta-
mento Invernale (12-14) include living rooms painted in accordance with
the function of the particular room;
the rooms in the winter apartments
were painted by Giacomo Bertoia,
assisted on occasions by Giovanni
de'Vecchi. The *Angel room*/Sala degli
Angeli (15) was painted most successfully with Biblical scenes by Raffaelino da Reggio and G.Bertoia. The
most impressive room in the palace is
the *Sala del Mappamondo*/Hall of the
Map of the World (16); the geographical pictures are the work of Antonio da Varese, and the other pictures
were contributed by Giovanni de'-
Vecchi and Raffaelino da Reggio
1574).

S.Teresa: The church was built *c.*
1620–30; it has a magnificent façade,
the principal work of Girolamo Rainaldi. The interior architectural detail
is impressive. Important contemporary altar painting: Madonna on
Mount Carmel, perhaps by Guido
Reni (high altar); St.Anthony by
Alessandro Turchi (right); St.Sylves-
ter by Giovanni Lanfranco (left).

Also worth seeing: *S.Maria della*

Consolazione (Piazza Vittorio Emanuele II): Lavishly decorated carved ceiling in the early baroque interior.

Environs: Carbognano: (4 km. E.): Village with atmospheric medieval centre. Carbognano was first mentioned in the 10C, and dates back to an ancient settlement, as shown by the Etruscan tombs found in the area. *Palazzo Baronale* (Piazza del Comune): Built for the Farnese in the 16C, and generally in good condition. Remains of what was probably a Roman temple dating from the first half of the 1C have been discovered at the edge of the village near the church of S.Donato.

Fábrica di Roma (7 km. E.): It is presumed that the village was founded by refugees from the town of Falerii Novi, abandoned in the 8C AD. It has been historically documented since the 11C, and was later a Farnese possession. *S.Silvestro* (Piazza del Duomo): Rebuilt in the Renaissance (mid 16C) on the site of an earlier church; part of the medieval building is still visible in E. section. Valuable frescos from the first half of the 16C

in the main apse. Opposite is the Farnese *palace.*

02041 Caspéria
Rieti   p.321 ☐ D

Part of the medieval ring wall has survived, and the charming little town has maintained much of its historic character. Numerous signs of Roman settlement have been discovered, and it is presumed that more are to be found under the present buildings. The town was owned by various families (including the Savellis and the Orsinis) and became part of the Papal States in 1592.

SS.Annunziata (on the S. edge of the town): Early baroque building by Girolamo Saraceni (completed in 1609). Outstanding baroque painting of the Annunciation on the high altar (mid 17C) by Giovanni Battista Salvi, known as Sassoferrato.

Parish church of **S.Giovanni Battista:** 13C Romanesque campanile

Caprarola, Palazzo Farnese

(later raised in the same style); the nave was widened in the 16&17C. In the apse is a painting of the Baptism of Christ by Giacomo Siciliano dated 1524. On the third altar on the right is a 16C carved figure of St.Sebastian.

Environs: Montefiolo (*c.* 1 km. S.): On the neighbouring hill is the former Capucine monastery of *S.Francesco:* The panel painting on the high altar is the only known dated and signed work of the Roman painter Girolamo Battacchioli.

S.Maria di Legarano (1 km. N.): There was a Roman country house on the site of this church, and the remains of a mosaic floor and various sculptures exhibited here were part of it. In the portal lunette is a fresco of the Annunciation by Bartolomeo Torresani (16C); on the right is a roughly contemporary portrayal of the plague saints Roch and Sebastian. The single-aisled interior has a ceiling with carved beams. On the left in the niche is a wall painting attributed to Alessandro Torresani (second half of the 16C) depicting the Marriage of Mary; 17C reliquary cupboard with

depictions of St.John the Evangelist and Sebastian (school of Antoniazzo Romano, late 15C). In the left arm of the transept Mary and Joseph, two painted terracotta figures which are all that remains of a 16C crib. In the right arm of the transept is a simple, painted wooden crucifix (15C). In the apse two frescos of the Madonna Enthroned (15C) and Christ in the Mandorla of the Cherubim (16C). On the high altar is a lively painted carving of the *Madonna*, the only signed work of Carlo Aquilano, dated 1489.

03043 Cassino

Frosinone   p.p.323☐H 5

The town of *Casinum* was founded by the Oscans and conquered by Rome in the Samnite wars; it became a colony in 309 BC. Thanks to its situation on the Via Casilina (Rome-Capua) it was an important centre of trade. After the fall of the Roman Empire Casinum and the abbey of Montecassino were often plundered and laid waste; in the 5C by the

Cassino, tomb of Ummidia Quadratilla

Cassino, amphitheatre (left), Montecassino, manuscript (right), 16C

Goths, Vandals, Heruli and under Theoderic, in the late 9C by the Saracens. In the late 9C the population fled to S.Germano, N. of the ancient town and built by Bertarius, Abbot of Montecassino; the modern town developed from this settlement, and the adapted ancient name was taken in 1871. In 1799 the town fell into the hands of plundering French revolutionary troops; in 1815 the Neapolitan King Joachim Murat was defeated here by the Austrians. Cassino was again completely destroyed in the Second World War in the course of bitter fighting for this cornerstone of the German front. There are more than 30,000 soldiers in the military cemeteries.

Rocca Jánula (NW; about 630 ft.): Ruins of the castle built in the second half of the 10C for the protection of S.Germano. The provisional peace between Frederick II and Pope Gregory IX was concluded here in 1230.

Terme Varroniane: Named after the villa of the Roman scholar Marcus Terentius Varro, which was sited here (116–27 BC). The largest spring in Italy rises from various points here.

Zona archeologica (SW edge of the town on the Via Casilina): Impressive Roman ruins have survived on the site of the ancient city: *Amphitheatre* (1C AD) of an unusual, almost circular shape (diameter *c.* 213 ft., walls up to 60 ft. high). Tomb of Ummidia Quadratilla (1C AD), who, according to an inscription, commissioned the amphitheatre. The building is cruciform in plan, and was consecrated as a *church c.* 1000 (it has been known as the Cappella del Crocifisso since the late 17C). In the interior are fragments of medieval frescos in the

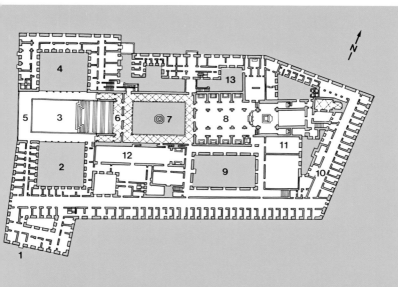

Byzantine style. *Theatre* semicircular diameter *c.* 164 ft.), now used for performances again. *Museo Archeolo-rico Nazionale:* Outstandingly well-organized modern museum with fine exhibits from the pre- and early historical periods, and from Roman times, documenting everyday life in Casinum.

Environs: Abbazia di Montecas-sino (9 km. W; 1693 ft.): The world-famous abbey is the mother monas-tery and spiritual centre of the Bene-dictine Order and one of the most important monastic establishments in Christendom. Benedict of Nursia (Norcia) founded a church of St.Mar-tin with attached monks' cells over the ruins of a temple of Apollo on the site of the ancient acropolis *c.* 529 (frag-ments of the 4–2C BC megalith wall are visible on the access road just before the final corner). The adjacent

Abbey of Montecassino 1 Entrance **2–4** Cloisters **5** Loggia **6** Atrium **7** Chiostro dei Bene-ficattori (Benefactors' cloister) **8** Church **9** Prior's cloister **10** Novitiate **11** Chapterhouse **12** Great refectory **13** Gardens

Oratory of St.John on the highest point of the hill on the site of the heathen sacrificial altar became the core of the later monastery church. Here Benedict drew up the rules of the Benedictine Order (his original manuscript was lost in a fire in the late 9C), and he was buried here in 547 next to his sister Scholastica, who died shortly before him. After sacking by the Saracens in 883 the monks did not return until 950, under Abbot Aligernus. The rebuilt monastery church was consecrated in 1071 (only a few fragments of the architectural decoration and the *bronze door*, cast in Constantinople, have survived).

Another fruitful period lasting into the period of the investiture controversy came to an end in 1230 when the monastery was violently occupied by the troops of Frederick II. The monastery was re-established in the second half of the 13C, but never rose to its former heights. It was made a bishopric in 1322, badly damaged by an earthquake in 1349, and subsequently rebuilt, then reduced to a commendatory in 1454. It was joined to the congregation of S.Justina in Padua in 1504, and this led to another period of activity and rebuilding. In 1727 the splendidly rebuilt baroque church was consecrated; the present reconstruction follows this design. The abbey was plundered by French revolutionary troops in 1799, secularized in 1806, declared a national monument in 1866 and returned to the Benedictine Order in 1929. The monastery was destroyed in an allied air raid in 1944 (the archives and the library were rescued to a large extent). The buildings were rebuilt to their original design 1949–57.

Church (8): Reconstructed after the Second World War. The church is one of the most magnificent baroque buildings in Italy as a result of the monumental quality of the architecture and the artistic splendour of the interior created by Giovanni Battista Contini, Cosimo Fanzago and Giovanni Rossini in the church consecrated by Pope Benedict XIII in 1727. The high altar is on the site of the tomb of St.Benedict and St.Scholastica; their relics were discovered in 1950, and are housed in a shrine. On the left and right are remains of the tombs of Pietro de'Medici, son and successor of Lorenzo the Magnificent, by Antonio and Francesco da Sangallo (1531–9), and of Guido Feramosca by Giovanni Merliano (1535–c. 1548) respectively. Under the choir is the only 15C *crypt* to have survived in the entire monastery, decorated by artists from the Benedictine monastery of Beuron in 1900.

Monastery buildings: Reconstruction of the Renaissance, Mannerist and baroque buildings (16–18C). The S. side is almost 400 ft. long. On the W. side of the cloister (3) is a loggia (5), which affords a magnificent panorama; opposite under the steps is

Abbazia di Montecassino (Cassino), interior of church

a surviving statue of St.Benedict by Pietro Paolo Campi (1736). Chiostro dei Beneficattori/Cloister of the Benefactors (7); originally built in 1510 to plans by Antonio da Sangallo and named after the statues of individuals who have done service to the abbey which stand here.

Cervaro (7.6 km. E.): This village dates back to the ancient settlement of Castrum Cerbarii, and in the Middle Ages was the property of the abbey of Montecassino; it was obliterated in the battle of Cassino (1944). It has been an agricultural centre since it was rebuilt. Outside (c. 2 km. N. on the road to Viticuso) is the pilgrimage church of *S.Maria di Piternis*, consecrated in 1408 on the site of an appearance of the Virgin.

Piedimonte S.Germano (9 km. W.): Originally the castle of the counts of Aquino, the village passed into the possession of the monastery of Montecassino as the result of an exchange of territory in 1061. It was rebuilt after being completely destroyed in 1944, and now houses various industrial enterprises.

Pignatoro Interamna (9 km. S.): A town dating back to the Roman colony of Interamna Lirinas, documented from 312 BC, and possibly originally a Volsci settlement, disappeared completely at the time of the decline of the Roman Empire. There are surviving sections of wall, ruins of an aqueduct and the necropolis beyond the Rio Spalla Bassa. The present village has existed since the Middle Ages, and was badly damaged in 1944.

S.Vittore nel Lazio (12 km. E.): In spite of severe damage in 1944 the village still has characteristic medieval corners, and a section of the fortifying wall has survived. Parish church of *S.Maria la Rosa:* Fine 13C pulpit in the nave (partially reworked in the 17C). *S.Nicola* (Via Roma): The 11C church has interesting frescos from various periods: wall paintings of the 12C Benedictine school, a cycle showing scenes from the life and works of the early Christian martyr Martha of Antioch (14C) and a 14C picture of the Last Judgement. Part of the original roof has survived.

02020 Castel di Tora
Rieti   p.321...E 3

This village, which still looks medieval, is near the site of the Sabine city of *Thiora*, as is shown by its name and that of neighbouring Colle di Tora, and various other traces in the surrounding area.

Parish church of **S.Giovanni Evangelista:** Expressive 16C Madonna painting; apse fresco of St.Anatol of Alexandria and the church patron (17C). Only the main tower of the castle which gives the village its name has survived.

Environs: Antuni: The Monte Antuni (2169 ft.) protrudes into the lake; on its peak are the ruins of the *medieval village* of the same name with the Castello del Drago.

Montecassino, church organ

00040 Castel Gandolfo

Roma   p.322☐D 4

The picturesque little town of Castel Gandolfo is set on the SW edge of the crater high above the Lago Albano; it is one of the *Castelli Romani*, and best known as the annual summer residence of the Pope. As necropolises prove it is on the site of *Alba Longa*, the oldest capital in the Latin league, destroyed by the Roman King Tullus Hostilius *c*. 600 BC; earlier research had presumed it to be on the NE and SE bank of the lake. Castel Gandolfo was founded again in the Middle Ages, and in 1279 was in the possession of the Savelli family, later it came into the Papal domain under Urban VIII; it was popular with visitors to Rome in the 18&19C.

Piazza del Plebiscito: The church of *S.Tommaso da Villanova* is on the E. side of the square with fountains. The church was built in 1661 by Gian Lorenzo Bernini on a Greek cross plan; the interior has stucco coffering and a high altar painting by Pietro da Cortona. The purposeful plainness of the neighbouring *papal summer residence* on the N. side of the square contrasts strongly with the massive baroque church. The residence was built by Carlo Maderna in 1624–8 under Pope Urban VIII, and has four wings set around an inner courtyard; it is not open to the public. The papal observatory was built in the rear buildings in 1936, and later the audience building, which can accommodate 8000 visitors, was added in the garden. The papal palace and the Villa Barberini have been extraterritorial possessions of the Vatican State since 1929.

Villa Barberini: Papal villa on the site of the earlier villa of Domitian; the remains of its baths, shrines of

◁ *Castel Gandolfo, Swiss Guard*

Castro dei Volsci, S.Nicola, frescos

nymphs and little theatre may only be visited with special permission.

Also worth seeing: Sculpture by Thorvaldsen is exhibited in the *Villa Torlonia*, in which Goethe once stayed.

Environs: Lago Albano (1 km. NE): There is a panoramic road all round the elliptical crater lake, which is over 550 ft. deep; the road leads from Castel Gandolfo to Marino inside the crater, keeping close to the bank of the lake. There is an interesting small *temple* of the Republican period, which can be reached by a cable railway, and the *Emissario*, a man-made underground channel 2.5 km. long and over 5 ft. high, built in 398&7 BC, and used since then to regulate the water level of the Lago Albano.

03020 Castro dei Volsci
Frosinone   p.323□G 5

The settlement dates back to a Volsci town, as is shown by remains of the ancient megalith wall and acropolis, and Roman country houses and baths; after being conquered by the Romans (late 4C BC) it was known as *Castriminum*.

Parish church of **S.Nicola:** Interesting 13C fresco cycle with Old and New Testament themes. *Monumento alla Mamma Ciociara:* Monument by Fedele Andreani (1964) for citizens of Ciociara killed in the resistance movement and during the last war.

Environs: Vallecorsa (10 km. S.): This may be the site of the lost Volsci settlement of *Verrugo*. There are remains of the defensive wall and medieval towers. *S.Antonio Abbate:* Crucifix dating from 1517 in the Gothic church. There is clear regression to the Romanesque in the architecture of the 15C church of S.Martino.

03023 Ceccano

Frosinone   p.323□F 5

The town grew up on the site of a Volsci settlement, called *Fabrateria Vetus* after being conquered by the Romans; in the 13C it was the centre of a small medieval state. An ancient satellite settlement known as *Fabrateria Nova*, which the most recent research suggests was located near here (and not at Falvaterra) was destroyed by the Lombards in 589 and then abandoned. Ceccano changed hands on numerous occasions from the late 16C and in 1504 finally passed to the Colonnas. The old town, on a hill in the middle of the modern industrial centre, was badly damaged by wars throughout the centuries and by heavy bombing in February 1944.

S.Maria al Fiume (on the Sacco bank): This church near the villa of the Roman Emperor Antoninus Pius and the temple dedicated to his wife Faustina (2C BC) was consecrated 1196. It was completely destroyed 1944 and rebuilt using the original materials, some from the Roman ruins, to the original Cistercian Gothic design. *Romanesque pulpit* and 13C *stoup* (first pier on the left). Collection of Roman inscriptions and finds from Fabrateria Vetus.

S.Nicola: This early-12C church was largely rebuilt at the end of the 13C.

Castle: Built in the 11&12C, much altered later.

Environs: Giuliano di Roma (km. SW): Remains of an ancient castle and tombs suggest a pre-Roman settlement (6–4C BC). The picturesque village on a slope is do

Cervéteri, necropolis, entrance to a tomb

nated by the 18C baroque collegiate church of *S.Maria Assunta*. Outside the village (0.5 km. N.): is the baroque pilgrimage church of *Madonna della Speranza* (1755–62) with a convent added in 1850.

Villa S.Stefano (15 km. S.): Tradition places a residence of the legendary Volsci king Metabo here; the ancient *round tower* was named after him. Finds confirm that the area was settled in the Roman period. Ruins of the Romanesque church of *S.Giovanni*, destroyed in 1944.

03024 Ceprano

Frosinone   p.323☐G 5

Fregellae was originally a Volsci town, then from 328 BC a Roman colony and faithful ally of Rome; it was sacked in the 3C BC by Pyrrhus, and later by Hannibal, and completely destroyed after a futile revolt against the Romans in 125 BC. In was here that Pope Gregory IX lifted the first excommunication against Emperor Frederick II; in 1266, as Dante was to mention fifty years later in the 'Divine Comedy' (Hell XXVIII 16-17), King Manfred of Sicily was betrayed in his struggle against Charles of Anjou, who had been given the fief of his kingdom by the Pope. In 1815 the Austrians defeated the former King of Naples, Joachim Murat, at Ceprano. He had distinguished himself as general to Napoleon I, became Marshall of France and married the Emperor's sister Caroline.

Environs: Falvaterra (9 km. S.): The most recent research suggests that Falvaterra does not date back to the abandoned ancient settlement of Fabrateria Nova (see Ceccano). The village has existed since the early Middle Ages, and this shows in the historical character of its little crooked alleyways, the pretty square and minimal remains of the *castle*.

S.Giovanni Incárico (9 km. SE): Apparently founded after the destruction of Fabrateria Nova. There is evidence of Roman settlement in the immediate surroundings, including

Cervéteri, necropolis, tumulus

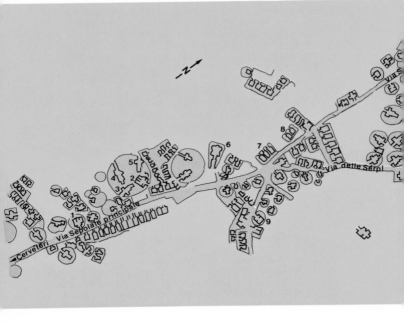

Cervéteri, necropolis 1 Tomb of the Chapters 2 Tomb of the Greek Vases 3 Tomb of the Deathbeds 4 Tomb of the Thatched Roof 5 Tomb of the Dolians 6 Tomb of the Reliefs (tomba bella) 7 So-called Little House (tomba della casetta) 8 Tomb of Marcie-Ursus 9 Four Chamber Tomb 10 Tumulus of Opheliae Maroi 11 Tumulus Mengarelli 12 Tumulus of the Colonnello

mosiac floors, sections of wall and the ruins of a temple. In the upper part of the village is the medieval core with remains of the wall and fortified towers.

00052 Cervéteri

Roma   p.320□C 4

There was a settlement on the tufa plateau above the coast even in the Iron Age (10C BC), called *Agylla* by the Greeks, *Cisra* by the Etruscans and *Caere* by the Romans. Sea trading and the mineral wealth of the nearby Tolfa mountains (see Civitavecchia) brought prosperity to the town (8–5C BC), during which time its citizens, along with the Carthaginians, asserted their right to supremacy in the Tyrrhenian against the Greeks (*c.* 540 BC); they were the only Etruscans to maintain a treasure house in Delphi, and they established important necropolises. The decline of the town started with the destruction of the principal harbour at Pyrgi (see S.Severa) by Dionysos of Syracuse in 384 BC and its subjugation to Rome in 353 BC, and it later became completely insignificant.

It was not until the ancient citadel was restored in the 10&11C that the town began to revive. In the 13C the inhabitants, suffering from malaria, founded the new settlement of *Ceri* 5

Cervéteri, necropolis, wheel ruts

km. to the E., and called the old town Cervétiri (Caere veteris). In the same century the citadel passed to the Venturini family, later to the Orsinis, who sold it to the Ruspolis in 1674.

Necropolises: Several Etruscan *cities of the dead* have survived around the terrain; the most important one (7–1C BC) is on the hill *Banditaccia*, to the N. The view along the ancient streets and squares is dominated by series of monolithic chamber and hall graves and accumulations of tumuli hewn out of the tufa and covered with grassy mounds of earth. Along the *Via Sepolcrale principale* eight tombs on the left are the most interesting: the *Tomba dei Capitelli* is so called after the scrolled capitals on two octagonal piers which bear the weight of the heavy coffered ceiling in the main chamber. On the walls and in the three rear grave chambers the

women's graves are like little houses without roofs, and the men's are like stone beds. In the largest tumulus on this side of the road (Tumolo II; 7–5C BC) are the *Tomba dei Vasi greci*, which is similar to the Tomba dei Capitelli in its system of two side chambers, subsequent main chamber and three adjacent grave chambers, the *Tomba dei letti funebri* with beautifully designed death beds, the *Tomba della Casa con tetto stramineo*, the oldest tomb, looking rather like a house with a thatched roof, and the *Tomba dei Dolii*, which has two chambers in which painted vases as well as red and white terracotta vessels were found. After another large tumulus, one reaches the *Tomba dei Rilievi*, probably the most interesting of the tombs because of its furnishings. On the left-hand side of the road the sequence continues with the *Tomba della Casetta*, with six chambers linked by arched windows and doors, the *Tomba di Marce-Ursus*, so called because of a inscription naming the owner in the interior, both typical examples of 6–4C BC grave chamber architecture. Just before the small square in front of the Tomba della Casetta the *Via della Cirnice* branches off to the left; it contains the four-chamber *Tomba a quattro camere*, and to the E. the *Via delle Serpi*, which contains the *Tumulo di Ofelia Duranti Maroi*, completely opened up by excavation; Etruscan and Greek vases were found here. The *Tumuli del Mengarelli* and *del Colonnello* are outside the enclosing fence, and reached via the Via delle Serpi; they are two of the largest so far excavated. The latter is surrounded by ten smaller tumuli also dating from the early 6C BC.

Castle: Medieval Cervéteri only covers the SW corner of ancient Caere, and is dominated by a *Rocca* with defensive towers, a 13C castle. The *Palazzo Ruspoli* (16C), which since 1967 has housed the *Museo Nazionale Cerite*, which has fine collections of Etruscan grave goods, local black and imported Greek ceramics (8–5C BC), and the *church of S.Maria*, in which an earlier Romanesque church forms the transept. This and the campanile date from the 12C. In the interior are frescos which have been removed (16C) and a painting on the high altar signed by Lorenzo da Viterbo (Madonna and Child, 1472).

Environs: Necropoli del Sorbo (1 km. S.): *Tomba Regolini-Galassi*, discovered in 1938.
Necropoli di Monte Abatone (2 km. SE): Recent excavation including the fine tombs *Tomba Campana* and *Tomba Torlonia* (4C BC).
Palo (9 km. S.): Coastal town on the site of the ancient Alsium, one of Caere's three harbours. A *Roman villa* in three sections with magnificent coloured mosaics in the interior (4&3C BC) has recently been discovered near the Castello Odescalchi (15C, not open to the public), set in a park and with corner towers.

Cittaducale, Porta Napoli, round tower (left), S.Agostino, portal (right)

02015 Cittaducale

Rieti   p.321 _ E 2

Cittaducale was founded in 1309 by
Charles of Anjou, and was often
involved in fighting against Rieti as
the northern bastion of the Kingdom
of Naples. Parts of the medieval
defensive wall with towers have survived. A charter was granted in the
16C, followed by the right to mint
coins, conferred by the Aragon family
in recognition of the services of the
town. The little town is built on an
elliptical plan with straight streets
intersecting at right angles, and is
dominated by numerous medieval
houses.

S.Agostino (Piazza del Popolo): *Portal* dating from 1450 with some
Gothic elements; lunette fresco by
Lorenzo Torresani (1548). In the
interior are two fine 18C *baroque
paintings* by Giuseppe Viscardi (first
altar on the left and second altar on
the right).

S.Maria del Popolo (Piazza del
Popolo): Late Romanesque church
with Gothic rose window and Romanesque campanile. The interior was
rebuilt after earthquake damage in
1703. Second pier on the left: 14C
relief of the Annunciation; on the high
altar remains of a 15C fresco of the
Madonna; in the choir 18C baroque
painting and fine carved stalls.

Torre Angioina/Anjou Tower
(Porta Napoli): Massive round tower
dating from 1380.

Also worth seeing: S.Cecilia
(Piazza Correto): Elegant portal
(1471) with bust of God the Father.
S.Maria della Fraternità (Via
De'Rossi): The brotherhood was by
tradition active socially; the late
Romanesque church contains various
wall frescos from different eras.

Environs: Cotilia (8 km. E.): The
healing springs were in use even in
Sabine times; the Roman Emperor
Vespasian (who died here in 79 AD)
and Titus also visited the 'Aquae
Cutiliae'.
S.Rufina (5.5 km. NW): The village
church of *S.Maria del Popolo* has two
frescos by Lorenzo and Bartolo Torresani (16C).

02010 Cittareale

Rieti   p.321 □ F 2

Cittareale was founded in 1261 and
named after Charles I of Anjou; it was
almost completely destroyed by an
earthquake in 1703. The church of
S.Silvestro was built on the site of a
Roman temple, and used some of its
walls.

Rocca di Re Manfredi: Impressive
ruin of a late 15C and 16C fortress
with semicircular towers and walls
clad in ashlar. Its traditional name
suggests an earlier 13C building of the
Hohenstaufen period.

*Cívita Castellana, cathedral, centre
portal*

Cívita Castellana, cathedral, lion on centre portal

01033 Cívita Castellana

Viterbo   p.321 □ D 3

Former Faliscan capital; the tribe was closely connected culturally and politically with the neighbouring and superior Etruscans from the 8C BC.

There is a long tradition of ceramic production; excavations of the ancient town have revealed terracotta sculptures from at least five Falsican temples dating from the 6–3C BC, to the N. and S. of Civita Castellana (Celle, Vignale, Sassi Caduti to the N.; Lo Scaso to the S.). The tombs on the W. edge of the city contained metalwork and jewellery, but also unique examples of red-figured vases from the Falerii workshops, which in their time were known throughout Etruria. These and many other specimens of Etruscan artistry are displayed in the Villa Giulia Museum in Rome.

S.Gregorio (by the Via della Tribuna): This little Romanesque church in the form of an Egyptian cross (T-shaped) has retained its original character. There are fragments of 15C fresco decoration in the transepts.

Cathedral **S.Maria** (Via Garibaldi) This Romanesque cathedral is of particular art-historical interest because of outstanding Cosmati work. The *crypt* (8C) implies an earlier building dating from the time of the town's foundation in the Middle Ages. In 1210 the Roman marble artist Jacobus and his son Cosmas built the magnificent vestibule with its high central arch in front of the façade; the *inlaid frieze* is one of the finest achievements of Cosmatesque mosaic. The three lavishly decorated

Cívita Castellana, 17C fountain

 portals are lively accents in the otherwise plain façade (*c.* 1200): the main portal is the work of Master Laurentius (father of Jacobus); *mosaic picture in the lunette* of the right-hand side portal by Jacobus. The Romanesque basilica formerly had a nave and two aisles, but was redesigned in the baroque style in 1736–40 as a single-aisled church with connected side chapels. The original Cosmati-work floor survived. The sections of the former *choir screen* with inlay work and exotic fabulous creatures by the Cosmati artists Lucas and Deodatus dating from 1237 (old sacristy on the left by the presbytery). Remains of Romanesque wall painting. 14C fresco on the S. transept altar, 15C panel picture on the N. transept altar. The *hall crypt* has nine aisles and some ancient columns; it was built in the 8C, probably on the site of a Falisco-Roman shrine.

S.Pietro (Piazza Matteotti): Lavish, stylistically coherent baroque interior (18C). The Adoration of the Christ Child by Antoniazzo Romano (second altar on the right) and of S.Bernadino of Sienna by Sano di Pietro (first altar on the left) date from the 15C. 17C *fountain* in the square.

Castle (Via Roma): Home of the National Museum. The massive pentagonal Renaissance building with some round bastions was begun in the last few years of the 15C by Alexander VI (Rodrigo Borgia) on the site of a 10&11C defensive building. In the early 16C Julius II had it completed by his fortress architect Antonio da Sangallo the Elder; he was responsible for the massive octagonal tower (almost 80 ft. high), which makes it a significant example of military architecture. The Borgia rooms were painted in the 16C, partly by Amico

Aspertini and the brothers Federico and Taddeo Zuccaro. Remains of a Roman *amphitheatre* have been revealed near the castle.

Museo Nazionale Falisco (Via Roma, in the castle): The National Museum has a collection of ceramics, including finds from the Faliscan town and its tombs, and from Falerii Novi.

Also worth seeing: *Ponte Clementino* (Via 12 Settembre): The topographical situation of the town is clearly discernible in the interesting view of the Rio Maggiore from the high bridge built by Clement XI in 1709. *S.Maria del Carmine* (Corso Buozzi): This Romanesque church rebuilt in the late 16C still has its fine 12C campanile (with some ancient building materials). In the interior are Roman columns with differently decorated capitals.

Environs: Calcata (13 km. S.): Picturesquely-sited village with E. access through a medieval double gate. To the S. is the small Faliscan necropolis of *Narce*; the tombs date back to the period of the Villanova culture (*c.* 9–8C BC).
Corchiano (9 km. NW): Numerous Etruscan/Faliscan graves of differing types around the village (including the tomb known as 'Puntone del Ponte' about 3 km. N. on the road to Vignanello, strikingly architectural in design) indicate that the area was settled in ancient times. Traditional *crib play* at Christmas (Rappresentazione del Presepe vivente). In the church of **S.Biagio** (near the cemetery) is a cycle of important frescos (1468) by Lorenzo da Viterbo and the so-called master of Civita. Remains of the medieval *castle* in the village square. **Outside the village** (about 1.5 km. W. on the road to Fábrica da Roma) is the fine Renaissance church of *S.Maria del Soccorso;* the frescos in the Paradise chapel are attributed to the brothers F. and T.Zuccaro.

Faléria (10 km. S.): The 13C parish church of S.Giuliano and the massive Renaissance residence of the Anguillara are part of the medieval heart of the village.
Falerii Novi (5 km. W.): The town was built after the destruction of Falerii Veteres in 241 BC; it was abandoned from the 8C AD, and later given up all together. The massive *ring wall* (3C AD, 2.1 km. long, over 16 ft. high, over 6 ft. thick, has 50 towers and 8 gates, and is one of the most impressive examples of Roman town fortification. Entrance to the site of the ancient town is through the *Jupiter Gate* (Porta di Giove). Near the Porta del Bove, named after a carved bull' head, in the SE corner are the remains of the *theatre*, the *forum* and the *baths* *S.Maria di Fálleri:* Monumental ruins of a large, late-Romanesque Cistercian church (13C); the Cosmati-work portal by Laurentius and Jacobus is the surviving element of the decoration.
Ponte Terrano (*c.* 1 km. W.): The medieval bridge over the channel of the Rio Maggiore is built on the foundations of a previous Roman structure. There are also traces of an Etruscan water system in the remains of an medieval aqueduct on the opposite side. The centre of the ancient necropolis was in the river channel E. of the bridge.

00053 Civitavecchia

Roma   p.320☐B 3

Trajan commissioned the building of the port of *Centumcellae*, connected with Rome by the Via Aurelia in AD 106&7; it continued to exist until it was taken by Byzantium in 537&8. In 828 it was conquered by the Saracens. After restoration in the 15&16C the ancient installations were enlarged to become the main Papal port. Both the port and the medieval town were almost completely destroyed by air raids in the Second World War. Civi

and sarcophaguses). The collection of *bronzes and ceramics* in chronological order on the third floor is particularly worth seeing.

Environs: Allumiere (17 km. NE): The *Museo Civico* is housed in the Palazzo della Camera Apostolica (15C), with interesting finds from pre- and early historical, Etruscan and Roman periods (some from the ancient quarries, which are still worked today).

Tolfa (21 km. NE): The *Museo Civico* in the Town Hall in the tree-lined Piazza Vittorio Veneto has a worthwhile collection of material from Etruscan necropolises and Roman villas in the area.

Terme Taurine (4 km. E.): Ruins of luxurious baths with several frigidaria and tepidaria, a basilican calidarium and a large *swimming bath*; also a solarium, a reading room and a library. The baths are part of a large-scale Roman imperial villa, possibly Trajan's.

Civitavecchia, S.Francesco

...avecchia is now an industrial centre ...nd the most important port in ...atium, and has the principal ferry ...onnection to Sardinia.

...orte Michelangelo: The impressive rectangular harbour fortress (394 ...t. by 262 ft.) was begun by Bramante ...n 1508 for Pope Julius II on the ruins ...f the ancient harbour; work ...ontinued under Antonio da Sangallo ...he Younger and was completed ...nder Pope Paul II in 1557 by the ...uilding of Michelangelo Buonarot-...i's elegant octagonal castle.

...useo Nazionale Archeologico ...Largo Cavour): Lucidly presented ...ollections on pre- and early history ...n the former papal customs building, ...nd also on Greek art (Mycenean and ...rotogeometric ceramics), the Etrus-...ans (grave goods, remains of ...emples) and the Romans (sculpture

02022 Collalto Sabino
Rieti   p.323☐F 3

Originally a pre-Roman fortified Sabine settlement, still dominated by a massive 15C castle. Collalto Sabino was severely damaged by raids and plunder by hordes faithful to the Bourbons in 1861. The large-scale *castle* is a striking example of Renaissance fortifications, defiant and powerful, but with a certain austere elegance.

03010 Collepardo
Frosinone   p.323☐G 4

Historic village with defensive wall in good condition in parts and numerous medieval houses. Tradition holds that the settlement was founded in 543 AD by refugees from nearby Alatri.

The site is of particular mineralogical and morphological interest.

Grotto Regina Margherita (also *Grotta di Collalto*) : 492 ft.long grotto under the S. edge of the village with stalactites and stalagmites. *Pozzo Santullo* (also *Pozzo d'Antullo*): Doline which came into being as the result of the collapse of a former cave (diameter at the centre 312-328 ft., depth 230–262 ft.).

Environs: Certosa di Trisulti (6.5 km. N.): In the early 13C Carthusian monks under the orders of Pope Innocent III built a new complex near the early medieval Benedictine monastery of *S.Domenico*, abandoned in 1204; the new buildings were much extended and altered, particularly in the 18C, and thus provides an architectural survey of the various styles from early Gothic to baroque.
Vico nel Lazio (5.5 km. NW): This is a fine specimen of a medieval settlement, surrounded by a defensive wall in good condition. *S.Maria:* Interior fresco of St. Catherine of Alexandria (14C); other wall paintings of the same period in the 9C *crypt*, which has its original columns. Collegiate church of *S.Michele Arcangelo:* Two first-class works of art are the valuable *mosaic antependium*, dating from the 10C (formerly in the basilica of S.Maria Maggiore in Rome) and the carved *Madonna* (12C, originally in S.Martino).

02041 Collevecchio Sabino
Rieti   p.321 □ D 2

The settlement dates from the second half of the 13C, when the population of Colle Muziona in the malaria-ridden valley of the Tiber withdrew here.

Parish church of **S.Maria Annunziata:** 16C portal. The interior was redesigned in the baroque style in the early 18C. 13C painted wooden crucifix.

The *Palazzo Piacentini* is attributed to Antonio da Sangallo the Younger and the *Palazzo Pistolini* was built to designs by the architect Vignola (both 16C).

Outside (to the N.): *S.Andrea,* Church of a Capucine convent; the general quality of the paintings is high; there is a fine Adoration of the Magi (late 16C Venetian School).

02043 Contigliano
Rieti   p.321 □ E 2

The appearance of the central area of Contigliano, built on the site of the Roman settlement of Quintilianum has remained almost unchanged since it was brutally plundered by Vitellozzo Vitelli in 1501; fine Renaissance and baroque buildings.

Collegiate church of **S.Michele Arcangelo:** The dominant baroque building started by the Tessino architect Michele Chiesa was completed in the first half of the 18C. In the first chapel on the left is a picture of St.Vincenzo Ferreri (1350–1419) by Onofrio Avellino (1724). On the high altar is a painting of the Archangel by Filippo Zuccheti (1700).

Environs: Cottanello (13 km. W.) Village famous for its red marble quarries with a medieval ring wall which has survived in part. *S.Cataldo* (key available from the priest at Cottanello): This little late-12C church has an interesting fresco of Christ Blessing with Apostles, Saints and Benefactors dating from the period in which the church was built.
Montásola (21 km. SE): The medieval tower and the gateway to this village first mentioned in the 13C have been partially rebuilt. *S.Pietro* In the interior is a fresco of the Madonna with St.Peter and St.Francis (17C), perhaps by Domenico Rainaldi. *S.Maria delle Murelle* (near the

Cori, S.Oliva, fresco

cemetery): Two Roman inscriptions set in the 14C façade. There are remains of a Roman mausoleum nearby.

S.Pastore (*c*. 3 km. N.): Ruins of the former Cistercian abbey. The buildings were started in 1255, and have been under various church administrations, for some time as a commendatory, since the waning of the Middle Ages. The last commendatory abbots allowed the Gothic buildings to fall into decay in the early 19C, and the ruins make an impressive group.

04010 Cori

Latina   p.322☐E 5

Legend has it that the ancient city of *Cora*, (one of the oldest cities in Italy) was founded by the Trojan Dardanos or Coras of Argos. In the 5&4C BC the town was secured with a threefold *polygonal wall*, of which a section about 2 km. long has survived. It became a municipium under the Romans, but was less important in the imperial period. It was plundered by Totila and Barbarossa, and came into the possession of the church in the 15C.

Temple of the Dioskuri (upper town): Two elegant Corinthian columns over 32 ft. high with a fragment of the architrave and the remains of the cella have survived of the temple dedicated to Castor and Pollux, rebuilt *c*. 89 BC.

Temple of Hercules (Monte di Cori): The surviving pediment in the narthex is supported by eight Doric columns. The temple was built in 89–80 BC under Sulla. Its sandstone blocks reveal fragments of the original

Cori, S.Oliva, fresco

stucco. The rear tower comes from the church of *S.Pietro*, destroyed in the Second World War.

S.Maria della Pietà (lower town): The collegiate church (c. 1600) is built on the crepidoma of the former temple of Fortuna; it is lavishly furnished, with an 18C gilded tabernacle and a valuable 12C Paschal candelabrum with four clustered columns supporting a capital and set on a base of stylized lions' heads and feet.

S.Oliva (upper town): Double church consisting of a medieval place of worship decorated with fine frescos in the interior and a Renaissance church (begun in 1477) with an apse fresco of the Umbrian school (1507, Coronation of the Virgin) and a tunnel vault with frescos in the style of Michelangelo (1533, scenes from the Old and New Testaments).

02030 Fara in Sabina
Rieti   p.321 □ E 3

The mountain fortress and the town, still dominated today by stately houses, particularly those dating from the 15C (Piazza del Duomo) and the 16C (Via del Popolo), were founded in the 7C by the Lombards as their most important outpost against the domination of Rome. In the early 11C Fara was partly taken over by the neighbouring Benedictine abbey of Farfa, and after the imperial coronation of Henry IV in 1084 it was ceded to it completely. After the decline of the abbey in the 15C the town was finally handed over to the Papal States as the seat of the district governor.

Collegiate church of **S.Antonio** (Piazza del Duomo): Late 15C portal (coat of arms of the community on the architrave). There are numerous important works of art in the interior: St.Anne Instructing Mary, baroque painting by Vincenzo Manenti, 17C (on the left by the high altar); St.Anthony in the Desert, by Angelo Maria Camponeschi, 1790 (first altar on the left); crucifix with Mary and St.John the Evangelist, attributed to the school of Guido Reni (first half of the 17C), Cappella del Sacramento: *Tabernacle* designed by Vignola in the form of a classical rotunda (1563).

S.Giacomo (below the Piazza Guglielmo Marconi): Small early baroque church with generally balanced furnishings. Expressive baroque painting on the high altar depicting the beheading of St.James the Elder (17C).

Also worth seeing: *Defensive walls:* survived in part, particularly to the S. of S.Antonio and in the NW of the little town (with gate). *Palazzo Orsini* (Via della Repubblica): Splendid early-16C Renaissance building; two of the corbels on the gutter are carved in the form of bears' heads. *Piazza del Duomo:* Fountain with the Farnese arms, endowed in 1570 by commendatory abbot Cardinal Alessandro Farnese. The Palazzo Castellani is an austere Renaissance building.

Environs: Abbazia di S.Maria di Farfa (6 km. NW): The first abbey was built in the second half of the 6C, and was sacked in a Lombard raid in the 7C. The Benedictine Thomas of Maurienne founded the abbey again in the late 7C, and in the Carolingian period it developed through endowments and support from the kings, but also through the strict discipline of the Order, into a centre of spiritual and territorial power (directly subordinate to the Emperor from the time of Charlemagne). It was destroyed *c.* 900 by the Saracens, despite seven years of resistance, but rebuilt in the early 10C. It reached the height of its power in the 10–12C, both through its connection with the Cluniac reform under Abbot Hugo I and through the work of the scholar monk Gregory of Catina and the school of calligraphy which he founded, which became famous throughout the Western world. The abbey was the mother institution of numerous Cluniac foundations. Its possessions, according to Gregory's 'Chronikon' (early 12C) included 18 towns, *c.* 130 citadels, over 680 churches and monasteries, and also several estates, harbours etc. As it supported the Emperor in the investiture dispute it was made subject to the Pope by the Concordat of Worms in 1122, and thus began its political and economic decline. In 1769 the title of abbot was transferred to the Bishop of Sabina, the commendatory was removed in 1841 and combined with S.Paolo fuori le mura in Rome; the monastery buildings were sold in 1862. In 1919 the Congregation of the Order re-established the abbey under the Benedictine monks of S.Paolo; since 1925 the abbot of Farfa has been the cardinal Bishop of the suburbicarian diocese of Sabina e Poggio Mirteto. The monastery has been an Italian national monument since 1928.

Abbey church of **S.Maria:** Completed in 1492, this is a slightly displaced new building on the site of the Carolingian church. Orsini coat of arms over the late Gothic portal (Farfa was the commendatory of this noble family from 1421–1553); early 16C lunette fresco. Fragments of ancient or early Christian sarcophaguses in the masonry. Romanesque campanile (11C); remains of frescos of the Roman school from the time of the building of the church have survived on its base.

The extensive monastery area is reached through a late Romanesaque *portal* (late 13C), the work of the sculptor Anselmo da Perugia; lunette fresco of the school of Gentile da Fabriano (early 15C). The complex includes buildings from various periods (some using sections from the buildings destroyed in the 7C or early 10C). On the left of the church is the so-called *Palazziaccio,* the abbots' crenellated medieval defensive tower. Small 'Lombardy' *cloister* of the Romanesque period (13C) and 17C *Large cloister* (Chiostro Grande) with a collection of architectural fragments; on the left is access to a room at a lower level with a *Roman sarcophagus* (3C AD), showing scenes from a battle between the Romans and the Germani. An 8C fresco in the *crypt* shows it to be part of the abbey refounded by Thomas of Maurienne in the 7C. The *c.* 20,000 volumes in the *library* include sixty valuable 16C codices, incunabula and printed matter. The *museum* shows sculpture, paintings and liturgical objects from the Romanesque to the baroque periods.

Talocci (8 km. S.): The lost city of *Cures* is located somewhere in the archaeologically important surroundings of this little village; Cures was one of the most important Sabine cities and in Roman legend was the home of kings Titus Tatius and Numa Pompilius (715–672 BC). The name is retained in the modern *Passo Corese* and *Corese Terra*, and in the name of the river which connects them. *Grotte di Torri* (2 km. NW): Piece of masonry from the Sabine city made up of massive stone blocks fitted together without mortar, now part of a farmhouse; behind it are two parallel vaulted stone passages. *Arci* boundary (2 km. SW; the name suggests a former fortress): Near the church of S.Maria delle Grazie is the *Villa Silvestri*, with fragments of Roman pictorial work and two sundials set into its façade.

Toffia (6.5 km. NE): The church of the *Fraternità delle Ss.Stigmate* dominates the village, which is documented from the 10C; some of the buildings use the walls of the former castle as outer walls or foundations. In the interior of the church is a circular picture of the Madonna (late 15C) with some stylistic elements pointing to Raphael's teacher Perugino. 16C *Palazzo Orsini*, classical in design. Outside the village is the church of *S.Lorenzo*, sometime minster and seat of the bishops of Sabina. The simple 13C building still stands, but was partially altered in the 17C.

03013 Ferentino

Frosinone   p.323☐F 4

This is the most important archaeolo-

gical area in the province: there are outstanding buildings from the pre- and early Roman periods and the Middle Ages, the time at which Ferentino enjoyed its greatest success. The town is dominated by impressive, still largely coherent, sections of the 4C BC cyclopean defensive wall, with Roman additions, and some medieval towers and gates.

The Hernici town of *Ferentinum* was taken by the the Romans in 361 BC and destroyed by Hannibal in 211 BC. It was plundered in the Saracen raid in the 9C, and damaged by bombing in the Second World War.

Cathedral of **S.Ambrogio** (Piazza del Duomo): The Romanesque cathedral was built in its present form in the early 12C on the ancient acropolis. The interior has alternate Romanesque piers and ancient columns with Corinthian capitals. *Cosmati-work floor* (*c.* 1116) by the Roman mosaic artist Paulus. In the main apse is a Romanesque bishop's throne. The *ciborium* on the high altar, which is also decorated using the techniques of the Cosmati, was created by Drudo of Trevio in the 13C, and was commissioned by the Archdeacon of Norwich, who came from a local noble family; the palmette frieze was probably influenced by the Augustan Temple of Concordia in Rome, once famous for its architectural ornamentation. The Cosmati-work *Paschal candelabrum* and the marble sculptures at the side of the sacristy portal (left aisle) also date from the 13C; at the end of the aisle is a Renaissance *tabernacle*. The sacristy contains two valuable *ciboria* from a Lombard (early 9C) and a Roman baroque workshop (dated 1641) respectively.

On the right by the cathedral is the *bishop's palace*, built on the ruins of a presumed temple of the Hernici with Roman sections dating from the 1C BC.

Ferentino, cathedral, sanctuary with paschal candelabrum ▷

Ferentino, cathedral, bishop's throne

S.Maria Maggiore (Piazza dell'Os-
pizio): The 13C Gothic church is an
exemplary work of Cistercian architecture with characteristic Italian
variants (including rectangular apse,
tower over the crossing, nave and two
aisles). The building is austere, in
accordance with the rules of the
Order, but it is beautifully proportioned, with restrained but delicate
architectural decoration: the façade
has a fine *rose window*, a large central
portal (columns supported by lions
and freize with the Evangelists) and
different small circular windows
above the side portals; the transept
ends and choir wall also have rosettes;
the individual sections of wall are
topped with friezes; the louvres in the
octagonal tower over the crossing are
relatively large.

Acropolis: Impressive 4C BC Hernici
fortress with massive base on a square
plan; it was raised by the Romans (1C
BC). Little remains of the upper part
of the original building (the lower
sections of the present bishop's palace
and the base of some arches).

Mercato Romano/Roman market
(Via Don Morosini): Hall built in the
first half of the 1C BC on the SE side
of the castle wall; it has five high
vaults for shops.

Ancient city gates: Particularly
striking is the *Porta Maggiore* (also
Porta di Casamari), one of the access
points to the Hernici town, with two
arched openings parallel to each
other. Next to it is a paved section of
the Roman Via Latina. Beyond the
gate a path (on the left) leads to the
so-called *Bequest of Aulus Quintilius*.
The inscription suggests that Aulus
Quintilius left part of the income from
his estates to Ferentino; he died in the
early 2C AD, during the reign of the
Emperor Trajan. *Porta Sanguiniaria*
(near S.Maria Maggiore): This
narrow passageway shows the massive
nature of the town wall, and also the
individual layers of its construction.
Above the oldest section, made up of
cyclopean blocks (4C BC) is the
Roman addition (1C BC) at the level of
the gateway arch, and then the medieval section which raised the wall still
higher. The medieval *Porta S.Agata*
is flanked by ancient sections of wall;
there is a Roman inscription on the
outside. Nearby is the *Porta Stupa*
with archaistic sections and Roman
arch.

Also worth seeing: *S.Agata* (Via
Garibaldi): Baroque church dating
from 1750. *S.Francesco* (Via XX Settembre): Built 1277–82, and combining Romanesque and Gothic stylistic
elements. Former church of *S.Lucia*
(Via Antiche Terme): It is presumed
that the remains of the Roman bath
of Domitilla (second half of the 1C
BC) are under this little Romanesque
building. *S.Valentino* (Piazza Matteotti): The oldest sections of the

originally Romanesque church are the apse above the crypt, which is reached by a Romanesque outer portal, and the campanile. *Teatro Romano/Roman Theatre* (near S.Lucia): The remains of the theatre were discovered in 1921 in a little square; they date from the 2C AD (diameter 177 ft., height 39 ft., 3,500 seats). *Via Consolare:* S.Pancrazio: 8C high altar; No. 66: Romanesque house (12&13C); Nos. 275–77 (near the Piazza Mazzini): Palazzo Montelungo, also Palace of Innocent III, with Gothic portal; Nos. 279–287: Palazzo dei Cavalieri Gaudenti (13C) with Gothic arcade.

Environs: Bath of Pompey (3 km. SE): Healing spring known to the Romans, now in use again.

03015 Fiuggi

Frosinone   p.323☐F 4

This town (known as *Anticoli di Campagna* until 1911) is in two sections, Fiuggi Città and Fiuggi Fonte, and is one of the best-known spas in Europe. The therapeutic value of the springs has been known since the Middle Ages; distinguished patients include Pope Boniface VIII and Michelangelo Buonarroti.

Fiuggi Città: The old town, once a church possession, owned by the Colonnas since the 16C, has retained its historical character.

S.Biagio (Via A.Diaz): Two fine baroque paintings (first half of the 17C): Madonna Enthroned by Giuseppe Cesari, known as Il Cavalier d'Arpino, and the baptism of the church patron by St.Laurence, the work of Giovanni Battista Speranza. In the Collegiate church of *S.Pietro* (Via Umberto I) is a picture of the Ecstasy of St.Francis by a Roman baroque painter (17C).

Casino (Piazza Trentino e Trieste):

Elegant 1910 Liberty-style building. Palazzo del Commune: *c.* 1925, based on the medieval models of the Bargello in Florence and the Palazzo Pubblico in Sienna. Palazzo Falconia (Piazzetta S.Stefano): Wall paintings and a small collection of valuable furniture and utensils in the Sala di Napoleone of the medieval building.

Fiuggi Fonte consists largely of spa buildings, with some interesting hotels and houses. The numerous springs are brought together and made accessible for the drinking cures in the Fonte Anticolana and the **Fonte Bonifacio VIII**, housed in a striking complex of modern buildings; both buildings are set in extensive parks (14 and 80 hectares respectively).

Environs: Acuto (6 km. W.): This little place used to be one of the possessions of the Bishop of Anagni; it takes its name ('pointed') from its site on a conical hill. The medieval castle has been rebuilt as a magnificent house.
Piglio (15 km. NW): Long village with a picturesque approach (famous for the Cesanese red wine grown throughout the region), presumed to stand on the site of the Hernici settlement of *Capitulum*, founded in the pre-Roman period. Ruins of the medieval castle. The tall houses which give the village its characteristic appearance are also largely medieval.
Torre Caietani (6 km. E.): The name refers to the castle of Pope Boniface VIII, who came from the noble Caietani family, resident in Anagni; the size of the building (late 13C) can still be discerned from the ruins.

04022 Fondi

Latina   p.323☐G 5

The present country town has a *poly-*

gonal wall about 1.5 km. long (*c*. 200 BC), and the Roman castrum design of the ancient *Fundi* (founded by Hercules, according to legend) can still be discerned. One of the four city gates to the two main streets has survived *(Portella)*, and the modern cathedral square was originally the forum at the intersection of Cardo and Decumanus maximus (Via Appia, Corso Appio Claudio).

Cathedral of S.Pietro: The early medieval pillared basilica with nave and two aisles (4&5C) was built on the site of a Roman temple; it was rebuilt in 1036–9 and again in its present form in the 13&14C (restored in 1936). The sandstone façade has a Gothic portal with an interesting *tympanum* (Judge of the World with Apostles and angels). The raised choir has three square apses. An important feature of the lavish furnishings is the *pulpit*, dating from 1278 and decorated with Cosmati work; it has columns supported by two lions, a tiger and a ram. Note also the Campanian *panel painting* (Holy Cross) dating from the 12C. In the Chapel of the Holy Cross is the particularly fine *baldacchino tomb* commissioned by the local count Onoratio II for his father, in the style of Timo da Camaiano.

S.Maria Assunta: The Gothic campanile and the spacious interior with nave and two aisles are reminders of the original Gothic pillared basilica built in the shape of a cross in the style of the Italian churches of the Mendicant Order. The earlier church was rebuilt in 1490 in Renaissance style for Onoratio II, with a Renaissance façade and three decorated portals. The tympanum figures on the central portal are of interest (Madonna and Child, St,Catherine and Onoratio II) and a charming *Renaissance ciborium* dating from 1491 in the left arm of the transept.

Palazzo dei Caetani: The Catalan architect Matteo Forcimanya was responsible for the Catalan/Gothic decoration in the palace courtyard; he built the plain early Renaissance building 1466–77 for Onoratio II.

Citadel: The massive walls of this square building dating from the 13–15C are fortified by three round towers which were damaged in the war. The schism in the Western church began under the protection of this castle with the election of Robert of Geneva as Antipope on 20 September 1378. The Torrione, a massive round defensive and watchtower on a cubic base has survived near the citadel.

Also worth seeing: Gothic *cloisters* in *S.Domenico* and *S.Francesco*; Roman statues and architectural fragments in the latter.

Environs: Lido di Fondi (13 km. SW): The ruins of the *Torre S.Anastasia*, one of three medieval watchtowers on the piné-clad coast, are near the mouth of the Canale di S.Anastasia, which flows out of the Lago di Fondi.

04023 Formia

Latina   p.323☐G 6

At the time of Cicero, *Formiae* on the Gulf of Gaeta was one of the most important fortresses on the Appian Way. At the time it was considered to be Homer's city of the Laestrygones. Because of its splendid climate the town was a valued resort; it had many Roman villas, and was known for its fine wines. The two areas of *Castellone* with the octagonal Torre S.Erasmo (14C) and *Rione di Mola* with the remains of the Castello di Mola, built in the late 18C by Charles II of Anjou, have retained a picturesque medieval appearance.

Villa Rubino (Via Unità d'Italia): In

Tomba di Cicerone near Formia (left), Fossanova, room in which Thomas Aquinas died (right)

he garden are ruins of a Roman villa with stuccoed and painted remains of walls and arches from the former baths and nymphaeia; it is generally held to have been Cicero's Villa *Formianum*.

Roman fishponds (Porto): Ponds for fish-breeding, almost 10 ft. deep, once part of a luxury villa, have survived near the harbour next to the Villa Communale, the municipal park built over the remains of Roman buildings.

Antiquarium (Via Vitruvio): Archaeological material (rescued during the Second World War) has been on display in some of the rooms in the Town Hall since 1974; it includes Roman inscriptions in honour of various people, frescos, statues and a fine *Leda group*.

Environs: Tomba di Cicerone (3 km. W.): On the Via Appia in the direction of Gaeta is a ruined monument almost 80 ft. high which is generally considered to be the tomb of Cicero. The mortar cella ceiling inside the cone-shaped tomb on a massive square ashlar substructure is supported by a large column with shaft rings. Nearby are sparse remains of another tomb, called *Tomba di Tulliola* after Cicero's daughter Tullia.

Fossanova

Latina   p.323☐F 5

Former Cistercian abbey: In the 9C a monastery was founded by Benedictine monks on the edge of the Pontine marshes in a wooded area at the foot of the Lepini Hills (near to Priverno). In 1135 the abbey was taken over by French Cistercians whose Order had been founded in 1098 as a Cluniac branch of the Benedictines. They created the ditch which later gave its name to the monastery (fossa nova = new ditch), and used it to drain the marshy area, which then made it possible to build. In 1173 the monastery was rebuilt in accordance with their austere rule, determined entirely by the spiritual and the central force of renunciation. In 1187 they started to build a new church; the altar was consecrated by Pope Innocent III on 19 July 1208.

The monastery church, dedicated to Our Lady and St.Stephen, conforms entirely with the concepts of the Cistercians in its austerity, precision and formal harmony. In addition this church with nave and two aisles is considered to be the first and most typical Gothic church in Latium, particularly in the emphasis on height in the nave, the pointed arches and the groin vaulting in the interior. The façade is a clear example of the renunciation of all decor-

ation; there was originally a portico in front of it. Under the rosette and a blind pediment is a portal with staggered shafts, each with three responds. Above this in the tympanum there is fine *Cosmati work* in the lintel and lunette. The absence of any decoration (painting or sculpture) is a striking feature of the relatively light, clear interior; the nave and aisles are separated by piers of perfect design, their shafts are produced to meet at the point at which the arches spring; the nave opens into a choir behind the altar, again free of all decoration; the choir has three windows and a smaller lunette above them. The light is admitted at the sides through small clerestory windows. In the W. arm of the transept are fragments of 14C *frescos*, which, like the 14C *fresco of the Madonna* on the altar of the first chapel in the E. transept, were not placed here until a later date. The tower above the crossing of the church, which can be seen for miles around, is really slightly too extravagant in design to conform with Cistercian austerity. There are two octagonal

Fossanova, cathedral, views of the church

storeys divided by mullioned windows and surmounted with a pyramidal roof with a lavish lantern.

The **monastery buildings**, like the church, have survived in their original condition. The fine *cloister*, surrounded by the church and other monastery buildings, has 8C Romanesque columns on three sides, the fourth side, the eastern one, was built in 1280 and 1300 with twisted and smooth columns in various designs, their bases decorated with geometrical patterns and Gothic acanthus capitals with tri- and quadripartite arches. There is also a small *aedicule*, influenced by the Moorish style, and with fine double arches; in the middle of it is the marble wash-basin used by the monks for washing in the early morning and after work. Interesting among the former monastery rooms are the *chapterhouse*, divided into a cross design by two piers, and with rib vaulting dating from 1250, and the *refectory* behind the aedicule, with a staircase built into the arches on the S. side and a lectern (pulpit). N. of the coherent monastery buildings is the

former pilgrims' house, beyond a garden. From the entrance a small staircase tower with four tiers in the NW leads to the *room in which St.Thomas Aquinas died*; his death occurred here on 7 March 1274 on his journey to the second Council of Lyon. The room was later transformed into a chapel with coffered wooden ceiling. There is an impressive haut-relief in the high altar in the manner of Bernini, showing the death of the Saint. In the S. section of the monastery is the *Infermeria*, the former hospital in which the monks cared for the sick of the area.

00044 Frascati

Roma   p.322☐E 4

Since Roman times the little town of *Frascata* has been a resort popular for its coolness in summer; it was further enlivened by additional population from Tusculum (see environs) which was destroyed in 1191. The new settlement around the churches of *S.Sebastiano* and *S.Maria* was forti-

Frascati, S.Rocco (left), S.Pietro, façade (right)

Frascati, villa of Horatius Falconerius

fied with a town wall in the 14C. Frascati is of course famous for the golden yellow wine from the Malvasier grapes which grow on the volcanic tufa on the NW slopes of the Alban Hills, but also for the beauty of its numerous 16&17C villas.

Cathedral of S.Pietro: This cathedral with nave and two aisles was built in the 17C on a Greek cross plan; the splendid *baroque façade* was added by Girolamo Fontana in 1698–1700. 18C bell towers. The 17C interior, designed by Carlo Rainaldi and Prospero de Rocchi, has various interesting features, in particular the cenotaph of Charles Edward Stewart (d. 1788) by the main entrance, and also a Romanesque *wooden crucifix* (c. 1100, second altar on the right), a Madonna of the Rosary (third altar on the right) in the manner of Domenichino and a 14C picture of the

Madonna of the Roman school on the baroque second altar on the left. Girolamo Fontana was also responsible for the baroque fountain (1709) near the cathedral.

Chiesa del Gesù: The façade of this single-aisled 17C Jesuit church is attributed to Pietro da Cortona. In the interior are *frescos* by Andrea Pozzo the Roman master of trompe-l'oeil and a *trompe-l'oeil dome* painted on linen by his pupil Antarto Colli. It should be viewed for the best effect from a black marble disc to which a black marble strip leads.

Villa Torlonia (Villa Communale) The fine flights of steps and the *cascades* built by Carlo Maderna (1556–1629) in the present municipal park used to belong to the former Villa Torlonia. Only a small building, the 16C *Casina* has survived of the

Frascati, fountain in front of the Chiesa del Gesù

riginal Palazzo or Casino (destroyed 943&44).

Villa Aldobrandini (Villa Belvelere): Giacomo della Porta began to build this extensive palace on the hillside above Frascati in 1598, to a commission from Cardinal Pietro Aldobrandini; it was completed by Carlo Maderna and Giovanni Fontana from 1602–4. The state rooms are lavishly decorated with stucco and *paintings* by Taddeo and Federico Zuccaro, by Giuseppe Cesari (Cavaler d'Arpino) and pupils of Domenichino. The swiftness with which the building was completed and the choice of the most able architects and artists of the period made the building model for 17C Italian villa architecture. The palace is placed at the crossing of two paths which articulate the surrounding park, the most interesting part of which is up the slope from

the elegant rear façade with its lavish protruding central section. The Roman baroque architect Giovanni della Porta set the pattern for Italian garden design with his first production of a so-called water theatre here in 1602. The *water theatre* cuts into the hillside like an exedra with statues in the apse niches. The water pours down the steps and is finally drawn into the central pool by the figure of Atlas in the middle niche.

Other villas: There are several other villas worth mentioning to the S. and E. of Frascati (some of them not open to the public): the first villa in the area was the *Villa Falconieri*, built 1545–8 for Bishop Alessandro Ruffini. It was extended after 1650 by Borromini and has lavish interior fresco decorations, including a *Birth of Venus* by Carlo Maratta. The pool with cypresses which figures so frequently in the pictures of Arnold Böcklin is a feature of the park. The *Villa Lancelotti* (Villa Piccolomini), a 16C valley villa, has a 17C park in the Italian style with a water theatre dating from 1620. Cardinal Markus Sitticus of Hohenems commissioned the *Villa Monragone* from Martino Longhi the Elder in 1573–7. Gregory XIII, a regular guest of the Cardinal, established the basis of the modern calendar, which is named after him, when he sanctioned the Gregorian calendar here on 13 February 1587. Fontana's large-scale water theatre has fallen into disrepair. The *Villa Vecchia*, a plain rural villa (16C) with stables and barn was bought by Cardinal Markus Sittikus of Hohenems in 1567. The estate buildings were extended in 1567–9 by his architect Jacopo Barozzi da Vignola and came into the possession of the Borghese in 1613. In 1614 Cardinal Scipio Borghese bought the last of his four villas, the *Villa Borghese* (formerly Torlonia). Like the Villa Vecchia it is rural in character, and like the other villas has the Cardinal to thank for a large part of its elegant interior. Two other villas, the *Villa Muti* (1579) and the *Villa Graziolo* (1590) are worth mentioning for their frescos by Domenichino and his school.

Environs: Monte Porzio Catone (4 km. E.): This little medieval town was first mentioned in 1078; it is set on a hill surrounded by olive groves, and takes its name from the nearby villa of the Roman Porzia family. Interesting features are the *Piazza Borghese* with its fine views, and fountain set among elms and chestnut oaks, the baroque Borghese palace (17C) and also the baroque parish church of *S.Gregorio Magno* built in 1666 for the Borghese by Carlo Rainaldi. In the interior of the centrally-planned Greek-cross building is a Madonna of the Rosary (1666, left side altar) by Guglielmo Borgognone.

Tusculum (6 km. E.): Although the name *Tusci* betrays Etruscan origin, legend has it that Telegonos, the son of Circe and Odysseus, founded this quiet little country town which became well-known through later possessions of Cicero, Lucullus, Caesar and Tiberius. After the counts

Tusculum (Frascati), ancient theatre

of Tusculum had provided several Popes in the 10–12C and ruled Rome, their home town was razed to the ground by Pope Celestine III in 1191. The semicircular *theatre* with seats for 1500 spectators below the acropolis has survived in the best condition, but the essential features of the ancient town can be discerned from the remains of the *forum*, paved streets and foundation walls. As in the case of the amphitheatre built of tufa ashlar, some underground rooms and equipment are to be found, including vaulted passages, water systems (6&5C BC) and cisterns, as in the imperial villa of Tiberius, which for a long time was taken to be Cicero's Tusculanum.

03100 Frosinone

Frosinone   p.323☐G 5

The city of *Frusino* was founded by the Volsci and later inhabited by the Hernici; it was destroyed for leading the revolt of the Hernici against the Romans in 306 BC. It has been a centre of ecclesiastical administration since the Middle Ages, and later became the seat of the papal governor of the provinces of Campagna and Marittima. Since 1926 it has been the capital of the province of the same name, made up of this territory and part of the province of Caserta. Frosinone is also the centre of the *Ciociaria*, a cultural area in Latium known since ancient times, the central part of which includes Anagni, Guarcino, Sora and Frosinone. It was the home of Cicero, Juvenal, St.Thomas Aquinas, the painter Giuseppe Cesari, known as Il Cavalier d'Arpino, and several Popes. The name Ciociaria is derived from the sandal-like footwear 'ciocia', originally part of the equipment of Roman legionaries, worn in many regions of Italy since the Middle Ages. The Ciociaria is known for its lively folk customs, songs and costumes.

S.Benedetto (Piazza della Libertà: The medieval church was redesigned in the baroque style in 1750 and contains several interesting baroque paintings. In the square is a monument to Nicola Riciotti (1797–1844) and the victims of the War of Italian Unification, by Ernesto Biondi (1910).

Cathedral of **S.Maria Assunta** (Piazza S.Maria): Rebuilt after war damage in 1944. Well-proportioned campanile with sections from an earlier Romanesque building. Important works of art in the interior: Madonna with saints and angels by the Bolognese artist Giacomo Sementi (first half of the 17C); cycle from the Life of Christ by E.Fantuzzi, G.Ceracchini, G.Colacicchi, L.Montanarini, D.Purificato (1962&3); Stations of the Cross by Livia De Puydt Canestraro; statues of the two patrons of the city and 6C Popes, S.Silverio (silver figure by E.Quattrini, 1930) and his son S.Ormisda (bronze figure by C.Quattrini, 1960).

S.Lucia (Corso della Repubblica): Neoclassical church admirable for its coherence (early 19C).

Also worth seeing: *S.Maria della Grazie* (1738) with fine fresco of the Madonna, early 14C. *S.Maria della Neve:* Baroque church rebuilt after war damage. 15C triptych on the high altar: Madonna by F.Balbi (second half of the 19C). *War memorial* (Viale Mazzini) by Domenico Mastroianni.

Environs: Arnara (10 km. SE): The village has retained its medieval character and is a striking example of a historic settlement. It is dominated by the fortified Colonna residence (15&16C).
Ripi (9 km. SE): Founded in 1315 on the hill of S.Silvestro close to the village of the same name abandoned in the Middle Ages after repeatedly being laid waste (remains of a castle and a church).

Gaeta, Palazzo Ducale, Quartiere Medievale

04024 Gaeta

Latina p.323□G 6

In the imperial Roman period *Caieta* was partly a suburb and port of nearby Formia (q.v.), and partly a popular summer resort for wealthy Romans, including the Emperor Nero and Antoninus Pius. After a period of Byzantine rule the port was in the hands of Saracen pirates from 681–846, and part of the kingdom of Normandy from 1140. Frederick II extended the naval defences and Gaeta became an important base and trading harbour for the Kingdom of the Two Sicilies. The port came under fire as the last bastion of the Neapolitan Bourbons on their flight from Garibaldi in 1860&1, and as British point of disembarkation in 1943&4, and lost many of its original buildings.

Torre d'Orlando (Monte Orlando): The fortress-like *Mausoleum of Lucius Munatius Plancus* was built high above the sea and the ancient harbour *c.* 15 BC. Lucius Munatius Plancus had fought as one of Caesar's generals in Gaul, and had founded Lyon and Basel; he was later a governor (Asia, Syria) and a censor, and a friend of Cicero and Horace. The sandstone cladding of the 43 ft. high brick building is decorated with a *frieze* of war emblems in the Doric style.

Torre Atratina (Via Atratina, Porte Salvo): The *Mausoleum of Lucius Sempronius Atratinus* (78 BC–AD 7), the former commander (38–34 BC) of Mark Antony's fleet and later proconsul in Africa is 46 ft high and 374 ft. in circumference; it is a faithful copy of the Torre d'Orlando.

Cathedral of SS.Erasmo e Marziano: The original building was Romanesque, and consecrated by Pope Paschal II in 1106; so radical have the alterations been, including a reduction from six to four aisles and a nave (1778) and the addition of a neo-Gothic façade (1903), that the church would be of little significance were it not for the fact that the transept on the right-hand side of the cathedral, with biforium and triforium windows,

Gaeta, Torre d'Orlando

survived, and also the 187 ft. high *campanile*. S. Italian influence shows in the majolica decoration of the octagonal uppermost storey (1279). The finest decorative feature of the neoclassical interior of the cathedral is a marble *paschal candelabrum* (13C) over 11 ft. high. The massive column has forty-eight bas-reliefs of the Life of Christ and St.Erasmus and is in the tradition of the Roman triumphal column. The 16C carved choir stalls have been partially restored. The single-aisled crypt (17C) is lavishly decorated with marble reliefs, marquetry and stucco, and has an interesting baroque *bronze pulpit* dating from 1692. The third side chapel on the right leads to a separate aisle which was part of the earlier cathedral, in which there are fragments of the original wall paintings, and then, via a staircase with six monolithic Roman columns, into the bottom storey of the campanile. The *diocesan museum* near the cathedral shows 14&15C frescos, medieval sculpture and fragments from the cathedral and other medieval churches.

Chiesa dell'Annunziata (Lungomare Caboto): The elegant baroque façade was built in front of the earlier Gothic building, of which only the Gothic portal has survived, by Andrea Lazzari in 1621. The lavish baroque interior furnishings include the high altar, which is decorated with marble inlay, and carved choir stalls, also an *Adoration of the Magi* and a *Presentation in the Temple* by Sebastiano Conca (1680–1764) in the choir, an Adoration of the Shepherds on the right central altar and a *Crucifixion* on the left central altar, both 17C paintings by Luca Giordano.

Santuario della SS.Trinità

Gaeta, cathedral, campanile (left), paschal candelabrum in the cathedral (right)

(Monte Orlando): In the 9C a shrine visited by several saints and countless of the faithful was established near the former *Villa of Lucius Munatius Plancus*; the cisterns of the villa have survived. It is also called *Santuario della Montagna spaccata*, after the cracks in the mountain which, according to legend, were caused by the earthquake at the time of Christ's crucifixion. On the altar of the chapel of the Holy Cross is a large wooden Crucifixion scene (*c.* 1450). In the nearby Benedictine monastery (12C) are several interesting paintings by Sebastiano Conca (17C).

Citadel: The fortress dates back to the 8C, but the present building consists largly of extensions by Frederick II (1227), and new work under Charles II of Anjou (1289), Alfonso I of Aragon (1436) and Charles V (1536). It consists of two massive

squares reinforced with round bastions.

Also worth seeing: Despite damage in the Second World War it is worth visiting the old *Quartiere Medievale* with its steps, crooked alleyways and medieval houses (12–15C) and also the 10C Romanesque church of *S.Giovanni* (S.Giuseppe), which shows Byzantine influence.

01035 Gallese
Viterbo   p.321 □ D 2

The village is still surrounded by its medieval ring wall, and legend has it that Agamemnon's son Haliscus lived here; he was the founding father of the Faliscans, who were politically and culturally associated with the Etruscans. The characteristic, techni-

Gaeta, cathedral, font with lions in the portico

cally sophisticated system of drainage ditches in the tufa layer of the old town and the tombs found in the area are evidence of Etruscan settlement; there are no Roman remains, however. The first record of a citadel is in the 7C AD.

Cathedral of **S.Maria Assunta:** Spacious cathedral with nave and two aisles dating from 1796. There is a picture of the Assumption (18C) by Franz Unterberger in the apse; paintings of the Viterbo school (15C) in the chapel at the end of the right aisle.

S.Flaminiano (E. edge of the village): The building has an elegant porch, and in the interior frescos (side apses) and 15C tapestries.

Palazzo Ducale (Piazza Castello): The former medieval castle was rebuilt by Vignola in the second half of the 16C as a majestic ducal palace with a magnificent cour d'honneur. Collection of important works of art. Fine *park* at the rear.

Also worth seeing: *S.Agostino* (Via XX Settembre): Several 15C frescos.

00045 Genzano di Roma
Roma   p.322☐E 4

This little town on the Appian Way was founded in the 13C; it is picturesquely sited above the SW crater flank of the former Nemi volcano (see under Nemi) and is one of the *Castelli Romani*. Three main streets fan out up the slope from the central terraced square, the Piazza Franconi, which has several fountains. Each year one of these streets (Via Berardi) is covered with an extravagant and artistically designed carpets of flowers for the famous *Infiorita* flower festival at the feast of Corpus Christi.

Palazzo Sforza-Cesarini: The original castello (1235) on the edge of the crater above the town was conquered by Nicola Colonna and later came into the possession of the Sforza-Ceserani family. In 1621 Prince Giuliano Ceserani had the citadel rebuilt as a palazzo, from which the view over the prince's garden on the steep interior slope of the crater and Lake Nemi can be enjoyed.

Environs: Lanuvia (5 km. SE): The ancient *Lanuvium* is said to have been founded by Diomedes. A section of the Roman town wall, built of tufa ashlar, (to the W. of the present town), the remains of a *Temple of Hercules* and (near the Villa Sforza-Cesarini) of the *Temple of Iuno Sispes Mater Regina* and the Roman upper town have survived of the Roman municipium (from 338 BC), the home of the consul Licinius Murena, who was defended by Cicero (62 BC), and the Emperor Antoninus Pius (AD 86–161). Interesting features in the *collegiate church* in the old town are an elegant *Renaissance tabernacle* and a 15C wooden crucifix; the Palazzo Colonna (15C) and parts of the medieval town wall with defensive towers are also worth a visit.
Nemi (5 km. NE): This picturesque little village on the lake of the same name is one of the Castelli Romani and takes its name from the sacred shrine of Diana *Nemus Dianae*. Excavations in the 19&20C revealed the walled shrine (1 km. NW) with several buildings surrounding an altar, and also a little theatre.
The *Palazzo Ruspoli* on the Piazza Umberto I has a cylindrical medieval defensive tower but is otherwise in Renaissance style; there is a small collection of ancient marble fragments in the courtyard.
On the N. bank of Lake Nemi, the

level of which, like that of the Lago di Albano, is controlled by an outlet, is the *Museo Nemorense* with scale models of two ancient shallow-keeled ships (the originals were destroyed in 1944); the ships were built for the megalomaniac Caligula *c.* AD 40 for the sea battles which he organized on the Nemorensis lacus.

01010 Grádoli
Viterbo   p.320□B 2

Famous 'Festa degli Incappuccinati' (Feast of the Hood-Wearers) of the brotherhood Fratellanza del Purgatorio, which on the Thursday before the carnival collects food for the public feast (with entrance fee) on Ash Wednesday in memory of souls in Purgatory.
The parish church of *S.Maddalena* has a finely-carved pulpit and confessionals.

Palazzo Farnese: Elegant 16C Renaissance palace, perhaps the work of Vignola, who created many excellent buildings for the Farnese family.

00046 Grottaferrata
Roma   p.322□D 4

Abbazia di Grottaferrata: Graeco-Catholic Basilian monks still live in the abbey, which was founded in 1004 on the remains of a Roman villa by St.Nilus and built by his pupil Bartholomew of Rossano. The castle-like fortifications were added in the 15C under Cardinal Giuliano della Rovere, later Pope Julius II.

Abbey Church of S.Maria: The church in the monastery courtyard was consecrated in 1024 by Pope John XIX, rebuilt in 1190 and 1754, then

Grottaferrata, S.Maria, Cappella di S.Nilo, fresco ▷

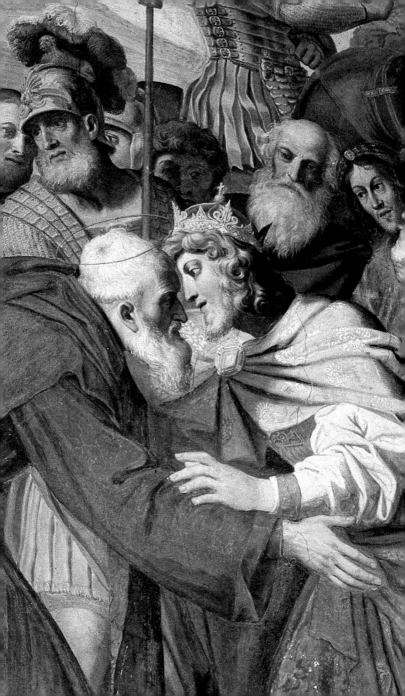

heavily restored in the 20C. In front of it is the fine 12C *campanile*; its five upper storeys are decorated with triforium windows and brightly-coloured majolica tiles. In the (restored) porch is a cylindrical Romanesque *font* (10 or 11C) with relief decoration, supported by four winged lions; there is also a 14C statue of the Virgin. The church was redesigned in the baroque style in the 18C; the nave and aisles are separated by Roman marble pillars. The entrance is a magnificent marble portal in the Byzantine style with Greek inscriptions, inlaid doors and a *tympanum mosaic* (11&12C, Deësis with portrait of St.Bartholomew of Rossano). The mosaic above the triumphal arch (feast of Penetecost), the frescos above it and the remains of a Cosmatiwork floor date from the 13C. The baroque altar wall with the icon of the Madonna of Grottaferrata (12&13C) were commissioned by Cardinal Francesco Barberini in 1655. Domenichino's frescos (1609&10) in the *Chapel of St.Nilus* represent the lives of St.Nilus and St.Bartholomew of Rossano.

Abbey museum: Collections on pre- and early history, and applied art from the medieval period to modern times, including an early medieval relief of the *Good Shepherd* and an episcopal *stole*, in the style of the Eastern church, in embroidered silk worked with gold (Life of Christ). The finest exhibits in the Lapidarium (Rooms I–III), which has sarcophaguses decorated with reliefs and Roman copies of Greek sculpture, are an *Attic grave stele* with a relief of a youth reading (5C BC) and a fragment of the *basalt statue* of the Pharoah Sethos I (*c.* 1300 BC).

Environs: Marino (5 km. S.): This is the largest of the Castelli Romani

◁ *Grottaferrata, abbey, marble portal, detail*

near the ancient *Castrimoenium* high above the N. bank of the Lago di Albano. It was mentioned in the 11C, and came into the possession of the Colonnas in 1419; Vittoria Colonna (1490–1548), the most famous daughter of the family, was born here. The wine festival known as *Sagra dell' Uva* is celebrated with great pomp on the first Sunday in October, and the fountain in the square flows with the heavy local wine. The *Fontana di Quattro Mori* with statues of Moors and sirens was erected in the Piazza Matteotti in 1642 to commemorate the Battle of Lepanto (1571), at which Marc Antonio Colonna commanded the papal fleet. The baroque collegiate church of *S.Barnaba*, with its majestic façade (1653) decorated with niches and statues is reached by way of the picturesque medieval *S. Lucia* quarter. Near the *Palazzo Colonna* (*c.* 1590), which has a large double staircase in front of it, is a small *Antiquarium* with ancient statues. The rococo interior of the circular church of the *Madonna del Rosario* (1713) is worth a visit, as well as the late-Renaissance church of *S.Maria delle Grazie*, which has an altar painting attributed to Domenichino (St.Roch). An interesting shrine of Mithras was discovered in a cellar in 1963 (house No. 12 in the street which leads from the Piazza Garibaldi to the station).

Grottaferrata, abbey church of S.Maria, campanile and façade

Marino (Grottaferrata), baroque collegiate church San Barnaba

---

01025 Grotte di Castro
Viterbo   p.320□B 1

Numerous tombs and urns confirm that this little town with its atmospheric medieval centre dates back to an Etruscan settlement. It is built on a steep slope, and many of the buildings and streets are shored up with massive walls.

S.Giovanni Battista (Piazza S.Giovanni): Baroque building by the Roman architect Girolamo Rainaldi dating from *c.* 1625.

Grotte S.Stefano
Viterbo   p.320☐C 2

It is assumed that the village was
founded on the site of an earlier
Etruscan settlement after Ferento was
destroyed and abandoned in 1172.

Environs: Montecalvello (6 km.
N.): Picturesque little village fortified
in the Middle Ages with the massive
palace of the former lords of Pamphili
(mid 17C).
Sippiciano (9 km. NE): Village with
medieval centre. *Outside* (*c.* 4 km. S.):
Piano della Colonna: Scant remains
(blocks from the walls and traces of
the drainage system) of the lost Etruscan settlement of *Moenia* with small
necropolises scattered around the
area.

03016 Guarcino
Frosinone   p.323☐F 4

This little medieval town on the site
of a Hernici settlement, under Roman
rule from the 4C BC, has survived in
good condition (scant remains of a
bathhouse are the only architectural
evidence of Roman settlement).

S.Michele (W. end of the village):
The campanile and the former cloister
(access from the left of the church)
have survived of the original Gothic
church; the nave was rebuilt in the
18C.

S.Nicola (Via del Monastero): The
18C baroque collegiate church (with
19C alterations) has a beautifully
carved pulpit.

Environs: Campo Catino (5840 ft.;
18.4 km. N.): Winter sport centre and
starting point for mountain tours in a
karst trough. *Outside* (*c.* 5 km.): *Colle
Pannunzio* (4921 ft.): An astronomical
observatory is under construction
here.

01010 Ischia di Castro
Viterbo   p.320☐B 2

Originally in the heartland of the
Papal States, Ischia, which has kept
its medieval centre, was assimilated
into the duchy of Castro, created in
1537 by Pope Paul III (Alessandro
Farnese) for his son Pierluigi, and
after the dissolution of the duchy in
1649 it reverted to the church.

Palazzo Ducale: The Farnese
Renaissance palace (*c.* 1540) designed
by Antonio da Sangallo remained
incomplete.

Antiquarium (in the local government building): The museum houses
interesting specimens of Etruscan art
from the necropolises around Castro,
and also fragments of medieval architecture from the former town of
Castro.

Environs: Ruins of Castro (*c.* 12
km. W.): A wooded hill on which isolated sections of buildings from the
town, destroyed in 1649, can still be
identified. The town is documented as
the seat of a bishop from the time of
the destruction of Bisenzio in the 8C;
it is on the site of an ancient settlement (perhaps Statonia?), shown by
the Etruscan necropolises to date
from the 8C BC, and from 1537 was
the principal town in the duchy of the

same name (its fortress built by Antonio da Sangallo *c.* 1542 was a famous example of military architecture). As the duchy had become increasingly burdened with debt, and its lords unable to discharge it, Urban VIII launched his struggle against the Farnese in 1641, but had to return Castro to the duke in 1642. The situation remained tense, and in 1649 the second Castro war broke out when a bishop appointed by Innocent X was murdered as he was travelling to Castro from Rome. As the Pope suspected the duke, his troops conquered the town after a three month siege, and destroyed it completely.

Farnese (3 km. W.): This little place gave its name to the family which can be traced back to the 12C; its members shared in the political, spiritual and artistic development of Italy as generals, holders of the highest ecclesiastical offices and generous patrons of the arts from the 15C onwards. *S.Rocco:* Particularly striking picture of St.Antony by Giovanni Lanfranco (first half of the 17C). Parish church of *S.Salvatore* (main

square): in the N. apse is a tabernacle in coloured marble and gilded wood presented by the Farnese family (late 16C). 17C baroque paintings: Paul III Celebrating High Mass by Antonio Maria Panico and Archangel Michael's Fight with Satan by Orazio Gentileschi. *Palazzo Farnese* (Main square): a Renaissance building. Below the village is the little church of *S.Anna* with frescos by Panico.

03036 Isola del Liri
Frosinone   p.323☐G 4

The Liri divides here into two main arms and several tributaries for some of its length, and forms the important Cascata Grande (maximum height 90 ft.) and Cascata Valcatoio; the volume and speed of flow of the water, bring about a moderate microclimate. Traces of settlement dating back to the early Iron Age.

S.Lorenzo (Piazza S.Lorenzo): This collegiate church was built in 1727

Farnese (Ischia di Castro),
S.Salvatore

Itri, S.Angelo

and has a picture of the martyrdom of the saint by Camillo Mariani.

Castello Viscogliosi: The 13C ducal castle was extended in the 16–19C. The park is famous for its atmospheric site and lush vegetation.

04023 Itri

Latina   p.323□G 6

This picturesque little town on the Appian Way was mentioned in 914; in earlier times travellers were afraid of its reputation for ambushes by robbers. Marco Sciarra, the robber chieftain lived here among others, who granted safe conduct to Torquato Tasso, and also Michele Pezza (1771–1806) who made history as *Fra Diavolo* and became generally known though the opera (1829) by Daniel François Auber.

S.Angelo: The 11C parish church has a *campanile* in front of it with Romanesque biforium windows and colourful majolica tiles. Gothic influence can be seen in the three pointed louvres in the topmost storey. The interior has a broad nave with two aisles; there are remains of 15C frescos in a niche (Crucifixion and Madonna and Child), and an interesting choir set on column-bearing lions.

Ruined castle: The former *castello* was badly damaged in the Second World War and its ruins tower above the jumble of medieval houses and little alleyways with arches. The medieval fortress is dominated by a square keep and a polygonal defensive tower with battlements. The lower sections are secured by smaller round towers and a massive round watchtower on the Via Appia.

Environs: Madonna della Civita (12 km. N.): The *Santuario Madonna*

◁ *Itri, S.Maria Maggiore*

della Civita is on the N. ridge of the Monte Grande, and commands unusually fine views (2208 ft. above sea level). In the neoclassical interior of the pilgrimage church, built by Silvestro de Donatis in 1820–6 on the site of a 14C church, is the *picture of Mary* held by legend to have been painted by the Apostle Luke; it was found hanging on a chestnut oak on 10 October 796. The fire-blackened icon was restored on the orders of Popes Pius VII in 1815 and Pius IX in 1877, who had it placed on the marble altar of the Neapolitan school which had been built around the chestnut oak in the 18C.

Labro, panorama

02010 Labro

Rieti   p.321 ☐ E 2

Despite violent struggles in the Middle Ages and early modern period the village still looks medieval and has remarkable unity.

Parish church of **S.Maria della Neve:** Plain building completed in 1508 on the site of the arsenal of the former castle. In the *Cappella Nobili Vitelleschi* (on the left of the entrance) is a screen with outstanding Renaissance carving. 15C font. There is a 16C fresco of the Annunciation which has been much painted over, perhaps by Bartolomeo Torresani. On the S. side of the church is the Romanesque *Cappella del Rosario* (rosary chapel).

Palazzo Nobili Vitelleschi: The residence was built in the 16C using the walls of the 10C castle, which was once famous throughout the area for the ease with which it could be defended. Along with Collalto, Orvinio and Rocca Sinibalda it was one of the most powerful in the province, until it was destroyed in the second half of the 15C.

Tre Porte: Three-arched gate in the centre of Labro and the starting point for all the streets following the outline of the former castle.

Environs: Morro Reatino (4 km. E.): Ruins of the medieval castle, once the northern bastion of Rieti on the border with the kingdom of Naples.

01010 Látera

Viterbo   p.320☐B 2

The town was first mentioned in 1013 and still has its historic centre. Good Friday procession with scenic representation of the story of Christ's suffering.

16C ducal **palace**. The splendid *fountain* was endowed by Pietro Farnese in 1648.

Environs: Onano (10 km. N.): The massive 14&15C castle and remains of the 14C defensive wall are evidence of the village's turbulent political past.

02016 Leonessa

Rieti   p.321☐E 2

Little town founded in 1228 with characteristic medieval houses (especially in the Piazza del Municipio) and fine 16&17C buildings in straight streets running parallel with each other.

S.Francesco (Via Ciucci): The building was consecrated in 1446; its straight-topped façade follows a design developed in the Abruzzi. The interior has a nave and two aisles, and, appropriately for the Rule of the Franciscan Order, which carries the requirement of austerity into buildings as well, it is predominantly simple. 14&15C *frescos* on the walls and columns. Splendid gilded 16C *tabernacle* on the high altar. In the Gothic chapel on the right (Cappella del Presepio) is a very expressive *crib* with painted terracotta figures, created by Abruzzi potters, probably followers of Paolo Aquilano, in the early 16C; on the left is a stylized painted carved figure of S.Biagio (late 14C), and on the right a terracotta statue of St.Sebastian (16C), both works of artists from the Abruzzi.The *portal* and decorations (1352) in the wall of

the N. aisle were transferred from the church of S.Donato della Torre, which has been pulled down. In the baroque chapel on the right next to it are two paintings by Giuseppe Viscardi (mid 18C) and a 16C carved crucifix.

S.Giuseppe da Leonessa (Corso S.Giuseppe da Leonessa): Baroque church consecrated in 1746; façade rebuilt in 1952. The ceiling pictures, paintings (miracles of the saint and events from the period of resistance to French rule), stucco and statues in the lavish interior were not completed until the 19C. 17C *reliquary* in chased silver containing the heart of the saint, born in Leonessa in 1556. Altar panel in the N. transept by G.Viscardi.

S.Maria del Popolo (Corso S.Giuseppe da Leonessa): Work started on the Gothic church in the mid 14C, but it was not completed until the 16C. The austere façade has a rose window and a fine late Gothic portal; the relief in the lunette has some Romanesque elements (the date 1514 presumably refers to a restoration). The interior was redesigned in the baroque style in the 18C.

S.Pietro (Piazza del Municipio): The façade of the Gothic church has a relatively large, lavish portal (1467) with an elegant ogee gable and sculptures combining late Gothic (dwarfs with hoods and leaf ornaments) and Renaissance elements (putti with garlands). In the interior, redesigned in the baroque style in the 18C, are traces of the original apse and fragments of 15C frescos. Large 16C picture, perhaps by Giacomo Siciliano, showing the handing over of the girdle to St.Thomas; 17C Coronation of the Virgin. In the *crypt*, also redesigned in the baroque style, is an Entombment with painted terracotta statuettes (mid 16C) by Abruzzi

Leonessa, S.Maria del Popolo ▷

artists; carved figure of St.Roch (early 16C); copy in painted wood of Michelangelo's Pietà in St.Peter's in Rome. On the N. side is the former *cloister* of the Augustinian monastery which used to adjoin the church. In the square is a *fountain* by Nicola di Giovanni (16C).

Environs: Albaneto (9 km. E.): *S.Maria Annunziata* with very fine baroque façade (2 towers); fine painted carved figures in the interior with nave and two aisles: 16C crucifix and St.Lucia and St.John the Baptist (17C).
Pianezza (10 km. NE): Essentially late medieval village. In the church of *SS.Agapito e Biagio* (with portal dating from 1522) is an unusual late-16C casing (designs of grotesques with bats' wings) with a painted carved figure of St.Antony (early 16C).
Terzone S.Pietro (12 km. NE): Church worth seeing for its interior, elegantly decorated in the baroque period. *S.Paolo* area: The Madonna in the church of *S.Erasmo* is the only known terracotta figure by Marino di Giovanni Frasca (1521).
Vallunga (2 km. NE): *S.Nicola di Bari* has a plain 16C façade and a splendid baroque high altar. Painting of the Madonna of the Rosary by Giacinto Boccanera of Leonessa (17C). 16C carved figure of St.Antony.
Volciano (8 km. NE): The large church of *S.Maria delle Grazie* has a fine portal dating from 1590 and houses some outstanding works of art: finely worked font, fresco of the Birth of the Virgin in a niche (both late 16C). Lavishly gilded high altar with late-15C miraculous image, flanked by the Annunciation (16C).

00056 Lido di Ostia

Comune di Roma   p.320 □ C 4

The modern seaside resort S. of Ostia was established after the First World War on the new alluvial land in the Tiber estuary; it is now a suburb of Rome. To the E. it is bordered by the extensive pine groves of the Castel Fusano, stretching 2 km. E. to the old coastline.

Castel Fusano: Sections of the *ancient road* of the Via Severiana have been revealed between the pines and chestnut oaks of the *park*, which was mentioned at the end of the 12C. It passed from the Fabians to the Roman Sacchetti family, who had the pine wood planted in 1713, and in 1755 to the Chigis, who for their part built the *Castello Chigi* (Castello Fusano) hunting lodge at the N corner of the park.

Environs: Laurentum (8 km. E.): Excavations on the former Roman coastal road, the *Via Severiana*, revealed numerous remains of *villas* of the imperial period and also of plainer residential buildings and an enclosure for animals. It is now known as Laurentum or Lauro-Laurentum, a settlement which cannot be placed historically or geographically in the formerly marshy and wooded area of Aeneas' landing place and appears to have become Lavinium (see Ardea; Environs).
Villa di Plinio (7 km. E.): Remains of a large villa of the imperial period (*c.* 100 AD), which may be identical with the country seat of *Laurentinum* Pliny the Younger's (AD 62–114) famous Laurentine villa.

Lucus Feroniae = 00065 Fiano Romano

Roma   p.321 □ D

The original Etruscan settlement (6–5C BC) was plundered by Hannibal in 211 BC. Augustus made it the Roman colony of *Iulia Felix Lucus Feroniae*. It flourished in the imperial period and there was vigorous building under Trajan, but Lucus Feroniae

Leonessa, S.Francesco, lion on portal

declined as Rome declined. The fact that there was no subsequent resettlement made it impossible to locate until 1952.

Volusian Villa: The Gens Volusia villa, discovered in 1961 and now almost completely excavated and restored, is reached from the Rome North service station on the Autostrada del Sole. A fragment of an inscription mentions the owner Lucius Volusius Saturninus, a member of the powerful family resident in Rome from the 1C BC. The building originally had three storeys arranged around a large atrium, and two of them have survived. In the residential area of the house the central tablinum, a triclinium on the left and a series of cubicula can be discerned, decorated with black and white and multi-coloured mosaic. In the *lararium*, on the W. side of the

early imperial columned courtyard, is a remarkable mosaic floor, and inscriptions and fragments of statues have been found.

Antiquarium: Houses inscriptions, implements and a model of Lucus Feroniae, as well as fragments and casts of sculptures found locally; in future they are to be housed in the newly-built *museum* near the entrance to the archaeological site.

Environs: Capena (9 km. NW): The *Etruscan town of Capena*, overthrown by the Romans in 395 BC, has been located near Civitucola, *c.* 3 km. NE of the modern wine-growing village of Capena; the principal triptych (Christ with the Apostles Peter and Paul; Annunciation) in the parish church of *S.Michele* in Capena is an important work by Antonio da Viterbo. The *necropolises* around the Etruscan town with shaft graves and other 8–3C BC tombs are more interesting than the remains of the acropolis on the Castellaccio Hill, with a temple dedicated to Augustus. Striking finds from the necropolises are now housed in the *Museo Preistorico Pigorini* and the *Villa Giulia* in Rome (q.v.).

Morlupo (14 km. W.): In the medieval old town near the *Castello Orsini* (13–16C) the baroque parish church of *S.Giovanni Battista* and the 15&16C altar pictures in the church of *S.Salvatore* are of interest. Near the cemetery on the road to Capena is the Romanesque church of *S.Leone* (11C); it has fragments of ancient sculpture set in the wall of the apse.

02046 Magliano Sabino

Rieti   p.321 □ D 2

The most striking features of this little town, with the exception of some medieval areas, are the streets and squares with stately 16C Renaisssance buildings, the period when the new town (founded 1495) became a significant force in the Papal States. Legend has it that the name is derived from the Roman patrician family of Manlius.

Madonna delle Grazie (Via Romana): This church was rebuilt in the 19C; the Romanesque crypt from the earlier building, with numerous 15C frescos, has survived. 15C Madonna of Mercy, a gift to his birthplace by the Venetian commander Mariano Falconi in the 16C; the magnificent robe is in chased silver (17C).

Cathedral of **S.Liberatore** (Via Cardinale di Lai): The basilica with nave and two aisles was consecrated in 1498 and radically redesigned in the baroque style *c.* 1735; the apse frescos date from this period. In the left apse is a painting by Rinaldo Jacobetti (1521) with the Coronation of the Virgin, and the birth and death of the son of a local nobleman by name of Uliano. Tempera picture of Christ Blessing by followers of Antonio da Viterbo (15C). Finely-worked 16C *statue of the Madonna*.

Also worth seeing: *Piazza Garibaldi* with the Palazzo Communale, built in the 16C and the Episcopal Seminar, one of the first institutions of its kind, established after the Council of Trent (1545–63) for the training of clergy. *S.Pietro* (Piazza Vittorio Veneto): Small 12C Romanesque church with ancient columns.

Environs: Foglia (6 km. S.): Fine wall paintings dating from 1605 in the church of *S.Maria Assunta*. Outside the village *archaeological site* (Zona Archeologica) with the necropolis named after the village.

01010 Marta

Viterbo   p.320 □ B 2

This fishing village (eels are a speciality) at the point where the river of the same name flows out towards the Tyrrhenian sea has historic narrow streets, some medieval houses and a promenade on the bank of the lake which make it one of the most charming places on the Lago di Bol-

Magliano Sabino, Palazzo Communale

sena. Marta was first mentioned in the 10C, and was always a church possession, except for a short period spent under the control of the Farnese family in the 16C. **'Barabbata':** Feast of reconciliation with procession to the plain Romanesque church (with Renaissance portal) of *Madonna del Monte* on 14 May, when farmers and fishermen dedicate fruits from the early harvest, young animals and implements.

Castle: Ruins of the building commissioned *c*. 1264 under Pope Urban IV, who was born in France (apparently using material from Bisenzio, which had been destroyed on the Pope's orders); it has a tower with an octagonal top storey (Torre dell'Orologio).

Environs: Isola Martana (2.5 km. NE): Amalaswintha, daughter of

Theoderic the Great, King of the Ostrogoths, was held prisoner on the island in AD 534&5, and finally drowned in the lake. Ruins of the 9C church of S.Stefano and the medieval castle.

04028 Minturno
Latina   p.323☐H 6

This little medieval town in the foothills of the Monti Aurunci has fine views; it was founded *c*. 580–90 by refugees from the ancient town of *Minturnae* (see below), which had been destroyed. It was called *Traetto*, and was ruled by various lords, including the dell'Aquila, Colonna and Carafa families, until 1879.

Cathedral of S.Pietro: The cathedral was built in the 12C and enlarged in the 13&14C; the three-storey Romanesque *campanile* in front of the façade has biforium windows decorated with inserted small columns. The 12–14C portico with inscriptions and architectural fragments leads to the interior, which is divided into a nave and two aisles by two rows of high columns; there are 17&18C baroque additions. The most valuable feature of the lavish furnishings are the *pulpit* (1620) decorated with splendid Cosmati-work and a *Paschal candelabrum* dating from 1264, also decorated with mosaic.

Castello: The appearance of the 12&13C castle with round main tower and numerous watch-towers has been altered by modern additions and rebuilding to provide accommodation. In the past it housed many famous visitors, including St.Thomas Aquinas, Alfonso of Aragon, Isabella

Minturnae 1 Ausonian settlement 2 Roman colony 3 Town walls 4 Porta Gemina 5 Aqueduct 6 Amphitheatre 7 Forum with two temples 8 Imperial temple 9 Theatre 10 British Military Cemetery

Colonna and Giuila Gonzaga, who was much pursued for her beauty. In the nearby *medieval quarter* picturesque alleyways, steps and medieval houses, some of them with inserted corner columns, have survived, despite bomb damage.

Environs: Minturnae (5 km. SE): The Via Appia leads through this little place, originally an Ausonian colony, enlarged as a Roman colony in 295 BC, and in the E. crosses the *Liris* river, the modern Garigliano; the early imperial harbour on its banks made the town prosperous for a time. The population was driven into the nearby Auruncan Hills by the unhealthy climate of the surrounding marshes and barbarian raids in the early Middle Ages. After this time it fell into decay, and was never rebuilt; the remains of the town have been excavated from 1817. In this way the foundation walls of parts of the Ausonian setlement and the Roman colony were revealed, and also the ring wall and its two gates. In the W. part of the town is the *aqueduct*, sections of which have survived; it comes as far as

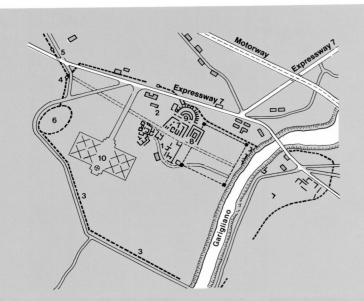

the W. Porta Gemina; the outlines of an amphitheatre can be discerned, but it has not yet been excavated. In front of the 1C BC Roman theatre are the remains of the baths near the central forum, and of several *temples*, of which the oldest (6C BC) was dedicated to the old Italic fertility goddess Marica. The theatre is in good condition; it has a radius of *c.* 130 ft., could seat approximately 4,600 spectators, and has a raised stage. Since 1961 it has been used for its original purpose: classical works are performed in the summer.

01014 Montalto di Castro

Viterbo   p.320☐A 2

This little country town on the ancient Via Aurelia, which dates back to the Etruscan market town of *Forum Aurelium*, was colonized *c.* 242 BC; it still has its charming medieval centre, some of which is still surrounded by the ring wall.

Castello Guglielmi: The 13–16C medieval castle has been largely rebuilt and converted to provide accommodation. *Il Mascherone:* Baroque fountain endowed by Pope Clement XI, with coat of arms and the mask which gave the fountain its name on the water pipe.

Environs: Castello and **Ponte dell'Abbadia** (12 km. N.): Interesting and impressive complex: the *castle* (12&13C) is a former abbey, presumably destroyed in the 10C by the Saracens, and given up, then rebuilt by the Cistercians; until 1850 it was a Papal customs point on what was once the N. border of the Papal States with Tuscany. Seat of the *Museo Nazionale di Vulci:* Large collection including particularly 10–5C BC ceramics.
The bold curve of the 105 ft. bridge over the Fiora gorge is impressive evidence of ancient building skills: the 4–3C BC Etruscan bridge outside the N.

gate of Vulci was reinforced *c.* 90 BC by Roman engineers.
Vulci (11.5 km. N.): Town lost after destruction by the Saracens in the 9&10C AD. In ancient times Vulci was one of the richest city-states in Etruria, famous for its bronze work and ceramic production (including black-figured vases in the 5C) at a high technical and artistic level. It was one of the last Etruscan centres to be conquered and forced into an alliance by the Romans, in 280 BC; its decline could not be arrested when the Roman colony of *Cosa Volcientum* was founded (the ruins of this Roman and of the medieval town, completely destroyed from 1330, are near the Tuscan coastal town of Ansedonia). Excavations have been under way since 1956, and have revealed the podium of an Etruscan temple and also Roman buildings and streets, among other things. The *necropolises* outside the town and largely beyond the Fiora are the among the most important of the many archaeological and art-historical features. Lucien Bonaparte, Prince of Canino and then

Castello Guglielmi in Montalto di Castro

owner of the site, which has proved to be one of the richest sources of finds in Italy, put the first excavations in train in 1828, after a chance find. Scientific excavation has so far produced *c.* 30,000 tombs in the Vulci necropolises, from the period of Villanova culture to approximately the 4&3C BC. The grave goods (a large number of which are in the Villa Giulia Etruscan Museum in Rome and the Archaeological Museum in Florence) include lavishly decorated bronze utensils, gold jewellery, statuettes and several thousand *Attic vases* of the highest quality (some more valuable than pieces found in Greece itself), which confirm the high level of trade between these peoples.

The most famous tomb is the grave chamber revealed in 1857 and named after its discoverer, the archaeologist Alessandro François (**'Tomba François'** in the 'Ponte Rotto' necropolis): The wall paintings found in the central chamber (2) of the complex, which dates from the 5&4C BC, and some of the side chambers (3–9), which are reached by the 65 ft. long passageway, or 'dromos' (1), were not painted until the late 2C or early 1C BC; they are now in the Villa Albani-Torlonia in Rome. The artificial mound of earth known as 'Coccumella' (among other variations on the name) is nearly 500 ft. in diameter; it is the largest known tomb in Etruria, and was probably also a sacrifical mound. The passageways leading to the treasure chambers, and the fact that certain spaces have been filled up with earth, have made the series of grave chambers into a labyrinth of which it is difficult to form a complete impression.

02040 Montebuono Sabino
Rieti   p.321 □ D 2

This village is a charming example of a medieval settlement with its ring wall almost complete, and little alleyways; some of the towers of the wall have been incorporated into later residential buildings.

Parish church of S.Giovanni Battista: This church was redesigned in the baroque style in the 17C; it has a 16C high altar panel and a 15C marble tabernacle of elegant design.

Environs: Fianello (8 km. W.): Historic village nestling around its medieval castle. *S.Maria Assunta* (near the cemetery): There are fragments of late Gothic frescos in the impressive ruins of this Romanesque church with crypt under the high choir; marble bishop's throne in the apse from the period in which the church was built.
Rocchete-Rocchettine (3 km. E.): Small village on a lonely, Romantic site, divided by the Aia brook; there are formerly threatening castles and

Montefiascone, S.Margherita ▷

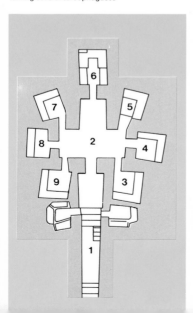

Vulci, Tomba/tomb of François 1 Dromos **2** Central chamber **3–9** Side chambers, each containing several sarcophaguses

old houses, some of which have been abandoned. In the parish church of Rocchete are two 17C baroque paintings by Girolamo Troppa, whose home was here.

S.Pietro (0.5 km. NW): The Romanesque church was started in the late 12C on the site of Roman baths; it was consecrated in the mid 13C; the chapel on the right of the apse is a Gothic extension dating from the 15C. Important frescos (though not all are in good condition) dating from the 14C to the late 15C: they include works of the Umbrian school on both sides of the entrance; a 14C Annunciation of the Florentine school above the arch in the right aisle; under the arch is a representation of historical personages and various saints. There are signed works by Giacomo di Roccantica dated 1451 in the semicircular apse, taken over from the baths.

S.Polo (4.5 km. S.): Three notable tempera pictures (15C) in the church of *SS.Pietro e Paolo*. Outside: *S.Maria della Noce* with extremely fine frescos dating from the 16C.

Tarano Sabino (2 km. S.) has kept its medieval character within the walls with defensive towers. Parish church of *S.Maria Assunta:* Interesting late Romanesque building (fragments of a Roman sculpture with a nymph and a satyr under the portal pediment); the campanile was completed in 1214.

01027 Montefiascone

Viterbo   p.320☐C 2

The earliest definite evidence of a settlement is of the period when the population was fleeing to the hills from the plain on the SE bank of the lake before the invading warrior hordes at the time of the fall of the Roman Empire. Montefiascone is known for the white muscatel wine which goes under the name 'Est, Est, Est'. Legend has it that a servant of the prelate Johannes Fugger, on a journey from Augsburg to Rome, was supposed to write 'est' (meaning

Montefiascone, S.Flaviano, Lower church **1**
Font

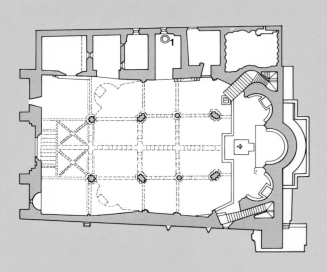

roughly 'there is some here') above the gates of all towns where he found good wine; he was so enthusiastic about Montefiascone's delicious wine that he felt moved to say it three times. The historic procession during the traditional wine festival in early August is a reminder of this incident.

S.Flaviano: This two-storey church, based on the principle of Chàrlemagne's Palatinate Chapel in Aix-la-Chapelle, consecrated in 805, is a unique work of medieval Italian architecture, both as a stylistic concept and in its execution. Special features include the aisle apses in the lower church, curving outwards like a bow from the central axis; this could possibly be a forerunner of the Gothic ambulatory, found particularly in French cathedrals. The *lower church* was started in 1032 on the site of an earlier church which probably dated from the 6C; the upper church was completed in the late 12C. Gothic façade dating from 1262; Renaissance loggia (first half of the 16C). Lavishly decorated capitals with some possibly Etruscan decoration; striking are the capital of the penultimate column on the right, with a figure pulling its beard or (on the other side, and likewise according to inscription) is putting fools in their place. There are important *wall paintings*, mainly dating from the 14C: right apse: Annunciation (1575). Main apse: Christ Blessing with St.Paul and St.Peter, with them the patron of the church. Left apse: Baptism of Christ (16C). On the left by the entrance: Crucifixion and Scenes from the life of St.Catherine of Alexandria (15C). Left aisle: (first chapel): Massacre of the Innocents, Entombment, Triumph of Death (15C); (second chapel): Crucifixion, St.Sebastian; (third chapel): among other subjects Madonna and St.Sebastian and St.Barbara, also a 12C font for baptism by immersion (1). *Upper church:* Basilica with nave and two aisles, connected to the lower church by an opening in the nave.

Cathedral of **S.Margherita** (Piazza S.Margherita): This impressive octagonal centrally-planned building was started in 1519, probably to designs

Montefiascone, S.Flaviano, fresco

Montefiascone, S.Flaviano

by the Renaissance architect Michele Sammicheli, and continued in the second half of the 17C by Carlo Fontana to a baroque design (his dome, which dominates the building and the town, was completed in the 19C) and concluded in 1840–3 with Paolo Garola's twin-towered façade. Painting of the school of Sassoferrato (17C; first altar on the left): terracotta composition by a follower of the della Robbia family (16C; second altar on the left); 19C wall painting. Stairs to the *crypt* on the left near the entrance.

Castle: (Via della Rocca): Ruins of the massive medieval papal castle.

Also worth seeing: *S.Andrea* (Largo Plebiscito) with Romanesque portal and interesting capitals. *City gate* (Piazza Roma): This was rebuilt in 1744, and leads to the oldest part of the little town, which was badly

damaged by severe earthquakes in the late 17C and early 18C.

Monteleone Sabino
Rieti   p.321 □ E 3

Monteleone still looks impressively medieval; it was built in the 10C over the ruins of the ancient Sabine town of *Trebula Mutuesca*. Numerous fragments of private and public buildings (parts of an amphitheatre, for example; some are incorporated in the medieval buildings), and pictures, particularly of the Roman period. Home of the Roman consul Lucius Mummius.

Parish church of **S.Giovanni Evangelista** with 15C portal and some 16C paintings. Excavations near the church revealed 4–2C BC clay ware. The various marble lions in the village square originally flanked the tombs in the ancient necropolis.

Environs: Poggio S.Lorenzo (6 km. NW): Remains of ancient buildings within the little village include what are presumed to be the ruins of the baths of Titus (second half of the 1C AD).
S.Vittoria (1.7 km. SE): This Romanesque church is very well worth seeing. It was consecrated in 1171, and stands on the site of an earlier church documented in the 9C as the tomb of the saint, who was killed at the time of the Emperor Decius (mid 3C), during the first general persecution of the Christians. Roman tombstones were incorporated in the walls of the façade with ornamental portal and eight-petalled rose window, as had already happened in the case of the 10C campanile. The interior with nave and two aisles was much altered until the 16C; the columns on the right-hand side were probably part of the early-Christian building which was the first on the site, in the late 3C. Frescos (including the patroness of the

church) and a painted 15C carved figure. The Roman *sarcophagus* which once contained the relics of the martyr is in a little room on the right near the altar. Ancient *architectural fragments* are displayed near the church.

Torricella in Sabina (8 km. N.): Tower of the 12C Brancaleone castle. parish church with fine rose window and a fine 15C *painting of the Madonna* of the Umbrian school.

Nepi, cathedral, crypt

01036 Nepi

Viterbo   p.321 □ D 3

The Etruscan town of *Nepet*, set in the country of the Faliscans, who were politically, economically and culturally connected with Etruria, was in the first place a heavily fortified bastion against Roman campaigns to conquer the Etruscan heartlands, further protected by the almost impenetrable forests in the Sabatine Hills in the S. However, when the Roman General Marcus Furius Camillus succeeded in taking Nepi and another town in 391 and 380 BC respectively, the Etruscan power base was rocked to its foundations, with serious consequences, particularly after the destruction of Rome's rival, the town of Veii, in 396 BC. Nepi became a Roman colony at first, and increased in importance with the Romans' destruction of nearby Falerii (now Civita Castellana) in 241 BC, and after the War of the Confederates in 89 BC it became a municipium with full rights of Roman citizenship. It was also much fought over in the early Middle Ages because of its strategic importance (as a bastion against raiders from the North heading for Rome), and was completely destroyed in 568 under the Lombard King Albuin, and resettled from the 9C.

Cathedral of **S.Maria Assunta** (Via Matteotti): Rebuilt in 1831 on the site of the earlier pre-Romanesque/Romanesque building (9–12C) destroyed in 1798, and retaining the portico and crypt. Particularly fine features of the interior are the baroque sarcophagus of St.Romanus (17C) of the school of Gian Lorenzo Bernini (high altar) and Giulio Romano's triptych (first half of the 16C). The large crypt with nine aisles dates from 1180, and was built on the foundations of a Roman temple of Jupiter.

Palazzo Communale (Piazza Umberto I): Work on this impressive building started under Antonio da Sangallo in the mid 16C and was completed to an elegant baroque design during the 18C.

Castle (near the Porta Romana): Impressive ruins of the massive castle built in 1450 by Rodrigo Borgia and rebuilt by the Farnese family in the 16C. Adjacent to it is part of the medieval town wall, incorporating two sections from the Etruscan defensive wall. The majority of the castle buildings still visible date from the 16C, after incorporation into the Papal States.

Also worth seeing: *Aqueduct:* Arches from the water system set up in the 6C AD and rebuilt in 1724; it follows the line of the ancient fortress wall in part. *Madonna delle Grazie* (near the Via Tor di Floridi): small church with plain Romanesque portal; in the interior stoup made up of Roman fragments; to the right of this is the *former Oratorium S.Biagio:* Portal made up of Roman fragments. Traces of apse painting from various periods. Small crypt.

Outside the village Etruscan and Faliscan tombs hewn in the rock have been discovered.

Environs: Castel S.Elía (2.5 km. E.): Village set on the Fontanacupa ditch with remains of the medieval wall with defensive towers. Underground tombs of the Faliscan/Etruscan period inside the village or in the rocky walls of the ditch. The *frescos* in the apse and transept of the basilica of *S.Elía* are an art historian's delight. Tradition has it that there was a Faliscan shrine here, on the site of which the Romans built a temple of Diana, as is clear from architectural frag-

ments. The Christian place of worship is said to have been founded by St.Benedict in 520; hermits had settled in the surrounding caves. The existing 11&12C Romanesque church is a new building extending the various earlier ones (8C building materials were found incorporated in the side portals). The plain interior makes a solemn and mystical impression; it is divided into a nave and two aisles by columns with lavishly decorated capitals, mainly from ancient buildings. In the left aisle are sarcophaguses and various old sections of the building, particularly from the Roman period. In the right aisle are various frescos from different periods, of which the best is a Madonna dating from 1448. The walls of the apse and the transept are covered with a most interesting cycle of wonderful *Romanesque frescos* (late 11–early 12C); the directness of their impact, despite some stylistic links with the East, is in stark contrast with the essentially static, monumental quality of Byzantine painting, so highly esteemed at the time in central and southern Italy.

Outside: *S.Croce in Sassonia:* German Franciscan monastery of the Saxon provincial Order with church of S.Giuseppe. The 144 steps of the staircase carved in the rock over fourteen years by the hermit Andrea Giuseppe Rodio (1743–1819) lead from here to the former hermit's cave, now the much-visited pilgrimage church of *S.Maria ad Rupes* (festival day 12 September). The object of pilgrimage in the little shrine (49 ft. long, 13 ft. high and 29 ft. wide) is a painting of the Madonna dating from the 16&17C.

04010 Norma

Latina   p.322□E 5

This little town was first mentioned in

Nepi, cathedral, dome painting ▷

the 8C, and is set on a high cliff 1,312 ft. above the Pontine plain, which in good weather can be seen just as clearly as the immediate surroundings; the fascinating view combines cleft limestone rocks, bare meadows and olive groves. The local people have never prospered, and so the old buildings have never been modernized. For this reason several picturesque groups of charming old-fashioned black farmhouses dating from the Middle Ages have survived.

Environs: Ninfa (8 km. SW): Pope Alexander was crowned in 1159 in the medieval settlement which was abandoned by the population in 1680 because of epidemics of malaria. It was destroyed by Frederick Barbarossa, then rebuilt in the 11&12C under the Frangipane and Caetani families. The ruined town has been exposed to the elements since the 17C, but has otherwise remained untouched; as it is only open to the public on the first weekend of the month it has been protected from the vandalism of tourists, and so the words of the historian Ferdinand Gregovorius, who spoke of the ivy-covered town on Lake Ninfa as a 'medieval Pompeii', still give a true indication of its present condition. The original *town wall*, the battlemented *Castello Caetani* (14–16C) and many *palaces* and *towers* have survived on the intact streets and squares. The *Villa Caetani* is a botanical garden established *c.* 1900 with more than 10,000 varieties of plant; it is now also a nature conservancy area (WWE) for small animals.

Norba (2 km. NW): This ruined town above Norma, popularly known as *Civita*, is the Latin settlement of *Norba*, founded according to legend by Hercules and later conquered by the Volsci and the Romans, then destroyed in 82 BC. It has a massive *town wall* 2.5 km. long and made up of polygonal blocks; there are three gates, and inside the wall one of the best-preserved and earliest Italic towns, arranged in places like a chess board, with parallel streets intersecting at right angles.

Ninfa, ruined town with Castello Caetani

Norba, detail of the ancient town wall

01028 Orte

Viterbo   p.321 □ D 2

This little town with a charming medieval centre goes back to the Etruscan settlement of *Horta* (Etruscan tombs nearby). Home of the Roman plebeian family of the Hortensii, which produced the famous orator and consul Quintus Hortensius Hortalus (114–50 BC). Because of its strategically advantageous site on the ancient Via Amerina, one of the principal routes between Rome and NE Italy, it was exposed to conquest by the Goths, Byzantines and Lombards in the early Middle Ages.

Cathedral of S.Maria Assunta (Piazza della Libertà): Impressive 18C baroque building; façade by Gregorio Castracchini (1901). High altar panel dating from the time when the church was built, painted by Giuseppe Bottani.

Museo Diocesano d'Arte Sacra/ Diocesan Museum in the church of *S.Silvestro:* 12C Romanesque building on the ruins of a Roman temple of peace, with Gothic additions on the N. side. The most valuable piece in the generally important collection of works of art, especially of the schools of Viterbo and Tuscany (13–15C) is an 8C Byzantine mosaic of the Madonna from the early Christian basilica of St.Peter in Rome.

Environs: Bássano in Teverina (8 km. W.): Early-11C Romanesque church of *S.Maria dei Lumi* with surviving fragments of medieval frescos.

Ostia Antica, old mill

02035 Orvinio
Rieti   p.321 ☐ E 3

The village was renamed (formerly *Canemorto*) in 1860, on the basis of the probably erroneous assumption that this was the site of the Sabine town of Orvinium, which has not yet been definitively located (see Corvaro: Environs Borgorose); it was the site of one of the four most important medieval castles in the province.

S.Maria dei Raccomandati: There are numerous frescos by Vincenzo Manenti in this plain 16C church; the figure in a white cloak on the left near St.Francis is a self-portrait. High altar with Madonna dei Raccomandatii dating from the period when the church was built.

S.Nicola: The original church was consecrated in 1536; the new baroque building is an oval design with a very fine, stylistically coherent interior.

Castello Malvezzi Cambeggi: The extensive medieval castle was later converted into a magnificent residence with a splendid park; the round tower and the defensive wall are striking features retained from the original building.

S.Maria del Piano (1.5 km. NE): Monastery church of a powerful Benedictine abbey, impressive, but starting to fall into ruins; legend has it that the abbey was founded by Charlemagne in thanksgiving for his vic-

Ostia Antica 1 Entrance **2** Porta Romana **3** Piazzale della Vittoria **4** Baths of the carriers **5** Baths of Neptune **6** Firemen's barracks **7** Theatre **8** Piazzale delle Corporazioni **9** Temple of Ceres **10** House of Apuleius **11** Mithraeum of the Seven Spheres **12** Corn store (horrea) **13** House of Diana **14** Drinking house (thermopolium) **15** Forum **16** Capitol **17** Temple of Roma and Augustus **18** Council chamber (curia) **19** Assembly hall (basilica) **20** Circular temple **21** W. gate of the former Castrum **22** Trinacria baths **23** Baths of Mithras **24** Storehouse (horrea epagathiae) **25** House of Cupid and Psyche **26** Baths of the Seven Wise Men **27** House of the Charioteer **28** Christian basilica **29** Overseas trade office (schola traiani) **30** House of the Muses **31** Living quarters and garden **32** Porta Marina **33** Small forum with shrine of the Bona Dea **34** Baths of Marciana **35** Synagogue **36** so-called Imperial Palace **37** Porta Laurentina **38** Campus Magnae Matris **39** House of Fortuna Annonaria **40** Museum

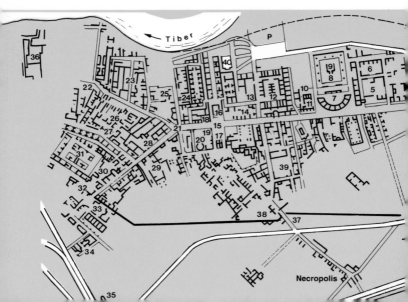

tory over the Saracens at Pozzaglia. Majestic and austere 11C Romanesque building; 15C portal.

00050 Ostia Antica

Comune di Roma   p.320☐C 4

The Roman port of Ostia is now 3 km. inland; it was originally on the former mouth of the Tiber *ostium tiberis,* from which it takes its name. Legend makes propaganda by claiming that it was founded by King Ancus Marcius, but excavations have revealed that this, the oldest Roman colony, was not founded until *c.* 340 BC. The military camp had privileges such as exemption from military service in Rome, and was used for the protection of the saltworks in the estuary and the increasing marine trade. Ostia was the Roman fleet's principal base by *c.* 300 BC, and it increased in importance as a port for Rome's provisions. After the town was plundered by Marius in 87 BC Sulla had the 2.8 km. long wall dating from the time of the town's foundation rebuilt. The town flourished in the 1&2C AD, at which time it had *c.* 80,0000 inhabitants. Because the Tiber was silting up, the Emperor Claudius moved the fleet to the newly-built *Portus Romae* on the coast N. of Ostia (see Environs: Fiumicino). Ostia's decline began when Portus Romae was declared autonomous by Constantine in 314.

Ostia Antica: Pope Gregory IV founded the settlement of *Gregoriopolis* a few hundred yards up the Tiber, N. of the 5C *Basilica S.Aurea.* The town which grew from this is now known as *Ostia Antica,* and on the site of the old basilica, in which St.Monica, mother of St.Augustine is buried, is the small Renaissance church of S.Aurea, built to plans by the Florentine architect Baccio Pontelli. The same architect was commissioned to build the triangular *fortress* W. of Ostia Antica by Cardinal Giuliano delle Rovere, later Pope Julius II. The citadel (1483–6) with battlemented castle incorporated a *defensive tower* built by Pope Martin V in the first half of the 15C. It is one of the first modern fortresses with casemates

Ostia Antica, Corinthian capital

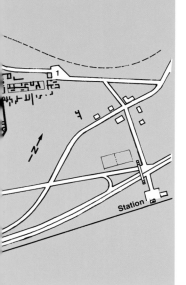

equipped for the use of firearms and guns.

Ostia Scavi: Excavation of the ancient town, buried under rubble and sand, began under Popes Pius VII and Pius IX in the 19C. Systematic scientific excavation has been under way since 1909, and so far about two thirds of the original area of the town has been revealed, giving a detailed picture of life there in ancient times.

Principal sights: Just inside the main entrance to the archaeological zone a small street on the left leads to the **Via delle Tombe** with numerous Republican and imperial *tombs*. Parallel to this street the *Via Ostenis* from Rome reaches the **Porta Romana**. This gate, built under the Republic and decorated with marble in the imperial period leads to the centre of the town and the *Decumanus Maximus*, the main street, 1.2 km. long, in which the most important public buildings are to be found.
On the left at the beginning of the street is the *Piazzale della Vittoria*

with the **colossal statue of Minerva Victoria,** copied from a Greek statue by Skopas (4C AD), and originally part of the decoration in the imperial period of the *Porta Romana*. Opposite the *baths of the cisiarii* carriage drivers) were built in a former warehouse (horrea) in the 1C AD. The floor mosaic shows scenes of daily life in Ostia.
Further into the town is the *Via dei Vigili* which on the right leads to the **Terme di Nettuno,** started under the Emperor Hadrian. There is a good view of the buildings and the floor mosaics (Neptune and sea creatures), which are in good condition, from the first floor. Adjacent to the N. is the **Caserma dei Vigili** (firemen's barracks) dating from the 1C AD; it has a *Caesareum* dedicated to the Emperor and *latrines* in good condition. Along the main street on the right is the **theatre,** built under Agrippa and extended under Septimus Severus and Caracalla in the early 3C; it has 2,700 seats, and plays are now performed here again in the summer. Behind it is the **Piazzale delle Corporazioni** with the former *temple of*

Ostia Antica, thermopolium, interior

Ceres. Around the square are the *offices* of 70 branches of businesses from all over the Roman Empire, as is shown by the coats of arms of the floor mosaics in the original colonnade.

W. of the theatre is the **House of Apuleius,** an impressive building with atrium in the Pompeian style, adjacent to which is the best-preserved of the 19 mithraeums in the town; according to the surviving mosaics it is called the **Mithraeum of the Seven Spheres.** In front of it are four little 2C *temples* on a common podium facing the Decumanus Maximus.

The next street, the *Via dei Molini* leads on the right to large *granaries* and *corn mills,* and to the *Via Diana,* between two-storeyed buildings. The building on the corner, the **Casa di Diana,** confirms that exterior balconies were used in ancient times; there is a *drinking house* (thermopolium) diagonally opposite.

The former military camp forms the square core of the town, the central **forum,** the heart of public life. The *Capitol* in the N. is dedicated to Vul-

can and the Dioscuri, with survivng ancient masonry from the period of Hadrian; opposite are remains of the marble-clad *Temple of Roma and Augustus* (1C AD) with the **Amazon Statue of Roma the Conqueror**. On the E. side of the square are the *forum baths* in the S. (2–4C), on the W. side in the N. the *council hall* (curia) and in the S. the originally marble-clad *basilica* for public meetings, with a *round temple* (3C) with spiral staircase adjacent. Near the Bivio del Castrum, the site of the original W. gate of the military camp, the Decumanus Maximus turns half left to the Porta Marina and the *Via della Foce* turns half right to the *Terme di Trinacria* and the *Termeu di Mitra* with fine wall paintings. The *Via Horrea Epagathiana* leads N. from here to the palace-like **warehouse** of the same name with monumental portal and courtyard with two-storey arcades; opposite is the atrium house **Domus di Amore e Psiche,** built in the 4C AD.

Between the *Via della Foce* and the *Cardine degli Aurighe,* which branch off from the Decumanus Maximus on

Ostia Antica, masks outside the theatre

the right, are the **Baths of the Seven Wise Men** with a round domed hall and lavish fresco and mosaic decoration, and the **Insula degli Aurighi** (house of the charioteer) with a fine façade; of interest on the Decumanus is the 2–4C **Christian basilica**, former baths turned into an early-Christian church with nave and one aisle. The *Schola di Traianum* diagonally opposite was the seat of an office for long-distance trade.

Shortly before the *Porta Marina* on the right are two houses which are slightly concealed: the **Casa delle Muse** with restored colonnaded courtyard amd rooms decorated with frescos and mosaic and behind that the **Casa a Giardino** (2C AD): this residence built around a rectangular park with two residential blocks in the gardens gives a good impression of Roman domestic culture.

Outside the *Porta Marina* is a little forum with the **Shrine of the Bona Dea**, *tombs* from the Republican period and the **Terme della Marciana,** with mosaic baths used until the 6C. The oldest **synagogue** in Europe (started in the 1C AD) in the

Ostia Antica, necropolis

SE and a palace of the imperial period, the so-called **Palazzo Imperiale** with an interesting *Lararium* and a little *mithraeum* NW of the baths, were, like the baths, originally on the beach. Near the S. gate, the Porta Laurentina are the triangular **Campus Magnae Matris** with shrines of oriental divinities and to the N. the **Casa della Fortuna Annonaria,** a late imperial palace with marble floors, mosaics, statues and frescos.

Museum: From the main entrance an avenue on the right leads to the *Museo Ostiense*, established in a former salt store built *c.* 1500 with a neoclassical façade dating from 1868. The eleven rooms have displays of objets d'art and utensils found in the course of the excavations.

Environs: Fiumicino (9 km. NW): The **Porto di Traiano** SE of *Leonardo da Vinci* airport is of greater cultural and historical importance than this lively fishing village and holiday resort N. of the estuary. The Emperor Trajan commissioned the hexagonal *artificial harbour basin*, completed in 103, as a result of the silting up of the Portus Romae, built by the Emperor Claudius in AD 42–46, and protected by moles. Forty columns on the six quays were used to moor up to two hundred ships. The **Fossa Traiana** has survived alongside the various ruins of warehouses, docks, baths, temples and arcades. This canal connected the harbour with the sea and the Tiber, and bore the name *Focem micinam*, which has survived with slight distortion as the name of the coastal resort of Fiumicino, not founded until 1825.

Isola Sacra (4 km. W.): The *necropolises of Portus Romae* were buried under sand until they were excavated, and have survived in very good condition. Approximately one hundred tombs show various 2–4C AD burial customs.

00036 Palestrina

Roma   p.322☐E 4

The ancient town of *Praeneste* dates back to Homeric times; in 499 BC it shifted its allegiance from the Latin Confederation to Rome. In 82 BC Sulla had the town destroyed and the citizens executed as associates of Marius. He spared the temple and the oracle of the goddess *Fortuna Primagenia*, to make his peace with her. Medieval *Palestrina* was built on the

Captions for the next two pages:

Palestrina, Archaeological Museum, 'The Nile in Flood', mosaic of the imperial period, details

site of the town destroyed by the Lombards, and the temple precinct. The bishopric became the property of the Barberini family from 1630. The town's most famous son is the great musical innovator Giovanni Pierluigi da Palestrina (1524–94).

Temple of Fortuna Primagenia: Bombing in the Second World War removed medieval accretions, and in 1952–5 excavation began of the upper temple of the shrine, set on four terraces on the slope and with an upper and a lower temple. The lower buildings were integrated by Sulla; they include the trefoil oracle grotto *Antro delle Sorti* (4C BC) and the *Temple of Juno* (3C BC), which are now underneath the cathedral, which has a medieval *campanile* and an episcopal seminary. The grotto on the left with remains of floor mosaics and the oracle room on the right with shallow

Ostia Antica, sarcophagus, detail

niches are usually accessible via the left-hand door of the seminary; they are closed at the time of writing. The upper shrine was set on the symmetrical *ramps* which have been excavated and the three *terraces with colonnades* connected by three central flights of steps. The square in front of them broadens towards the slope into a theatre-like exedra, which used to lead to the shrine with the statue of Fortuna Primagenia.

Archaeological Museum: Finds from the temple precinct have been on show in the Palazzo Colonna-Barberini since 1955; they include a remarkable chased *bronze mirror* and a *mosaic* of the imperial period.

Environs: Castel S. Pietro Romano (4km. N): High above Palestrina, this picturesque medieval town built above the former Acropolis of Praeneste, has retained its polygonal walled lay-out. There is a wonderful panorama stretching as far as Rome from the nearby ruins of the *Rocca dei Colonna* (14&15C).

Genazzano (11 km. E.): The medieval town is dominated by the medieval *Castello Colonna*, rebuilt in the 15C by Oddone Colonna (Pope Martin V), who was born here, and extended by Cesare Borgia. Important features of the town are the church of *S.Croce* with 13C frescos, the *Santuario della Madonna del Buon Consiglio* (13–17C) with a legendary miraculous image and fine Cosmati-work floor, and also the *Casa Apolloni* with external staircase and biforium façade (14C). Roman ruins in the area, including a *nymphaeum* with fine columns and arches.

Zagarolo (8 km. W.): There are numerous Roman reliefs and imperial architectural fragments in the masonry of the *town gate* of Zagarolo. The two monolithic granite columns near the *Palazzo Colonna* (14–17C) are also Roman spoils.

03018 Paliano

Frosinone   p.323 □ F 4

In the Middle Ages this town, settled

Genazzano, Castello Colonna (left), Palestrina, temple of Fortuna Primigenia (right)

since the 3C, and Palestrina formed the power base of the noble Colonna family, which included high church dignitaries, outstanding political and military figures and the Renaissance poetess Vittoria, Marchesa di Pescara, who was in touch with Michelangelo and other important intellectuals of the period.

Piazza Roma: Collegiate church of *S.Andrea:* Burial place of the Colonnas of Paliano. *Palazzo Colonna:* This impressive building in dark tufa was built for Filippo Colonna in 1620. Elegant fountain with putto in the centre of the square (17C).

Castello (now penal institution): Despite later rebuilding the main tower, which still dominates the building, and the double ring wall, still show the massive scale of the fortress built in the 16C by the military architect Fustino da Camerino for Marcantonio Colonna on the site of the medieval castle.

Environs: Serrone (8 km. NE): The site has been settled since ancient times, and the little town was repeatedly destroyed in various wars. The historic core includes remains of a *cyclopean wall* from the pre-Roman period and some Roman buildings, as well as the ruins of the 15C *Colonna castle.*

00018 Palombara Sabina
Roma   p.321□E 3

Old town: The streets and medieval buildings of the little Lombard town of *Palumbaria*, mentioned in the 11C, rise in a spiral around a pyramid-shaped hill, surmounted by the *Castello Savelli* (16C) and its 11C keep. The high altar painting by Antoniazzo Romano is worth seeing in the *Chiesa dell'Annunziata*, a Renaissance church redesigned in the baroque style.

S.Giovanni di Argentella: The Romanesque church of S.Giovanni d'Argentella is in a valley not far from the town (2 km. SW) in a cherry tree plantation, near the ruins of an abbey founded in the 8C by Basilian monks. There are Roman and medieval architectural fragments in the porch; the *niche fresco* in the façade (Madonna and Child) shows Byzantine influence. The four storeys of the tall *campanile* are pierced by single, double and and triple windows. The interior has a nave and two aisles, and interesting remains of 14C frescos and an *altar wall* with Cosmati-work decoration.

03020 Pástena
Frosinone   p.323□G 5

Pástena was founded in the first half of the 13C; it had a castle, and was built on the site of a lost Volsci settlement. It is famous for its caves, explored since 1926, which are among the most interesting and impressive in Europe.

Grotte di Pástena (4.5 km. N.): Two karst *caves with stalactites*, one above the other, with a common entrance (over 80 ft. high). The upper system of caves is extremely impressive; it is almost 700 yards long, and is open to the public.

02025 Petrella Salto
Rieti   p.323□F 3

Characteristic features of the atmospheric medieval centre of the little town are narrow, crooked streets and houses with typical 14&15C doors and windows, and also the ruins of the castle. In 1598 the castle was the scene of the murder of the feared and violent Count Francesco Cenci; despite the confession extracted under torture of the principal guilty party, the

Count's daughter Beatrice, whom he had ruthlessly ill-treated, and who was executed with her accomplices on the Ponte Sant'Angelo in Rome in 1599, the people declared her free of all guilt, as the murderess of a tyrant. Her fate and this moral dilemma are the subject of Shelley's tragedy of 1819 'The Cenci'.

S.Andrea (near the end of the village): Elegant façade dating from the first half of the 17C, still of Mannerist design. Lavish baroque altar. Near the church is the *Palazzo Maoli*, opposite the defiant *Seat of the Castellan of Colonna*, both 16C.

Parish church of **SS.Annunziata:** 12C Romanesque building with Gothic windows and fine 15C portal. The interior with nave and one aisle was redesigned in the baroque style; particularly fine is the painting of the *Rosary Madonna* (third altar on the right).

Environs: Capradosso (7 km. NW): This little village is based on the ancient settlement of *Cliternia*.

Petrella Salto, parish church

S.Maria: 15C late Gothic frescos (Last Judgement, Crucifixion and St.Sebastian and St.Maurus), all by the artist responsible for the majority of the wall paintings in the S.Giovanni baptistery in the church of S.Maria 'extra moenia'.

S.Maria Appari (also *S.Maria della Cerasa*) (0.5 km. S.): Pilgrimage church dating from 1562; the façade is elegant and rhythmical (tower 1672). The altars have alternate round and pointed gables.

03026 Pofi

Frosinone   p.323☐G 5

Founded in 1533, and owned for a long time by the Colonna family. Characteristic of the historic medieval centre are the defensive wall with towers, twisty streets, arches, and the 16C Palazzo Colonna, which has survived in good condition.

S.Antonio: 11C Romanesque church; single-aisled interior with frescos of the Last Judgement. In the more modern part of the village on the S. slope is **S.Pietro**, with a 19C high altar picture of the Madonna with St.Peter and St.Paul by Peter of Copenhagen in the style of the 15C Umbrian school.

The **local museum** (in the Palazzo Communale) has a collection including prehistoric clay goods and bones of animals.

02047 Poggio Mirteto

Rieti   p.321☐E 3

This little town consists of a historic core, still partially surrounded by the 14C defensive wall, and a modern section including the long *Piazza Martiri della Libertà* beyond the *Porta Farnese* (1512 with coats of arms of the community and the heraldic lilies of the Farnese family).

The remains of Roman buildings in the area (including the *baths of Lucilla*) are evidence of settlement in ancient times; charter from 1837. In 1841 Poggio Mirteto became a suburbicarian bishopric and since 1925 has been combined with Sabina.

Palazzo Episcopale (Piazza Dottori): Massive medieval building of austere appearance rebuilt in the 15&16C (especially noticeable around the windows); 19C portal.

Cathedral of **S.Maria Assunta** (Piazza Martiri della Libertà): Monumental building (1641–1725) with harmoniously articulated façade. Interior: 18C stucco with ornaments, and also scenes and figures from the New Testament and the history of the church. On the high altar signed painting by Giuseppe Romano (1617). Baroque altars from the period when the church was built in the chapels. Above the square **baroque church of S.Rocco** dating from 1785.

S.Paolo (near the cemetery): There are stylistically interesting frescos in the single-aisled interior of the 12C Romanesque church with 13C Gothic alterations: they include the Triumph of Death (late 13C) with verses in contemporary dialect; Annunciation and Entombment (14C); the frescos dated 1521 in the choir are the work of Lorenzo Torresani.

Environs: Bocchignano (3.5 km. SE): The village still has some of its medieval ring wall, and also houses packed closely together, some of them on ancient foundations, giving the place an impressively historic feel. Parish church of *S.Giovanni Evangelista* with three-storey campanile surviving from the original **Romanesque** building, which otherwise has been largely reconstructed.
Castel S.Pietro (3 km. E.): Fragments of Roman sculpture and interesting stones with inscriptions have been built into the entrance to the courtyard of the largely rebuilt *Palazzo Bonaccorsi*. In the *cemetery chapel* Gothic frescos of the Madonna Enthroned, dated 1422.
Montópoli in Sabina (3 km. S.):

Capradosso (Petrella Salto), panorama

Priverno, Palazzo Comunale

The defensive tower, which is in good condition, and the campanile of the Gothic church of *S.Michele Arcangelo* dominate the medieval centre of the village. The consistent design of the buildings in the residential area makes them worth seeing; they date from the Renaissance and are reached through a 16C gate. Remains of private and public ancient buildings, sculpture and utensils have been discovered right up to the present day, and they are evidence of the relatively dense population of the area in ancient times.

Baroque monastery church of *S.Maria delle Grazie* (on the edge of the village) with carefully designed interior featuring good stucco and wall paintings of the school of Vincenzo Manenti (mid 17C).

Poggio Catino (5 km. N.): The towers of the medieval ring wall, part of which has survived, were incorporated in later buildings. Home of the scholarly Benedictine Gregorio, whose important works include the early-12C Chronicle of the Abbey of Farfa. The fragments of Roman wall found near the cemetery (1C BC) are held by local tradition to be part of the baths of Sulla.

02030 Poggio Nativo
Rieti   p.321 □ E 3

S.Paolo: Remains of marble decoration (probably 13C) on the portal and floor of the interior; the skill with which it was executed points to the Cosmati group of artists.

Environs: Osteria Nuova (4 km. W.): *Grotta dei Massacci:* Tomb constructed of massive stone blocks; the entrance to the passageway leading into the interior is supported by a monolith over 12 ft. long.

03037 Pontecorvo
Frosinone   p.323 □ G 5

This little town, rebuilt after being almost completely destroyed in the battle of Cassino in 1944, has had a lively history. It consists of the historic district of Civita and the left bank of the Liri and the modern area of Pastine on the plain. The citadel was built in 886, and named after an existing bridge over the river which was apparently crooked (pons curvus); the modern name of the town is just an Italian version of this, and not a reference to the traditional popular derivation 'crow bridge', on which the coat of arms is based. In the 18C Pontecorvo was conquered by the King of Naples, and in the Napoleonic Wars was alternately under the Popes and the French.

Parish church of **S.Bartolomeo:** This church was built on the remains of the 9C castle and reconstructed, after being destroyed in the war, alongside the surviving campanile. There is assumed to be an ancient shrine of Flora under the church of **S.Maria Immacolata**. Various frescos (early 17C) in the apse attributed to Giuseppe d'Arpino, known as Cavalier d'Arpino.

Environs: Espéria (13 km. S.): Parish church of *S.Maria Maggiore:* The original Romanesque building near the Madonna di Loreto chapel was redesigned in the baroque style in 1745. In the interior is a picture of the Outpouring of the Holy Spirit, by Taddeo Zuccaro (second half of the 16C). On the right near the church is the present *Palazzo della Pretura*, started for Fabrizio Spinelli in 1474. Door dating from 1481. Ruins of the medieval *castle* near the little baroque church of *S.Maria delle Grazie*.
Santuario di **S.Maria di Monte Léucio** (5.5 km. NW): Lonely church dating from 1513 at the top of the hill of the same name (1542 ft.).

04015 Priverno

Latina   p.323□F 5

The medieval town of *Piperno* came into being on the ridge above the river Amaseno after the acropolis of the ancient *Privernum* (see below) was destroyed by the Saracens. The late medieval buidings of the picturesque little town show clear influence of French Gothic.

Cathedral of S.Maria Assunta: This cathedral at the top of a magnificent flight of steps in the *Piazza Vittorio Emanuele II* with its many fountains was consecrated in 1283; it was rebuilt in 1782, and lost much of its original Gothic-Cistercian austerity. The portico with three arches leads to the interior with nave and two aisles, which has been completely rebuilt, with the exception of a few

Priverno, cathedral, column ▷

columns in the choir; it contains the head reliquary of St.Thomas Aquinas (fourth chapel on the right). Below the high altar is a fine 17C *wooden sculpture* (body of Christ).

Palazzo Communale: On the right near the cathedral is the Gothic Town Hall (13&14C); the lower storey has two long runs of arches. The upper storey is decorated with biforium windows and a little bell turret.

S.Giovanni (Via Orsini): Small church with sections from the original Gothic building. Frescos of various periods (14C and later).

Environs: Privernum (3 km. N.): The ruins of this town, originally a Volscian, and conquered by the Romans in 394 BC, were discovered in 1899 near the church of *Madonna di Mezz'Agosto*. Excavations are still not complete; so far they have revealed the foundations of two *temples* and several *villas* of the Republican era.

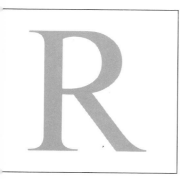

Rieti

Rieti   p.321 □ E 2

Capital of the province of the same name. The interesting historic centre

◁ *Priverno, S.Giovanni, Madonna fresco*

with numerous important medieval ecclesiastical and secular buildings and quarters with a great deal of atmosphere (especially around the Via Romana, Via del Porto, Via S.Ruffo) is still largely surrounded by the 13C town wall. Ancient *Reate*, once a Sabine centre, was subjugated by Rome in 288 BC. It was a regional centre of administration under the Lombards and the Franks. Gregory IX received Emperor Frederick II here in 1234, and canonized St.Dominic; Nicholas IV also crowned Charles of Anjou King of Naples here in 1289.

S.Agostino (Piazza Mazzini): 13C Gothic church with campanile from the earlier Romanesque building (12C); the rose window (1901) is imitation Gothic; 14C marble portal: lunette fresco of the Siennese school (1354). The interior was redesigned in the baroque style in the late 18C.

SS.Camillo e Ruffo (Piazza S. Ruffo): The interior of this church founded in the 14C and later much rebuilt was redesigned very skilfully in the baroque style in the 17C.

S.Francesco (Piazza S.Francesco): Early Gothic building (1245–53) dating from about two decades after the death of St.Francis of Assisi, the founder of the Order. Portal still Romanesque in design; baroque lunette fresco by Vincenzo Manenti (17C). Rose window in similar style dating from 1926. The Rule of the Order required simplicity in architecture as well as in other matters, and the interior is accordingly austere, with later side chapels and baroque additions dating from 1635. Important apse frescos revealed recently with stylistic traits of the school of Giotto (first half of the 14C).

Cathedral of **S.Maria Assunta** (Piazza Cesare Battisti): Originally a 5C basilica rebuilt in 1109 and consecrated in 1225; the crypt was completed as early as 1157, the chapels were added later. Massive Romanesque campanile dating from 1252 by the architects Andrea, Enrico and Pietro, who practised in Rome in particular; on the base are fragments of a fresco by Marcantonio di Antoniazzo (1510) representing the miracle of the bell; peal of four bells cast in the 18&19C.

The spacious interior was almost completely redesigned in the baroque style in 1639. Left-hand aisle: in the first chapel remains of a Madonna fresco by Antoniazzo Romano (1494); the third chapel was rebuilt in 1843 from designs by Giuseppe Valadier; at its side is a child's tomb by Federico Fiorentino, 1511; in the fourth, the Barbara chapel, decorated by Gian Lorenzo Bernini, Carlo Fontana and other baroque artists, is a statue of the town's revered patron saint by Giovanni Antonio Mari (1657) from a design by Bernini; there are also several figures of saints and scenes from the life of Barbara (18C). Frescos by Pietro Paoletti in the choir (1829). Right aisle: in the first chapel painting of the Madonna with St.Vincent and St.Nicholas of Bari by Bartolomeo Torresani (1528); fine 16C carved figure of St.Roch (second chapel); Guardian Angel by Andrea Sacchi in the third chapel, which was painted by V.Manenti in the course of the baroque redesign of the church; Manenti, working with the stucco artist Gregorio Grimani, was also responsible for the Cappella del Sacramento (1629), which contains two paintings by Giovanni Francesco Romanelli dating from 1653. The right aisle gives access to the interesting nine-aisled *hall crypt* with lavishly decorated columns.

S.Pietro Martire (Via dalla Molina): This little 13C Romanesque church has an extraordinarily lavish baroque interior (17C). Magnificent heavy wooden ceiling by local master carver Andrea Massini (1628), gilded by Ludovico Gonnetti (1653). On G.Grimani's high altar is a Martyrdom of the Patron saint dating from 1657; side paintings by V.Manenti. Side altars by Antonio Ravazzini (1682); St.Agatha (right) by A.Manenti (1616).

Rieti, S.Agostino, portal capital (left), S.Francesco, portal (right)

S.Scolastica (Via T.Varrone): This baroque church (1696–1717) is of general artistic interest: it is on a Greek cross plan and was designed by A.Ravazzini, who was also responsible for the stucco, designed by Francesco Fontana. High altar by Filippo Brioni; painting by Girolamo Pesci. Torment of Andrew by A.Sacchi on the right-hand altar.

Palazzo Comunale (Piazza Vittorio Emanuele II): The original Town Hall building was 13C, rebuilt in the 16C; the austere design of the earlier building is visible in the Via della Pescheria, façade by F.Brioni (1748); some alterations were made in 1909 when the building was being repaired after severe earthquake damage. It houses the *Biblioteca Comunale/Town Library* and the *Museo Civico/Municipal Museum*.

Palazzo del Governo, also *Palazzo Vincentini* (Piazza C.Battisti): Late Renaissance building (late 16–early 17C) designed by Giovanni Domenico Bianchi, and incorporating some parts of an older building.

Palazzo Vecchiarelli (57 Via Roma): This splendid palace, built *c.* 1597–1618 by Carlo Maderno, combines late Renaissance and early baroque design. The fine courtyard with portico and loggia, and fountains on the façade side, shows skilful articulation of enclosed space.

Palazzo Vescovile (Piazza Marino Vittori): Work started on the bishop's residence, one of the great secular buildings of the period, in 1283 under the direction of the architect Andrea. In 1288 the so-called papal loggia on two massive arches was built in front of it; one of the stones in the loggia is a memorial to the marriage in 1185 of Henry VI of Hohenstaufen to Constanza, the daughter of the King of Sicily. There is a spacious portico divided into two aisles by cruciform pillars on the ground floor. Above this is a hall of unusual dimensions 1329 ft long, 50 ft. wide and 40 ft. high; Renaissance door dating from 1535. Two other rooms were painted by V.Manenti in the first half of the 17C.

Town wall: Fragments of the Roman

Rieti, cathedral (left), foliage on central portal (right)

fortification have survived in the Via della Peschiera (tower), Via Roma and Via Pelliceria. The impressive medieval construction, dating mostly from the 13C (with later additions), with battlements and square and semicircular towers, has survived almost completely on the N. border of the old town. *Porta d'Arce:* This town gate was rebuilt to its original mid-13C design after being destroyed in 1944; it stands at the beginning of the Via Salaria, the old salt road and one of the ancient arterial routes connecting Rome and the N. Adriatic coast.

Teatro Flavio Vespaiano (Via Garibaldi): Municipal theatre by Achille Sfondrini (1893). The atrium has frescos on allegorical subjects by A.-Calcagnadoro (1909), who a year before had created the stage curtain showing the Conquest of Jerusalem by Vespasian's son Titus (AD 70). The ceiling painting by Giulio Rolland (1901) in the auditorium shows the triumph of Titus.

Museo Civico/Municipal Museum (in the Palazzo Communale; Piazza Vittorio Emanuele II): Interesting Roman sculpture and inscriptions at the foot of the steps on the ground floor. The collection includes prehistoric finds, objets d'art and utensils, particularly of the Roman period, and also fine paintings, sculpture and gold objects from the 13–20C; *Room 8* is devoted to the work of A. Calcagnadoro.

Also worth seeing: *Churches: S.Antonio Abbate* (Via Vignola): This church founded in 1337 was rebuilt in 1570–1611 to plans by the leading Roman architect Giacomo Vignola, who made a significant contribution to the style and dynamics of architectural baroque, a movement which was in its infancy; the church remained incomplete, however. Adjacent is the Municipal Hospital (Ospedale Civile), which was founded at the same time. *S.Benedetto* (Via S.Bene-

detto): Michele Chiesa's baroque version (1718–23) of the original Gothic monastery church has an outstanding, stylistically homogeneous and artistically distinguished interior. *S.Eusanio* (Via S.Eusanio): This building extended in the 15C contains several outstanding 15&16C frescos, some of which have only recently been revealed. *S.Giovenale,* also *Madonna della Scala* (Via Garibaldi): Baroque version, dating from 1741, of a church built in the 15C. To the left of the right-hand altar is the tomb of the poetess Isabella Alfani, wife of the poet A.M.Ricci, with a relief by the Danish sculptor Bertil Thorvaldsen (1829); on the right of the altar is the tomb of Rosa Carmela Ricci, sister of the poet, by Giuseppe Fabris (1842). *S.Giuseppe* (Via Garibaldi): Small and atmospheric baroque rebuilding of the church founded in the 12C. High altar panel with death of St.Joseph and Holy Family on the right-hand altar by V.Manenti. On the left-hand altar St.Leopardo, a youthful work by A.Calcagnadoro (1895). *S.Lucia* (Via S.Lucia): Since it was redesigned in the baroque style in the second half of the 17C, the originally plain 13C building has housed some fine works of art: marble high altar (1682) with stucco by A.Ravazzini; painting of the Resurrection by Cesare Tuppi (1599); statues of St.Francis and St.Clara (1696). The altar on the left was endowed by two sisters of the Order and nieces of G.L.Bernini; painting of St.Laurence at prayer by Ciro Ferri (1655). *S.Pietro Apostolo* (Via Roma): A Gothic wooden door dating from 1462 with very fine carving by Jacopo Santilli was set into the 13C Romanesque portal of this otherwise plain church founded in 1153; façade renewed in 1919. Interior stucco by Bartolomeo Bernasconi (1750). The high altar transferred from S.Domenico was created by F.Brioni in 1747. St.Alexander on the left-hand altar by A.Manenti (1623). *Secular buildings:*

Rieti, cathedral, crypt ▷

The present *Palazzo della Casa di Risparmio* (Via Garibaldi) by M.Chiesa is a good example of 18C secular baroque architecture; portal by Giuseppe Gubleyras (1818). *Palazzo Ricci* (Via T.Varrone): Elegant late-18C neoclassical building designed by Giovanni Stern. The poet A.M.Ricci died here in 1850. *Palazzo del Seminario* (Piazza G.Oberdan): G.Vignola built this impressive group of buildings using the former Palazzo del Podestà (first half of the 14C), of which the *Arco del Seminario* was also part; the first priests' seminary following the guidelines laid down by the Council of Trent was established here in 1564.

Environs: Franciscan places of pilgrimage in the Sacred Valley (Valle Santa) of Rieto (each of the buildings may only be visited if escorted by a brother of the Order): *Fonte Colombo* (5.5 km. SW): According to tradition this is where Christ revealed to St.Francis the final version of the Rule of the Order to be followed by the Minorites. These events and some miracles performed

Rieti, Palazzo Vecchiarelli, courtyard

by the Saint during his various stays here are the subject of numerous works of art which are kept in the building. There is a large 15C Gothic fresco in the portal arch of the church of *SS.Francesco e Bernardino*, consecrated by Cardinal Nicolas of Kues in 1450; in the interior two wooden reliefs by Giovanni da Pisa (17C); the modern stained glass windows are by Duilio Cambellotti. On the left near the church is a path leading past the Stations of the Cross (18C) to the Chapel of *S.Maria*, which St.Francis had built in 1217 over his place of worship, the Sacred Grotto (Sacro Speco); the 13–15C paintings are not in good condition; on the left wall is a Magdalen wrapped in her hair (late 14C) and perhaps the blessed Kunigunde (15C); on the left in the window jamb is St.Francis' symbol of the 'cord' and St.Clara (16C). Further into the wood is the chapel of *S.Michele* with the bed of the founder of the Order hewn in the rock. A small monastery museum has been established in some of the cells of the hermitage near the so-called *Conventino di S.Bernardino*.

La Foresta (5 km. N.): The monastery is presumed to have been founded in the existing church of S.Fabiano in 1225, immediately after Francis of Assisi had stayed there. This is where the miracle of the vineyard is said to have taken place: a vineyard was almost completely trampled down by a crowd of people who had rushed to the Saint, but it was blessed with a second and even more lavish crop of fruit.

Greccio (18 km. NW): Outside the village on a little spur is the monastery, founded in 1260 and later much rebuilt in an equally plain manner: the *Cappella di S.Luca* was consecrated in the grotto in which St.Francis celebrated mass before a real crib on Christmas night 1223; this led to the custom of Christmas cribs, to which the Franciscans are particularly devoted. A fresco attributed to the Master of Narni of the Umbrian school (1409) above the altar represents the birth of Christ and the so-called Greccio crib. In the little 13C church of *S.Francesco* is an altar painting of the Descent from the Cross (16C); on the left wall is the remarkable picture of the Madonna, perhaps by Biagio di Antonio (15C), above an interesting 14C fresco showing the Announcement of Remission of Sin by the Saint. In the adjacent oratory is a 16C painting of the Saint drying his suffering eyes. The ascetic *dormitory* has also survived as it was in the second half of the 13C. Parish church of *S.Michele Arcangelo:* The campanile was originally the tower of the medieval castle. On the left-hand altar is a fine 16C painting of the Madonna. *S.Maria del Giglio:* This little 18C church has three outstanding rococo stucco altars.

Poggio Bustone (20 km. N.): The monastery founded in 1235 is on a cliff above the village, which has the ruins of a medieval castle; St.Francis frequently spent time in the area from 1209: in the plain church of *S.Giacomo* (mid 15C) are remains of wall paintings dating from the period in which the church was built, and several 16&17C frescos. In the cloister is a 15C fresco of the Madonna and Scenes from the Life of the Saint (17C); other baroque wall paintings near the entrance to the monastery buildings and in the refectory. A rather difficult path leads to the *hermit's cell* on a steep rock on the hill; it was turned into a tiny chapel in the 17C.

00040 Rocca di Papa

Roma   p.322☐E 4

This little town was first mentioned as a papal castle in 1181. It is one of the Castelli Romani and is spread like a fan on the N. flank of Monte Cavo. It was destroyed in 1541 and 1556, and few of the medieval buildings have survived, except in the highest part of the town, known as the *Quartiere dei Bavaresi* since Ludwig of Bavaria stationed a garrison here in the 14C.

S.Maria Assunta: The original archpriest's church was built 1664—

Rieti, town walls

Rocca di Papa, market place (left), Santuario Madonna del Tufo (right)

1754 on a Latin cross; it was damaged in the earthquake of 1814 and rebuilt 1815–45 to plans by Domenico Palmucci. The neoclassical façade adopted elements of the Doric Order and has side bell turrets. Important features in the single-aisled interior are an altar picture of the Assumption of 1739 signed by Corrado Giaquinto in the right arm of the transept and a 19C plaster copy of the Münster marble Pietà by Wilhelm Theodor Achtermann in the first chapel on the right; in the first chapel on the left is a panel picture (Madonna and Child) of the 14C Siennese school.

Also worth seeing: The *Santuario Madonna del Tufo* (16C, 1.8 km. S.) with a fresco (Madonna and Child) by Antoniazzo Romano behind the high altar is worth a visit, and so is the little *Gipsoteca* with Achtermann copies near the Chiesetta del Crocifisso.

02040 Roccantica
Rieti   p.321 ☐ E 3

Castle: The village's name comes from the 'Rocca', once known as a formidable fortress; it was later rebuilt, retaining one of the round towers. The surrounding streets follow the line of the walls.

S.Caterina d'Alessandria (below the castle; it may be possible to obtain a key from the address posted at the time of your visit): In the interior is an important Gothic fresco cycle (condition inconsistent), signed and dated 1430 by Pietro Colaberti.

Parish church of **S.Maria Assunta:** The mid-16C painting attributed to Bartolomeo Torresani, showing the Madonna Enthroned with Saints, is particularly striking. The high altar panels showing the Assumption and the Baptism of Christ are 17C baroque works.

Also worth seeing: *S.Valentino:* Little Gothic church with massive campanile; now a war memorial.

00040 Rocca Priora

Roma   p.322□E 4

The highest of the Castelli Romani is on a chestnut-clad hill with fine views which was settled in the Bronze Age. In the Middle Ages the town of *Arx Periura* was dominated by the Annibaldi family; in the 14C it came into the possession of the Savelli family, and in the late 16C it passed to the Pope.

Piazza Umberto I: In this medieval square is the parish church of *S.Maria Assunta* with massive façade and campanile; all the interior except the 15C choir and transept has been rebuilt; also in the square is the *Palazzo Baronale,* built over the Savelli castle by Virginio Vespigniani in 1880. The town arms and the arms of the Savelli family on the church portal (15C) leave no room for doubt about the family's dominant position in those days.

Environs: Monte Compatri (5 km. NW): This charming medieval village is built around the conical hill of the same name; at the top of the village is the domed church of *S.Maria Assunta,* which is visible for miles around; it was commissioned by Scipione Borghese in 1663. The keep of the former citadel was changed into a campanile by Luca Carmini in 1876. The same architect was responsible for the dome, choir and transepts of the church; the spacious neoclassical interior has Doric columns and the painting in the first altar on the right (St.Abbot Antony, St.Roch and St.Sebastian) of the 16C Venetian school is of interest.

03038 Roccasecca

Frosinone   p.323□G 5

This little town dates back to a citadel founded in 994 by Abbot Manso of the Benedictine Abbey of Montecassino and today consists of the abandoned medieval section known as Castello and the more modern settlement of La Valle, which is sited lower down the hill.

Castle: Imposing ruins of the castle of the counts of Aquino, rebuilt in the 12C and standing directly on the rock. Legend has it that Thomas was held prisoner by his brothers in the *round tower;* they were opposed to his entry into the Dominican Order, but he managed to escape from them.

Castello: The medieval quarter is reached via a Gothic gate; it was abandoned after heavy bombing in 1944 in the course of the Battle of Cassino. The historic layout with characteristic alleyways is easily discerned despite this.

In the church of *S.Maria Annunziata* are baroque pulpit and choir stalls dating from the 17C. Behind the church are the ruins of the 13C early Gothic birthplace of St.Thomas Aquinas (No. 32).

S.Tomaso: The Romanesque church with Gothic elements and the monastery attached to it have both almost completely disappeared.

Environs: Caprile (2 km. SE): There are two 16C paintings attributed to the Neapolitan Francesco Santafede in *S.Maria delle Grazie.*
Casalvieri (14.8 km. N.): Early-17C painting of the Temptation, probably by Fabrizio Santafede, and some contemporary carved figures in the *parish church* at the highest point of the village. Traces of human settlement in the Palaeolithic period have been found nearby.
Castrocielo (5 km. SE): Medieval

Ronciglione, Castello

refoundation; the original village had the same name, and was grouped around the castle (now in ruins); it was abandoned because of shortage of water. The shrine of Mary *S.Maria di Monte Asprano* is a popular place of pilgrimage.

Colle S.Magno (6.2 km. E″): This mountain village was also founded by the former inhabitants of old Castrocielo. Of the medieval fortifications a tower and parts of the walls have survived.

02026 Rocca Sinibalda
Rieti   p.321□E 3

The village has a picturesque site above the Turano valley, and has retained its historic character in a most impressive fashion; the castle which dominates it is the most impressive of the four medieval castles in the province—the other three are Collalto, Labro and Orvinio.

Castello: Cardinal Alessandro Cesarini commissioned this building on the site of a smaller medieval castle; work started *c*. 1530 under the Siennese painter and architect Baldassare Peruzzi and was probably continued after his death in 1536 by his son, with some alteration of the original design. The plan of the magnificent set of buildings, which combined the functions of defence and a gracious residence, is roughly in the shape of an eagle with outstretched wings.

Environs: Longone Sabino (11.5 km. E.): *Outside:* A footpath 1.7 km. long leads from the crossroads in the direction of Vaccareccia to the church of the former Benedictine abbey of *S.Salvator Maggiore.* The monastery was founded from Farfa in the 8C and soon became powerful and influential under the Carolingians. It was rebuilt in the 10C after being destroyed by the Saracens. As it owned a great deal of land it became involved in frequent conflict with Rieti, began to decline in the 15C, was dissolved in the 17C, and since then has fallen into ruins. The church was much altered in the 17C, but has fragments of a Cosmatiwork marble floor and wall paintings dating from the high Middle Ages.

01037 Ronciglione
Viterbo   p.320□C 3

Small, historic country town on the S. slope of the Cimini mountains, of extraordinarily attractive appearance: there are numerous buildings of high quality from various periods and a characteristic medieval quarter (*Borgo Medioevale*) with atmospheric alleyways and Romanesque and Renaissance buildings, and the impressive baroque *Via Roma.*
Famous *carnival* with traditional events.

Ronciglione, Piazza del Duomo with cathedral and Gentili fountain

S.Maria della Pace (Viale della Pace): The church was much extended in 1689; it contains a large baroque altar with a painting of Maria della Pace of the Viterbo school (15C) and St.Catherine and St.Peter, parts of a former triptych by Antoniazzo Romano (second half of the 15C). On the N. wall Christ with St.Andrew, baroque copy of a painting by Federico Barocci dating from 1538.

S.Maria della Provvidenza (Via Borgo di Sopra): Small medieval church (restored 1742 and 1954) with an elegantly proportioned Romanesque *campanile* (12C). There are frescos from various periods, but those dating from the 15C in the apse are the finest.

Piazza del Duomo: *Cathedral of SS.Pietro e Caterina Martire:* This impressive baroque building (1671–

95) was built to designs by Carlo Rainaldi; it is also worth seeing for its stylistically coherent interior. The paintings on the side altars (on the left by Giuseppe Ghezzi; on the right triptych by Gabriele di Francesco and Assumption by Francesco Trevisani) date roughly from the time when the church was built, but the high altar panel is attributed to the school of Giulio Romano. The lower church of *S.Maria del Suffragio* was used as an ossuary until 1873. Near the cathedral are the ruins of the high medieval *castle* with round corner towers. *Municipio/Town Hall:* Former 16C apostolic palace. *Fountain* by Antonio Gentili with the heraldic motifs of the Farnese family, unicorn and lily.

Also worth seeing: *Oratorio della SS.Annunziata* (Via di Monte Cavallo/Via Plebiscito): The interior of this 17C baroque place of worship has largely retained its lavish decoration. *Porta Romana* (Via Roma): This elegant early baroque building (early 17C) to a design by Giacomo Vignola is at the beginning of this street with a fine sequence of baroque buildings. *S.Andrea* (Via Borgo di Sopra): Ruined Romanesque church with very fine early Gothic campanile by Galasto of Como (1430), incorporating fragments of decorative marble slabs. *S.Maria degli Angeli* (Via di Montecavallo): The Romanesque church was much rebuilt, as demonstrated particularly by the Gothic capitals of the interior columns and the striking 16C Renaissance portal.

Environs: S.Eusebio (*c.* 3 km. SE near the Via Cimina in the direction of Rome): Small 11&12C Romanesque church. Columns with interestingly decorated capitals and remains of 13C frescos in good condition in the interior.

04017 S.Felice Circeo

Latina   p.323☐F 6

The Latin, later Volscian settlement of *Circeii* became a Roman colony in 393 BC. After various raids by barbarians and Saracens the strategically important town came into the

possession of the Knights Templar in 1250 and passed to the Caetani family in 1301.

Acropolis: The refuge fortress (4&3C BC) of the ancient Circeii is over 600 ft. above the little town with its fine views; the trapezoid *cyclopean walls* of the fortress are almost 17 ft. high. The ancient round building inside the walls protected the cisterns, which were important to refugees in time of siege.

Old town: Remains of polygonal walls in the ancient lower town have survived in the Via Rossi. The defensive tower *Torre dei Templari* (*c.* 1250) in the nearby Piazza Vittorio Veneto belongs to the *Casa dei Cavalieri* (13C house of the Knights Templar) in the Piazza Lanzuisi.

Also worth seeing: Interesting features on the coast below S.Felice Circeo are the *Grotta Guattari* (near the Albergo Neanderthal), in which a 60,000 year old skeleton of a Neanderthal man was found in 1939, and two 16C watch towers, the *Torre Vittoria* and the *Torre Fico*.

Environs: Fonte di Lucullo (6 km. NW): A *Roman grotto* in which building was done under Domitian was discovered in 1904 in a wooded meadow on the S. bank of the *Lago di Sabaudia*, which is now part of the Circeo National Park.
Monte Circeo (7 km. W.): According to the ancients, this island, now part of the headland as the result of alluvial accretion, was the site of the palace of the sorceress Circe. From the summit (1775.ft) there is a fine view as far as Rome, Ischia and the Ponza islands in clear weather.
Villa di Domiziano (8 km. N.): The remains of the extensive imperial *Villa of Domitian* (1C AD), with baths, nymphs and cisterns have been revealed in the *Parco Nazionale di Circeo* since 1934. A number of Roman copies of Greek statues came

from here, including the Kassel Apollo and the Satyr with Flute (Vatican Museums, see Rome).

01020 S.Lorenzo Nuovo
Viterbo   p.320☐B 1

Striking example of urban baroque architecture with straight streets intersecting at right angles and leading to a large octagonal square in the centre. Pius VI had the settlement built under the direction of Filippo Prada in 1775–9, as the village of S.Lorenzo Vecchio (the ruined castle on a rocky spur is still visible) had to be abandoned because of malaria.

00058 S.Severa
Roma   p.320☐B 3

Castello: The *castle*, built *c.* 1000 on Etruscan foundations, is picturesquely sited on a broad sandy beach with rust-red cliffs 1 km. SE of the historic centre of the modern resort with several little churches and palaces. In the 14, 16 and 18C three battlemented walls fortified with towers were built around the maritime fortress, and the picturesque settlement developed in their protection.

Pyrgi: The Etruscan town of *Pyrgoi* flourished in the 7&6C BC as the principal port of Caere (see Cervéteri); it was fortified as a colony with Roman citizenship in the 3&2C BC and destroyed by the Saracens in the 9C. Interesting features are the ruined harbour installations, which are below sea level, the walls of the Roman *castrum*, a ruined Roman villa (N.) and above all the remains of a *shrine* (SE of the citadel) destroyed by Dionysios of Syracuse in 384 BC, and in which small gold slabs (5C BC) found in 1964 confirmed that the Etruscans traded with Carthage.

Environs: S.Marinella (7 km. W.): Important features are the remains of the ancient port of *Punicum* (see Cervéteri) on the beach and the much rebuilt *Castello Odescalchi* (15C) and two *Roman bridges* on the Via Aurelia.

03049 Sant'Elia Fiumerápido
Frosinone   p.323☐H 5

An arch from a Roman bridge, now isolated in a field, and other traces of ancient building are evidence of Roman occupation of the site. The local dialect still retains features introduced by Greek colonists who settled here in the 10C.

S.Elia (also *S.Maria Nuova*): Font and a relief fragment on the N. side from the Carolingian period (9C). 17C baroque organ.

Ognissanti (at the W. end of the village): The little church dates back to the 11C and has fine frescos of the Benedictine school.

Municipio: The medieval former church of *S.Biagio* was incorporated in the Town Hall building.

Environs: S.Maria Maggiore (*c.* 1.5 km. N.): Part of the 11C mosaic floor and medieval apse frescos also of the Benedictine school; apostles named in uncial script under the Madonna with two angels.

02038 Scandriglia
Rieti   p.321☐E 3

Medieval and Renaissance buildings dominate the village. According to tradition St.Barbara of Nicomedia, one of the fourteen auxiliary saints, who died in 306, is buried in Scandriglia.

Parish church of **S.Maria Assunta:**

The medieval foundation was redesigned in the baroque style in the 18C. Two 16C paintings are particularly worthy of attention: Madonna Enthroned with Saints (second altar on the left) and Baptism of Christ. There is also a painted carved figure of the Madonna (early 16C).

Also worth seeing: Late Gothic *Palazzetto Anguillara-Orsini*, dating from the 15C, with lavishly decorated double-arched windows on the first floor. On the S. edge of the village is the medieval pilgrimage church of *S.Nicola di Bari.*

Environs: Ponticelli (6 km. NW): At the N. end of the village is an ancient statue of a Roman in a toga, found nearby. *S.Maria del Colle:* This 13C Romanesque building is particularly interesting for its frescos. The 13–16C wall paintings show various stages of stylistic development, particularly Gothic and Renaissance. Characteristic examples are the 13C Annunciation fragments of the Roman school, the 14C Crucifixion with traits of the Siennese school and the 15C St.George.
S.Maria delle Grazie (4 km. SW): This lonely monastery church has a miraculous image of the Madonna and an outstanding painting of the Madonna Enthroned with St.Francis and St.Antony of Padua, attributed to the late-15C Umbrian school.

00037 Segni
Roma   p.323□F 4

Porta Saracena: The NW town gate in the *c.* 2 km. long *cyclopean wall* of the former Volscian town of *Signia* is constructed of gigantic polygonal blocks; the architrave consists of monolithic rectangular supports almost 10 ft. long.

Acropolis: The remains of the fortifying walls show the extent of the

former mountain city above Segni. The church of *S.Pietro* with its squat campanile was built in the 13C above the cella of the former *temple of the Capitoline Gods* (3C BC).

Environs: Valmontone (14 km. N.): Mattia de Rossi was responsible for the fortress-like *Palazzo Doria* (1662), with several rooms with frescos of a high standard in the upper part of this medieval village, and also for the *collegiate church* (1685–9), which is next to the palace. The domed church is oval in plan, and the façade is adorned with two campaniles with onion domes and a concave columned portico.

04010 Sermoneta
Latina   p.322□E 5

This little town has fine views, and is set on a ridge above the Pontine plain which has been settled since prehistoric times. The narrow alleyways and rustic houses are surrounded by a medieval town wall with semicylindrical defensive towers.

Cathedral of S.Maria Assunta: This 13C church has been much altered; it was built in the Cistercian Gothic style (see Fossanova) above a former temple of Cybele and has a five-storey *campanile* with biforium windows and decorative majolica. The tympanum fresco (Madonna with Child and Saints) was painted by Pietro Coleberti in the 15C. Interesting features of the interior are the fresco of the Judgement of the World (damaged, 15C) on the interior wall of the entrance, 17C carved choir stalls and a 15C painting by the Florentine Benozzo Gozzoli (Virgin with Angels).

Castello Caetani: The town is dominated by the 13C castle, which is in good condition; it was rebuilt as a fortress by Antonio da Sangallo the

Elder for Pope Alexander IV *c.* 1500. The 138 ft. *keep* towers above it. The rooms were decorated with frescos in 1470. Charles V (1536) and Pope Gregory XIII (1576) were among the distinguished figures who stayed in the castle.

Environs: Abbazia di Valvisciolo (3 km. N.): *SS.Pietro e Paolo*, the church of the Basilian abbey founded in the 8C was built in 1240, and architectural details show the hands of those later associated with it: the small cross of the Knights Templar can be seen in the *rose window* above the main portal, and the handwriting of the Cistercian builders of Fossanova is discernible in the circular openings above the pointed windows of a rectangular choir and in the design of the responds. The bases and capitals of the columns in the charming *cloister* (restored 1959–62) are reminiscent of Casamari.

04018 Sezze
Latina   p.323□F 5

Teatro Italiano: This medieval town in the hills is known in Italy for its passion play, performed on Good Friday in the *natural amphitheatre,* with the Pontine plain as a backdrop.

Antiquarium: Prehistoric exhibits from the caves in the area, some of which are painted, also finds from the Latin-Roman town of *Setia*, including a fine 1C BC floor mosaic.

03010 Sgúrgola
Frosinone   p.323□F 5

Madonna dell'Arringo: Very fine 14&15C frescos in the interior, especially a Madonna dating from 1375. This is said to be the place

Sermoneta, S.Maria Assunta ▷

where Sciarra Colonna assembled his soldiers for the conspiracy against Pope Boniface VIII; the Pope was brought into his power in Anagni (q.v., under Palazzo Bonifacio VIII). The Gothic church by the cemetery once belonged to a Cistercian abbey and contains an outstanding medieval fresco.

Outside: *Villa Magna* (on the S.Pietro hill): Considerable remains of a Roman country house of the period of the Emperor Nero (mid 1C AD).

Environs: Morolo (6 km. SE): Some scholars locate the lost Volscian town of Ecetra here or on the site of the neighbouring town of *Supino*. Remains of the castle and the fortifying wall have survived from the medieval period. Birthplace of the sculptor Ernesto Biondi (1855–1917). Passion play on Good Friday with about one hundred and ten participants, moving to different performance areas in the village. In the collegiate church of *S.Maria Assunta* is a large baroque painting of the Assumption by Sebastiano Concha

(18C). The mineral spring of S.Antone bubbles up to the SW at a height of 3,297ft.

Pátrica (17.5 km. SE): This village on a steep rocky spur dates back to the Roman settlement of *Patricum*, as is shown by some remains (including those of an aqueduct). The imposing ruins of the Colonna family's medieval *Castello delle Tomacella* is in an impressive position; Pátrica came into the possession of this family after changing hands on various occasions. In the parish church of *S.Giovanni Battista* is an expressive neoclassical altar painting of the Baptism of Christ by Nicolò Lapiccola (second half of the 18C).

S.Leonardo (4 km. SW): Very old place of worship near a spring.

Supino (12 km. SEE): Several archaeological finds in the village and the surrounding area led to the assumption that this was the home of the Ecetrans, the sworn enemies of Rome, as reported by the Roman historian Livy. The most important archaeological project is a recently discovered Roman bath on the 'Cona del Popolo' site, which has very fine

Abbazia di Valvisciolo (Sermoneta), cloister

mosaic floors (including Poseidon and sea creatures) and marble coverings. Colourful *azalea show* on a Sunday in May, fixed annually. *S.Cataldo* (Piazza S.Pietro): New building dating from 1700 on the site of an early-14C Romanesque building, and designed by the Roman architect Guarino Guarini. Striking features of the harmoniously proportioned centrally-planned building with twelve sides are subtle spatial effects and stylistically coherent decoration. The statue of the church patron on the second altar on the right near the entrance is a youthful work of Ernesto Biondi (1870).

03039 Sora

Frosinone   p.323□G 4

The town dates back to a settlement of the same name founded by the Volscians on Monte Casto (1791 ft.) which was finally conquered by the Romans after vicious fighting in the Second Samnite War in 302 BC. The history of the town has been a succession of wars, revolts and disastrous earthquakes since the early Middle Ages. The carnival procession is famous beyond the immediate area.

Cathedral of **S.Maria** (Piazza Indipendenza): A previous Romanesque building dating from the early 12C (Sora was the seat of a bishop from the early Christian period) was rebuilt in the Cistercian Gothic manner after destruction in the first half of the 13C using the surviving portal; it was altered again in the 17C. The baroque furnishings were destroyed by fire and the interior was restored to its Gothic form. The podium of a late-4C BC Roman temple was discovered under the cathedral.

Also worth seeing: *S.Francesco* (Piazza Umberto I) with a large window in the choir; this part of the church is square to conform with the architectural requirements of the Cistercians. On the second altar on the left is a 15C fresco of the Virgin of Mercy. *S.Restituta* (Piazza S.Restituta): The Romanesque church collapsed in 1915 and was rebuilt in

Sperlonga, grotto of Tiberius

its original form; the central portal survived. On the ground floor of the campanile is a votive chapel to the war dead. *Monument* of the ecclesiastical historian and cardinal Cesare Baronio (1538–1607) dating from 1963 (Piazza Palestro).

Environs: Fontechiari (12 km. SE): The name of the village suggests springs in the surrounding area. Historic centre still largely surrounded by the medieval defensive wall; the parish church of *SS.Giovanni Battista e Evangelista* is generally well worth seeing, and so is the defiant tower of the castle of the Boncompagni family (16C).
Monte S.Casto: Remains of the walls of the pre-Roman Volsci acropolis. At the highest point is the impressive ruined medieval castle, rebuilt after destruction in 1229 by Frederick II's troops, and extended in the 15C.
Pescosólido (7.5 km. NE): The area has been settled since early historical times; the name of the village is derived from the Oscan language (Pesclum Sodolum, roughly 'hard rock'). Completely rebuilt after being wiped out by the earthquake of 1915. 16C painting of the baptism of Christ by Giuseppe Capricci in the *parish church*.
S.Domenico (4.5 km. SW): In 1101 the patron saint of the church founded a monastery, presumably on the site of the birthplace and country seat of the Roman orator and statesman Marcus Tullius Cicero (106–43 BC), at the time part of the territory of the city of Arpinum (now Arpino). From the early 13C the monastery belonged by papal decree to the Cistercian abbey of Casamari (see Veroli), and the churches of both establishments were rebuilt following the plain but harmonious design favoured by that Order. (The buildings were largely reconstructed after severe damage in 1915). Wooden sculpture of the founder on the high altar by Tiburzio Vergelli (second

half of the 16C). The splendid three-aisled *crypt* with delicately ornamented vault arches and some columns or capitals which are finely carved was part of the earlier 11C Romanesque building. Piers from a Roman construction near the Liri bridge.

01038 Soriano nel Cimino
Viterbo   p.320☐C 2

This is presumed to be the site of the town of Surrina, founded by the Etruscans or Phoenicians, lost after destruction by the Romans. The present town goes back to the new medieval foundation of *Surianum*. In October *Sagra delle Castagne* (chestnut feast) with historic procession.

Castello Orsini (Via della Rocca; now penal establishment): This massive battlemented fortress at the highest point in the village, much extended under Pope Nicholas II in 1278, is one of the most impressive castles in Latium, with bastions, curtain walls and defiant principal tower in good condition.

Collegiate church (Main square): Excellent 18C centrally-planned building. The medieval quarter leads off the main square.

Palazzo Chigi-Albani (below the main square): Splendid building with access terrace and two wings started by Giacomo Vignola in 1562. On the terrace is the Fontana Papacqua (also Regina delle Acque), one of the most imaginative Mannerist fountains (the palace is not generally open to the public).

Environs: S.Eutizio (5 km. E.): An Etruscan necropolis and 3C AD catacombs have been discovered next to the church.
S.Giorgio (footpath *c.* 1 km. beyond the Porta Romana): Small Romanes-

que church with tympanum decorated with figures in the façade (restored in 1937) and fine apse.

04029 Sperlonga
Latina   p.323□ G 6

This picturesque small fishing town on a rocky plateau above the sandy beach of S.Angelo has retained much of its original character; striking features are the *Truglia watch-tower*, town walls and gates, and white-washed houses in peaceful alleyways.

Environs: Grotta di Tiberio (2 km. E.): In AD 4–26 Tiberius commissioned a natural theatre and a triclinium for feasts in the originally stuccoed grotto of his *imperial villa*, excavated in 1957, from the Greek sculptors Athanadoros, Hagesandros and Polydoros (known for their Laocoön group in the Vatican). The three larger then life size *groups* (scenes from the Odyssey) and a large number of other sculptures can be seen in the nearby Museo Nazionale.

00028 Subiaco
Roma   p.323□ G 6

This picturesque small medieval town dates back to the ancient *Sublaqueum*, an imperial villa belonging to the Emperor Nero, commissioned by him on a site just below three artificial lakes. The dammed waters of the Aniene fed the longest Roman aqueduct *Anio Novus* (87 km.). Benedict of Nursia (Norcia) settled in the valley as a hermit in the early 6C.

Cathedral of S.Andrea: The domed church has an impressive façade with two low side towers, and was built 1766–95. In the neoclassical interior is a *Miraculous Draught of Fish* by Sebastiano Conca. Fine *paraments* in the sacristy.

Rocca Abbaziale: The castle was built at the highest point in the town in the 11C by Abbot Giovanni to protect the monasteries. The defiant fortress with massive *defensive tower* and a *clock tower* later passed through the hands of the Borgia, Colonna, Barber-

Monastero di S.Scolastica near Subiaco (left), Cosmati-work cloister (right)

Monastero di S.Benedetto (also: Sacro Speco) near Subiaco

Monastero di S.Benedetto (Subiaco), fresco in the Shepherds' grotto, c. 800

ini and Orsini families. There is a fine view of the town from the high garden with architectural fragments from Nero's villa.

Also worth seeing: The charming *Quartiere Medievale* near the Piazzetta Speccata and the plain church of *S.Francesco* on the W. edge of the town, built in 1327 over the former oratory of S.Pietro al Deserto are worth a visit. The church has an altar triptych signed by Antoniazzo Romano in 1467 (Madonna and Child, St.Francis and St.Antony of Padua).

Environs: Monastero di S.Benedetto (3 km. SE): St.Benedict lived in the *Sacro Speco* cave for three years, and the monastery clinging to the slope grew up around it (rebuilt in the 14C in the Cistercian Gothic style). It has an upper and a lower church. The history of Italian wall painting from the 9–15C can be followed in the *frescos in the entrance corridor* (Umbrian school, 13C), in the *upper church* (Umbrian border school of 1430 and 14C Siennese school), in the *lower church* (14C Siennese school and Roman Magister Consolus, *c.* 1280) and in the *Cappella di S.Gregorio* (Roman school with Byzantine traits, 12C). At the entrance to the chapel is a portrait of St.Francis painted during his lifetime in 1224. The earliest fresco (*c.* 800) is in the *Grotta dei Pastori* (Madonna with Child and saints). The sculpture of St.Benedict seated in the Sacred Grotto was created in 1657 by Bernini's pupil Antonio Raggi.

Monastero di S.Scolastica (2 km. E.): Only surviving monastery of the 13 founded by St.Benedict and his followers before the Order moved to Montecassino (q.v.) in 629. Pope Leo VII presented the citadel of Subiaco and surrounding land to the monastery, which was dedicated to the Saint's sister, in 937. It was at the

Sacro Speco, Annunciation, 14C ▷

height of its powers in the 11–13C. The first Italian printing press was established here by the Germans Pannartz and Schweynheym in 1464. *Campanile* with triple louvres and arch friezes. The interior of the church, redesigned in Cistercian Gothic style in the 13C; neoclassical interior 1769–76. A staircase leads from the sacristy with ceiling frescos (Life of Mary) by Carlo Maratta to the caves of St.Scholastica, with a fresco cycle dating from 1426 in the *Cappella degli Angeli*. A further staircase leads to the so-called *Cosmati cloister*, built in two main phases; the S. section was built by Master Iacopo c. 1200, the rest by his son Cosma and Cosma's sons Luca and Iacopo in 1227–43. There are spoils from Nero's villa among the delicate columns with some smooth and some twisted shafts.

Villa di Nerone (2 km. E.): The ruins of the imperial villa are below the monastery of St.Scholastica; the foundation walls in opus reticulatum can still be discerned.

01015 Sutri
Viterbo   p.320☐L 3

The town derives its generally interesting and picturesque appearance from elements of Roman and Etruscan architecture, some of which has only survived as fragments, or been incorporated into later buildings. There is also striking medieval architecture, particularly the Romanesque campanile of the cathedral and the remains of the medieval town wall, some of which was built on ancient foundations. The general impression of rough charm made by the town is enhanced by the blackened tufa in the walls of the historic buildings. According to legend the town was founded by the Pelasgians. Sutri is

◁ *Sacro Speco, St.Francis of Assisi, 1224*

Sacro Speco, Redeemer, fresco, 15C

Villa di Nerone near Subiaco

first documented historically as an Etruscan centre, on a typical site, easy to defend, on a plateau at the confluence of several water courses. The name is probably derived from Saturn (Sutrinas in Etruscan). In September *Sagra del Fagiolo* (bean festival) at which beans are prepared to a traditional recipe and served in characteristic clay dishes.

Cathedral of S.Maria Assunta

(Piazza del Duomo): The original Romanesque building was radically rebuilt in the 16–18C. Surviving parts of the earlier church are the campanile (1207), parts of the Cosmati-work floor in the nave, two columns and the spacious *crypt* with seven aisles with walls decorated with Cosmati work. In the second chapel on the left is a panel picture of Christ Blessing in early 13C Byzantine style. In the ambulatory is a Renaissance altar endowed by Pius V, a bishop of Sutri (second half of the 16C).

Madonna del Parto

(Via Cassia, near the Villa Staderini): This unusual and interesting little church was built in an Etruscan tomb which in the Roman period contained a shrine of the cult of Mithras. The wall painting, applied directly to the smoothed tufa of the portico, shows scenes from the legend of St.Michael. The oldest fresco is the Birth of Christ above the altar (the church is dedicated to Mary the Assister at Births). Near the entrance to the villa are the ruins of a medieval citadel, the so-called *castle of Charlemagne*.

Amphitheatre

(Via Cassia): This relatively small building (180 ft. by 148 ft.) with an oval arena was probably cut into the tufa outcrop in the Augustinian period (second half of the 1C BC) complete with seats, using a dip in the ground.

Cimitero/Cemetery:

Burial place since the Etruscan period. The chapel of *Madonna della Cava* contains some Etruscan materials; the name is probably derived from the adjacent early Christian catacomb. Etruscan tomb openings in the embankment on the left.

Palazzo Communale

(Piazza del Comune): Collection of Etruscan, Roman and medieval architectural fragments, inscriptions and archaeological finds.

Also worth seeing: *Piazza della Rocca:* Square with 13C Romanesque house. Nearby is *S.Silvestro* with a Roman sarcophagus which has been turned into the high altar. *Porta Vecchia* (NE end of the town): Medieval town gate with fragments of Etruscan and Roman masonry.

Environs: Archaeological zone (1 km. SE on the strada statale): Small 6–4C BC Etruscan necropolis with niches in the rock for urns with ashes, and for bodies. Near the church of *S.Maria della Grotta* and the *Grotta d'Orlando*, where Charlemagne's sister is said to have hidden with her illegitimate son, the later hero Roland.

Bassano Romano (7 km. SW): *Palazzo Odescalchi* (visit by request): The medieval castle of this village founded in the 12C was completely rebuilt in the 16&17C by the Anguillara and Giustiniani families, and became the present splendid group of buildings. Numerous rooms with excellent frescos of the late Mannerist period (early 17C) with representations of Biblical and mythological material by Francesco Albani, Bernardo Castello and Domenichino. Twelve marble busts in the 'Sala dei Cesari'. *Outside* (1.5 km. NW) is the baroque church of *S.Vincenzo* with twin-towered façade, endowed by Vincenzo Giustiniani (17C).

Capránica (5 km. NW): This town, which has a picturesque medieval quarter, was probably founded by the Etruscans. *S.Francesco* (Borgo Vittorio Veneto): The original Romanesque building with Gothic alterations contains, behind the high altar, the important Gothic tomb of the twin brothers Francesco and Nicolò Anguillara, who died in 1406 and 1408 respectively. In the church of *S.Maria* is an impressive panel picture of the Roman school (last altar in the left-hand aisle); 15C St.Ter-ence, St.Roch and St.Sebastian. *Madonna del Piano* (NW end of the village): The church has an elegant mid-16C façade by Vignola and a fine single-aisled interior with beautiful wooden ceiling and stucco. The frescos date from the first half of the 16C and are attributed to Antonio Caracci or Francesco Cozza.

01016 Tarquinia
Viterbo   p.320☐B 3

This little town set on a hill is world famous for its Etruscan art treasures. It has medieval quarters and some monumental individual buildings, and was named in 1922 after the Etruscan city which used to be sited on the neighbouring hill to the NE, La Civita. Ancient *Tarchuna* (Tarquinia is the latinized verion of the name) was held by legend to have been founded by Tarchon, a son or brother

Tarquinia, National Museum, winged horses, 3C BC

of Tyrrhenos (Greek 'Tyrrhenoi' = Etruscans), who emigrated from Greece in the 13–12C BC; there is no historical evidence of settlement older than the 9C tombs of the Villanova period, however. The town's increasing importance from the 7C BC is shown by its political development as one of the pillars of the Etruscan Confederation of Twelve Cities and also by the first-class artistic quality of the tombs and grave goods in the surrounding necropolises. It was also the cradle of the dynasty of kings which ruled Rome in the 7–6C BC, until, according to legend, the Tarquinians were driven out after the suicide of the Roman Lucretia, in 510 BC; she had been raped by Prince Sextus Tarquinius. These events, and the Greek naval victory at Cumae in 474 BC over the Etruscan fleet was the start of the long but inevitable decline of Tarchuna: it was taken by the Romans in 308 BC. Tarquinia, sited on the Via Aurelia (leading from Rome to Bordeaux or Tarragona), and with full rights of Roman citizenship, had access to the sea, and was an important centre of Roman trade. The city was so badly damaged by Germanic campaigns against the declining Roman Empire and the struggle for its inheritance that the inhabitants moved in the 7C BC to the neighbouring hill, that is to say the site of modern Tarquinia, and ancient Tarquinia was depopulated for this reason, and as a result of malaria, from the 9C; this is confirmed by historical records.

The new settlement was called *Cornietum* (Italian Corneto), and developed into a lively centre of maritime trade and also agriculture; it was an important source of supplies for Rome. In the 12–14C it was a free community; many turbulent centuries followed for the area, which had many lords and was much fought over.

Necropolises in Tarquinia, fresco in the Tomba dell'Orco ▷

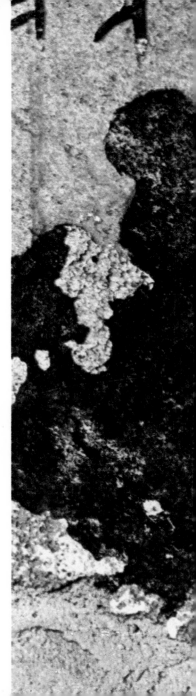

Excavations: There is a good view of the Etruscan, Roman and early medieval *city* form the Porta Nuova on the E. edge of modern Tarquinia. The ruins include sections of the 4C BC ring wall and the massive lower part of a temple now called 'Ara della Regina' (*c.* 253 ft. by 115 ft.); the terracotta relief of two winged horses now in the Tarquinia museum was probably part of its architectural decoration; there are also remains of several buildings (including the so-called Baths of Tullius) and ceramics. *Gravisca* (6 km. SW): Since 1969 excavations have revealed the hitherto unknown *Etruscan port* (6&5C BC) near the resort of Tarquinia Lido, and also a little above that remains of the Roman colony of *Gravisca*, founded in 181 BC. Its own port on the site of the earlier installation fell into ruins in the late ancient period and was not reopened until the 18C, as *Porto Clementino*, with the exception of a short upsurge of activity in the 15C; it was in existence until it was bombed in 1944.

Tomba della Caccia e Pesca

The town: Tarquinia is one of the most atmospheric and interesting towns in Latium. The ring wall is 3.2 km. long (9–10C, with some later additions), and other extraordinary architectural features surviving from medieval Cornietum are the 18 tall residential or defensive towers which have survived in good condition or been damaged to varying extents; the towers date mainly from the 13C, and there are also other ecclesiastical and secular buildings from this period. The Via Antica, Via Giordano Bruno, Via dell'Orfanotrofio, Via S.Pancrazio, Via Porta Tarquinia and side streets, Via delle Torri, Piazza S.Martino and Piazza S.Stefano are all worth seeing.

Tomba dei Leopardi

S.Francesco (Via Porta Tarquinia): This early Gothic church built towards the end of the 13C conforms

◁ *Tomba di Triclinio, dancing flautist*

Tomba delle Leonesse, wall fresco 'The Dancers'

Black-figured vase from Attica

Tomba degli Auguri, detail of frescos

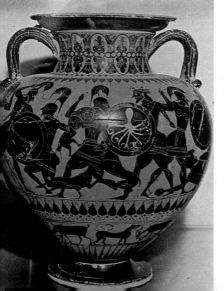

Tomba dei Leopardi, dancers and musicians, 5C BC

with the architectural standards of the Franciscan Order both in its Latin cross plan and in the austerity of its architecture. Massive 16C campanile. Fine baroque stucco in the interior (right-hand altar chapel). The adjacent 13C monastery building with large cloister was rebuilt in the 15&16C.

Cathedral of S.Margherita (Piazza del Duomo): Some Gothic features (particularly the triumphal arch) have survived in the E. from the earlier medieval building, badly damaged in 1642, and also Antonio da Viterbo's outstanding frescos with scenes from the lives of Mary and the saints (1508).

S.Maria di Castello (in the citadel NW of the town): This Romanesque building started in 1121 and consecrated in 1208 is the finest example of medieval architecture in this town, which has many fine churches from the period of its greatest economic success (12–14C). Central portal (1143) by Piero da Ranuccio, and biforium windows by Niccolò da Ranuccio. The rib vaulting in the interior with nave and two aisles is of particular interest as an innovation in 12C Italian architecture. The altar ciborium (1168), the pulpit (1209) and the mosaic floor in the left aisle and parts of the nave are specimens of the originally lavish Cosmati work by the Ranuccio family.

Palazzo Vitelleschi (Piazza Cavour): The massive complex was built 1436–9 for Cardinal Giovanni Vitelleschi, who lived in Tarquinia; it incorporates sections from earlier buildings (some houses and parts of the town wall). It dates from the period of transition from Gothic to Renaissance and shows characteristics of both styles. Houses the *Museo Nazionale Tarquiniese*.

Museo Nazionale Tarquiniese (Palazzo Vitelleschi; Piazza Cavour. Details of guided tours of the Monterozzi necropolis are also available here): The museum provides a thorough view of Etruscan art from its beginnings in the Villanova period until it died out in the 1C BC at the

Museo Nazionale Tarquiniese, recumbent woman

time when the Etruscans were absorbed into the Roman Empire. The finds are almost all connected with the central *cult of the dead*, intended to equip the deceased for the life to come: this led to the building of elaborately painted tombs (6–2C BC) which in the final stages were like dwelling houses in their design; to sarcophaguses with recumbent figures of the dead man or woman with idealized or portrait features (2–1C BC; to grave goods of lavish dimensions. The most spectacular of the exhibits not related to the cult of the dead is the sensitive terracotta relief of two winged horses (early 3C BC), probably a fragment of the gable decoration of the great temple, the so-called *Ara della Regina*.

In the courtyard are Etruscan sarcophaguses, objects from the Roman period and parts of medieval buildings. The *ground floor* and *first floor* contain a systematic collection of utensils and works of art from the Villanova period to the 1C BC. This chronological display clearly shows the development of *methods of burial* and the cult of the dead: the cremation tombs are typical of the Villanova period (called 'pozzo' graves because they look like fountains); they contained the ashes of the dead in decorated urns made of brownish-black clay (impasto) and various other vessels. From the 7C BC burial tombs were used; these were walled and covered with mounds of earth or hewn into the rock, and from them developed the chamber grave with various sections (from the 6C). A characteristic feature of the Tarquinia necropolises is their painting representing individual scenes from the life of the deceased or of the imagined afterlife (on the walls in each case) and decorative ornamentation (on the ceiling). The custom of providing *grave goods* for the afterlife has provided us with an enormous selection of utensils and ornaments. The 'Salone d'Armi' is the most magnificent room in the palace (1st floor, Room 6). *Second floor:* Reconstructions of several tombs from the Monterozzi necropolis with frescos removed from the walls there, particularly in the austere 5C BC classical style.

S.Maria di Castello, interior

S.Francesco, interior

Also worth seeing: *SS.Annunziata*
(Via Marcantinio Barbarigo): Church
built towards the end of the 13C; the
exterior with its portal in the Norman
Sicilian style and rose window, and
the plain interior, have survived from
the original Romanesque building.
S.Giovanni Battista (Piazza S.Gio-
vanni Battista): The 13C Romanesque building was originally a
commandery of the Knights of Malta.
The architrave of the left-hand portal
is part of a Roman sarcophagus illus-
trating the probably Christian subject
of a man praying, with two shepherds.
The apses are Gothic, the interior of
the central portal Renaissance.
S.Pancrazio (Via S.Pancrazio): The
church dates from the second half of
the 13C and combines Romanesque
and Gothic elements. Lavishly decorated Cosmati-work portal; Gothic
lunette. Sicilian-Norman zig-zag
ornamentation in the three relatively
shallow apses (the left-hand apse was
rebuilt to its original design). Pure
Gothic interior. To the left of the
church are remains of the former
priors' palace. *Piazza Matteotti:*
Palazzo Communale, 13C Romanes-

que building with tower raised in the
18C and rebuilt façade. *S.Maria del
Suffragio* with lively baroque façade.
Baroque fountain dating from 1724.
Via S.Giacomo: At the NW end above
the Marta valley is the 13C Romanesque church of S.Giacomo (façade
rebuilt later); its little hemispherical
dome is based on the Arabian-Byzan-
tine designs of S. Italy. Also the elegant Romanesque former church of
S.Salvatore.

Necropolises: The most interesting
of the ancient burial places is the
Monterozzi necropolis on the S. hill of
the Etruscan city (i.e. 5 km. SE of the
modern town). It may only be visited
by guided tour, and a preparatory
visit to the Museo Nazionale is
recommended. The site was discovered in the 15C as a result of accidental finds; it was used in the 7–2C
BC and therefore shows evidence of
various kinds of burial practice. The
necropolis achieved world-wide fame
for the unique painting of the 6–2C BC
tombs; they are of the utmost art-
historical importance, not only as
masterpieces of Etruscan painting,

S.Maria di Castello

but as detailed evidence of pre-Roman painting with stylistic allusions to Greek monumental painting, which has been lost almost without trace.

Methods of excavation: For centuries the site was ploughed up in the search for lucrative finds, and also badly damaged by diggers with an academic interest but insufficient technical equipment, but in the present century archaeologists were able to harness technical progress: in 1935 the first series of aerial photographs was taken, and they made it possible to recognize not only the bumps in the ground but also the lighter patches indicating the chalky material removed from deeper tombs, which showed up against the darker fields. Examination of the ground by geophysical methods (e.g electrical measurement of the resistance of the earth), started in 1956 and continuing to the present day, also made successful location possible, and this led the engineer C.M.Lerici and the foundation named after him at Milan Polytechnic to make sensational discoveries, even in parts of the site where investigations were considered complete.

Wall painting technique is well known: In the older tombs dating from the end of the 5C and the beginning of the 6C BC the pictures were painted directly on to the smoothed rock face. Gradually the practice was introduced of applying an initial coating of clay (sometimes with thin veins from plants as a binding agent); the outlines were scratched into this and colour was added while the clay was still damp ('al fresco'). In the Hellenistic-Roman period (3–1C BC) the outlines were often omitted, and individual areas and details were differentiated by coloured shading. The basic colours red, yellow, green, blue, white and black were prepared from plants and minerals; later the range was increased by mixing colours. Male skin tones were kept darker than women's as a matter of principle. The *pictorial themes* of the tombs were always scenes from the life of the deceased, the funeral feast and the burial ceremony.

Tempio di Giove Anxur above Terracina

The guided tour covers selected grave chambers, changed at regular intervals: they include the late-6C BC. *Tomba dei Giocolieri* (jugglers' tomb) and the *Tomba della Caccia e Pesca* (hunting and fishing tomb), dating from the same period. *Tomba del Barone* (tomb of the baron), late 4C BC. *Tomba Giglioli* probably early 2C BC. *Tomba dei Tori* (tomb of the bulls), mid 6C BC. *Tomba degli Auguri* (tomb of the augurers), second half of the 6C BC. *Tomba delle Leonesse* (tomb of the lionesses), late 6C BC. *Tomba dei Leopardi* (tomb of the leopards), 5C BC.

Environs: Gravisca and **Lido di Tarquinia** (6 km. SE): See under 'Excavations'.
Monte Romano (16 km. E.): Fine 16C Renaissance buildings throughout the town, possibly on the site of the lost ancient town of Aria.
Luni sul Mignone: A path through the fields leads to this tufa plateau above the estuary of the Vesca in the Mignone, settled from about the 9C BC to the 14C AD, about 5 km. S. of Monte Romano. Swedish excavations established the existence of an Etrus-can city in a characteristic hilltop position for ease of defence, and on the site of an pre-Etruscan settlement; a fragment of the wall of the 6C BC Etruscan fortifications has survived in the E. Blackish-brown impasto clay vessels, utensils in black Bucchero clay and red-figured Greek vases are among the finds; only fragments of the mid-2C BC Roman amphitheatre have survived; it seated over 6,000 spectators.

04019 Terracina

Latina   p.323☐F 6

This Roman colony founded on the site of a Volsci settlement in 329 BC first flourished as a result of the building of the Appian Way, which reaches the sea here near the characteristic rock needle known as the *Pisco Montano*. Modern life in the town is largely centred on the *Borgo Marino* (S. of the Appian Way), which has a marina and bathing beaches.

Cathedral of S.Cesario: The

Terracina, cathedral (left), excavations in cathedral square (right)

Piazza Municipio , the former forum, is at the centre of the medieval section of the town (N. of the Appian Way). The *Temple of Roma and Augusta* opposite the ruins of the *capitol* (1C BC) was used as an early Christian church. The Romanesque church built above it was consecrated in 1074 and extended in the 12C. There is a fine view of the medieval town from the lavishly decorated 13C campanile. 18 Roman temple steps lead to the *portico*, decorated with a 12C mosaic frieze; the six Roman columns have lion bases. The interior has been redesigned in the neoclassical style, but the 12&13C floor, the *paschal candle* (1216) and the *pulpit* with five columns set on lions (1245) are decorated with Cosmati work.

Museo Archeologico: The cereal tower *Torre Frumentario* 13C in the modern Town Hall contains Roman inscriptions, reliefs and statues found in and around Terracina.

Environs: Tempio di Giove Anxur (3 km. E.): The 1C BC *Corinthian temple* of Jupiter Anxurus on a massive terrace supported by arched piers, is on the summit of Monte S.Angelo (745 ft.), the Roman *Mons Neptunus*, from which there are fine views; the temple is next to the ruins of the *Acropolis Anxur*, and is in good condition. The statue of Jupiter was originally placed in front of the rear wall of the cella.

Torre del Epitaffio (7 km. NE): This is the largest of the Roman *tombs* in the Terracina area; it has square foundation walls (*c.* 30 ft. by 30 ft.) and is almost 60 ft. high. Although there is no historical proof, it is said to be the tomb of the Galaba family, or of Cicero's daughter Tullia (see Formia). A *gatehouse* (1568) with an inscription dedicated to Philip II shows the former boundary between the Papal States and the Kingdom of Naples.

00019 Tivoli
Roma   p.322☐E 4

The ancient Latin town of *Tibur* came into being in a strategically favourable

Tivoli, S.Lorenzo cathedral

Tivoli, S.Silvestro

Tivoli, well outside S.Silvestro

position above the waterfalls of the Aniene, which flows rapidly out of the Sabine Hills into the Campagna at this point. Tibur was Roman from 380 BC; it flourished under the Emperor Hadrian; the municipium was a much-loved source of summer coolness, but dreaded as a place of banishment.

Temple of Vesta (Via della Sibilla): The 2C BC *circular temple* has ten of the original 18 Corinthian columns and is held to be a former shrine of Vesta. The adjacent *rectangular temple* (2C BC) has a portico on four Ionic columns. The temple survived in good condition until the Middle Ages, which explains why it was used as a church; it appears in many pictures as late as 1800.

Cathedral of S.Lorenzo: The 12C *campanile* with short pyramid-shaped spire was part of the Romanesque building. In the interior of the pillared basilica with nave and two aisles (rebuilt *c.* 1650) are a historically interesting carved *group of figures* (Descent from the Cross, fourth chapel) dating from the 13C and a 12C triptych (Redeemer with Mary and John, third chapel on the left).

Villa d'Este: Cardinal Ippolito d'Este (son of Duke Alfonso and Lucretia Borgia) acquired the site of a former Benedictine monastery in 1550 and transformed it into one of the most important Mannerist villas. The *palace* has three storeys with frescos by Livio Agresti, Taddeo and Filippo Zuccaro among others. The *garden*, which is symmetrically laid out on descending terraces, has particularly attractive *fountains* and cascades; they are illuminated on summer evenings, and make a most charming picture.

Villa Gregoriana (Largo S.Angelo): In 1826–35 Pope Gregory XVI had the Aniene diverted through two tunnels in the rock (Traforo Gregoriano) because of the danger of floods; the water falls 525 ft. from the tunnel openings. There is a good view of the *Cascata Grande* (354 ft.) from the two upper terraces of the *English garden*, which was laid out in and around the original course of the river, incorporating the *Siren grotto* and the Neptune grotto.

Also worth seeing: The Romanesque church of *S.Silvestro* is on the picturesque *Via del Colle* with its medieval houses and Roman ruins. The church has 12&13C apse frescos revealed in 1909–18 (Christ with the 24 Elders of the Apocalypse, Virgin and Child with the two Johns and 12 Prophets, legend of Sylvester). The church of *S.Giovanni Battista* (Viale Trieste) has choir frescos attributed to Antoniazzo Romano (1475), and

Tivoli, Villa d'Este ▷

Tivoli, Villa Adriana, building with three exedrae

Villa Adriana, ruins of the Villa of Hadrian, built by the 'Philosopher Emperor'

Tivoli, Villa Adriana, Canopo ▷

the fortress of *Rocca Pia* is also of interest; it was built in the 15C for Pope Pius II on the ruins of a *Roman amphitheatre;* it has four battlemented round corner towers.

Environs: Ponte Lucano (6 km. W.): The five-arched *Roman bridge* carrying the Via Tiburtina over the Aniene was of decisive strategic importance in the Emperor Barbarossa's Italian campaign of 115 and in the struggles of the Colonna family in 1241 and the Orsini family in 1485. The nearby *Plautian tomb*, designed like a round tower, dates from the early imperial period.

S.Gregorio da Sassola (13 km. E.): This picturesque little town, dominated by the *Castello Branaccio* (with drawbridge) is of interest in terms of town planning as a result of the striking contrast between the *Borgo Medievale* quarter with narrow alleyways and medieval buildings and the 17C *Borgo Pio* area, laid out by Charles Pius of Savoy after the plague epidemic of 1656.

S.Maria di Quintilio (3 km. N.): The Christian shrine by a spring, with an 11C Byzantine icon in its interior (Madonna and Child), is named after the nearby ruins of the expansive Roman *villa of Quintilius Varus* (2C AD); the shrine is set in an olive grove, and is the high spot of a walk in the area.

Villa Adriana (6 km. SW): In 118–38 the Emperor Hadrian commissioned extensions to an earlier villa (1C BC) below Tibur, and it became an extensive and magnificent building. The two sections of the Villa of Hadrian are only loosely linked; their design reflects houses admired by the 'philosopher emperor', who loved building, (see Pantheon, Castell Sant' Angelo in Rome) on his two journeys around the Roman Empire.

A first impression is gained from the *model of the villa*, an attempted recon-

Villa Adriana, Villa of Hadrian, detail ▷

Tivoli, Villa of Hadrian 1 Entrance **2** Model of the Villa of Hadrian **3** Cento Camerelle **4** Philosophers' Hall **5** Villa dell'Isola **6** Greek Library **7** Roman Library **8** Library courtyard **9** Baths and Solarium **10** Large Nymphaeum **11** Vestibule of the Three Exedrae **12** Small Baths **13** Gymnasion

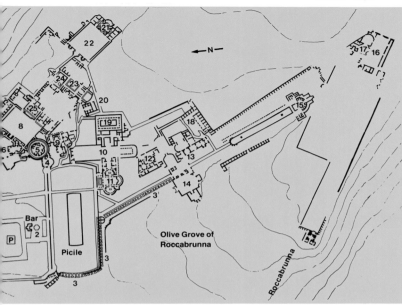

and Large Baths **14** Vestibule of the Baths **15** Serapeum **16** Academy **17** Temple of Apollo **18** Praetorium **19** Colonnade with Fishpond **20** Main Guardroom **21** Vestibule of the Four Conches **22** Piazza **23** Doric Atrium **24** Triclinium and Nymphaeum of the Palace **25** Colonnade of the Palace **26** Guest room with mosaic floor **27** Tempe pavilion **28** Tempe terrace **29** Nymphaeum with Temple of Venus **30** Casino Fede (headquarters of the 18C excavations)

Tivoli, Villa d'Este

struction near the car-park bar. The name of the colonnaded *Picile*, 761 ft. by 318 ft., is loosely derived from the Athenian Stoa Poikile and is built around a garden court with central pool. The SW corner of the building is supported by a lower building with four storeys containing the so-called *Cento Camarelle*, numerous small rooms, perhaps used as accommodation for the imperial guard. From the SE corner the philosophers' hall with niches leads to the circular and colonnaded *Villa dell'Isola*, the centre of which is isolated by a ring moat. To the N. are the multi-storeyed buildings of the so-called *Greek and Roman library* with triclinia with towers and a rectangular library court. S. of the so-called Great Nymphaeum, in form and size like a stadium, are the *large and small baths*, with vestibule, sports hall and elaborate facilities for cold, tepid and hot baths.

Further to the S. is the *Canopus*, the only copy of an historical building in the villa to bear a name which is historically verified. Hadrian had copies of Greek statues set up on the edges of the artificial canal (394 ft. long), including the koroi from the Erectheion); along with other statues, portrait busts and carvings from buildings they can now be seen in the *museum* W. of the canal. To the S. the Canopus, in the manner of its Egyptian model, joins the semicicular *Serapeum* buildings.

The so-called Praetorium with three rows of cells behind the Great Baths leads to the former *Imperial Palace* with the vestibule with four conches on the colonnaded *Piazza d'Oro* in the S. In the centre are the hall of the Doric Piers and the Triclinium and Nymphaeum of the palace. To the N. is the palace colonnade on the library court. A wooded artificial terrace,

Tivoli, Villa d'Este, 100 fountains

called the *Terrazza di Tempe* after the Thessalonian Tempe valley leads past another semicircular nymphaeum with a little temple of Venus to the remains of the *Greek theatre*, in which some rows of seats have survived.

02049 Torri in Sabina

Rieti   p.321 □ D 2

This medieval foundation has maintained the historical character of a strongly fortified town.

Parish church of **S.Giovanni Battista:** An early medieval 7&8C font with Christian symbols is the most interesting interior feature of this church, started in the 15C and complete in 1549. Early-17C high altar panel; Virgin sheltering suppliants under her cloak by the neo-classical painter Vincenzo Camuccini (first half of the 19C); Ecstasy of St.Theresa and St.Liborius and St.Anselm of the 17C Umbrian school.

Environs: Cantalupo in Sabina (5.5 km. SE): In the parish church of *S.Biagio:* 17C baroque paintings. *Palazzo Cesi-Camuccini:* Medieval citadel rebuilt in the 16C as a residence for Cardinal Pierdonato Cesi by Giovanni Domenico Bianchi; parts of the original structure were retained. Majestic late Renaissance façade with portico and loggia; the pilasters are decorated with Doric and Ionic capitals. In the interior, fine Mannerist frescos of the school of the brothers Federico and Taddeo Zuccaro (second half of the 15C). Most of the treasures from the museum here have been sold.

S.Maria in Vescovío (5.5 km. SW):

This former cathedral (until 1495) is eminently worth seeing; it is set on the lonely site of the city of Forum Novum, founded by the Romans and once a flourishing town, but reduced in the Middle Ages to scraps of walls and isolated archaeological finds. Tradition has it that the Apostle Peter founded the first Christian congregation in the town while staying here for an extended period. The original church was destroyed along with the rest of the town in the course of a Saracen raid in the late 9C; the church was rebuilt a few years later, but the town remained uninhabited, and fell completely into ruins. After further damage the church was rebuilt once more in the early 14C, incorporating quite large sections of both earlier buildings and some of the furnishings.

The oldest part of the single-aisled church is the E. section with the architecturally very interesting 9C semicircular *crypt*, with two rooms; fresco dating from the time when the church was built. The early Gothic fresco cycle in the nave (early 14C), possibly by a follower of Pietro Cavallini, is of interest.

Vacone (6 km. N.): There are traces of Roman settlement around this village, which is documented as having been settled since the 1C. *Parish church* with Romanesque features. Triptych by a follower of Antoniazzo Romano (mid 16C).

03010 Trevi nel Lazio

Frosinone   p.323☐F 4

The village with its characteristic historic centre is still dominated by the ruins of the defiant Caetani castle on the site of the pre-Roman acropolis (remains of the massive ashlar blocks from this building are still visible).

Tuscania, collegiate church of S.Maria Maggiore, portal ▷

Tuscania, S.Maria Maggiore, tympanum on left side portal

Before it was taken by the Romans ancient *Treba* was the central settlement of the Italic Equi tribe. In the mid 15C Trevi nel Lazio was destroyed in the struggle for the Kingdom of Naples.

The collegiate church of **S.Maria Assunta** contains two Gothic chalices and a valuable alabaster Birth of Christ in the 16C Mannerist style.

Chapel of **S.Maria del Riposo:** The frescos are of great folk and art-historical interest; they are signed by the otherwise unknown painter Petrus and dated 1483.

Oratorio di **S.Pietro:** Baroque sculpture of the church patron with angels (1705) by Giovanni Gramignani and Lorenzo Ottone.

Complesso Civico/Civic Centre:

Modern buildings offering various facilities, including an amphitheatre opened in 1983.

Environs: Filettino (10 km. NE): Highest community in Latium (3527 ft.) with medieval centre. Outstanding 13C frescos in the *funerary church.* The *Palazzo Caetani* was destroyed in a revolt against the family in the 17C and fell into ruins.

01017 Tuscania

Viterbo   p.320☐B 2

This extremely attractive little town has been continuously occupied since it was founded by the Etruscans in the 7C BC; it has maintained its medieval core within the 12&13C ring wall, which has survived largely intact. The Etruscan necropolises are important

Tuscania, S.Maria Maggiore, detail of main portal (left), rose window (right)

archaeologically and in the history of art.

It has long been posssible to read Etruscan *script*, which is based on a Western Greek alphabet and runs largely from right to left, but the *language* itself still presents problems of understanding. Despite various deciphering methods (etymological, comparisons with other languages, combinations etc.) and approximately ten thousand known texts, it has so far been possible to establish the meaning of a few hundred words only.

Etruscan *Tusena* was one of the twelve members of the Confederation of Cities. It is presumed that the site of the acropolis was the hill on which the church of S.Pietro now stands. Tuscania was conquered by the Romans in the late 3C BC, but retained its economic importance. (There are remains of Roman baths dating from the Augustan period on the Strada S.Maria Maggiore.) From the early 14C until 1911 the town was known as *Toscanella;* it was a possession of the Papal States from 1377. It was badly damaged by earthquakes on numerous occasions, most recently in 1967 and 1971, and was also plundered and damaged by Charles VII's troops in 1495.

Duomo/Cathedral (Piazza Bastianini): The basilica was rebuilt in the 18C and has retained the Renaissance façade of the earlier building (16C). Small art collection with works particularly of the 14&15C schools of Sienna and Viterbo in the *chapel of SS.Giusto e Giulano* (right-hand aisle). The 16C *fountain* is attributed to either Bramante or Vignola.

S.Maria Maggiore (at the foot of the S.Pietro hill, originally within the town walls, which in this area were

Tuscania, S.Pietro, rose window

destroyed in the 15C): Important Romanesque church with Gothic features. It was founded in the 8C on the foundations of a heathen temple, and rebuilt in the very late 12C, in keeping with the original spatial arrangements and retaining individual sections and furnishings. The fine façade reflects the design of S.Pietro in its lavishly decorated portal with columns (in the walls Peter and Paul, in the tympanum the Madonna Enthroned with the Lamb of God and the Sacrifice of Abraham), dwarf gallery with lavishly decorated columns and rose window. In the right-hand side portal the capitals are already Gothic, but the apparently three-dimensional zig-zag arch of the left-hand portal is still characteristically Norman. Massive Romanesque *tower* in front of the façade. The spacious interior is divided up by piers and columns; the Romanesque

capitals have adopted classical leaf ornamentation.

S.Maria del Riposo (outside the walls near the Porta S.Marco; houses the *Museo Civico*): Renaissance church built on the site of a Romanesque predecessor *c.* 1495; the fine portal was added to the plain façade in 1522. *Museo Civica/Municipal Museum:* Contents include characteristic 2–1C BC terracotta sarcophaguses from the necropolises around Tuscania, also an extraordinary collection of 12–17C ceramics, rescued from the wells of medieval houses.

S.Pietro (SE edge of the town, formerly within the town wall, which has been destroyed at this point): In the square in front of the church are the ruins of two massive defensive towers and the former bishop's palace. The former cathedral is sited

Tuscania, S.Pietro, eagle

on what is presumed to have been the Etruscan acropolis, and is one of the most interesting medieval Italian ecclesiastical buildings. The foundation church dates back to the late 8C; the E. section and crypt were largely retained in the 12C Romanesque rebuilding. The new building was completed in the 13C with the addition of the three-dimensionally articulated façade, which served as a model for S.Maria Maggiore, built shortly afterwards; the rose window fell out in the earthquake of 1971, but it has been reconstructed and replaced; symbols of the Evangelists in the spandrels. On the left are medallions in tendril-work showing the Lamb of God with prophets and archangels, including a relief of a dancer which is probably Etruscan. The tendrils on the right grows out of a snake fettered by demons as a symbol of evil. Half figures of bulls appear at the sides; the dwarf gallery is flanked by two gryphons.

Museo Civico / Municipal Museum: See S.Maria del Riposo.

Also worth seeing: Impressive ruins of the medieval *castle* SE of S.Pietro. *Palazzo di Lavello* (Via Torretta): Originally 14C seat of the counts, rebuilt in the 15C and much altered subsequently. Nearby (in the Via Torre di Lavallo, with some Renaissance buildings) is the defiant early-15C Lavallo tower. *S.Maria della Rosa* (Largo della Rosa): This 14C buidling combines Romanesque (persisting despite the late date) and early Gothic features, and is in some ways a simplified version of the churches of S.Pietro and S.Maria Maggiore. Large areas of 16C Renaissance wall paintings in the left-hand aisle; splendid high altar by Giulio Perino d'Amelia (second half of the 16C); a niche contains the painting of the so-called Madonna Liberatrice, who is said to have sent a storm to put an end to the plundering of the town inë 1495. *Silvestro* (at the end of the Largo della Rosa): This plain, small, late-14C church still has Romanesque features. On the interior of the façade is a representation of the Tree of Jesse dating from the period in which the church was built.

Environs: Necropolises: The 7–2C BC tombs in the area have continued to yield utensils, statuettes, weapons and items of bronze jewellery until the present day, also vessels decorated with reliefs made in characteristic black Etruscan clay (so-called Bucchero), and stone and terracotta sarcophaguses. The tombs include *Castelluzza Peschiera* with the famous cubic tomb (Tomba del Dado) and *Cipollara* (3–7 km. N. in the direction of Marta) and *S.Giuliano* (10 km. W.). An extraordinary find was a set of figured dice, the values of which, recorded in Etruscan, have still not been deciphered (Cabinet des Médailles, Paris). The most famous of the tombs around Tuscania is the *Grotta della Regina*, 1.5 km. to the S. near the church of Madonna dell'O-livo; twenty-six passages lead off in all directions from a space in the centre of this labyrinthine Roman building with columns hewn from the rock.

01018 Valentano

Viterbo   p.320□B 2

Village still partially surrounded by the 15C fortifying wall; principal town in the duchy of the same name after the destruction of Castro in 1649.

Collegiate church: Three baroque altar pictures: Madonna of the Rosary of the school of Carlo Maratta (second altar on the right), and panels attributed to Sebastiano Conca (third altar on the right and left). The bells were rescued and brought here from Castro when it was destroyed.

Castle: 15C Farnese family building, rebuilt later, with some elegant sections.

Palazzo Comunale (Piazza Cavour): Two standard measures set in the masonry between coats of arms, the measurement of length valid in the duchy of Castro and a measure for building bricks.

Town gates **Porta Magenta** (1779) and **Porta S.Martino** (first half of the 15C).

Vasanello

Viterbo   p.321□D 2

The town founded by the Etruscans was probably the fortified Roman road station of *Castrum Amerinum* on the Via Amerina.

S.Maria: 11C Romanesque church with portico; archaic capitals on the columns. On the N. side remains of the medieval fortifying wall. Equally remarkable capitals in the interior. 12C frescos in the side apses. Renaissance font in a fine niche. Three-aisled crypt under the raised choir.

S.Salvatore: The campanile of the 10C Romanesque building was partially built of paving stones from the ancient Via Amerina. Numerous frescos in the interior, particularly of the late 15C.

Castello: The castle built in the 12C by the Orsini family was altered later. There is a ceramics firm in in the impressive building, which houses a permanent exhibition giving an impression of local production, which is rich in tradition.

Antiquarium (in the baroque Palazzo Comunale): Regional finds of the Etruscan-Faliscan and Roman periods; reconstruction of a 2C AD tomb; medieval ceramics.

01010 Veiano

Viterbo   p.320☐C 3

The village was largely rebuilt after being destroyed in the 17C (there are some medieval sections); it dates back to the Etruscan settlement of *Vicus Veianus*, according to tradition a foundation by refugees from Veii, taken by the Romans in 396 BC.

Parish church of **S.Maria Assunta:** Rococo rebuilding (18C) with small portal of the original Renaissance church.

Chapel of the Santacroce family: Renaissance funerary chapel designed by Antonio da Sangallo the Younger (first half of the 16C).

Palazzo Altieri: Renaissance building completed in 1518.

Environs: Oriolo Romano (8 km. S.): Founded in 1560 by Giorgio di Santacroce. *Palazzo Altieri:* Started in the 16C and completed in the late 17C with fine late-Mannerist decoration (lavish stucco and interesting frescos). Collection of 265 portraits of Popes in the 'Galleria dei Papi', based on a gift of Pope Clement X (Emanuele Altieri), and constantly brought up to date since his time. 17C baroque fountain in the square.

Veio = 00123 Isola Farnese

Comune di Roma   p.321☐D 3

At the time when it was at the height of its powers, in the 8–6CBC, ancient *Veii* was the largest city in S. Etruria. It was captured by the Romans in 396 BC after a siege lasting ten years, and Etruscan dominance began to decline. It was a colony under Caesar, and raised to the status of municipium by Augustus. After the reign of Hadrian it was allowed to fall into ruins. The first excavations were conducted in the 17&18C. Systematic excavation in later centuries including our own have revealed the celebrated Apollo of Veii and the early Corinthian Chigi vase, both now on display in the Villa Giulia in Rome (q.v.).

Archaeological Zone: The monuments are distributed over a high plateau between two deep valleys cut by streams (about three to four hours on foot). Particularly worth seeing are the remains of a *swimming pool* and the lower part of a *Temple of Minerva* with surviving sacrificial altar. As well as a number of sacrificial gifts and lavishly decorated ceramics, some of them from Euboea, the famous statue of Apollo was also discovered here (see above), and the temple was for a long time known as the Temple of Apollo for this reason. The old *Etruscan Road* and fragments of the Roman city have survived near the Isola Farnese.

Environs: Isola Farnes (0.5 km.

SE): The village is set on a steep tufa cliff and dominated by the medieval *Castello Ferraoli*, once a possession of the Orsini and Farnese families. There are fine frescos in the plain 15C *village church* with nave and two aisles: Coronation of the Virgin in the apse, and Madonna and Child on a pier, dating from the 15&16C.

Ponte Sodo (2 km. N.): The way past the Temple of Minerva (see above) leads past the little Cascatella della Ninfa waterfall to the almost 250 ft. long *Ponte Sodo* (5C BC), an Etruscan tunnel in the rock used both for the drainage of the area and the provision of drinking water in time of siege, and to the fine *Tomba Campana* (key with the keeper of the Temple of Minerva)

00049 Velletri

Roma   p.322□E 4

This town with superb views is set on the SE slopes of the Alban Hills; it was captured by the Romans in 338 BC and named *Velitrae*. It was laid waste by Alarich in 410, and became a bishopric in the 5C, but the medieval town did not really recover fully until the 12&13C. It has been a church possession since the 16C, and was conquered by Fra Diavolo (see Itri) for the Bourbons in 1799.

Cathedral of S.Clemente: A new church was built in the 13&14C on the ruins of a Roman temple (2C BC) and a 4&5C basilica; the campanile collapsed on to the nave in the 17C and the church was rebuilt (1659–62). The *Renaissance portal* was created in 1512 to plans by Traiano da Palestrina. The pillared basilica with nave and two aisles has a raised choir (14C) over the Romanesque crypt, which is decorated with 13–15C frescos. The upper part of the ciborium is 13C Cosmati work.

◁ *Velletri, Torre Trivio*

Velletri, cathedral, Renaissance portal (left), Pallazzo Ruspoli (right)

Museo Civico: The *municipal museum* is housed in the *Palazzo Comunale*, built in 1573–90 by Giacomo della Porta, and rebuilt after bomb damage. The museum has an important collection of local archaeological finds, including Volscian terracotta, fragments of Roman statues and a late-2C BC Roman sarcophagus decorated with reliefs.

03029 Véroli

Frosinone   p.323☐G 4

Evidence of the historic past of this little town, which is well worth seeing, are remains of the cyclopean wall around the acropolis of the city founded by the Hernici, and medieval towers; the wall was raised by the Romans after their conquest of the city in the 4C BC; it was badly damaged by the earthquake of 1350. Charming medieval quarter of S.Leucio; Via Cavour with Romanesque and Gothic buildings.

Cathedral of **S.Andrea:** The new baroque building (18C) retained the rose window and base of the original Romanesque church. Two pictures by the Polish baroque painter Thadeusz Kuntz in the last two chapels on the left. Choir stalls dating from the period in which the church was built. The church treasure (access to the treasury from the right aisle) includes valuable masterpieces of the gold- and silversmith's art dating from various centuries.

S.Maria Salome: Gothic version (second half of the 14C) of a church built in the early 13C, probably after the discovery of the bones of St.Maria Salome (mother of the Apostles James

Casamari (Véroli), abbey portal (left), group of columns (right)

and John); it was redesigned in the baroque style *c.* 1733.

Also worth seeing: *Castle:* Imposing ruins of the medieval building in which Popes John X and John XII are said to have been held prisoner. Very near to the castle is the little Romanesque church of *S.Leucio* (1C) with scant remains of wall paintings. *S.Agostino* (Via Vittorio Emanuele): Madonna by Giacomo Sementi in the second chapel (first half of the 17C). Adjacent on the left is the medieval 'Casa Reali', with an otherwise rare specimen of a Roman calendar of the Augustan period set in its walls ('Fasti Veruliani'). *S.Erasmo* (Via Garibaldi): Romanesque church redesigned in the baroque style in the 18C. *S.Maria dei Franconi* (Via dei Franconi): Façade and the right-hand side chapel from the original Romanesque chruch (12C). In the interior fragments of

medieval wall paintings and a fresco by followers of the Zuccaro family (late 16C).

Environs: Cistercian Abbey of Casamari (15 km. SE; part of the municipality of Véroli): The Benedictine abbey was founded in 1095, probably on the site of the Roman *Cereatae Marianae*, home of the Roman consul and general Gaius Marius (156–86 BC); the abbey went over to the Cistercians in 1151 and was rebuilt immediately afterwards, developing within the specifically Gothic architectural standards of this Order into one of the most important centres of medieval culture in central Italy. It was reduced to a commendatory in 1430, and destroyed by French troops in 1799. It was restored to the Congregation and now houses a theological institute, a boarding school and a meteorological station. Archi-

Casamari, church interior

tectural fragments of the Roman town in the courtyard on the left. To the right of the entrance is the *apothecary* with liqueur factory founded in 1762. The *church* was built in 1203–17 by William, a brother of the Order, and is one of the finest Gothic monuments in Italy. Altar ciborium by Carlo Rainaldi (*c.* 1670) from SS.Apostoli in Rome; fragments of the high altar of the original church in the altar of the choir side chapels. *Cloister:* N. portal and twin columns are masterpieces of stonemasonry. To the E. access to the *chapterhouse*. The *refectory* (121 ft. long by 36 ft. wide) was restored to its original form. The adjacent *library*, despite considerable losses from its original collection, still has many valuable manuscripts and incunabula. *Museum:* The collections are housed in 14C Gothic rooms and include finds from primeval, early historical and Roman times, paintings, particu-

larly from the 15–17C, records and liturgical vessels.

01019 Vetralla
Viterbo   p.320☐C 3

Small town of partly medieval appearance on the site of an Etruscan town abandoned in the Roman period; it was reoccupied from the 7C AD. Near S.Maria di Forcassi (2 km. NE) remains of the Roman forum of Casii.

Cathedral of **S.Andrea** (Piazza Umberto I): The church was rebuilt by Giovanni Battista Contini in 1711–30 and shows early traits of the neoclassical style. Apart from the mainly contemporary paintings by Domenico Muratori, Ludovico Mazzantini, Giacomo Triga and Marco Benefial there is a 12C portrait of the Madonna (N. transept). Pews and organ from the period in which the church was built.

S.Francesco (Piazza Vittorio Emanuele): The 11C Romanesque church goes back to an earlier 8C building, most of the lower part of which has survived. Portal with plant decoration. Fine column capitals in the interior; parts of the Cosmati-work floor. Wall paintings in various styles.

Also worth seeing: *SS.Filippo e Giacomo* (Piazza Marconi): Viterbo school fresco of the Madonna (early 16C) on the right pier beside the sanctuary; 15C tabernacle. *Palazzo Franciosoni* (Piazzetta Franciosoni) and *Palazzo Vinci* (109 Via Cassia) of the school of Vignola in very late Renaissance style (second half of the 16C). *War memorial* (Parco della Rimembranza) by Pietro Canonica. The *round tower* (Piazza della Rocca) is all that remains after the bombing of 1944 of the medieval castle, which was turned into a monastery in 1669.

Environs: Cerracchio (4.6 km. W. near the bridge over the River Secco): Small Etruscan necropolis with tombs of various kinds.
Norchia (15 km. W.): 5–2C BC necropolises SE and NE of the Etruscan town of *Orcle* (Latin *Orgola*) which are of interest for the various kinds of tomb found there, especially cubic tombs and the temple tombs unique to this site. The town was abandoned in the Middle Ages; some of the Etruscan defensive wall has survived (especially near the older necropolis, to the S.). S. of the ancient town are remains of a Roman mausoleum, the so-called *Toraccia*. In the Cava Buia gorge opposite, it is possible to follow a section of the Roman Via Clodia, with Latin inscriptions, a ruined bridge and crosses scratched in the tufa by medieval pilgrims. Ruins of medieval buildings: Romanesque church of S.Pietro (12C); town gate;

the medieval castle survived until 1435.
Poggio Montano (*c.* 3 km. NW): Small necropolis dating from the late Villanova period (*c.* second half of the 7C BC).

00029 Vicovaro
Roma   p.321 □ E 3

Sections of the two cyclopean ring walls of the ancient Aequi town of *Varia* still surround parts of this charmingly sited medieval town. It was abandoned in the 9C after being conquered by the Romans and plundered by the Lombards. In 1191 the newly established town of *Vicus Variae* passed to the Orsini family.

S.Giacomo: Domenico di Capodistria started to build this octagonal church in 1454. Late Gothic and Renaissance meet in the *portal* with pilasters and niches, and decorated with carved figures and reliefs. In the tympanum two angels with the arms of the Orsini family; above that is a niche statue of the patron of the church.

Also worth seeing: The parish church of *S.Pietro* (1755) has a baroque façade with two low towers (1775). Two round towers and walls from the former Orsini palace have survived in the courtyard of the adjacent *Palazzo Cenci-Bolgnetti* (18C), with Gothic portal.

Environs: Anticoli Corrado (12 km. NE): The medieval town is dominated by the 11C *Castello Massimo*; in the period between the wars it became known through artists such as Antonio Mancini, Arturo Martini and Oskar Kokoschka, and still has more than forty artists' studios; their work can be seen in the *Casa Corti*. The

Viterbo, S.Maria Nuova, interior ▷

Noah's Ark fountain in the Piazza is the work of Arturo Martini.

Licenza (8 km. N.): In the Palazzo Baronale which has a battlemented defensive tower is the Horace Museum with finds from the Villa Orazio (see below), including architectural, mosaic and vase fragments and everyday objects of general interest.

Monumento di Basso (4 km. SW): On the edge of the Via Tiburtina near the attractive ruins of a former *Orsini castle* is the elegant *tomb* of the Roman military tribune Gaius Memmius Bassus, dating from the *Imperial period.*

S.Cosimato (2 km. E.): This Romanesque church built over a Roman villa was rebuilt in the 17C. Frescos of the Umbrian school (15&16C) in the single-aisled interior and elegant *Renaissance tabernacle* on the high altar. Roman remains in the former Renaissance garden.

Villa d'Orazio (6 km. N.): Horace's *Roman villa* at the foot of the Mons Lucretilis was a gift from his patron Maecenas *c.* 33/32 BC; it was rediscovered in 1911. The opus reticulatum foundation walls reveal a complete set of *baths,* a *colonnaded courtyard* with pool, and twelve rooms, some with mosaic floors, arranged around the courtyard.

rebuilt medieval castle completed in 1575; extensive park. Baroque fountain dating from 1673 on the left.

Late Renaissance **gate** designed by Vignola at the beginning of the generally interesting Corso Mazzini.

Environs: Canepina (4 km. W.): *Madonna del Carmine:* The Renaissance stucco has largely survived intact in the side chapels. Elegant Renaissance church of *Santa Maria Assunta* dating from 1513&14 in the historic centre. The medieval castle was rebuilt for residential purposes, retaining two round towers.

Vallerano (1 km. W.): Vallerano has a medieval core and was originally an Etruscan foundation (small necropolises). Parish church of *S.Andrea:* 18C baroque church. In the interior Madonna painting dated 1478 and signed by Carolino da Viterbo. *Madonna del Ruscello:* Renaissance building (completed in 1609) with excellent contemporary furnishings: pews and organ front by Giovanni Battista Chiuccia and Alessandro Vibani; paintings by Pomarancio, Lanfranco, the local artist Paolo Menicoccia and by Santo Vandi (second half of the 17C) in the chapels.

01039 Vignanello
Viterbo   p.320□C 2

Charming wine-growing town with some streets which have retained their historic buildings in entirety. Collegiate church of **S.Maria** (Piazza della Repubblica): Impressive baroque church completed in 1723 with splendid organ. The high altar panel is attributed to Annibale Carracci.

Palazzo Ruspoli (privately owned: visits possible by previous arrangement): This Renaissance palace with corner towers and battlements is a

---

01100 Viterbo
Viterbo   p.320□C 2

Viterbo was originally founded by the Etruscans, and traces of the acropolis on the cathedral hill (Piazza S.Lorenzo) have survived. Although it was very badly damaged by bombing in 1944 it is the still the best example of a medieval town in Latium: the 5 km. long *ring wall* (1095, second half of the 13C, some 17&18C additions) has survived almost without gaps; unique, almost   unchanged   *S.Pellegrino*

Viterbo, S.Maria Nuova, fresco c. 1400

 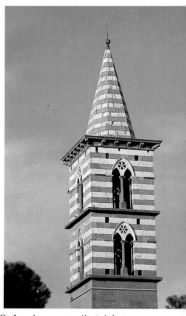

Viterbo, S.Maria Nuova, cloister (left), S.Angelo, campanile (right)

quarter, very heavily built on, especially in the 13C; numerous Romanesque and Gothic churches and houses (especially the *Casa Posci*, 102 Via Saffi), large palaces and twelve *towers* associated with particular families (there were originally two hundred). After being conquered by the Romans the town became the colony of *Vicus Elbii*. From the 11C onwards it was involved in the struggles between Pope and Emperor, Pope and Antipope; it declared itself for the church in the late 8C and from the 13C remained true to the Guelphs, who were opposed to the Emperor. In the 13C it was the permanent or temporary residence of Popes Alexander IV, Clement IV, Hadrian V, Nicholas II, and scene of the election of Urban IV, Gregory X, John XXI, Nicholas II and Martin IV. The circumstances surrounding this last election in 1281

(the inhabitants had taken two cardinals prisoner in the cathedral and were excommunicated) led to Viterbo's rapid decline into a provincial town in the Papal States. Capital of the province of the same name from 1927.

S.Francesco (Piazza S.Francesco): Gothic building dating from 1236 (partially rebuilt in 1373), restored after serious war damage. Exterior pulpit (15C) in the SW corner of the façade. S. transept: on the left is the Gothic tomb of Hadrian V (d. 1276), with recumbent figure, and lavishly decorated with Cosmati work; it is probably an early work of Arnolfo di Cambio. On the right are fragments of the tomb of Pietro di Vico, also lavishly decorated with marble inlay, probably by Pietro Oderisi; di Cambio died in 1268; the family had been heirs to the office of City Prefect of

Viterbo, Palazzo Podesta (left), detail (right)

Rome since the early 12C. N. transept: on the right is the Gothic tomb of Clement IV (d. 1268) by P.Oderisi; the features of the recumbent figure almost have the quality of a portrait. Beneath is the tomb of one of his nephews, Cardinal Pierre Le Gros de St-Gilles. Near the façade late Gothic tomb of Cardinal Gerardo Landriano, who died in 1445. In the square *war memorial* by F.Nagni.

Cathedral of **S.Lorenzo** (Piazza S.Lorenzo): This church was built by Lombard architects in the 12C, probably over the remains of a Roman Temple of Hercules on the site of the Etruscan acropolis, and was rebuilt to a Gothic design in the mid 14C; the façade was rebuilt 1560–70. Adjacent on the right is a Romanesque chapel (baptistery) from the original building. The interior, restored to its original Romanesque form after

bomb damage, is divided into a nave and two aisles by 20 monolithic columns with interesting capitals. Remains of the original floor covering in the nave. On the left near the entrance is the tomb of John XXI (d. 1277); in the adjacent niche remains of 14C frescos. Right aisle: in the baptistery font by Francesco da Ancona (1470) and wall paintings of the Umbrian school (mid 15C). In the subsequent baroque chapel, tomb of Letizia Bonaparte, cousin of Napoleon III, with a bust by Jean Dupré. In the next chapel is an altar panel by Giovanni Morandi (1697); martyrdom of two saints by Lodovico Mazzanti (1724). On the aisle wall fine *Madonna* by Benvenuto di Giovanni (late 15C) and St.Laurence by Marco Benefial (18C). In the right apse St.Stephen and St.Laurence. High altar panel by G.F.Romanelli (17C). In the left apse 'Madonna della Car-

Viterbo, Palazzo dei Priori

bonara', important 12C panel picture; 15C fresco of the Madonna. In the fourth chapel Christ Blessing, probably by Liberale da Verona (1472). Bust of Cardinal Gallo, perhaps by Antonio Canova, above the sacristy door. In the fifth chapel Holy Family by G.F.Romanelli.

In the **Canonry (Canonica)** is a lavish collection of valuable paraments, of which some are held by tradition to date from the 6C. In the *Chapter Library/(Biblioteca Capitolare)* are some fine codices, including the 'Pantheon' of Gottifredo Tignosi, illustrated with 14C miniatures.

On the S. side of the cathedral is the **Palazzo Papale/Papal Palace** (now bishop's residence): one of the most harmonious of 13C Italian secular buildings. The residence built 1257–66 was extended in 1267 by the

addition of the early Gothic loggia (and the large flight of steps leading to the portal) with filigree tracery; the side facing the valley has been missing since the 14C. In the centre is a well (15C), consisting partially of fragments of the original 1268 version. The palace was the scene of conclaves for the election of Gregory X, John XXI and Martin IV.

S.Maria Nuova (Piazza S.Maria Nuova): The church was built in the 12C on the site of an earlier building; it was damaged on numerous occasions, the last being 1944, and rebuilt in its original Romanesque form. Ancient head of Jupiter over the portal; 13C exterior pulpit on the NW corner. Interesting art-historical features of the interior are a fresco dating from 1293 depicting Christ Crucified, with Mary and several saints (14C Barbara figure), and also a sequence of 14–16C *wall paintings* by masters of the Viterbo school: Matteo Giovannetti (left-hand aisle, Christ Crucified, with Mary and saints; mid 14C); Franceso Antonio (in a niche in the right-hand aisle, Christ Crucified, with Mary and saints; in the left aisle Bearing the Cross and portraits of saints, all 15C); Antonio da Viterbo (in a niche in the left-hand aisle St.Jerome with St.Laurence and St.John the Baptist; *c.* 1500). Carved column capitals in various designs; 15C ceiling decoration. Access to the monastery from the right-hand aisle; the Romanesque cloister may date from the 8C and has outstanding examples of the medieval mason's art.

S.Elisabetta, also **S.Maria della Peste** (Piazza dei Caduti): The elegant octagonal Renaissance building dating from 1494 is now a memorial for war dead.

S.Maria della Verità (Piazza Crispi): Romanesque monastery church founded in the early 12C and extended by the addition of the 13C Gothic transept. In it are various 14–

16C frescos and the principal work of Lorenzo da Viterbo, his decoration of the Gothic *Mazzatosta chapel* (on the right): the frescos were completed in 1469 (restored from fragments after the bombing), and are of outstanding quality in overall composition and in the organization of the individual scenes, in the gradations of light and colour and in the precise and lively execution of detail. On the W. wall of the church copy of Melozzo da Fori's Annunciation (original painted in the second half of the 15C in the Pantheon in Rome) and several saints, perhaps by Lorenzo da Viterbo. In the left aisle Virgin Suckling the Infant Christ (14C); St.Fabian with the plague saints Sebastian and Roch by a follower of Antoniazzo Romano (late 15C); Trinity of the school of Antonio da Viterbo (early 16C). The large *cloister* is a harmonious blend of early-13C Gothic and 14C high Gothic. The monastery was dissolved in 1870, and now houses the *Museo Civico/Municipal Museum.*

S.Rosa (Via di S.Rosa): Neoclassical building of 1839–49 with dome painted by Giuseppe Cellini (1908), the funerary church of St.Rosa, whose body is buried in the second altar on the right. Opposite (second altar on the left) is an altarpiece by Balletta (1441). Altar panels from the second half of the 19C to the early 20C by Belisario Sillani (third altar on the right), Francesco Podesti (high altar), Vincenzo Pontami (third altar on the left), Giovanni Michele Wittmer (first altar on the left). The earlier building, lavishly decorated with frescos by Benozzo Gozzoli in 1453, was completely destroyed in 1632; early 17C copies of these Renaissance paintings in the Municipal Museum. Nearby (Via Casa di S.Rosa) is the birthplace and residence of St.Rosa *(Casa di S.Rosa).*

S.Sisto (Piazza S.Sisto): Romanesque church built in the 9C over an

Viterbo, Papal Palace

ancient temple, and extended in the 12C (including apses); the main apse is let into the town wall. The lower storeys of the original campanile (9C) have survived; a secular tower was raised to form the new campanile in the 12C. Interesting capitals in the interior (particularly on the fifth pair of columns). Near the steps to the extraordinarily high choir are two Romanesque pulpits. High altar made of 4&5C fragments. On the right-hand wall is a valuable *gold ground picture* by Neri di Bicci (15C).

Fountains: Fontana Grande (Piazza Fontana Grande): Oldest (started in 1206, restored in 1424) and largest fountain in the town. *Fontana dei Leoni* (Piazza delle Erbe) 17C with fine animal carvings. *Fontana della Morte* (Piazza della Morte) with 13C upper section. This square also contains the Romanesque *Loggia della*

Morte with deep arcade. *Fontana di Piano Scarano* (Piazza Fontana di Piano): Fountain dating from 1367, still in very good condition.

Piazza del Plebiscito: Historic centre of the town. *Palazzo dei Priori:* Dominant building (1460 to mid 16C) with commanding courtyard façade; elegant 17C fountain in the courtyard. Lavish fresco decoration in the individual rooms, including a late Renaissance cycle by Baldassare Croce with paintings of the myths and history of the town (Sala Regia); ceiling paintings of the Miraculous Deeds of the Madonna della Quercia (15C; Sala della Madonna); chiaroscuro frescos dating from 1558 (Sala del Consiglio/ Council Chamber); in the chapel baroque stucco, ceiling paintings by Filippo Cavarozzi and Marzio Ganassini (*c.* 1610) and altar panel by B.Cavarozzi (early 17C). *S.Angelo:* The original Roman building was redesigned in the baroque style in 1746. According to legend the Roman sarcophagus on the right near the portal is the tomb of Galiana, celebrated for her great beauty, murdered by a spurned baron in the first half of the 12C. In the interior Renaissance altar painting (15&16C). *Palazzo del Podestà*, started in 1247 and altered on numerous occasions; tower (144 ft.) dating from 1487.

Piazza S.Pellegrino: Considered the finest surviving group of 13C buildings in Italy, and centre of the medieval quarter, which is very well worth seeing. The Romanesque church from which the square takes its name was partially rebuilt in 1889.

Palazzo Farnese (Via S.Lorenzo): Late Gothic building dating from the early 15C with graceful courtyard. Possible birthplace of Alessandro Farnese (1468–1549; later Pope Paul III). Adjacent medieval house with large archway and remains of the Etruscan acropolis.

Palazzo Papale/Papal Palace: See S.Lorenzo cathedral.

Rocca/Castle (Piazza della Rocca): The castle started for the papal legate in 1354 was completed under Paul III. Fountain dating from 1575 to plans by Raffaello da Montelupo and Vignola.

Teatro Comunale/Town Theatre (Piazza Verdi): Neoclassical building by Virginio Vespignani (1844–55); stage curtain by Pietro Gagliardi.

Museo Civico/Municipal Museum (Piazza Crispi; housed in the former convent buildings of of S.Maria della Verità): Includes outstanding Etruscan-Roman medieval and modern departments with excellent examples of local and regional art.

Museo delle Confraternite (Piazza della Morte, Palazzo di S.Tommaso): This collection devoted to the works of the socially active fraternities contains documents and various objects associated with these institutions, constituted in the 12C.

Also worth seeing: *Chiesa del Gesù* (Piazza del Gesù): This little 11C Romanesque church with animal sculptures on the sloping tops of the façade was the scene of the stabbing on 14 March 1272 of the nephew of King Henry III, Henry Duke of Cornwall, by Guido and Simon de Montfort. They were avenging the death of their father, the brother-in-law of Henry III and leader of the opposing barons, in the struggle against Edward, the heir to the English throne. Romanesque well with bowl in the square. Opposite the church massive Borgognone tower. *Chiesa Del Gonfalone* (Via Cardinale La Fontaine): This baroque church built 1665–1726 is lavishly provided with frescos and paintings by local 18C

Viterbo, Palazzo dei Priori, fountain ▷

artists. *Palazzo Chigi* (Via Chigi): 15C Renaissance building near a massive medieval tower. *Palazzo Gatti* (Via Cardinale La Fontaine): Characteristic 13C building. *Palazzo Santoro* (Piazza Verdi; houses the *Biblioteca Comunale/Municipal Library)*: Elegant Renaissance building completed in 1466. The library founded in 1810 has a collection of valuable manuscripts, documents and printed works, and also a Bible with annotations believed to be in the hand of St.Thomas Aquinas. *Town gates:* Porta Romana: Magnificent baroque building on the ancient site by Bernardino Parenzo (1653), with additions made in 1705. Porta del Carmine and Porta S.Pietro are example of medieval gates in good condition. *S.Giovanni in Zoccoli* (Via Mazzini) dates from the 11C and is pure Romanesque in style; the 12C façade is decorated with a rose window set between symbols of the Evangelists. Romanesque bishop's throne (main apse); altarpiece by Balletta (1441; right-hand side apse). Spindle-shaped 14C fountain in the neighbouring Piazza Alighieri. *S.Ignazio* (Via Saffi): Baroque church dating from 1671; fine painting of the Madonna by Cavarozzi (early 17C) and magnificent organ. *S.Maria della Salute* (Via Ascenzi): Small centrally-planned baroque building (14C) with splendid portal: The Fourteen Works of Brotherly Love, Crucifixion, Ascension and Christ in Purgatory. *SS.Trinità* (Piazza della Trinità): Rebuilt as a baroque church with impressive dimensions (consecrated 1727). Altar panel of S.Maria Liberatrice by Donato d'Arezzo (early 14C; S. transept). Renaissance cloister (1514) with fresco cycle by Giacomo Cordelli and Marzio Ganassini (16&17C).

Environs: Acqua Rossa (*c.* 9 km. N.): Excavations by Swedish archaeologists revealed an Etruscan settlement with necropolises founded in the 8C BC and which disappeared *c.* 500 BC. The acropolis is of particular interest as a rare example of an early Etruscan residential area. The many finds furnished much information about daily life in this period.

Bagnaia (5 km. E.): Village with an interesting medieval quarter, at the height of its powers in the 16&17C. *Villa Lante:* One of the finest palaces in Italy. Building started in 1477 and was completed under Cardinal Giovanni Franceso Gamabara 1566–78 by Vignola and collaborators, who were working at the same time on the palace for the Farnese family, relations of the Gambaras. Cardinal Alessandro Montalto commissioned the superficially identical left-hand pavilion and most of the fountains in the park in 1585–90. The former hunting lodge was rebuilt after destruction by bombing and occupying troops in 1944&5; geometrical Italian garden on several terraces with the Fontana del Quadrato. *Gambara pavilion:* The loggia walls are decorated with views of the finest contemporary villas in Latium; ceiling painting by Raffaelino da Reggio; in the adjacent hunting and fishing rooms landscapes by Antonio Tempesta; frescos in the upper storey probably by Raffaelino da Reggio and Battista Lombardelli. *Montalto pavilion:* pictures and views by Agostino Tassi; in the upper storey frescos by Giuseppe Cesari, known as the Cavalier d'Arpino; architectural painting by A.Tassi. Subtle cascade and various fountains on the various levels of the terrace.

Bagni di Viterbi/Viterbo Baths (3–5 km.W.): Thermal springs used by the Etruscans and by the Romans, the latter in very splendid buildings, for therapeutic purposes; the best known is the Bulicame crater pool with sulphurous steam rising from it mentioned in Dante's 'Divine Comedy' (Hell XIV, 79–81). Work on the existing building started in 1846.

Bomarzo (19 km. SE): Bomarzo dates back to an Etruscan settlement and is dominated by the *Palazzo Orsini*, built 1525–83. Below Bomarzo to the NW is the *Parci dei Mostri* (monster park), created *c.* 1580 for the Orsini family; the park is a masterpiece of Mannerism, a characteristic synthesis of buildings, landscapes, and gardens with sculptures and fountains. Vignola's Tempietto is near the present entrance. The so-called Crooked House is an architectural joke: right angles were deliberately avoided. The huge masks and fantastic animals from which the park takes its name confront the visitor among the other figures which he meets on his walk through the park.

Castel d'Asso (9 km. SW): The Etruscan town founded in the 7C BC and known by its Roman name of *Axia* is presumed to have been sited on the plateau above the confluence of the Arcione and the Rio Secco. The ruins of the medieval castle are on the site of the settlement which later disappeared. Archaeological zone: The Etruscan necropolis on the other side of the Arcione (outside the main settlement, as always) has several 4–2C tombs. Particularly striking are the unusual dimensions of the *Great Tomb (Tomba Grande)* and the inscriptions on the Orioli tomb.

Férento (10 km. N.): Ruins of the Roman town of *Ferentium,* built in the 3C BC on the site of a conquered Etruscan settlement. The theatre (open-air performances in the summer) has survived in good condition, apart from the once lavish architectural decoration; the tufa ashlar of the walls, which still rise to a height of over 30 ft. in places, and the arches are dry-stone constructions. Underground Etruscan and Roman tombs throughout the area. The ruins on the hillside of the 9&10C church are evidence of the medieval town of the same name which has disappeared without trace since it was destroyed in 1172.

S.Maria della Quercia (2 km. E.): This pilgrimage church built 1470–1525 is one of the most harmonious Renaissance buildings in Latium. Above the façade (1509) is a pediment with relief (two lions guarding the miraculous image in the oak tree); in the portal tympanums terracotta (1508) by Andrea della Robbia. The columns and pilasters at the top of the steps are the remains of a portico. In the tower (1481–84) the bells S.Maria (1528) and S.Agata (1654). In the nave is a coffered ceiling designed by Antonio da Sangallo the Younger (1518–25). On the high altar marble tabernacle by Andrea Bregno (1490) with miraculous image (1417); in the apse vault circular picture of the Madonna della Quercia by Truffetta (1519). Choir stalls with inlay work (1514). Baroque organ.

S.Martino al Cimino (7 km. S.): Generally interesting village, rebuilt in the' 17C within the medieval ring wall on the basis of contemporary ideas of town planning. *S.Martino:* The early-13C Gothic Cistercian church deviates from the specific architectural standards of this Order, particularly in having twin towers (probably 14C) and a polygonal rather than a square choir. The chapterhouse, the refectory with finely-executed architectural detail, and parts of the cloister have survived. Other parts of the building were incorporated in the Palazzo Doria-Pamphili, commissioned by Olimpia, the influential sister-in-law of Pope Innocent X in the mid 17C.

Vitorchiano (9 km. NE): This village, which has been settled since Etruscan times, is well worth seeing for its medieval centre. In the Middle Ages a faithful ally of Rome against Viterbo; the appearance of the official Roman abbreviation S.P.Q.R. ('The Roman Senate and the Roman People') on numerous door and window jambs and in the coat of arms dates from this period. The 13C defensive wall has survived in good condition; the towers were largely 15C additions.

Alphabetical list of the sights of Rome

Index of places included

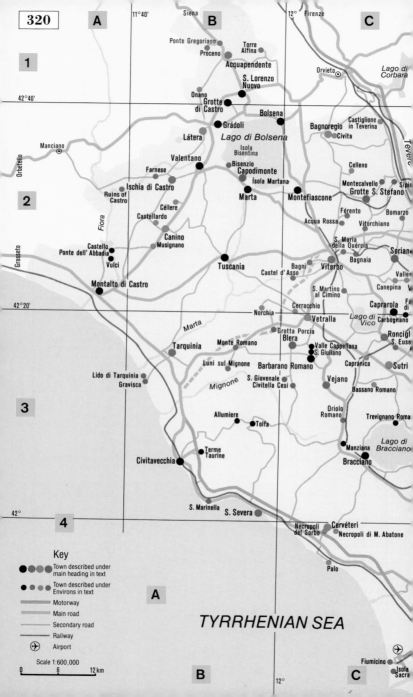

320

A   11°40'   Siena   B   12°   Firenze   C

1

Ponte Gregoriano
Proceno
Torre Alfina
Acquapendente
S. Lorenzo Nuovo
Orvieto
Lago di Corbara

42°40'

Onano
Grotte di Castro
Bolsena
Bagnoregio
Castiglione in Teverina
Civita

Grádoli
Látera
Lago di Bolsena
Isola Bisentina
Valentano
Bisenzio
Capodimonte
Celleno
Manciano
Orbetello

2

Farnese
Ísola Martana
Montecalvello
Sipic
Grotte S. Stefano
Ischia di Castro
Marta
Montefiascone
Ruins of Castro
Céllere
Castellardo
Férento
Bomarzo
Acqua Rossa
Vitorchiano
Canino
Musignano
S. Maria della Quércia
Soriar
Castello
Ponte dell' Abbadia
Bagnaia
Flora
Vulci
Tuscania
Bagni
Castel d' Asso
Viterbo
Valle
Grosseto
Montalto di Castro
Canepina

42°20'
Norchia
Cerracchio
Vetralla
Lago di Vico
Caprarola
Fa di
Carbognano
Marta
Grotta Porcia
Blera
Roncigl
S. Euse
Tarquinia
Monte Romano
Valle Cappellana
S. Giuliano
Caprànica
Sutri
Luni sul Mignone
Barbarano Romano
Lido di Tarquinia
Gravisca
S. Giovenale
Civitella Cesi
Vejano
Bassano Romano
Mignone

3

Oriolo Romano
Trevignano Roma
Allumiere
Tolfa
Manziana
Lago di Bracciano
Terme Taurine
Bracciano
Civitavecchia

42°
4
S. Marinella
S. Severa
Necropoli del Sorbo
Cervéteri
Necropoli di M. Abatone
Palo

Key

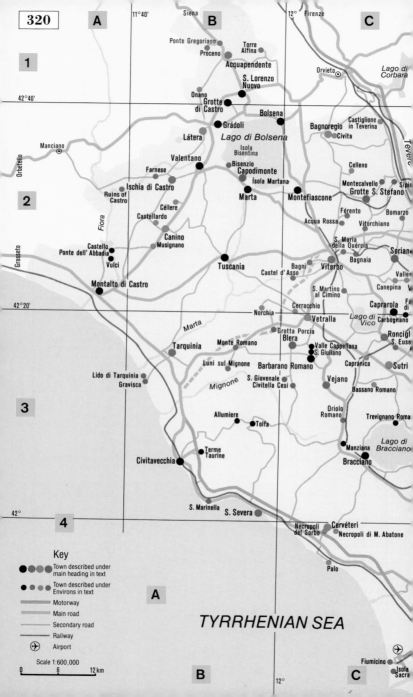 Town described under main heading in text

• • • • Town described under Environs in text

━━━ Motorway
━━━ Main road
─── Secondary road
─── Railway
⊕ Airport

Scale 1:600,000

0   6   12 km

A

TYRRHENIAN SEA

Fiumicino
Isola Sacra

B   12°   C

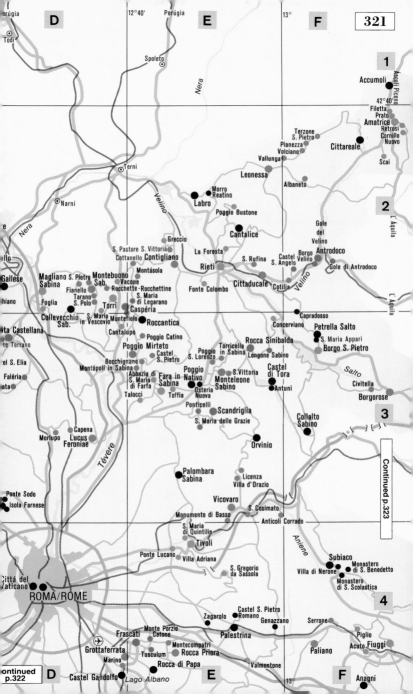

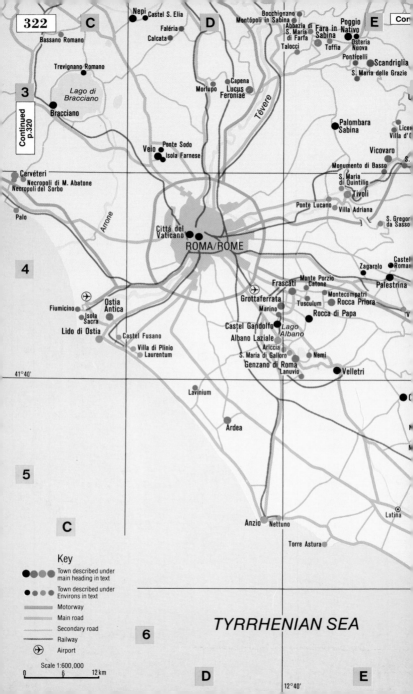

322

C

D

E

Cor

Nepi
Castel S. Elia
Faléria
Calcata

Bocchignano
Montópoli in Sabina
Abbazia di
S. Maria
di Farfa
Talocci

Poggio
Nativo

Fara in
Sabina

Toffia

Osteria
Nuova

Ponticelli

S. Maria delle Grazie

Scandriglia

Bassano Romano

Trevignano Romano

3

*Lago di
Bracciano*

Bracciano

Morlupo

Capena
Lucus
Feroniae

Tévere

Palombara
Sabina

Lice
Villa d'(

Continued p.320

Veio
Ponte Sodo
Isola Farnese

Vicovaro

Monumento di Basso

S.

Cervéteri
Necropoli di M. Abatone
Necropoli del Sorbo

S. Maria
di Quintilio

Tivoli

Palo

Arrone

Ponte Lucano

Villa Adriana

S. Gregor
da Sasso

Città del
Vaticano

ROMA/ROME

4

Zagarolo

Castel
Roma

Palestrina

Fiumicino

Ostia
Antica

Frascati

Monte Porzio
Catone

Grottaferrata

Montecompatri

Rocca Priora

V

Isola
Sacra

Lido di Ostia

Tusculum

Marino

Rocca di Papa

Castel Gandolfo

*Lago
Albano*

Castel Fusano

Albano Laziale

Villa di Plinio
Laurentum

Ariccia

S. Maria di Galloro

Nemi

Genzano di Roma

Lanuvio

Velletri

41°40'

Lavinium

Ardea

5

Latina

C

Anzio
Nettuno

Torre Astura

Key

Town described under
main heading in text

Town described under
Environs in text

Motorway

Main road

Secondary road

Railway

Airport

TYRRHENIAN SEA

Scale 1:600,000

0   6   12 km

6

D

12°40'

E

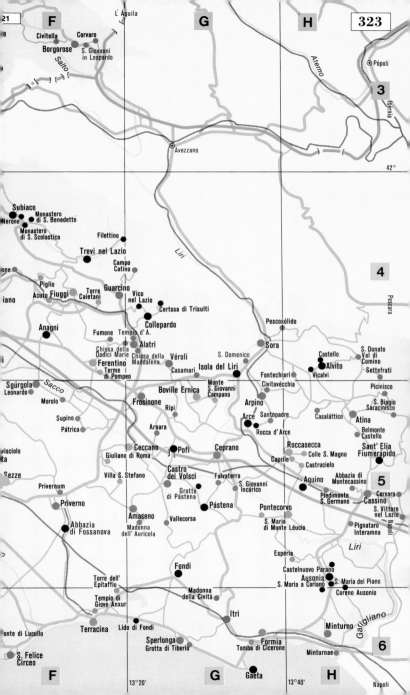